Ivan the Terrible

Ivan the Terrible

A Military History

Alexander Filjushkin

Frontline Books, London

Ivan the Terrible: A Military History
This edition published in 2008 by Frontline Books, an imprint of
Pen and Sword Books Ltd, 47 Church Street,
Barnsley, S. Yorkshire, S70 2AS
www.frontline-books.com

ISBN: 978-184832-504-3

CIP data records for this title are available from the British Library
and the Library of Congress

For more information on our books, please visit
www.frontline-books.com, email info@frontline-books.com
or write to us at the above address.

Typeset by Wordsense Ltd, Edinburgh
Printed and bound in Great Britain by Biddles Ltd, King's Lynn

Contents

List of Illustrations   vii
List of Maps   xi
Acknowledgements   xiii

Introduction   1
Chapter 1. Russian Military Forces in the Sixteenth Century:
    The Infrastructure of the Russian Army   17
Chapter 2. Who Were the Enemies of Russia in the Sixteenth
    Century? A Brief Review of Their Military Potential   57
Chapter 3. The Russian Crusades: Ivan the Terrible
    Against the Muslims   92
Chapter 4. From Offence to Defence: The Military Policy
    of Ivan the Terrible Against the Muslims in the 1560s and 1570s   118
Chapter 5. Ivan's Baltic Wars   142
Chapter 6. The Dispute Over Russian Lands:
    Ivan's Policy towards Poland and Lithuania in the
    Third Quarter of the Sixteenth Century   175
Chapter 7. The Military Disaster of Ivan the Terrible   207
Epilogue   258

Notes   267
Appendix I: Chronology   273
Appendix II: List of Rulers   278
Appendix III: State of Troop Alertness and the Mobilisation
    Potential of the Armies of Countries Participating in the
    Wars of Ivan the Terrible   282
Appendix IV: Comparison of Eastern European Armies
    of the Sixteenth Century   283
Bibliography   287
Index   295

Illustrations

PLATES
(*between pages 114 and 115*)

Colour

1. Russian tsar Ivan the Terrible in the so-called 'Copenhagen portrait'
2. Portrait of Ivan the Terrible from the seventeenth-century manuscript 'Titulyarnik'
3. Sixteenth-century German propaganda image of the Russian tsar
4. Tsar Fyodor Ivanovich, son of Ivan the Terrible
5. Tartar warriors of the sixteenth century
6. Russian warriors of the sixteenth century
7. Lithuanian nobles
8. Polish hussars
9. Polish knights
10. The tsar's throne (1551) in the Kremlin
11. The main Russian crown or 'Monomakh's cap'
12. The throne of Ivan the Terrible
13. Ivan the Terrible entering the Cathedral Square in the Moscow Kremlin
14. A sixteenth-century torture chamber
15. The Russian icon 'The militant church'
16. The siege of the Russian fortress
17. The capturing of Kazan
18. The Lublin Union in 1569, from a painting by Jan Matejko
19. Tatar raid on the Russian fortress of Pronsk
20. Lithuanian ambassadors in Moscow
21. The siege of Marienburg
22. Fragment from 'The Defence of Pskov' by Karl Brullov
23. Stefan Bathory at Pskov

Black and White

1. Marble bust of Ivan the Terrible
2. The king of Rzeczpospolita, Stefan Bathory
3. The fortifications of Pskov
4. Ivangorod from the Estonian side of the Narva
5. Fortifications of the Pskovo-Pechersky monastery, built in the 1560s
6. Underground church in the
7. A chapel and cross at Savkina Gorka, the outpost of Voronach
8. Fortification towers of the Russian fortress Izborsk, situated to the west of Pskov
9. The 'Thick Margaret' Gun Tower and Olevuste Church in Revel (modern-day Tallinn)
10. The Virgin's Tower and the Dome Cathedral, Reval
11. Ruins of the bishop's Cathedral in Dorpat (modern-day Tartu)
12. A modern view of the Livonian knights' castle in Riga, Latvia
13. The City Hall and the House of Dark-haired Guild in Riga
14. Modern reconstruction of the fortress of the Livonian Order at Fellin (modern-day Viljandi)
15. The ruins of Fellin today
16. Old Ladoga, Russia's oldest fortress
17. Ruins of the Higher Castle of Vilno
18. Fortress of Narva, the famous Livonian castle and port
19. 'The Cattle Driving Tower' in the Swedish fortress of Vyborg
20. St Basil's Cathedral
21. Wawel, the ancient residence of the Polish kings in Krakow
22. Livonian cannon 'Revel's Lion'
23. Battle of Pskov depicted in a nineteenth-century Russian engraving
24. Exterior view of the sixteenth-century Pokrovsky Tower
25. Interior view of the Pokrosky Tower

LINE ART

1	Grand Prince Ivan III	2
2	Grand Prince Vasiliy III	3
3	Tsar Ivan the Terrible	5
4	Moscow in the sixteenth century	6
5	The crowning of Ivan the Terrible in 1547	12
6	Map of Russia by Antonio Jenkinson, 1593	18
7	Russian warrior	21
8	Moskovites	23

9 Russian cavalryman — 27
10 Russian nobles on military service — 31
11 Russian *strelets* — 32
12 Fortifications of Novgorod the Great — 44
13 Wooden fortifications on the line of abatis — 46
14 Fortress Ladoga — 48
15 Fortress Krasnaya — 50
16 Fortress Sitna — 50
17 Fortress Sokol — 50
18 Fortress Turovlya — 50
19 Bastions in the Moscow Kremlin — 51
20 European mercenaries — 53
21 Further types of European mercenary — 55
22 Tatars — 61
23 A fight between Tatar and Polish troops — 63
24 Map of Grand Duchy of Lithuania by Martin Kromer — 75
25 Krakow, the capital of Poland in the sixteenth century — 76
26 Polish *sejm* in 1506 — 77
27 Vilno, the capital of the Grand Duchy of Lithuania — 78
28 Lithuanian warrior — 81
29 Polish–Lithuanian troops at battle — 82
30 Map of Livonia, 1574 — 85
31 Riga in 1547 — 87
32 Map of Sweden by Abraham Orthely — 90
33 Ivan the Terrible, in the image and likeness of St George, defeating Kazan Khan Yadegar — 106
34 Russian freight ship — 144
35 Fortress Oresheck, Noteburg in Sweden — 146
36 Sigismund II Augustus — 149
37 Russian merchant — 151
38 The castle of Kokenhusen — 154
39 Duke Magnus — 167
40 Polotsk in the sixteenth century — 176
41 The Russian banner of the Polotsk raid with holy symbols — 177
42 German leaflet about the Russian capture of Polotsk in 1563 — 179
43 Fortress Ula — 183
44 German leaflet on the battle of Ula in 1564 — 184
45 The Polish *sejm* of 1570 — 189
46 The Russian tsar's confirmation of his oath before foreign diplomats — 191

47 Henry Valois, king of Rzeczpospolita   195
48 Emperor Maximilian II   196
49 Riga   201
50 Polotsk   209
51 The siege of Polotsk in 1579   210
52 A leaflet on King Stefan's challenge to the Muscovy tyrant   217
53 A leaflet on the capture of Luki the Great in 1580   221
54 Smolensk   222
55 A feast in the tsar's court with foreign ambassadors   226
56 Fortress Pskov   230
57 Jan Zamojski   235
58 'Russia under Ivan the Terrible'   245
59 'Crimes of the Turks'   246
60 The cover illustration from Oderborn's book on Ivan the Terrible   250
61 The punishment of Livonian women and children by Russian
    troops   253

Maps

Introduction

1   Russia in 1533   4

Chapter 1

2   The defence system on Russia's southern border   28

Chapter 2

3   Crimean khanate in the sixteenth century   59
4   Kazan khanate in the mid-sixteenth century   67
5   Astrakhan khanate and Nogay Horde in the sixteenth century   70
6   Turkish possessions in eastern Europe in the sixteenth century   73
7   Kingdom of Poland and Grand Duchy of Lithuania
    in the first half of the sixteenth century   79
8   Territorial ambitions of the Grand Duchy of Lithuania and
    Russia, and lands lost by the Grand Duchy of Lithuania
    in the late fifteenth and early sixteenth centuries   83
9   Livonia in the first half of the sixteenth century   86

Chapter 3

10   The siege and capture of Kazan in 1552   101

Chapter 4

11   The Tatar raids in 1572 and the battle of Molodi   134

Chapter 5

12   Trade routes in the Baltic in the sixteenth century   145
13   Military operations in Livonia in 1558   157
14   Military operations in Livonia in 1559   162
15   Military operations in Livonia in 1560   169

16   The partition of Livonia between Poland, Grand Duchy
     of Lithuania, Russia, Sweden and Denmark after 1561   173

Chapter 6

17   The Russian–Lithuanian War 1561–70   187
18   The raid by Ivan the Terrible's army in Livonia in 1577   199

Chapter 7

19   Military operations in 1579 in the 'Moscow War'   213
20   Military operations in 1580 in the 'Moscow War'   215
21   Military operations in 1581 in the 'Moscow War'   229

All maps © Alexander Filjuskin, 2008.
Please note that these maps are intended as sketches to aid the reader and are not drawn to scale.

Acknowledgements

I would like to thank all my friends and colleagues who have helped me while writing this book. I am particularly grateful to Alexey Lobin (Russia), Anti Selart (Estonia), Andrey Yanushkevich (Byelorussia), William Urban (USA), Sergey Bogatyrev and Michael Leventhal (Great Britain). Special thanks also to the Russian historical journal *Rodina* and its editor, Yury Borisenok, for permission to use many of the illustrations, which are the property of this publishing house. And I would like to thank Kate Baker, of Frontline Books. Her advice and skilled assistance made my work on the book thoroughly enjoyable.

My obligation to Olga Uverskaya, Alexander Mitrophanov and Galina Yakovleva is considerable. The translation of this book has been possible only with their help. Olga Uverskaya has worked on the Introduction and Chapters 1 and 2, Alexander Mitrophanov on Chapters 3 to 7 and Galina Yakovleva on Chapter 7 and the Epilogue. It is also important to thank Philip Sidnell for all his hard work and meticulous editing, which considerably improved the text. He saved me from many complicated problems and I am most grateful.

My creative labour was only made possible by the support of my family. My apologies that I was so pressed for time and did not find enough time for them; they deserve better. The encouragement of my wife, Svetlana Smirnova, was great, and I finished the book thanks to her above all others. My sons, Egor and Fedor, showed patience and indulged their father's work. And my mother, Svetlana Filjushkina, unquestioningly trusted in my abilities to perceive the military policy of Ivan the Terrible, even when I wasn't sure that it was possible for an ordinary person to comprehend the cruel deeds of the first Russian tsar.

At the heart of different parts of this book lies my research, supported by several scientific organisations at various points in my life. Initially, it was St Petersburg State University and Voronezh State University. Then I received grants from the American Council of Learned Societies (1999 and 2000); a

Queen Yadwiga scholarship from the Jagellonian University (Krakow, Poland, 2000), grants from the Russian Ministry of Education (2001–2002), Russian scientific organisation ANO-INOCENTER with the support of Keenan's Institute, Carnegie Corporation and Foundation of the John D and Catherine T MacArthur Foundation (USA, 2004); and a scholarship from the German Gerda-Henkel Foundation (2004–2006). I am exceedingly grateful to all these organisations.

Alexander Filjushkin
Berlin, St Petersburg, Tolmachevo, 2008

Introduction

Having been told that the pope had huge authority all over the world, Joseph Stalin narrowed his eyes cunningly and asked: 'And how many divisions does the pope have?' These words reflect the criterion by which a country's political significance has been appraised in Russia since ancient times: military power. The size and quality of the armed forces, their ability to win wars, have always been appreciated more than any other characteristics of the state's level of development and higher than the ability of the country to gain the sympathies of its neighbours and maintain friendly relations with them. Knowing this, we must admit that Russian politicians of the late nineteenth century had reason to say: 'Russia has only two allies: its army and its navy.'

When did the Russian military factor start playing its role in world and European history? In, for example, the early Middle Ages, throughout the Crusading era (1095–1291), the Hundred Years War (1337–1453), the Wars of the Roses (1455–85), the West did not know anything about Russian armies. Minor wars against Sweden and German military orders in the Baltic region, like the casual clashes with the Grand Duchy of Lithuania, were just local conflicts of which Europe had only very vague notions. Nobody could see in those insignificant campaigns what later would be called a 'Russian military threat'.

It was only towards the end of the fifteenth century that, as Karl Marx wrote:

> Astonished Europe, at the commencement of Ivan's reign [Ivan III]* hardly aware of the existence of Muscovy, hemmed in between the Tartar and the Lithuanian, was dazzled by the sudden appearance of an immense empire on its eastern confines, and Sultan Bajazet† himself,

---

* The great prince of Moscow, Ivan III (1462–1505), increased the territory of the Russian state more than sixfold (from 430,000 to 2,800,000 square kilometres) during his reign.

† Bayezid I (1354–1403), nicknamed Yildirim ('the Thunderbolt'), was sultan of the Ottoman Empire from 1389 to 1402. He captured Serbia, Bulgaria, Macedonia,

Grand Prince Ivan III (German
engraving, sixteenth century)

before whom Europe trembled, heard for the first time the haughty language of the Muscovite.[1]

A contemporary Russian philosopher, Vadim Tsimburski, interprets Russia's entrance onto the world stage in the fifteenth century as a geopolitical blast: 'The Russians exploded the old intra-continental Eurasia of nomads.'[2] As a result of this explosion, the entire historical development of eastern Europe, from the fifteenth century to the present day, has been inextricably connected with Russia's influence.

However, Ivan III's time was merely a prelude to the moment when Europe started talking of Russian wars. Ivan III was concerned with internal problems rather than with external ones. He was primarily engaged in consolidation of Russian lands and creation of the new Russian state. The main enemy at the time was the disintegrating Golden Horde, from which Ivan claimed independence in 1480. In 1502 Ivan managed to defeat one Tatar state using the forces of another one: the Crimean khan, acting as the Great Prince of Moscow's ally, beat the Great Horde by the River Tikhaja Sosna and put an end to its existence as a state. Russia's participation in international coalitions against the Habsburgs, in 1483–91 and 1492–98, was exclusively financial

Fessalia, Hungary and Bosnia and established a protectorate over Byzantium. Timur-i-Lenk (Tamerlane), having crushed Bayezid in the battle of Ankara (1402), captured Bayezid and displayed him in an iron cage.

Grand Prince Vasiliy III (German engraving, sixteenth century)

and diplomatic in nature. Some minor wars on the outskirts of Europe (for instance, with the Livonian Order in 1500–3) were just a latent symptom of a future westward advance.

Ivan III was at war with the external enemies for twenty years out of forty-three, that is 47 per cent of the whole length of his reign. His son, Vasiliy III (1505–33), dedicated twelve years to wars out of the twenty-eight that he ruled the country, 43 per cent of his reign. Under Ivan the Terrible's son, Fyodor Ivanovich (1584–98), wars lasted only six years, which, nevertheless, also amounts to 43 per cent of his time as ruler.

But it was Ivan IV 'the Terrible' (1533–84), grandson of Ivan III, who set the record, in both absolute and relative terms, for the duration of wars Russia was taking part in. Out of the fifty-one years of his reign Russia was campaigning for thirty-seven of them and nearly all years of peace (1533–47)

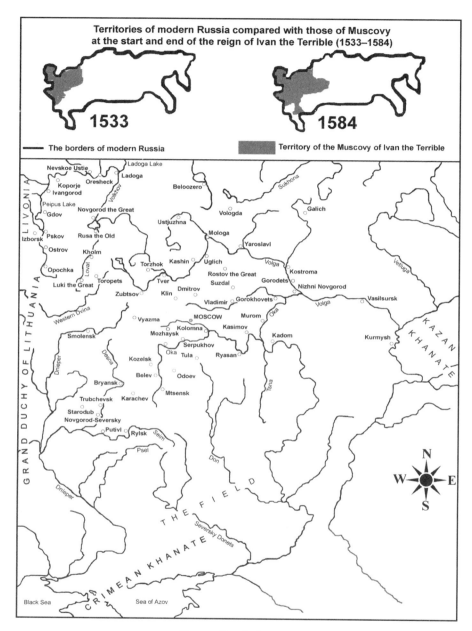

Map 1. Russia in 1533

were during the tsar's childhood. During the period from 1547 (when Ivan came of age and started ruling on his own) to 1584, there were only three years in which Russian troops were not fighting!

Tsar Ivan the Terrible
(German engraving, sixteenth century)

This extremely high intensity of fighting caused the emergence of the phenomenon of the so-called 'wartime generations', hitherto unknown in Russia where times of fighting had alternated with periods of peace. Under Ivan the Terrible a whole generation had been born and grown up in wartime. Those children had not seen their fathers. They just knew that the fathers 'were sacrificing their heads somewhere for the tsar's sake'. A young nobleman started military service when he was fifteen, was sent straight onto battlefields and had to serve until he was seriously wounded or disabled. Very few warriors survived to retire for reasons of old age and decrepitude.

The fact that war had become an essential part of the life of the Russian aristocracy is confirmed by rare extant autobiographical texts from the sixteenth century. Relating the events of their lives, people remembered war episodes before anything else. Thus, Prince Andrey Kurbsky wrote to Tsar Ivan the Terrible:

In front of your army have I marched – and marched again; and no dishonour have I brought upon you, but only brilliant victories, with the help of the Angel of the Lord, have I won for your glory, and never have I turned the back of your regiments to the foe. But far more, I have achieved most glorious conquests to increase your renown. And this, not in one year, nor yet in two – but throughout many years have I toiled with much sweat and patience; and always have I been separated from my fatherland, and little have I seen my parents, and my wife have I not known; but always in far-distant towns have I stood in arms against your foes and I have suffered many wants and natural illnesses, of which my Lord Jesus Christ is witness. Still more, I was visited with wounds inflicted by barbarian hands in various battles and all my body is already afflicted with sores.[3]

Apart from the nobility, war determined the lifestyle and living conditions of other social strata. It was war that formed the appearance of Russian cities. At the beginning of the sixteenth century there were about 160 cities in the country, inhabited by some 300,000–350,000 people. Moscow, with 100,000 people, was the largest city of Russia and Novgorod the Great, with 26,000 inhabitants, the second largest.

Structurally, towns were divided into two parts: *gorod* and *posad*. The former was usually reinforced by a wall and occupied by the administration and clergy of the town. The city garrison was also quartered there. In addition, there were siege yards (*osadnye dvory*) where inhabitants of the town could hide in case of danger. During periods of peace these *dvory* stood empty, being looked after by a yard watchman (*dvornik*) who was responsible for their safety.

In addition to governors (*namestniks*) and the tsar's appointed military commanders (*voevodes*), towns were administered by an elected govern-

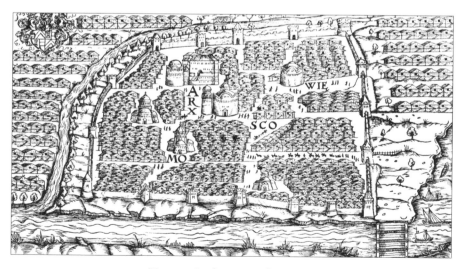

Moscow in the sixteenth century
(fragment from a contemporary German map)

ment, and in this they differed significantly from European burgomasters or councillors. The institution of an elected town commander (*gorodovoy prika-zchik*) appeared in Russian towns in 1511 and became widespread from the 1530s. They acted as commandants and were responsible for tax collection. *Prikazchiks* were in charge of a particular group of citizens – conscripts (*sluz-ilije ljudi po priboru*; literally 'serving people from conscription'), who served in a local garrison as artillerymen (*pushkars*), gate-defenders (*vorotniki*) and *pischal*-wielders (*pischalniks*; the *pischal* being an early form of matchlock musket, similar to the arquebus). These citizens received payment in the form of 'bread' (provisions) or money from the tsar. But, since the government always paid its subjects poorly and irregularly, most *sluzilije ljudi* had to keep shops in the *posad* or tend farms in order to make their living.

Posads, of which only those in large cities could afford fortifications, were inhabited by merchants and craftsmen. The city marketplace with its numerous workshops and shops was to be found there. The majority of the *posad* population paid the state a special tax and had to do a number of services for the government (so-called *chernoye tjaglo*, or 'unskilled obligation'). Some territories (called *belye slobody*, literally 'white districts' or 'free districts') were released from these services. As a rule, these belonged to monasteries.

A main difference between a Russian city of the sixteenth century and a European one can be easily seen from the above description. In the centre of the latter a market square, a city hall, houses of wealthy citizens and residences of merchant guilds and trade corporations were located. By contrast, a Russian city had as its centre a fortress, with only the troops and representatives of the authorities always settled inside it. A marketplace and houses of merchants and craftsmen were very often built outside the city fortifications. This shows the dissimilarity of the cultural priorities. For a European city its economy and self-governance were a matter of major significance. Russians saw the city's principal task as strengthening its defensive potential, for which strong military power was necessary. A town in Muscovy was first of all a military and administrative centre and, only after that, a trade and craft centre.

This characteristic of Russian cities was conditioned by the influence of the Tatar Yoke of the thirteenth to fifteenth centuries, when protection of the city walls gave the only opportunity to survive Tatar raids. Towns were built mainly as fortifications and administrative centres. By the sixteenth century the external danger had decreased, at least for the towns in the central regions. But this decrease was too little to forget about the danger completely and give up old cultural orientations. In the sixteenth century, Moscow, the capital of the country, was set on fire by the Tatars twice, in 1521 and 1571. Southern Russian towns were also attacked by the Tatars dozens of times. In 1521,

1541, 1571 and 1591 Tatar invasions threatened the central lands of Russia. Cities on the Russian–Lithuanian border were assaulted several tens of times. That is why the defensive functions and the status of a city as a military centre retained their importance throughout the sixteenth century.

The peasantry did not avoid the influence of warfare either. Until the end of the sixteenth century Russian peasants were personally independent and not obliged to do military service. In the event of enemy attack they could be mustered to serve in the militia, but the instances of gathering the militia even within separate territories were already extremely rare in the sixteenth century. Usually, when large towns were under siege the local peasant population had no choice but to take part in the defence of the town where they had found shelter.

Still, both peasantry and townsfolk ('black people', the inhabitants of *posad*) performed certain military duties for the tsar's benefit, including: *pososhnaya*, service in special detachments, the equivalent of pioneers, engaged in picking up dead bodies, building siege fortifications etc; *jamskaya*, providing carts for the government's needs; and *postroynaya*, participation in building the city fortifications. Moreover, urban population had to give, among other taxes, money for the maintenance of *streltsy* (regular units of arquebusiers) and the purchase and production of gunpowder. Thus, peasants and town-dwellers of the fifteenth and early sixteenth centuries contributed 20–30 per cent of their annual income in total, the greater portion of these taxes being intended for military needs.

Yet the Russian peasantry suffered not only from taxes and heavy duties but also from the war, which contributed directly to the dramatic change of their class status. The ceaseless wars waged by Ivan the Terrible meant a nobleman spent most of his time on the battlefields, not on his estate. He was not able physically to manage it and control the peasants on his estates. Wealthy nobles could afford to hire a manager and not to visit their estates for many years. But the aristocrats of more modest means faced the threat of a total loss of labour force on their lands. While a nobleman was at war, his peasants ran away from him to his richer neighbour (or were forcibly driven by this neighbour – a practice known as *svoz krestian*). Having discharged his duties, a nobleman returned home at last, only to find himself ruined, his fields and household neglected and his peasants gone in an unknown direction. This phenomenon of an exodus of peasants (forced or otherwise) was called *pustoshit' pomestje* ('to empty an estate').

The authorities were seriously troubled by the problem. Firstly, it encouraged desertion as nobles would leave their duties and return to their lands to save them from ruin and to fight the neighbours for the rustled peasants.

Secondly, a bankrupt nobleman, owner of an 'emptied' estate, was not a full-value warrior anymore as he could not maintain and equip himself. By the end of the Livonian War (1580s) there was only about 20 per cent of the prewar population left in the lands around Novgorod the Great. And these were the very lands which had been distributed among the nobility to form a Muscovite noble cavalry, the heart of the Great Prince of Moscow's army, several decades before!

The government solved the problem by introducing serfdom in the late sixteenth century. From that moment the peasants became attached to the nobleman, who was their owner and so they could not leave him. Fugitives were hunted down and, as soon as they were caught, put into special military detachments. The introduction of serfdom took about seventy years. It started at the very end of Ivan the Terrible's reign, in the 1580s, with the establishment of the so-called 'forbidden years' (*zapovednye leta*), a temporary prohibition on the transfer of peasants from one owner to another for a period of several years, applied to a specific region. The process was completed only in 1649 when the state statute book, *Sobornoe Ulozhenie* (*The Code of Law*), was created. *Sobornoe Ulozhenie* prescribed a lifelong and relentless search for runaway peasants.

It is indicative that the process of introducing serfdom started simultaneously with the unsuccessful (for Russia) end of the twenty-five-year-long Livonian War. That was the moment when the issue of the preservation and maintenance of the nobles' army became especially severe. The nobles did not want to fight, being aware of ruin and poverty waiting for them at home. Since the state had called them up for service, let the state guarantee their financial security and the presence of the labour force in their estates. The government met the demands by turning peasants into serfs. Thus, the war factor of the late sixteenth century caused the enslavement of the whole class of hitherto personally free rural workers. This measure played its role in unleashing the first civil war in Russian history in the early seventeenth century, known as the 'Time of Troubles'. The unwillingness of the peasants to submit to such a cardinal change in their social status was one of the prime causes of the war.

It is clear, therefore, that in the sixteenth century war affected the fate of all secular classes of Russian society. For some war was a *modus vivendi*, others woke up one fine morning to find themselves serfs. The very appearance of the country, most notably in the urban culture, was formed by the real or imaginary menace of war. All Ivan the Terrible's military doctrine was conditioned by this constant feeling of the total militarisation of life.

In spite of the despotic character of his reign, Ivan the Terrible could not force his subjects to fight for almost forty years relying only on compulsion and tyranny. A new, comprehensible and widely accepted ideology of conquest must have been created and brought to the masses. Under Ivan the Terrible, Russia's highly developed foreign policy doctrine rested upon the interpretation of the role played on the historical scene by Russia. That interpretation was based on belief in the exalted destiny and historical mission of the Orthodox people. This messianic idea emerged a hundred years before Ivan the Terrible, when Russia rejected the Florence Union, an alliance with the Roman Catholic Church, in 1439. Under the threat of the Ottoman invasion, the Union was signed by the Byzantine Orthodox Church – the Constantinople Patriarchy – to which the Russian Church was officially subordinated. Byzantium's behaviour was viewed in Russia as treachery. And in 1448 the Russian Orthodox Church placed itself out of Byzantium's authority and became independent.

After the events of the period from 1439 till 1448, Russians became convinced that they were the last true believers in the world. All other nations, practising Roman Catholicism, Islam or (from the sixteenth century) Protestantism, were going the wrong way. This thought gave rise to a feeling of peculiarity and particular responsibility for the fate of the Christian religion laid upon Russians by God. An idea appeared of Russia being a New Israel and the mission of Russian tsars was similar to that of kings of Israel. They were predestined to lead their people to the Kingdom of Heaven and to deliver the light of the true religion to other peoples (including those conquered by Russia).

This doctrine did not lead to the idea of crusades; Ivan the Terrible had no intention of forcibly implanting Orthodoxy on neighbouring countries. That was not the aim of his wars. Russian occupying troops built Orthodox churches in conquered countries for their own needs, but didn't force the inhabitants to change faith or convert to Orthodox views. The consequence of the Orthodox ideology was that Russians felt their absolute rightfulness and superiority over other peoples in any situation.

Here is an interesting episode. In 1578 the diplomats of the Grand Duchy of Lithuania (GDL), wishing to please the Russian tsar, named him 'not the last' among the worldly lords. That caused a burst of indignation. The boyars (the highest ranking of the nobility) declared on behalf of the tsar:

> This is humiliation not praise. 'Not the last' is merely 'not the worst' but where there are twenty or more people there 'not the last' might be the tenth or the fifteenth one . . . But we, as far as God's will is, do not know anyone

above us: neither the fifteenths, nor the tenths, nor the fifths, nor the sixths, nor any others. But everywhere, with God's mercy, we are the first among sovereigns.[4]

The feeling of superiority and messianic ideas agreed with the eschatological expectations. In 1492 it was seven thousand years since the creation of the world, and the Russian system of chronology started with this event. That's why the year 1492 was awaited with fear. According to the prophecies of Mefody Patarsky, Gregory Korinfsky and Mefody Victorin: 'Humankind has been predestined to live for seven thousand years from the Creation to the End of the world'.

The prophecies appeared to be coming true: in 1453 Constantinople was seized by the Ottomans. In Russia the event was received with mixed feelings of satisfaction and horror: satisfaction at the thought of the treacherous Byzantines, who had signed the Union with Rome, justly punished; and horror caused by the collapse of the world, predicted by Mefody Patarsky, that had to follow the fall of Constantinople.

What did the Chosen People, the New Israel, feel on the eve of Doomsday? Russian Orthodox believers became more and more convinced about their particular mission and their superiority over all other peoples. It was taken for granted that only Russians would represent mankind on Judgement Day since all the others – Catholics, Protestants and Muslims – were just unworthy of it.

In 1547 Ivan the Terrible was crowned and became the first Russian tsar. Moscow Metropolitan Macarius, who conducted the ceremony, defined the significance of the title of tsar, and the new role of the Orthodox tsar, as follows:

> O Grand Prince Ivan Vasilievich, God-crowned Tsar of the whole of Russia, accept from God as a gift this sceptre to rule the standards of the Great Empire of Russia, watch over and protect it [the Empire] with all your strength[5]

Russia's change to tsardom was an event of huge importance. The realisation of the idea of God's realm on earth has been considered a historical mission of the Russian tsars and the ultimate aim and meaning of Russian history since that moment. For example, in a monument to the official ideology, *Stepennaja Kniga* (*The Book of the Stages*, 1563) the past of the Russian lands was depicted as seventeen stages of a staircase, leading Russia to God's realm. The book draws direct parallels between Russian history and the Holy Scriptures. Thus, Prince Vladimir's kin were named 'the New Israel's kin' and

The crowning of Ivan the Terrible in 1547
(from a Russian chronicle, sixteenth century)

Vladimir himself was compared to David, Yaroslav the Wise to Solomon, and Ivan III to Jesus Navin (Joshua). The reign of Ivan IV was claimed in the book to be the climax of both Russian and world history.

Henceforth, any actions of a Russian tsar, including wars intended for glorification of the Orthodoxy and chastisement of 'wrong-believing' neighbours, were accepted as righteous and justified. And here the roots of Ivan the Terrible's tyranny and aggression lie.

In what geopolitical context did Moscow see itself? It felt encircled by enemies, a state of God's beloved people in a ring of 'wrong-believers': Catholics, Protestants and Muslims. Ivan the Terrible used to talk about the 'four sabres' ceaselessly fighting against him: the Crimean, Kazan and Astrakhan khanates and the Nogay Horde; and beside them the 'fifth sabre' – the Grand Duchy of Lithuania.

Ivan IV's diplomats divided all the surrounding countries into two types: 'brotherly nations', related to Russia on the principles of 'love and friendship', and 'neighbours', which were the objects of hostility and potential adversaries in war. The notion of 'friendship' included, apart from good-neighbour diplomatic relations and free trade, a readiness to enter into political or even military alliance. But the highest level of friendly relations was 'love', which meant willingness to 'stand as one against the foes'. Such a formula allowed the origin of this category to be connected with the Christian belief that 'no one has greater love than he who gives up his life for his friends' (John, 15:13). The formula of an alliance implied: 'the one who is your friend becomes a friend of ours; the one who is an enemy of yours is our enemy'.

On the basis of these views an interesting episode took place in Anglo-Russian relations. In 1582, when Ivan tried to contract a military and political alliance with Queen Elizabeth, Russia demanded from England a list of its enemies: since from that moment they were to become the enemies of Russia as well. The Russians were even ready to send troops for English coastal defence. In return, Ivan IV wanted Elizabeth to acknowledge Russia's enemies (first of all the Kingdom of Poland, GDL and Crimean khanate) as Britain's enemies too. England was expected to be prepared to take up arms against them. The English diplomats managed to find a splendid answer by which the Russian diplomats were completely stumped: 'Give us a list of your enemies and we'll try to make you friends'.[6] The treaty between the two countries was not concluded; such diplomatic language could not be understood at Ivan the Terrible's court.

What was the scheme used by Russian diplomats in international affairs? First of all, the results of Ivan the Terrible's conquests had to be legalised. In sixteenth-century Russia the chief means of expanding the land was the forcible annexation of neighbouring territories: 'towns and lands are not acquired whilst sitting at table'.[7] Victorious wars and subjugation of peoples were regarded to be distinctive features of the true tsar and Russian rulers were extremely anxious to appear true tsars.

But any invasion must be justified. And here the other discourse prevailed: the subjugation of bordering lands was accepted as restoration of the ruined state body. Moscow's ideological paradigm said that Rus had been a single whole once, then it had disintegrated and Russia's historical mission consisted of its revival. That's why all annexations of the supposedly foreign territories were stated to be, in fact, measures for restoring Russia within its original God-given borders. The policy applied not only to the former principalities of Ancient Rus but also to the neighbouring non-Russian lands. All the space from the Volga region to the Azov and from the Baltic Sea to the Northern Black Sea coast, as one annalist of the sixteenth century puts it: 'This is the whole of Russian land.' For all that, Russia was not regarded as an ethnic or state community but merely as the hereditary estate of the Rjurikovichi, the dynasty of the Moscow grand princes. As Sergey Bogatyrev keenly observed, the idea of a patrimonial estate seems to have been the only comprehensible concept for Moscow diplomats and they have become highly skilled in manipulating this concept in their reasoning.[8]

As the idea of Moscow recovering its native territories (not conquering new ones!) prevailed, the explanation of why these territories had been lost became urgent. The argument was extremely simple but nevertheless effective. These lands were 'traitors'. The majority of punitive operations of Muscovite troops aimed at the deposition of local dynasties were, in accordance with the political discourse of the time, justified as forced measures aroused by the urgent need to punish the traitors. The principle applied to both Russian and non-Russian territories.[9]

From the standpoint of Muscovite chroniclers, the subjugation of Kazan by Ivan the Terrible in 1552 was a penalty for treason. After all, Ivan III's troops captured Kazan as early as 1487 and up to 1535 it was officially considered to be a Russian protectorate. Having taken advantage of Ivan IV's infancy, Kazan had betrayed Russia and, consequently, was justly punished by its aggression. Furthermore, the Cheremises, a people from the Volga region, settled on the khanate's territories, were declared the descendants of lowly fugitives from Rostov (a small town in Central Russia), who in their time had fled there to avoid christening. The seizure of Astrakhan in 1556 was declared to be in response to the treason of a puppet khan, Derbish-Ghali, enthroned by the Russian army in 1554.

The conquests in Livonia, according to Muscovite ideology, were also in response to the 'treasons' of Livonian cities. 'Livonian Germans' were considered to be bondsmen of the Great Prince of Moscow 'from olden times'. But 'Livonian Germans' were not going to submit and refused to pay tribute that would have symbolised their obedience to Russia. That's why the tsar assailed them in wrath. The war with Lithuania that interceded for Livonia broke out also because of treason. Since Livonian towns had betrayed Ivan and gone over to Sigismund, the Russian tsar had legal ground and God's blessing to fight the traitors.

By the 1560s Ivan the Terrible brought the scheme of armed annexation of neighbouring lands to perfection. In response to a petition by a country's population, a Muscovite prince raises a ruler to the throne, the ungrateful population then betrays and dethrones this ruler and God punishes the land for its 'falsehood' with the tsar's campaign. However, at the sight of Muscovite regiments, the population has a chance to rapidly repent of the 'treason' and forward another petition to the tsar, again asking to admit them to his citizenship. That is how the subjection of Novgorod the Great, Tver, Kazan, Astrakhan and even Livonia were depicted in Ivan the Terrible's chronicles.

Russian princes in their turn 'showed their mercy' by making the wrongdoers swear fealty and 'granting' a new ruler.

Only in the sixteenth century did the world learn what Russia's wars were like. In 1558 Russia started the first war in its history with European countries, known as the Livonian War (1558–83). On the battlefields the Russians fought with Poles, Lithuanians, Livonians, Swedes, as well as mercenaries from the German lands, Scotland, Italy, France and Hungary. The Vatican and Denmark were also involved in the conflict. To comprehend the character of their new enemy, whose onslaught was being compared to Ottoman aggression against 'the Christian world', Europeans had to have a closer look at it. Thus, because of war, the rest of the world became more interested in Russia.

In conclusion, the concept of Moscow as the 'Third Rome', frequently connected with the Russian political ideology of the sixteenth century in historical literature, must be mentioned. In accordance with the concept, Moscow accepted the functions of the world centre of Christianity, which originally belonged to Rome, then to Constantinople (the 'Second Rome') and at last were transferred to Moscow (the 'Third Rome'). There was to be no 'Fourth Rome'.

It must be emphasised, however, that the concept of Moscow as the 'Third Rome', invented by Philophey, a monk of the Eleasar's monastery in Pskov in the years 1523–4, was not an essential part of Russian political doctrine during Ivan the Terrible's reign. It was of exclusively clerical character during that period. It was the idea of the 'New Israel', not the 'Third Rome', that was used to ground the notion of Russia's particular significance and destiny. The idea of 'Moscow, the Third Rome' gained political influence only in the 1580s, after Ivan the Terrible's death; specifically, in 1589, The Fifth Ecumenical Moscow Patriarchy was established and Moscow became a world religious centre, adopting the role that had hitherto been played by Constantinople. But this was at the time of Ivan's successors.

The present book recounts a history of Ivan the Terrible's military policy in the west and the east. This was a new type of war, hitherto unknown in Russia, intended for the annexation, or even utter destruction, of foreign countries. In the course of these wars, three states (namely the Livonian Order, Kazan khanate and Astrakhan khanate) were swept away forever. The conquest of Siberia, which would become a cornerstone of the future Russian Empire, began in that period – in 1582 – though its history is not covered because it was a private initiative and, furthermore, was not not completed until the seventeenth century, long after Ivan the Terrible's death in 1584. Military organisation was established as the foundation of Russian social structure. The government applied military methods to the population, launching campaigns against its own subjects (notably the notorious massacre in Novgorod in 1570, committed by the *Oprichniki**). Ivan the Terrible's wars have fostered a negative image of Russia in Europe and assigned it to a certain place within the world system. The remnants of this influence can still be found today. To understand its essence one should scrutinise its source – Ivan the Terrible's military policy.

---

* The *Oprichniki* were members of the tsar's special guard in existence between 1565 and 1572. Used as an instrument of repression, they had extraordinary powers for the 'struggle against traitors', which they used to unleash a reign of terror on the population. They were organised on the lines of a religious order, Ivan the Terrible having the title 'Father Superior'. They wore rough black habits and carried brooms and severed dogs' heads, to symbolise their role in sweeping and gnawing out treason. Ivan the Terrible reputedly wore the silver-plated head of an Alsatian on his chest, the teeth of which chattered in time with his steps.

I

Russian Military Forces in the Sixteenth Century

The Infrastructure of the Russian Army

Russia was not involved in the so-called European 'military revolution' that began in the fifteenth to sixteenth centuries. This consisted of giving up the system of feudal, knightly warfare, the growing role of artillery and professional mercenaries and various changes in armament, strategy and tactics.[1] In Russia there was nothing of the kind. Of course, some technical innovations reached Russia. Artillery and firearms were known and used but their appearance did not lead to any significant changes in military organisation. It is generally agreed that firearms were not popular in Russian armies as long as the main enemies of Muscovy were the Eastern steppe armies of Tatars. They tended to be slow to adopt firearms because they hindered speed of manoeuvre. Only in the second half of the sixteenth century, when the West became Ivan the Terrible's main enemy, did firearms become widespread.

As a result, Russian armed forces could successfully hold out against the armies of approximately equal development. Russians defeated Tatars as well as armies from northern Caucasian, Volga region and Siberian states. Success was achieved in wars with the Livonian Order, Grand Duchy of Lithuania and in a clash with the Ottoman army, the first one in the history of relationships between the two powers. But Russian armies could oppose Polish troops only with difficulty, and the very first collision with the mercenaries of a new European type, sent against Russia by Stefan Bathory in 1578, led Moscow to the brink of a military catastrophe.

The Russian army under Ivan the Terrible was irregular and organised according to a class principle. All nobles were obliged to perform lifelong service. Units of commoners were of two types. Firstly, musters of the so-called *datochnije ludi*, irregular detachments composed, as a rule, of townsmen and gathered in a case of emergency; secondly, units of professional soldiers who were paid money and bread for their service. The latter were not similar to European mercenaries. A warrior did not sell his sabre to the one who paid more (as it was in Europe) but went to the only possible employer, the

Map of Russia by Antonio Jenkinson, 1593

Orthodox tsar. The fees he got for it were quite small and the payments were not regular. That was not an advantageous bargain. The money given by the state was not intended to enrich a warrior but to provide him with the minimum necessary to perform his duties.

The only difference between this type of service and service for aristocrats was that a nobleman could not choose whether to serve or not. Enrolment to the commoners' units was voluntary and available for ordinary folk, the only condition being that they could not be slaves. Of course, the absence of compulsion was illusory in many cases. Local authorities could force a person to enrol in the *datochnije ludi*. But military recruiters were not known in Russia. Russian society was prejudiced against European mercenaries, such behaviour was considered shameful. Russians were convinced that a man should fight for his faith, tsar and motherland. To be paid for the service was mean-spirited. Participating in a war was a duty not a commercial undertaking.

The Russian army included cavalry, infantry, artillery and auxiliary units. Cavalry can be regarded as the main arm and the foundation of the Russian armed forces in the sixteenth century. Operations involving large cavalry formations were the primary tactic of the Russian army in the sixteenth century: clashes of mounted detachments on campaign, 'avalanche' charges of cavalry, assaults on neighbouring lands, raids on the enemy's territories and so on. In the event of Tatar intrusions, Russian troops tried to avoid pitched battles in wide open spaces. They either took the defensive behind their fortifications or used the same tactics as the Tatars did: for example, cavalry raids, outflanking manoeuvres, cavalry strikes and counterstrikes.

The cavalry consisted of four parts. The first, the mainstay and elite of the army, comprised the nobility. Every noble was obliged to bring with him a certain number of warriors who were provided for and armed at his expense. Most of these, consisting largely of house-serfs or 'fighting servants' (or slaves – the so-called '*boevye cholopy*') though some of them could be professional soldiers, served with their master and constituted the second portion of the cavalry. The Cossacks (discussed later) were the third component and the fourth was made up of cavalry regiments of Kazan, Astrakhan and Nogay Tatars that had pledged allegiance to Russia. The latter were frequently used in western campaigns. These were all light cavalry; Russia did not have a heavy cavalry force.

In the sixteenth century, the techniques of cavalry fighting did not yet bear any trace of the effects of the mass introduction of gunpowder weapons. The use of firearms spread to the Russian cavalry only in the seventeenth century, when flintlock guns became common. As long as the only guns available were matchlocks requiring up to ninety-five actions to load and fire each shot, the mass employment of firearms by cavalry was impossible.

The use of firearms was the privilege of the infantry, which was of secondary importance and used only in situations where they were absolutely necessary, such as garrisons and sieges. In contrast to Europe, there were no pike-armed infantrymen in the Russian army. This is connected with the fact that Russian infantry at this time did not employ a linear formation to repulse enemy cavalry attacks. In principle, Russians tended to avoid field battles against mounted troops unless there were any fortifications or, at least, natural obstacles such as rivers, ravines or forests, to take cover behind.

The dominant force of footsoldiers in Ivan the Terrible's day were the *streltsy* (literally 'shooters', from the word *streljat,* meaning 'to shoot at somebody'), who were equipped with firearms. These were a new type of soldier which emerged in the middle of the sixteenth century and rapidly became numerous. They were recruited in the typically Russian manner of hiring for money and 'bread'. The appearance of *streltsy* reinforced the Russian army greatly. Almost all victories at the time were won with the assistance of *streltsy* and owing largely to their efforts.

Under Ivan the Terrible the role of the artillery (*narjad*), which was singled out into a special branch, became much more significant. Russian artillery was divided into three types: fortress, siege and field. The siege artillery was the most highly developed and, as contemporaries reported, was competitive with that of Europe. The use of field artillery, on the other hand, was underdeveloped. To exploit field cannon, a special device was invented and named *gulyay-gorod* (literally: 'walking town'). This was a mobile wooden fortress made of high shields mounted on wheels. *Gulyay-gorod* could be moved around a field while arrows and gunfire were delivered from its shelter. The device proved particularly effective against Tatar cavalry.

The Russian army of the sixteenth century did not have any specialised auxiliary detachments. Military medical services, support services and an engineering branch did not yet exist. The universal auxiliary troops (*posokha*) were recruited from the common people (peasants and townsfolk). They were labourers, multi-purpose gangs for all eventualities. *Posokha* helped to drag heavy guns and carts during marches, hacked paths through forests, built temporary bridges, dug siege and defence fortifications, picked up those who had been wounded on battlefields and gathered dead bodies and trophies. When necessity demanded, *posokha* participated in combat operations and even in assaults on fortresses, but the quality of these militiamen was too low for them to become the shock troops of the army.

Posokha detachments were not maintained on a permanent basis but were mustered occasionally for specific campaigns, after the completion of which they were disbanded. Enrolment in the *posokha* was treated like a special duty, being a part of the state service (that is, service performed for the tsar personally). There were cases when every third or fourth adult male of a certain region was taken for the *posokha*. Those performing such service were paid by the state to give them the means to maintain themselves during campaigns.

Russian warrior (German engraving, sixteenth century)

The structure of the Russian army went back to the Middle Ages and had not changed much by the sixteenth century. The regiment still remained the principal tactic unit. At the start of a campaign all the army was divided into several regiments, as had happened a century or two previously. The usual deployment was in a battle line divided into three divisions: left wing, centre, right wing. The left flank was protected by the so-called 'regiment of the left hand' (*polk levoy ruki*), the right flank by the 'regiment of the right hand' (*polk pravoy ruki*). The centre was greatly reinforced and was the main body both in offence and defence, attacks on the wings and outflanking manoeuvres being rare. In the centre a 'guard regiment' (*peredovoy polk*) was thrown forward, or from the second half of the sixteenth century it was a so-called *yertowl*, a mobile cavalry detachment used for reconnaissance. Immediately behind it was placed the 'advanced regiment' or vanguard (*storozhevoy*), and behind this the main force or 'great regiment' (*bolshoy polk*) was drawn up. The high command of the army was located in the great regiment and artillery was usually attached to it, either field artillery (*maliyj narjad*) of a medium calibre or heavy siege cannon (*bolshoy narjad*). The size of regiments varied from 2,000 to 5,000 people.

What was the overall strength of the Russian army under Ivan the Terrible? A precise answer is impossible. Visiting foreign diplomats gave numbers ranging from 100,000 to 300,000. Figures provided by Russian sources are noticeably lower. All military appointments were recorded, along with the size of the regiments indicated, in special 'Rank Books' (*razrjadnye knigi*). According to them, the maximum strength of the noble cavalry in the 1560s was around 30,000–35,000, and in the seventeenth century approximately 15,000–20,000 people. Obviously, the truth lies somewhere in the middle because the rank books did not always include 'fighting servants', *streltsy* and Cossacks and, therefore, underestimated the size of the army. By the middle of the sixteenth century the efficient part of it apparently fluctuated from 50,000 to 100,000 people. By the end of the century, because of deaths in the Livonian War, the crisis of the noble service system and the increased rate of desertion, this figure was reduced.[2]

'WE HAVE ONLY ONE RIGHT – TO DIE FOR OUR TSAR!':
RUSSIAN NOBLES AND MILITARY SERVICE

Analogous to Europe of the Middle Ages, the sixteenth-century Russian community could be divided into 'those that pray' (*oratores*), fighters (*bellatores*) and workers (*laboratores*). But there were two essential differences. Firstly, Russian *laboratores* were weak, few in numbere and, in contrast to their European equivalents, could never become a middle-class

Moskovites (German engraving, 1576)

bourgeoisie. Secondly, Russian *bellatores* did not possess any lands. They were only conditional, temporary owners of their lands and depended on the state authorities for everything. Their relationship with the state materially differed from those in Europe.

In most medieval European countries these relationships were determined by the formula of vassal dependence which, apart from the obligations put upon a vassal by his overlord, guaranteed certain rights and privileges of feudal immunity. Russia did not experience the vassal system of the European type. Relations between a lord and his subject developed according to the different principles here. The Russian tsar represented the highest authority. In relation to him, all subjects, regardless of their social status (boyars, nobility, townsfolk or clergy), were in an equally servile and dependent state. That means that there was the only one 'superior person' in the country while all others were 'inferior'. It is indicative, therefore, that the expression 'I am your slave' (*Az esm' tvoj cholop*) became an official form of address used by aristocrats towards the tsar.

Russian noblemen possessed neither property nor any legal guarantees of their position. The consequence of such conditions was that real opposition to the arbitrary nature of the authorities could not appear in Russia until the nineteenth century. Not a single attempt was undertaken to create ruling institutions of a parliamentary type on a regular basis. 'Slavish consciousness' and fear of the tsar's wrath were instilled in Russian nobility at a genetic level.[3]

All this became apparent in the specific institutional setting of the Russian monarchy. In 1547 the Russian ruler adopted the title of tsar. Ideologically the tsar's status noticeably differed from west European kingship. Though a king had always been regarded as an anointed sovereign he had not been considered to be an immediate representative of God. This function had been attributed to the pope. A Russian tsar was a direct representative of God on Earth. His position rested on the principles formulated by Paul the Apostle: 'Let every person be subject to the governing authorities. For there is no authority except from God, and those that exist have been instituted by God. Therefore he who resists the authorities resists what God has appointed, and those who resist will incur judgment' (Romans 13:1–2). This norm taken as a moral basis in Russian medieval society of the mid sixteenth century affected even *Domostroy*, a book containing regulations of everyday life and housekeeping!

Hence, any rebellion against the throne was considered a transgression against God, an awful sin. This fact, by the way, reveals one of the reasons why the idea of the defence of personal rights has not acquired wide dissemination in Russia. The overwhelming majority of the population easily submitted to tyranny. The remonstrance against it used to be attributed either to criminal elements ('rebellious people') or to disturbers of the conventional moral standards. The latter included those who fled abroad as the first Russian dissidents (such as Prince Andrey Kurbsky in the sixteenth century and a minor clerk, Gregory Kotoshikhin, in the seventeenth century) or criticised the Orthodox Church and its ideology (Russian 'free-thinkers').

This also explains the essential distinctions in mentality and ethics of Russian and European aristocrats. Russian noblemen's system of values had faithfulness to the tsar and the Orthodox Church at its heart. This was evident in many aspects. Thus, a challenge to a duel in order to vindicate someone's honour was an acceptable norm for Europeans. For Russians, a duel was a crime, a needless murder: the only proper way to kill or to die was to do so in battle, for the tsar's sake. European aristocrats thought it disgraceful to wait on the lord of the manor at table. It was servants' task. Russian nobles, for their part, did not see anything blameworthy in it. On the contrary, to offer cups and dishes to the overlord used to be the highest honour. It is revealing that the names of many ranks from the court (*dvorets*, meaning 'palace') hierarchy have been related to table service: *stol'nick* ('a man serving at table'), *chashnichiy* (a man bringing a cap'), *kravchiy* ('cup-bearer') and so on.

What was the basis of such a subordinated position of Russian nobility and such all-embracing power of the tsar? Russian serving noblemen did not own their lands, they received their estates as temporary possessions. Of course, this did not mean that in practice nobles' lands were constantly being confiscated and distributed anew. Since all the male members of a given family served there was no sense in the endless 'shuffling' of the estates (*pomestje*). As a rule, the estate was kept by the family passing on from one kinsman to another until the family had no men able to do the service. Usually elder sons parted from the father and got an additional plot of land as an 'allowance'. The younger sons were allotted estates cut from their father's. Besides, the serving aristocracy tended to secure the temporary estates for the kin, turning them into patrimony (*votchina*). A patrimonial estate was not the occupier's property either. It was, just like a *pomestje*, held on the conditional terms and granted in return for service. But it was granted to a whole family, not a single representative of it. Therefore, it could be inherited *de jure*, not only *de facto* as was the case with a *pomestje*.

Throughout the sixteenth and seventeenth centuries, Russian nobles longed to unify *pomestjes* and *votchinas* into a single form of possession with the power of alienation and rights both of demise and purchase and sale. But these rights were obtained only in Peter the Great's time when, in 1714, *pomestje* as a form of landownership was liquidated. And nobles' right for the lands was legalised only in 1785 in 'The Charter Bestowed to Nobility' (*Zhalovannaya gramota dvoryanstvu*) when Empress Catherine II declared that a nobleman could be deprived of his property by the court's decision only in cases of lese-majesty. Until then, the authorities could on legal grounds take away lands and other property from any person at any time. That's why Russian nobles, until the eighteenth century, felt a kind of refined pride in saying that they had only one right – to die for their tsar's sake.

How did the system of noble service look in the sixteenth century? An aristocrat began his service at the age of fifteen, when he was called a 'newcomer' (*novick*). He could serve in one of the two existing types of nobles' militia. The most widespread and less prestigious was the so-called 'enrolment from towns' (*vybor iz gorodov*). The nobles, also known as *dvory-ane* or *deti boyarskie* (boyars' children), were mustered in the administrative centres of the districts (*uezd*) where their estates were situated. These detachments were called after the name of the central settlement of the *uezd*: the Novgorod nobles, the Kostroma nobles, the Tver nobles and so on.

In every district the special lists of the nobles obliged to enrol for service from the given *uezd* were compiled. Since 1556 the lists have been called *desyatnjas* ('the list of scores'). *Desyatnjas* were of two types: *verstalnye* ('list of incomes'), fixed money and lands given by the state, while *razbornye* ('list of information about service') recorded information about new appointments, investitures, wounds and so on. These papers were sent from the districts to a special department in Moscow, the Razryadniy Prikaz (the medieval Russian prototype of the Military Ministry). Copies of *desyatnjas* were sent to the Pomestniy Prikaz (department controlling land ownership of nobles).

The nobles were divided into different social levels (so-called *stati*, or 'ranks') according to their gentility, riches, services in battle. For example, in 1550, Muscovite nobles of the first rank received a subsidy of twelve roubles, those of the second rank received ten roubles and the third rank only eight roubles.

In 1556 Ivan the Terrible promulgated new legislation on military service – the so-called '*Ulozhenie o Sluzhbe*' ('Codex of Military Service'). Now every nobleman was obliged to appear before the regiment in person and to raise one cavalryman with horse and armour from every hundred *chets* of his estate (one *chet* was about 5.6 hectares, or 5,600 sq. m). If a noble man was poor, had a small estate and could not provide enough soldiers, the requirements of the duty were lowered. Average size of estates during the reign of Ivan the Terrible was from 100 to 400 *chets*. But in practice some had less or more (especially if they held land not only as *pomestje* but as *votchina* too).

If a nobleman had collected more warriors than he was obliged to, he received subsidiary money according to the armament of these people. For example, a complete set of armour was worth 4.5–5 roubles; a sabre 3 roubles and a helmet 1 rouble.* If a nobleman could not collect sufficient warriors to meet the requirement, or the equipment of those raised was deficient, he was liable to pay a fine proportionate to the shortfall in men or arms.

How did the system work in practice? We have only a few *desyatnjas* of Ivan the Terrible's time, but still we can give some examples. In 1556, 174 nobles were obliged to arrive at the muster in Serpukhovsky district. Of these ninety-two turned up, bringing 668 warriors with them. These figures require some comment. Firstly, the substantial proportion of absentees (*netchikis*) is striking. But this is not evidence of widespread evasion of military service so much as a demonstration that the Russian state had a shortage of nobleman for state service. Of those noblemen who were absent in this instance, eight were in captivity, three took up posts in local

---

* For comparison, a horse cost between 60 kopecks and 10 roubles (100 kopecks = 1 rouble); a cow 10–25 kopecks; and a sheepskin coat of ordinary quality 15–30 kopecks. The price of 1 *chetvert* (about 210 litres) of corn varied between 10 kopecks and 1.5 roubles (in bad years), with an average of 20–30 kopecks; 1 kg fresh meat cost around 16 kopecks; one barrel of milk no more then 25 kopecks; 100 eggs 3–4 kopecks; 1 kg butter 1–2 kopecks and 1 kg salt 0.2 kopecks.[4]

Russian cavalryman (German engraving, sixteenth century)

administration and four were ill. Others were serving in remote fortresses, escorting embassies abroad and so on. Only two of the eighty-two men were deserters!

Secondly, the considerable quantity of additional men (668, around seven 'fighting servants' for each of the 92 noblemen) was conditioned by the nobles' desire to receive the subsidies, not directly by the extent of the estates of Serpukhov's gentry. Many of the noblemen exceeded the requirements of the *Ulozhenie o Sluzhbe*. For example, Andrey Sabyrov had estates of about 999 hectares and was obliged to collect seventeen fighting servants, yet he put twenty-nine at his commander's disposal and received a tidy sum from the state.

However, this eagerness to exceed the standards of service had a negative result: noblemen could not equip all their servants with armour as it should be. So, in this example, 164 warriors from 668 were declared unfit for combat. Some of them had no horses, there being only 445 saddle horses and 32 pack

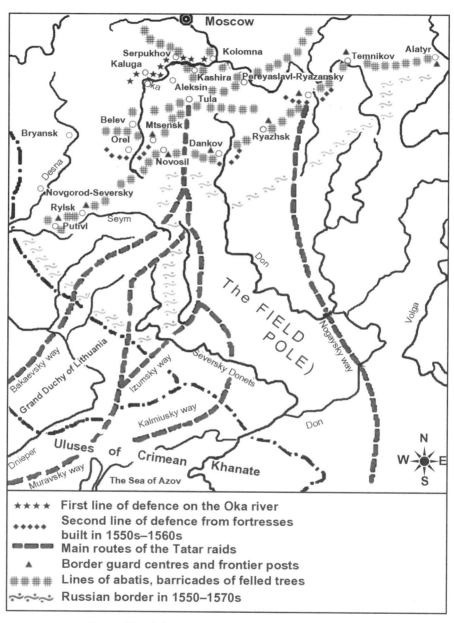

Map 2. *The defence system on Russia's southern border*

horses between them. Only 210 soldiers were fully armoured, 219 had only partial armour and 164 were only lightly protected. It is interesting that the state demanded the noblemen provide horses and armour only. Spears, sabres, battle-axes, bows and arrows were given by the state free of charge.[5]

In addition to the 'enrolment from towns', the troops of the nobility were completed by the Moscow nobles, which consisted of *stol'nicki*, *stryapchi*, *dvoryane moskovskie* and *zhiltsy*. The *stol'nicki* and *stryapchi* were lower court ranks. *Dvoryane moskovskie* were the ordinary Moscow noblemen. *Zhiltsy* were directly responsible for the tsar's palace and provided safety for the grand prince and his family. The name *zhiltsy* comes from the Russian for the verb 'to live' (*zhit*), since they lived close to the sovereign.

The principles of service were equal for Moscow and provincial noblemen. But Moscow's nobility were exceedingly rich. Their estates were 280–560 hectares and they received 20–100 roubles annually. Many of them had *pomestje* estates and *votchina* at once. It is interesting that the typical number of Moscow noblemen was modest, around 2,000 or 3,000, yet the great extent of their lands allowed them to gather many fighting servants. The strength of the tsar's regiment could amount to 20,000 people!

The military service was 'in siege' (in fortresses, *gorodovaya* or *osadnaya*) or regimental. The first was not prestigious. Service in fortresses was for noblemen who were poor or in ill health, perhaps as the result of wounds. The regimental service was more important. It was divided into 'remote service' (a campaign into foreign countries) and 'boundary service' (*beregovaya*, literally 'at the bank', since the main, southern frontier of the Russian state was on the bank of the river Oka).

Junior commanders in the regiments were *golovy* (from *golova* or *glava* – 'head' or 'chief'). They usually commanded one or several hundred warriors. The highest military post was *voevode*. There was a kind of hierarchy among the highest *voevodes*. The *voevode* of the great regiment was the main commander. After him in seniority came the *voevode* of the regiment of the right hand then of the guard regiment, and, finally, of the regiment of the left hand. Since the number of *voevodes* in each regiment varied from two to four, there was a separate hierarchy within them running from the first *voevode*, the second *voevode* and so on.

The appointment of individuals to any post was determined by order of precedence (*mestnichestvo*). According to this the places in the hierarchy that could be occupied by the member of a certain kin were defined by the places (*mestos*) taken by his ancestors' service. For example, if the forefathers of the Troecourovi noble clan had occupied positions higher than those of the Buturlini's kinsfolk, nobody from the Troecourovi family could take a post where he would be subordinated to some of the Buturlini. It would be not a simple dishonour but would throw the whole of his kin back in the order of precedence.

During a war such restrictions could be very dangerous. So, one of the first military reforms of Ivan the Terrible was the denunciation and disaffirmation of this system in 1549 and 1550. But even Ivan the Terrible could not cope with the Russian aristocracy's arrogance. An order of precedence continued to determine official appointments in spite of all the authorities' attempts to extirpate this faulty practice. It was only successfully abolished ninety-eight years after Ivan the Terrible's death. In 1682 the authorities found a solution of simple genius: according to the tsar's decree all the Rank Books were burnt. Noblemen could not start quarrels related to *mestnichestvo* since the documents which had been the basis of all the arguments on the subject were physically destroyed.

Apart from the sense of duty, the prospect of booty and land allotments by the tsar, what were the motives for the Russian nobleman's service? The system of encouragement and reward in Ivan the Terrible's army was quite limited. Both distinguished *voevodes* and common warriors might, as a great honour, be allowed to 'see the tsar's eyes', that is to attend a special audience with the tsar. A warrior could be rewarded with a special order, a gold coin, the so-called *ugorsky zolotoy*. Or he could be granted additional land as a *votchina* or *pomestje*, or be given gifts of clothing, jewellery and so on.

The advancement of distinguished *voevodes* up the scale of rank was possible. Successful commanders were promoted to higher positions. But this movement was restricted by the order of precedence and was not a major motivating factor. Every nobleman understood the limits he could reach and he knew as well that he would not go a step higher regardless of any services he had performed.

Obviously, fear of the tsar's wrath was a major stimulus. Apart from the dishonour for a warrior and all his kin, military defeat very often resulted in violent punishment from the tsar. The punishment of the actual culprit frequently led to repressions against the other, absolutely innocent, members of his kin and to the confiscation of the patrimonial estates, which could be a catastrophe for the family. For example, we know the fate of the *voevodes* who surrendered the town of Tarvast to the Lithuanians:

> And as soon as the Tarvast *voevodes* came from Lithuania to Moscow and the Tsar and the Great Prince put his disgrace upon them for they had surrendered the city to Lithuanian people, and the Tsar sent them to towns

into prisons and ordered [his officers] to take from them their *pomestjes* and *votchinas* and distribute them.[6]

This fear of not fulfilling the tsar's orders, breaking an oath of loyalty to him and failing in their martial and Christian duties, was the most important motivation for the Russian nobility during Ivan the Terrible's wars.

A NEW TYPE OF SOLDIER: STRELTSY

Hand-held firearms probably appeared in Russia in the late fifteenth or early sixteenth centuries. We cannot say more precisely because the Russian word *pischal* meant for a long time both a light cannon, and the hand-held matchlock musket or arquebus. The first mass use of hand-held *pischals* in a field battle was in 1480, when the army of the Great Prince Ivan III stood

Russian nobles on military service (German engraving, sixteenth century)

31

Russian strelets *(Pen and ink, seventeenth century)*

against Akhmat Khan's Great Horde troops near the River Ugra. The Tatars tried to make a forced crossing of the river but were kept off the fords by archery and *pischal* fire.

The existence of detachments of *pischalniks* was mentioned in the beginning of the sixteenth century. Their numbers ranged from several hundreds up to a thousand or more people. *Pischalniks* of the first half of the sixteenth century were mostly mentioned in connection with Moscow, Pskov and Novgorod the Great, that is with the capital and the northwest of Russia, which were more open to European influences, including military culture. From 1512, *pischalnik* detachments served on the southern borders. They participated in Russia's war for Smolensk in 1512–22 and in the campaigns against the Kazan khanate.

Ivan the Terrible established a new kind of troops – *streltsy*. The date of their foundation cannot be fixed precisely. The term was mentioned in the chronicles as early as 1530. *Streltsy* are also known to have participated in the Kazan campaign of 1546–9, but there is no certainty that the new *streltsy* and not old-style *pischalniks* are referred to. It is known for certain that three thousand of a new type of troops was mustered in 1550 and these troops were called *streltsy*. This force consisted of six units (*prikazes*), each of five hundred warriors, under chiefs appointed from the nobles: Grigory Zelobov-Pusheshnikov, Matvey Diyak Rzevsky, Ivan Cheremisinov, Vasily Funikov-Pronchischev, Fyodor Durasov and Yakov Bundov. In addition, every *prikaz* had five subordinate officers, also appointed from nobles and each commanding a hundred men. The new troops were quartered in Vorobjova Sloboda (in Moscow, where the State University now stands).

There were several important innovations in these new troops. First of these was their armament. They were equipped with a hand-held *pischal*, a sabre and a berdiche, a battle-axe with a broad crescent-shaped blade which doubled as a prop while firing the *pischal*. Thus the *streltsy* were defined as units specialising in fighting with firearms from their inception.

The second innovation was in their terms of service. Like the nobles, *streltsy* were liable for service for their whole life, but, in contrast to the nobles, they were full-time regulars. The noble cavalry were disbanded at the end of a campaign, the aristocrats going home to live on their estates till a new campaign began. *Streltsy* performed their duties all year round.

Thirdly, the *streltsy*' posts were hereditary: after a warrior died he was replaced by his son or brother. Fourthly, it was initially planned that the state would pay these in money for their service. The allocation of estates was designed only for noble commanders. In practice, however, these plans were not fulfilled; being always short of money the state found it easier to distribute estates and also turned a blind eye to the mercantile activities of provincial *streltsy*.

Nevertheless, the financial position of Moscow's *streltsy* was better than that of the others. By the end of the sixteenth century there were between 7,000 and 20,000 people, according to various sources. The rank and file got a salary of 4 roubles per year, 12 quarters (that is 72 *poods* or 1,152 kg) of rye and the same quantity of oats. Each commander of a hundred got 12–20 roubles and an estate; commanders of half-hundreds 6 roubles and commanders of tens 5 roubles. Chiefs of *prikazes* got 30–60 roubles and an estate of 300–500 quarters in area. In addition, Moscow *streltsy* annually received from the treasury cloth for their uniform and salt, 32 kg for ordinary soldiers and 80 kg for commanders of half-hundreds. The salt was very profitable to resell.

Streltsy very quickly became the backbone of Russian fortress garrisons. They were a part of the so-called 'serving people' or *sluzhilye po priboru* (that is, a 'recruit in the army'). But the standards of welfare in the provinces were much worse. The ranks got 2 roubles a year; commanders of ten 2 roubles and 25 kopecks; half-hundred commanders received 2 roubles and 50 kopecks and hundred commanders 10 roubles. On top of this they received provisions of 576–672 kg rye per year and the same quantity of oats.

A fifth innovation was the establishment of a state institution, the Streletsky Prikaz, specifically for the management and organisation of the troops. The first mention of it dates back to 1571 though it might have been established earlier. The Prikaz looked after the *streltsy*, their departure to the places of service, organised training and the provision of their armament. The Prikaz was also the main court for *streltsy*.

An important feature of the recruiting process was the practice of bail. Since *streltsy* applied for the service they had to bring guarantors who could confirm that they were 'good fellows': reliable, God-fearing, rather wealthy, physically strong and able to perform the service faithfully. Sometimes they were also required to be married. In the presence of witnesses and representatives of the authorities the guarantors swore that a candidate possessed all the aforementioned qualities. There were two variants of the procedure: either a new *strelets* (the singular of *streltsy*) was spoken for by the whole male population of the *strelets*' neighbourhood (*sloboda*), or it could be done by six or seven elderly, trustworthy warriors.

Streltsy were settled densely in one part of the town (in the *posad* as a rule) not far from the fortifications which they had to defend in an emergency. Exclusive *streltsy slobody* appeared in towns very quickly. Frequently these were separated from the town by either natural obstacles (rivers, ravines or similar) or artificial ones (*nadolbis* – barriers of vertical beams driven in the ground at a sharp angle). In case of a siege all the *streltsy* had special siege yards inside the fortress where their families could find shelter.

Every *strelets* received a site on which he built a house at his own expense and started a household, usually with a garden and a vegetable patch. This practice was called 'household settling' and the authorities paid a subsidy for it. In the sixteenth century this amounted to 1 rouble. After the *strelets*' death the house remained with his family, but someone from the family could be recruited to take his place with the *streltsy*. A *strelets* could sell the house only if he was transferred to another town, in which case he bought a new house with the money received from the sale.

Since *streltsy* were frequently sent to other garrisons, confidence in their reliability and loyalty was essential. And this trust was important not only for the authorities but also for the other warriors of the garrison; they wanted to know that their new companions in arms would not betray them and flee. To guarantee this, an institution of mutual responsibility was introduced. It can be seen especially clearly in the newly built towns where the newly recruited *streltsy* garrisons were being sent. The *streltsy* divided into two parties and one party publicly swore their faithfulness to the other one.

One more distinctive feature of *streltsy* troops was the kind of uniform they wore as a result of attempts by the authorities to standardise their clothing. A degree of similarity in clothing was required in the other branches of troops: for example, clothes worn over the armour should have been of the same colour. But these requirements did not find much approval among nobles and their fighting servants, perhaps due to the practical difficulties. *Streltsy* got their equipment from the state so uniformity was more achievable.

The introduction of the uniform was achieved by distributing the same material for making clothes. A Muscovite *strelets*' everyday garment consisted of a long-skirted (heel length) kaftan made of rough grey, black or brown broadcloth with wide sleeves that narrowed at the wrist. The full-dress uniform included a long-skirted red kaftan (sometimes made of velvet) with gilded lacing on the chest, a lofty hat decorated with sheepskin (for the poorer warriors) or sable fur (for the wealthy ones), a nice cross-belt (white, as a rule) and heeled boots with turned-up toes. By the end of the sixteenth century *streltsy* wore red, yellow and blue kaftans, depending on the regiment they belonged to.

In battle, head protection was most important, so iron helmets, hemispherical in shape with narrow brims, were worn. Under the kaftans, chain mail or other protective armour (lamellar or leather) was worn. *Streltsy* did not wield shields or lances. The mounted *streltsy* of the tsar's guards were armed with bows in addition to firearms, which were still considered unreliable.

THE COSSACKS

The image of a Russian Cossack was sharply imprinted in European minds after the seizure of Paris by Alexander I's troops in 1814. Parisians were highly impressed with the uninhibited behaviour of the tall bearded men that bathed their horses in the Seine, seduced numbers of Parisian women and turned the word '*bistro*' into the name for a fast-food service (in Russian, '*bistro*' means 'quickly!'). Since that time the word 'Cossack' has been associated with freedom-loving and wild warriors from Russia, equally irrepressible in a battle, a feast or pillage.

The Cossacks of the sixteenth century did not bear much resemblance to their legendary descendants who routed Napoleon Bonaparte's army. The history of the Don, Volga and Dnieper Cossacks goes back to early times. In the Middle Ages the Don was home to the so-called wanderers (*brodni-kis*) – free people unwilling to subdue to any Russian prince. They earned their living by hunting, fishing and mercenary work and did not shrink from attacks on merchant caravans. In the thirteenth to fifteenth centuries, the size of this population rose as a result of the Tatars' incursions into eastern Europe and the establishing of the Golden Horde's power. Steppe and forest-steppe regions accepted society's outcasts, those who had lost all their property and also those who did not want to obey any kind of power – neither Russian princes nor Tatar *murzy*. During these centuries the ethnic composition of this freedom-loving population changed but the most significant element remained the Tatars, natives of the Golden Horde.

In the first half of the sixteenth century the Azov, Crimean, Belgorod, Astrakhan, Gorodets, Kazan, Meschera, Ryasan, Putivl, Don and Horde Cossacks were known. Then they steadily united into larger communities. Russian and Turkic ethnic elements assimilated with the Cossacks as well. In the 1540s the first Cossack settlements, fenced with the simplest fortifications (a rampart with a palisade), appeared on the Don river. It strengthened the Cossacks' positions and enlarged the influx of deserters from the central *uezds* of Russia.

Two different social groups appeared under the name of Cossacks in the sixteenth-century army. A particular kind of serving people (*po priboru*) – serving Cossacks – appeared in the second half of the century. They occupied a position lower than that of *streltsy* and artillerymen. Recruitment was voluntary and Cossacks were enrolled from townsfolk, free and poor people. As remuneration for their service the Cossacks got a salary and provisions (similar in structure and amount to the remuneration of the town *streltsy*) and small plots of land, sufficient to maintain a family. Some wealthy Cossacks possessed estates and were known as *pomestje* Cossacks.

Like *streltsy*, the serving Cossacks used to settle in towns in particular *slobody*. They performed frontier, regiment and town duties. The detachments of a garrison were headed by a Cossacks' *golova* subordinated to the town's *voevode* or to the siege *golova*. In the latter case they were subordinated to the Streletsky Prikaz and Razryadniy Prikaz. The serving Cossacks were formed into detachments of five hundred. Like *streltsy* regiments, these were in turn divided into hundreds, half-hundreds and tens. *Pomestje* Cossacks were recruited into the noble regiments.

Serving Cossacks were divided into infantry and cavalry. Their armament consisted of sabres, lances, bows and sometimes firearms. The Cossacks represented a kind of intermediate layer between the military elite – the noble cavalry and the specialised troops of *streltsy* and artillerymen – and *posokha* warriors. In general, Cossacks served in garrisons but their detachments can quite often be found in the lists of troops participating in long campaigns during

Ivan the Terrible's time. The average strength of the town Cossacks of the period is estimated by historians at between five and ten thousand people.

Besides the serving Cossacks, Ivan the Terrible's Moscow started collaborating with the 'free Cossacks' living outside Russia along the Don, Volga and Dnieper rivers. They were not subjects of the Russian tsar and relations with them were regulated by the diplomatic department – Posolsky Prikaz.

Here the word 'Cossack' came to be used for the designation of a freedom-loving and bellicose population of the basins of steppe and forest-steppe rivers. This word has a Turkic origin and means 'a free person', 'a daring fellow'. The authorities started regarding desertion to the Cossacks as a malevolent disobedience to the state power. But at the same time it could not be denied that a Cossack sought a heroic and martial fate. That's why a special term was used for the designation of such an escape – 'to leave for daring'. Moscow Great Prince Ivan III wrote in irritation: ' . . .and he will go through his wilful stupidity to the Don's daring'. The Moscow authorities avoided dealing with the Cossacks, proclaiming that 'those brigands live on the Don without our knowledge and escape from us'.

The Cossacks gained their main income from agricultural activity and armed raids into neighbouring lands; in other words, from pillage. But merchant caravans were not enough for everyone so Cossacks entered the service of the East European states – Russia, the Grand Duchy of Lithuania and sometimes even in the Crimean khanate. Usually the enrolment was not individual; the Cossacks applied for service collectively. The Cossack detachments were headed by *atamans* elected by the common 'Cossacks' circle'. The *atamans* chose a place where the service would be the most profitable. Here their function was close to the role of the European captains of mercenary detachments. But a captain acted as a recruiter as well, while a Cossack *ataman* usually led only the Cossacks from his own *stanitsa* (a Cossack settlement). There were, however, spontaneously formed detachments of free Cossacks, but such groups (it's better to call them gangs) appreciated an unrestricted life and opportunities for unpunished plundering rather than abiding by terms of service.

The Cossacks were employed from time to time by Russian leaders long before Ivan IV. But Ivan the Terrible was the first of the Russian rulers to turn the Cossacks' energy, their hatred of the Tatars and their habit of living at the expense of pillage to his own advantage on a substantial scale. Those who regularly ravage borderlands can be asked to guard these lands from other robbers. The Cossack detachments in the southern Russian steppe became a cover force for Russia against Tatar raids. In return they were paid money, the government sent them arms and ammunition and winked at the Cossacks' liberties and the practice of sheltering fugitives – 'There is no extradition from the Don!'

The first information concerning Moscow's collaboration with the Don Cossacks dates from 1549 when Ivan the Terrible ordered the Cossacks to assail the Crimean region. In 1550 the Cossacks and the nobles from Ryasan participated in the battles with the Nogay Tatars near Ryasan itself. The Cossacks took an active part in the defence of the southern Russian borders, especially in the organisation of the frontier service. Still, from the very beginning, the collaboration was not easy. In 1557 the Volga Cossack *atamans*, Vasiliy Meschersky and Pitchuga Putivlets, killed *ataman* Lyapun Philimonov, who had been sent from Moscow, and plundered the tsar's treasury being carried to Astrakhan by ships. Ivan the Terrible, unable to bear this, sent detachments of nobles and Cossacks loyal to him to the Volga. The brigands were killed. That is the first known incident of a direct military clash between the Cossacks and the central Russian power. But it was not until 1581 that the Volga region was cleared of Cossack robbers. Some of them moved to the River Don, while others went to the River Yaik, where they founded a new Ural Cossacks' community. From 1591 the Ural Cossacks started serving in the Russian army.

Ivan the Terrible willingly employed free Cossacks in his troops since they were splendid warriors. The Cossacks were famous for their horsemanship, perfectly wielded cold steel and their archery and quickly became familiar with firearms. A Cossack charge frightened any enemy. And the Cossack light cavalry could be compared only with that of the Tatars. Moreover, the Cossacks acquired excellent skills in the field of reconnaissance. They were superb as scouts, spies and messengers.

Yet the rebelliousness and licence of the Cossacks were irritating. It was not merely the prospect of insubordination to Muscovite *voevodes*, but also the probable political complications caused by the Cossacks' unauthorised military operations, which threatened to spoil relations with the Nogay Horde, the Crimea, the Ottoman Empire and the Grand Duchy of Lithuania. The agreements achieved by Russian diplomats with the greatest difficulties might be cancelled with a single dashing raid on a Tatar settlement or an Ottoman fortress. That's why the Moscow government, while sending the Cossacks their salary and ammunition, from time to time tried to repudiate them officially in every possible way, proclaiming that the Ottomans, the Nogays and the Tatars were welcome to kill them as much as they wished. The tsar was not going to come to their defence. In 1574 a decree for the southern towns was issued ordering the immediate hanging of any free Cossack (but not a serving one) that happened to appear in a town.

Relations with the Cossacks slightly improved only in 1584 when Ivan the Terrible's son, Fyodor Ivanovich, resumed large payments of money and provision and started providing the Cossacks with arms. In 1592 the Russian government managed to win over the Cossacks of Zaporozje. Moscow planned to create an army for operations against the Crimean Tatars founded on the Cossack troops. But the central authorities tried to encroach upon the Cossacks' liberty and privileges so by the 1590s the relationship had already gone bad again. The Cossacks performed their independent military actions and were being hung and imprisoned in Russian towns in accordance with the tsar's decree. During the Time of Troubles the Cossacks constituted a huge proportion of rebel armies.

RUSSIAN ARTILLERY IN THE SIXTEENTH CENTURY

Artillery has been known in Russia since 1382. The first cannon, known as *tyufyaks*, were stationed without gun carriages on the fortresses' walls and used to fire stones. For a long time artillery was exclusively for use in, or against, fortresses and it is only from the end of the fifteenth century that there is information concerning the employment of guns in battles in the open field. The development of Russian artillery became rapid in the late fifteenth century after the Gunnery Yard was founded in Moscow. Some researchers consider the Yard to be the first Russian factory. Russia eagerly invited foreign military experts and engineers specialising in artillery. In 1488 the whole complex of foundries and workshops for modern gun production was built by Italians.

The distinctive feature of artillerymen was that they were subordinated to several different state departments: to the Pushkarsky Prikaz (known since 1577) for technical aspects; for matters of service to the Razryadniy Prikaz and the territorial *prikazes* – the Novgorod and the Ustjug *chetverty* (literally 'quarters', but in late medieval Russia a territorial administrative department). Those serving in the artillery were divided into combatant and non-combatant ranks. The combatants comprised *pushkars* ('gunners') and *zatinshiks* (gunners who manned the *zatinnye pischals* described below). The non-combatant ranks included *vorotniki* (literally 'masters of the gate', from the Russian *vorota*, 'gate'), state smiths, state carpenters, state watchmen and deliverymen, so-called 'masters of town construction' (*gorododelcy*), bell-makers, gun founders, 'masters of well-sinking' (*kolodezniki*), draughtsmen and their pupils.

Artillerymen like any other serving people (*po priboru*) lived in separate *slobody*. They were not numerous. In small fortresses there were only several tens of them. In southern fortresses the number of artillerymen varied from five to forty-five people for a town. Such small numbers of artillerymen indicates a strange phenomenon: there were less of them than there were cannon in the fortresses. For instance, there were forty-six artillerymen in Ivangorod in 1556, while eighty-two people were necessary for manning the fortress' guns. In Pronsk during the second half of the century there were fifty-six guns and forty-two *zatinnye pischal*s minded by only twelve *pushkars* and twenty-one *zatinshiks*. In Dedilov, forty guns were serviced by fifteen *pushkars* and twenty-five *zatinshiks*. That meant that in an emergency the guns were operated by members of artillerymen's families, other warriors of the garrison and even common townsfolk. This fact shows that artillerymen were not an isolated and privileged corporation keeping the secrets of their skills as used to be the case in Europe.

Recruitment from the *posad*'s craftsmen was voluntary, and the service became hereditary. For the newly recruited artillerymen the recommendation of old *pushkars* was necessary. The novice swore loyalty, promised to be honest, not to steal, not to drink and not to give away the secrets of the art of artillery.

Artillerymen got plots of land (from 0.5 to 6 hectares per person), money and provisions comparable to that of the serving Cossacks. Muscovite *pushkars* got 2 roubles a year. During campaigns provisions were distributed on special terms: for example, in 1556 in Nevel the *pushkars* received 1 rouble, 2 *poods* salt, 12 buckets rye and the same of oats per year. Salt and grains could be substituted with money according to their price. The authorities also paid a one-off grant for the household's equipment ('for settling').

What kinds of armament did Ivan's the Terrible artillery possess? There were several types: *zatinnye pischals, tyufyaks, pischals, pushki* and *sorokas*.

Zatinnye pischals

Zatinnye pischals (or *gakovnitsy*) were large-calibre versions of the hand-held *pischal* for fortress use. These were of 20–30 mm in calibre and up to 120 calibres in length. They were stationed on the fortress walls, each operated by two people. Each *zatinnye pischal* was braced against the wall with a special hook (*gak*) situated towards the muzzle, which served to diminish the recoil of firing. *Zatinnye pischals* were very effective at a range of 300–400 m. But their effectiveness was limited in comparison to heavier artillery pieces. Another disadvantage was the difficulty of loading; the barrel got clogged with powder rather quickly. By the end of the sixteenth century this kind of weapon was unpopular.

Tyufyaks

Tyufyaks (from the Turkish *tyufeng*, 'gun') were small-calibre guns for firing clusters of small shot or stones. The barrel was made of iron plate or cast in brass and was conical to ensure the spread of the projectiles. The length of the barrel was 40–120 cm. In the sixteenth and seventeenth centuries these guns were generally employed as fortress artillery.

Pischals

Confusingly perhaps, in this period the term *pischal* was used not only for the hand-held weapons of the infantry but also for a broad category of artillery pieces. In this context, *pischals* were usually long-barrelled, small-calibre guns for direct fire on a flat trajectory. Each had a forged barrel 200–250 cm long and a calibre of 13–40 mm. Unlike *zatinnye pischals* the barrel was mounted on a wooden gun-carriage, to which it was fixed by means of iron cramps. *Pischals* could have trunnions, foresights and iron mantlets with slits. By the middle of the sixteenth century wheeled gun-carriages had appeared.

The term *pischal* was also given to guns that European practice would have classified as *kartauns*, *shlangs* and *polushlangs*. *Kartauns* were short-barrelled cannon with a shot weighing 25 lb. *Shlangs* and *polushlangs* (from the German *Schlange*, 'snake') were long-barrelled cannons. The barrel's length was 4–7 m and the shot weighed 7.5–54 lb. The weight of these cannon was usually in the range of 700–1,000 kg, but sometimes exceeded a ton. Both *kartauns* and *shlangs* were being made according to the patterns brought to Russia by foreign master gunners.

In 1545 a batch of sixteen *falkonettes* (*valkoneyka* in Russian) were founded in Moscow as per Italian samples. They were long-barrelled, small-calibre pieces firing a ball of up to 3 lb. The guns were mounted on wheeled gun-carriages.

Pushki (cannon)

Later becoming the generic term for cannon, in the fifteenth and sixteenth centuries the Russian word *pushki* was used for guns designed for indirect, high-trajectory firing. This could be either a mortar ('the upper cannon') or a howitzer (*gafunitsa* – a mortar with an elongated barrel allowing it to fire at a smaller angle than an ordinary mortar could afford). These were heavy guns meant for sieges and could throw balls weighing 90–240 kg.

Sorokas (sorokovije pischals, shutikhas, 'organs')

Sorokas were multi-barrelled, small-calibre guns. The number of barrels ranged from three to a hundred. There were two methods of fastening the barrels, either side by side, sometimes in several tiers to form a box, or in the form of a revolving drum or barrel. The barrels fired in turns, a special mechanism carrying the igniting spark from one fuse to another. Due to the series of shots the fire of this weapon could cover a large sector, but the serious disadvantage of *sorokas* and organs was the length of time required to reload all the barrels, resulting in a slow overall rate of fire.

Russian guns fired stone, iron, lead, brass and cast-iron balls; with stone, iron and lead small shot (*drob*). The slag from forges was often used as ammunition. Composite shells were also made, for example by pouring molten lead over stone balls, or molten lead or tin over iron pieces (*usechka*). The balls were kept in special boxes, the prototype of future caissons. The largest balls would stand waist-high. Beside these, incendiary shells (*ognistye kuli*) were being produced in the form of small balls wrapped in several layers of thick paper soaked with combustible mixture and tied tightly with linen ropes.

In 1578–81 the Polish army employed heated shot or 'scorching balls' (*kalenie yadra*) as incendiary ammunition while advancing upon Russia. The balls were heated in a fire before being loaded into the cannon barrels. In order to avoid this igniting the powder, the balls were wrapped in wet grass. These balls, having hit a wall, broke apart and scattered small fragments that stuck into wooden walls. Since the spread of these splinters was quite wide, they created numerous blazes over a vast area that hindered attempts at fire-fighting. Later such *kalenie yadra* appeared in the Russian army.

Explosive shells were not used by the Russian artillery of the sixteenth century, though they sometimes employed their forerunners: hollow balls filled with combustible mixture. Tubes loaded with powder and bullets could be riveted on the outside, and the balls might then be put into tarred bags braided with ropes and soaked in sulphur. Such balls were used as incendiaries and the chaotic shooting that resulted when the tubes of bullets were ignited was intended to frighten the enemy.

In the second half of the sixteenth century, Russian artillery became more standardised. Forged barrels were decreasing in number (they remained mainly in the small-calibre artillery of obsolete type). Founding from iron, brass and cast-iron was rapidly developing. The government aimed to establish production of ordnance in accordance with standard examples. For that purpose calibrating compasses (*kruzala*) were used. They were first mentioned in 1555 but were probably applied even earlier. By means of these compasses, the diameter of a gun's barrel and the diameter of a ball were measured. The so-called *polutornaya pischal* became the pattern for a gun taking a 6 lb shot and with a barrel of 280 cm in length.

In Ivan the Terrible's time there were plenty of famous artillery masters, both Russian (for example, Andrey Chohov and Stepan Petrov) and foreigners (the German Kaspar Kuns and Lithuanian Bogdan), in Russian service.

On the whole, Russian artillery in the sixteenth century was the most developed branch of troops, nearly equal to the European level. Most of the victories of the Livonian War, successful sieges and stormings were made possible by the might of the guns and the skill of the artillerymen. All foreign observers noted their high level of expertise.

RUSSIAN STRONGHOLDS

In the sixteenth century urban agglomeration became central to the Russian state. The fact is confirmed by an unprecedented rise in city building. At the beginning of the sixteenth century there were 160 fortified centres in Russia and in the course of the century between 55 and 70 new ones were built, not counting the rebuilding and modernisation of old fortresses. That means that during only one century the number of settlements of the urban type increased by 34–44 per cent! The pace of construction was constantly accelerating; 180 new cities had been built by 1620 and 226 by 1650. It was a real transformation in the country's appearance and the organisation of life within it. The new centres were built very quickly: a large fortress city took one to two years, while a small town was ready in two to three weeks.

What distinguished sixteenth-century cities from preceding ones was the fact that from that time all Russian cities were built according to the tsar's decree and to a previously worked out plan with the use of elaborate estimates and designs. Any unauthorised erection of towns was forbidden. And if such activity took place, instructions were sent from Moscow ordering the town to be rebuilt in accordance with the ideas of the tsar's *voevodes*.

City fortresses of the sixteenth century were of three types. The first, and most widespread, were traditional medieval wooden fortresses that were rebuilt and modernised. These were polygonal, with an irregular shape following the contours of the site. The outer ring of fortifications consisted of a moat or natural obstacles (gullies, steep slopes, rivers or other areas of water). Moats could be 3–10 m deep and 5–25 m wide, or occasionally even wider. That surrounding Moscow's Kremlin was 8 m deep and 35 m wide! In large cities the walls of the moat were reinforced with stonework, beams, palisades and wicker fences. Through specially built canals the moat could be filled with water from a nearby lake or river.

The second compulsory element of the fortifications was a rampart. The outer slope, facing the enemy, was steep and the inner one gentle. Frequently an earthen terrace was made at the back of the rampart in order to simplify passage along it for the defenders. The height of a rampart was 3–5 m or more and the depth 10–20 m or more. The rampart was built up using the earth excavated to make the moat, but it was not a simple earthen mound. It was strengthened with a frame made of several rows of beams driven in the ground with the space between them filled with clay or stonework of airbricks. The outer slope of the rampart was turfed.

On top of the rampart there was a wooden fortress wall. Its simplest version was a *tyn* or *ostrog*, a continuous fence or palisade, 2–5 m high, formed of pointed beams driven into the ground. Usually the rampart in front of the *ostrog* was protected by wooden forked branches fixed in the ground. On the inner side of the *tyn*, slanted wooden props were placed. These were sharpened (hence they were called *igls* – 'needles') and often went through the *tyn*, their points projecting on the outside. Their function was, as with the points on the palisade, to prevent any attempt to scale the *tyn*. Archers and *pischalniks* were usually firing from the top of the *ostrog*. For this purpose shorter flat-ended timbers (*polati*) were hammered into the ground along the inner side of the wall. These served simultaneously as firing posts and as buttresses. In large *ostrogs*, perpendicular timber walls were built inside the palisade and flooring

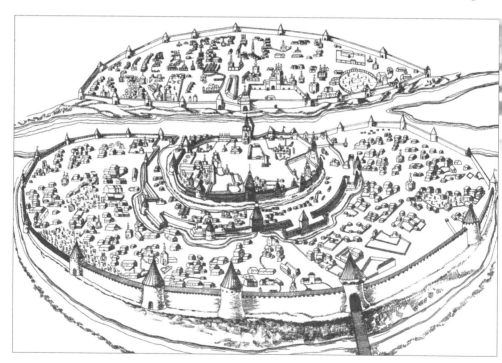

Fortifications of Novgorod the Great (part of a Russian icon, eighteenth century)

44

fixed across them to form a shooting platform. Some of the bays created between these walls could be filled up with earth, increasing the strength of the palisade.

At certain points along the *ostrog*, two- or three-storeyed wooden towers were built to house the artillery and as stations for archers. The towers controlled the weak sites of the *ostrog*: irregularities of the terrain, bends or openings in the rampart. As a rule, the *ostrog* surrounded the *posad* or *selitebnaya* parts of the town, that is the parts inhabited by the bulk of the city's population.

In the centre of a town a *gorod* was situated. It served as a protection for administrative centres, major churches, siege yards and the residences of the *voevode* and wealthy citizens. In contrast to the *ostrog*, where beams were driven in the ground vertically, the *gorod*'s fortifications were made of large rectangular timber frameworks laid horizontally and stacked up, fastened at certain intervals with short cross pieces. From the inside the frameworks were filled with earth (if they were not intended for special facilities such as armoury or storage of casks with water for fire extinguishing).

Usually the fortifications included two parallel walls 2–4 m apart connected with intermediate walls (*pererubs*) every 1.5–4 m. The space between the walls was divided into wide and narrow squares. The former were left empty, while the latter were filled with earth. The hollow squares were intended to hold the fortress defenders and, as a rule, two embrasures and a door were cut into each one.

Such a wooden fortress wall could be of two types of construction. The first and more ancient one was called *gorodnyi*. In this case the frames forming the squares were built separately and then put together like children's bricks. The advantage of this method was in the quickness of erection and ease of maintenance. The disadvantage was that heavy rain caused soil subsidence so some of the *gorodny* shifted and broke the line of the wall, which, naturally, affected its durability.

If the *pererubs* were fastened together like the framework of a peasant's log hut (*izba*), this continuous and solid construction was named *tarases*. Strictly speaking, the *taras* had a hollow, comparatively small frame frequently used as a kind of wooden casement, a platform for cannon and *pischals*. Since the embrasures were situated low above the ground they were called 'the embrasures of the low battling'.

Usually the height of such a wall reached 4–6 m. Along the upper perimeter of the walls there were fighting platforms, or battlements (*zabralos*), covered with a wooden gable roof. *Zabralos* had embrasures in their walls and in the part of the floor that projected beyond the outer side of the wall, overhanging

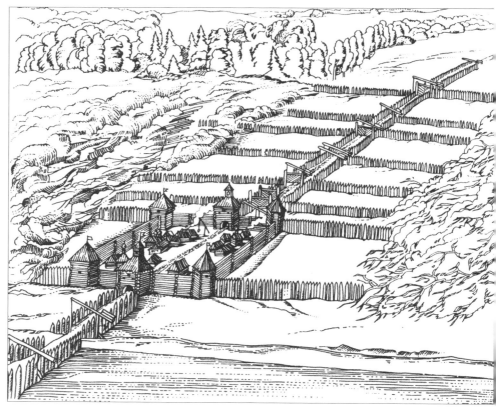

Wooden fortifications on the line of abatis (modern reconstruction)

any attackers at the wall's base. Small-calibre *pischals* and archers could be stationed on the *zabralos* and thick beams (*katocks*) were dropped from them or rolled down the outer slope of the rampart onto the assailants.

The role of towers (they were called *strelitsas* or *kosters* in Russia, the word *bashnya*, 'a tower', only becoming widespread in the sixteenth century) in the wooden fortresses increased significantly in the sixteenth century. As is clear from their names, towers began to be distinguished according to the specific function: 'passing-by' tower (*proezgaja*), gate tower (*vorotnaya*), corner tower (*naugolnaya*), 'blind' tower (*glukhaya*), guard tower (*karaulnaya*) and so on. As a rule, towers were quadrangular, more seldom polygonal or round, in shape with hipped roofs made of boards. The tips of the boards were sometimes decoratively sharpened in the form of points or spears. High towers were crowned with watch-towers and reached 20–30 m in height.

Towers projected several metres from the line of the walls in order that assailants might be brought under a flanking crossfire from two towers at once.

For that purpose towers started to be built closer together and the stretches of wall between them (so-called *pryaslos*) were made straight to prevent them impeding the defensive fire.

Both on the top of the towers and the fortress walls, so-called *oblams* were erected. An *oblam* was built on a frame wider than the main structure, with its walls protruding 20–30 cm beyond the wall. Thus, a tower was a large cuboid put upon a smaller base and resembled a giant mushroom. The *oblam* had no floor, that is to say the overhang was open below, forming a downwards firing slit, or machicolation, along the whole perimeter of the tower. This was convenient for striking enemies close to the walls, right under the defenders, with arrows, spears, boiling tar, water and sewage poured down on them.

The embrasures of the towers, generally, consisted of small rectangular openings 8–10 cm wide, meant for hand-held firearms, and larger ones of 30–40 cm across, for artillery pieces. Usually embrasures were not decorated at all externally (rarely they were framed with boards). Embrasures were located on the lower and middle floors, but mainly on the upper level, since the field of fire was wider there.

Apart from their primary defensive purpose, towers functioned as living quarters for the garrison, storage facilities, sometimes as bell towers or chapels and sometimes as state offices, housing guardhouses, *prikazes* and prisons. Depending on its dimensions, a fortress could possess anything from three or four, to some dozens of towers.

Modernising traditional wooden fortresses was an adequate solution to defence where the opponents of Russia were the Tatars. To the south and east of the country, neither the Crimean, the Nogay nor the Kazan Tatars mastered effective tactics of storming fortresses, nor employed artillery much during sieges. In principle, if there were sufficient ammunition and provisions, the garrison was at full strength and with a certain steadfastness of the defenders, such fortresses could successfully withstand the Tatar assault. This type of fortress (with *ostrogs* prevailing) became the main type of Russian stronghold during the colonisation of Siberia in the late sixteenth and the seventeenth century. Cheapness, simplicity and speed of building allowed the erection of a fortress that could be too tough for local tribes in a matter of weeks.

The second category of stronghold consisted of stone fortresses built in the fourteenth and fifteenth centuries and rebuilt later (such as Ladoga, Koporje, Oresheck, Yam, the fortifications of Moscow, Kolomna, Pskov, Novgorod the Great and some others) and of those polygonal stone fortresses built in the sixteenth century (such as Kitay-Gorod in Moscow). These fortifications were for the most part of brickwork into which individual large boulders had been inserted. The walls were 10–20 m high and 2–12 m thick. They contained three levels of embrasures: embrasures of 'the low battling', low above the ground; of 'the medium battling' and *mashikulys* – embrasures overhanging the fortress walls and towers and allowing downward shooting. Firing was also possible from between stone merlons made in the form of a swallow's tail, according to the fashion brought by European architects.

The main concentrations of firepower, however, were the towers. They protruded far beyond the line of the walls and were 25–30 m high. Theirwalls were 3–12 m thick. The towers were multi-storeyed (from three to five levels) with numerous embrasures along the perimeter and special ventilation for the escape of gunpowder gases. The embrasures were basically meant for flanking fire along the walls. Stone towers, like wooden ones, were roofed with boards.

A typical Russian polygonal fortress of the sixteenth century is Moscow's Kitay-Gorod (literally 'Middle Town', derived from Mongolian *kita*, 'middle'). The construction of Kitay-Gorod was begun as early as 1534, in the very first year of Elena Glinskaya's reign as regent for her underage son, Ivan the Terrible, and was completed in 1538, when Ivan was eight. In that year Elena was poisoned by boyars and one of the all-too-common periods of unrest began within the Russian state.

The construction was carried out the following way. Along the proposed line of the walls, a continuous course of 1–1.5 m oak beams was driven into the ground as piles, on which wooden cages filled with stones were placed. Rubble was piled over these and then the whole structure covered up with earth. With its width reaching 12 m, this formed the foundation of the future fortress. The walls protected an area of 69 hectares to the northeast of the

Fortress Ladoga (German engraving, seventeenth century)

Kremlin (from the Spasskaya and Nikolskiye gates) and their overall length was 2.6 km. The walls were 6.5–9 m high with wall-walks up to 4 m wide that allowed the movement along the walls of guns each pulled by two horses.

The warriors took cover behind the rectangular merlons each of which had three embrasures: a central one for an artillery piece and the outer two for firing handheld firearms. On the walls there were *mashikulys* (machicolations) for firing downwards towards the foot of the wall. On the inside of the walls were situated deep niches (*petchuras*), with embrasures for 'low battling'.

Kitay-Gorod was reinforced with fourteen round, polygonal and rectangular towers. Special underground passages (*slukhi*) were dug under the towers to prevent enemy saps. On the walls of the passages brass plates were fastened. Their vibration signalled that the enemy was undermining the tower.

Beyond the walls, Kitay-Gorod was protected by a moat 8 m deep and 17 m wide. Pointed stakes were inserted in its base. It is possible the moat was partially filled with water from the local springs. The only way into Kitay-Gorod was through the drawbridges and specially strengthened and armed gate towers.

Kitay-Gorod was a model and very strong Russian fortress of Ivan the Terrible's epoch. The twist of fate was that it was never assaulted by the enemy. It has never saved Moscow from foreign incursions, though Russian troops had to storm it during the civil war of the early seventeenth century (the Time of Troubles). Russians were furious that the stronghold was so unassailable that it seemed nearly impossible to seize.

The third type of fortress, first appearing in the late fifteenth century, was represented by the so-called 'regular fortresses', which, as their name suggests, were of a regular shape and which were used exclusively for defence. The first Russian fortress of the kind was Ivangorod, built in 1492 by Italian architects on the bank of the River Narova, right opposite the Livonian fortress of Narva.

In 1514–20 the first fortress of this type in central Russia was built. Tula was rectangular in shape, had a perimeter of 1,066 m and occupied 6 hectares. It had nine towers and walls 10 m high and 2.8–3.5 m thick. The building of any constructions within 200 m of the fortress was forbidden, to ensure a clear field of fire.

During the years of the Livonian War, Ivan the Terrible erected fortresses of the regular type in the occupied territories to serve as strongholds of Russian power. In particular, a number of such fortresses (Krasnaya, Kozyan, Sitna, Sokol, Turovlya, Susha) were built around the captured Lithuanian town of Polotsk in 1563–78.

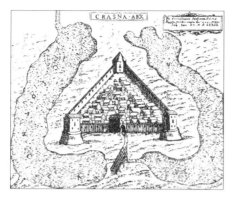
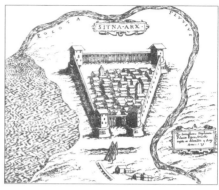
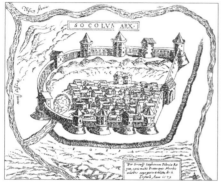
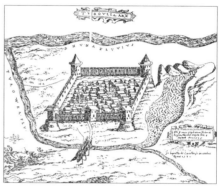

Top left: Fortress Krasnaya (Polish engraving, 1579)
Top right: Fortress Sitna (Polish engraving, 1579)
Bottom left: Fortress Sokol (Polish engraving, 1579)
Bottom right: Fortress Turovlya (Polish engraving, 1579)

In the sixteenth century, European technical achievements started slowly penetrating into the Russian art of fortification. It is easy to notice from their descriptions that Russian fortresses were adapted for the destruction of poorly protected enemies assaulting in a human 'avalanche' and thus getting right under the flanking fire from the towers and under boiling water and tar, *katocks*, spears and arrows from the walls. But the fortresses were not designed for sieges employing artillery and foreign firearms. The primary Russian enemies, the Tatars, did not use artillery in their assaults. Livonians and Lithuanians did not employ siege guns too much, so the problem could still be solved by strengthening the walls. The walls were made thicker or covered with earth and turf so cannonballs simply buried themselves there. The grass got dry very quickly, so such Russian wooden fortresses had a peculiar, yellow-green, 'shabby' look. The turf covering protected a fortress from incendiary shot

Bastions in the Moscow Kremlin

and gave some shelter from the shells with which the enemy tried to break the wall. But there was a disadvantage: the walls became uneven and it was much easier for assailants to climb up the turf, grass and earth.

There was a duel between the shell and the wall. Russian architects at that time knew next to nothing about the tactical requirements of building fortresses able to withstand a large-scale siege employing massed artillery. Only in rare cases were single elements of European fortifications being built by, or with the assistance of, foreign specialists. Thus, during work on the Moscow Kremlin towards the end of the fifteenth century, Italian architects erected outer bastions near four towers (Spasskaya, Arsenalnaya, Nikolskaya and Konstantinovskaya – see page 52) and a fortification near the bridge by the Troitskaya Gates (Kutaphiya Tower). Fortifications of bastion type were built in Kitay-Gorod, in the Kremlin of Nizhni Novgorod and in some other places. But they were intended mostly for hindering the attackers' access to the main fortifications, not for counter-artillery fighting. Thus in this aspect the development of Russian fortification was inferior to European.

*

FOREIGN SPECIALISTS AND ADVISORS IN THE RUSSIAN ARMY

Foreign military specialists were frequently engaged to work in the Russian army from the late fifteenth century. Initially they were Italians and Germans, that is natives of the Italian cities of the Holy Roman Empire. They mostly specialised in artillery. It is known that in 1507 four Scottish makers of cannon made an attempt to emigrate to Russia but it is not known whether they managed to reach remote Moscow.

Under Ivan the Terrible the quantity of foreigners employed in the Russian army quickly increased. At the same time the national make-up of mercenaries had changed. The lower proportion of Italians was apparently connected with the difficulty in getting to Russia from the Apennines, but the number of Germans, Lithuanians and Tatars had significantly risen. Immigrants from new countries also appeared: English, Dutch, Danes, French, Swedes and Scots.

How many mercenaries were there in Ivan the Terrible's army? Jerome Gorsey wrote 'about 1,200'. Another Englishman, Giles Fletcher, reported:

> Of mercenary soldiers that are strangers (whom they call *nemcy*) they have at this time 4,300 of Poles; of Circassian that are under the Poles about 4,000; whereof 3,500 are abroad in his garrisons; of Dutch and Scots about 150; of Greeks, Turks, Danes and Swedes, all in one band, 100 or thereabouts.[7]

According to Russian sources, the entries of the Rank Books in 1578 reported four hundred serving *nemcy* in Moscow. Russians called all Western Europeans *nemcy* because the latter could not speak Russian and, therefore, were considered dumb (*nemoy* in Russian). In Russian cities foreigners resided in particular neighbourhoods, or *slobody*.

Russia needed Europeans above all as specialists in military arts. That's why artillerymen, military engineers, gunsmiths and builders were in the greatest demand. The important role of Italian and German professionals in the formation of Russian artillery has already been mentioned. It was Italian masters, Antonio Solary and Aristotle Fiorovanti, who built the main Russian fortress, the Moscow Kremlin, in the late fifteenth century. By Ivan the Terrible's time the number of foreign artillerymen and masters had decreased, but during the late fifteenth and first half of the sixteenth century foreigners trained and prepared Russian officers and specialists.

However, some of the foreigners, having remained in service, played a vital part in Russian military history. Thus in 1552 a German engineer, called by the Russian chronicle 'Razmysl' (which means 'wise man'; apparently he was 'cunning and skilful in the destruction of towns') commanded the field-engineering works against the walls of the Tatar capital, Kazan. It was he who

European mercenaries (German engraving, sixteenth century)

detonated a mine under the stronghold's walls which broke the underground passage leading to the water supply. The blast caused the rapid capitulation of the city, which could not do without water. In 1572, in the battle of Molodi, an important role was played by the European mercenary detachments whose firing seriously crippled the Tatar cavalry.

Under Ivan the Terrible European mercenaries were in less demand as teachers and masters than in their direct function – as skilful warriors. Detachments of firearm-wielding cavalry mercenaries appeared (similar to European *reiters*, though the term was not used in Russia). The Europeans were divided into 'hundreds', later called companies. At the company level Russians did not interfere in command. Foreigners had their own commanders subordinated only to the general headquarters of the army. The authorities tried to staff the companies with people of the same nationality. They were used particularly in campaigns directed southwards against the Tatars, where highly trained warriors equipped with modern weapons proved to be most effective.

The Englishman Jerome Gorsey related the occasion when Tsar Ivan employed a squadron of Scottish gunners under Jamie Lingett's command. They had been captured with the Swedish detachment and were to be executed, but Ivan then decided to part Scottish mercenaries from the Swedes, Russia's immediate enemies in the war. As an alternative to the gallows, the Scots were offered lifelong service for the Russian tsar. Gorsey wrote:

> Money, clothes and daily allowance for meat and drink was given them, horse, hay and oats; swords, piece, and pistols were they armed with. Poor snakes afore, look now cheerfully. Twelve hundred of them did better service against the Tatar, than twelve thousand Russes with their short bow and

arrows. The Krym, not knowing then the use of piece and pistols, struck dead off their horses with shot they saw not, cried: 'Away with those new devils that come with their thundering puffs', whereat the emperor made good sport.[8]

Foreign mercenaries got to Russia in different ways. Some of them were recruited in Europe by Russian diplomats; others travelled in search of employment on their own initiative. The cases in which captives were re-recruited to serve the Russian tsar were also quite numerous. The mercenaries either got paid in 'feedings' (foodstuffs) and money or were given estates as remuneration for their job. As a kind of bonus, money and clothing were given at the beginning of their service. The horses got 'feedings' of hay and oats.

To get a feeding (*kormlenie*) due to him a mercenary had to show a special document, a 'feeding memory', where the rates of the allowances were indicated. Theoretically, a warrior should have received a portion of meat and alcohol (*myod*, literally 'honey') daily, but usually he took the provisions once every ten or fifteen days, or even monthly. Alternatively, he could have the monetary equivalent, or food money (*kormovie den'gi*), instead. The mercenaries preferred the money for they quickly faced the reality of receiving the provisions: the best part of it was simply being embezzled. The German mercenary Heinrich Staden wrote that *myod* for foreigners was of two kinds: good and bad, dilute. The special staff (*sitniks*) took the mercenary's cask and filled it with bad 'honey'. If a warrior showed indignation the issue resulted in an uproar and the mercenary was left with nothing. But if he bribed the *sitnik*, the latter let the mercenary into the cellar where he could chose any beverage he wanted, having tried all of them.

The foreigners complained that at the distribution of provisions for several days at once the officials invariably kept the tenth part 'for their labours'. Since the 'feeding memory' was given for a year's term, if its holder died during that year the 'feeding' due to him continued to come in but went straight into the officials' pockets.

The scheme of allotting estates to mercenaries was more complicated. The foreigner got a special document, or memory, saying that the tsar granted the warrior a certain quantity of land. The document was sent to the Pomestniy Prikaz. But the Prikaz did not bother with searching for non-occupied land. So the mercenary had to enforce it on his own, in a strange country and, in many cases, not even knowing the Russian language. He had to seek out a childless land-holding widow who had not yet been deprived of most of her late husband's land. The widow got a small lot of land 'for living' and the rest of the estate went to the mercenary according to the dimensions indicated in the memory.

Further types of European mercenary
(English engraving, early seventeenth century)

Nevertheless, European mercenaries arrived in Russia in greater and greater numbers. In the late fifteenth and early sixteenth centuries, Russian diplomats abroad had to enquire secretly where to find a military specialist ready to move to Russia. As an ambassador of the Holy Roman Empire, Sigismund von Herberstein related a curious story when a Russian envoy in Innsbruck sent an agent to the local prostitutes to get some information through them about any gunsmiths in need of a job.

A hundred years later, in the late sixteenth century, such contrivances in recruiting abroad were already unnecessary. Foreign mercenaries travelled to Muscovy and willingly entered Russian service. In the seventeenth century they would form whole regiments. Partly the surge was connected with the 'catastrophe of peace', when the shortest cessation of wars in Europe caused the appearance of a huge mass of aggressive, starving people who could earn their living only by selling their fighting skills. Finding themselves out of work, they were ready to sell their talents anywhere.

It is also worth mentioning that the mercenaries were attracted to Russia by the very high salary (by European standards) and the prospects of getting land, which was quite difficult for a mercenary in his native country. Foreigners were well protected legally and enjoyed some juridical privileges. And lastly, nobody forced a serving foreigner to convert to Orthodoxy.

The only problem was that there was no way out of Russia during Ivan the Terrible's reign. Russian military service turned out to be for life. One could only flee the country secretly or do something so extraordinary that permission was granted to go home to Europe. The German mercenary Heinrich Staden wrote:

> It is not so easy for a foreigner to do the wrong sufficient to get a capital punishment. But only if he is caught planning escape abroad, then only God can help him! It seldom happens that a foreigner dares to flee the country because the road to it is straight and wide and the way leading from here is much too narrow.[9]

2

Who Were the Enemies of Russia in the Sixteenth Century?

A Brief Review of Their Military Potential

THE MUSLIM ARMIES

The Tatar states that rose up from the remnants of the Golden Horde in the fifteenth century and claimed to be its political successors were the primary enemies of Russia in Ivan the Terrible's time. They differed from each other in their political intentions and military might. At the same time, the culture of warfare was similar in all these states, varying only in details and the stages of development. It was Eastern military culture. The Tatar armies were steppe armies with particular tactics, quite different from the powers further to the west.

The Crimean Tatars

The Crimean khanate was a young state in eastern Europe. Historians often cite the name of Hadji-Girei (1433–65) as its first independent ruler. Sometimes an exact date when the Crimea gained its independence is found in historical literature – the year 1443. But this independence did not last for long; in 1475 Ottoman troops disembarked on the Crimean shore. In 1478 the Crimean khanate officially became a vassal of the Ottoman Empire.

Initially, relations between Russia and the Crimea were very friendly. Both countries were interested in an alliance against their common enemy – the Great Horde (the rump successor of the Golden Horde). But their purposes differed. Moscow longed to rout the Great Horde and finish off the 'Tatar threat'. The Crimea in its turn was the Horde's rival for power over the Tatars of eastern Europe and the nations submitted to them.

After the Great Horde's downfall in 1502, Russian–Crimean relations deteriorated rapidly as the foundation of their friendship had disappeared. The Crimea claimed to be the historical successor of the Great Horde's power over eastern Europe, aspiring, in fact, to the role the Great Horde had played lately. In 1507 the Crimean khan, Mohammed-Girei, gave the Polish King Sigismund I a *yarlik* (a document entitling its holder to collect tribute in certain regions) for fifteen Russian towns. That meant, firstly, that Russia and the Crimea became enemies and, secondly, the Crimean Tatars made an attempt to gain command of eastern Europe as their Golden Horde forefathers had done. From 1507 there was protracted military confrontation between Russia and the Crimean khanate. The affair was settled only in 1783 when the Crimea was seized by the Empress Catherine II's favourite, Prince Grigory Potemkin, without a single shot.

Under Ivan the Terrible, Russia was in a state of open armed conflict with the Crimea. The Tatars launched serious assaults on Russian lands in 1535, 1539, 1541, 1542, 1544, 1552, 1553, 1555, 1556, 1560, 1563–5, 1568–74, 1576, 1578 and 1580. Russian troops and their allies, the Don Cossacks and detachments of the Lithuanian Prince Dmitry Vishnevetsky who had entered Russian service, attacked the Crimean territories each year during the period 1556–62. The Cossacks often raided Crimean land in the following years and in 1574–6 there was full-scale war by the Don and Dnieper Cossacks against the Ottomans and the Tatars in the Black Sea region.

In the sixteenth century the Crimean khanate occupied the lands of the whole Crimean peninsula except the coastal zone with the main ports and trade centres that belonged to Turkey. The Crimea also possessed steppe lands without distinct borders in the northern Black Sea and Sea of Azov areas. Their boundaries disappeared in the 'Wild Field' (*Pole*) – the no-man's land of steppe between Russia and the Crimean khanate. The borders of these Crimean *ulusy* (an *ulus* is a rural or administrative division) were thought to reach the Molochnaya river (or perhaps even as far as the Mius river) in the east. In the north, on the left bank of the Dnieper river, the boundaries reached the Konskiye Vodi river and in the west they went beyond Ochakov to Akkerman. It is therefore hard to define the total area of this Tatar state. The Crimean peninsula with adjacent territories occupies 26,000 sq. km, including a steppe zone of 19,165 sq. km and a mountainous zone of 5,812 sq. km. A satisfactory calculation of the total area of the *ulusy* is impossible as only their approximate borders are known.

The population of the Crimean khanate in the sixteenth century constituted approximately 350,000 people, about 150,000 of whom lived in steppe while the other 200,000 resided in towns, highlands and agricultural regions of the Crimea. The population was multi-ethnic, with Crimean Tatars prevailing but also a great deal of the population (especially urban population) comprised Greeks, Karaims, Armenians, Jews and Turks. Islam was the predominant religion but there were Christian and Jewish communities in the towns as well. Life was submitted to *sharia* law and all the Tatars were convinced of

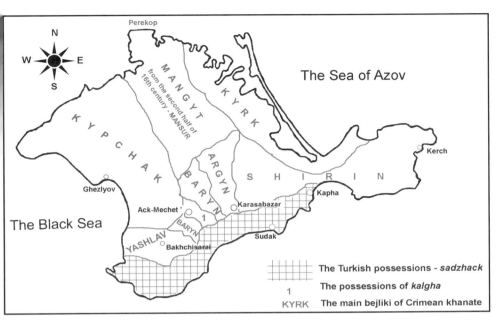

Map 3. Crimean khanate in the sixteenth century

the necessity of Holy War (*gazzavat*) against Christians. The closest Christian countries were Russia and the Grand Duchy of Lithuania.

The state was headed by the khan from the house of the Gereis who governed as a personal ruler. The khan's appointment had to be confirmed by the Ottoman sultan's order (*firman*). The khans received the symbols of their power form Istanbul. On the very first request of the sultan, the khans were obliged to set out against any enemy. But the Ottomans did not constantly interfere with their remote vassal's affairs, which gave the khan a certain, though rather limited, freedom of action. One of the main sources of the khan's income was the so-called *sauga*, the fifth part of any booty that had to be given to the khan.

There was a council of nobles, which was founded in the image and likeness of the Turkish model. It consisted of two parts, the small *divan*, which was restricted in numbers, and the big *divan*, which was larger and included the representatives of the most noble and influential aristocrats, the *bej-carachei*. The khanate was divided into parts called *bejliki*, belonging to the main Tatar clans: for example, Shiriny, Baryny, Arginy, Cedzhety and Jashlavy (Suleshevy). The clans distributed land to their junior members (*murzy*). The common people were united in communities with communal ownership and labour (*dzhaamaty*).

59

The main cities of the khanate were Bakhchisarai (the capital), Ack-Mechet' (the seat of the heir to the throne, *kalgha*), Solkhat, Kyrk-Er (Chuphut-Kale) and Karasabazar. In towns the slave-trade flourished, especially that of captive Christians from Russia and the Grand Duchy of Lithuania. All seaports belonged to Turkey, with the one exception of Ghezlyov. In the highlands, fruit growing, beekeeping and winegrowing prospered, while agriculture was practised in the lowlands. In the steppes north of the Black Sea there was migratory stock-rearing, mainly horse- and sheep-breeding.

The Tatars did not intend to seize the lands of their enemies – Russia and the Grand Duchy of Lithuania – even less to conquer these states. Apart from the immediate capture of booty, the goal of Tatar campaigns was to frighten their enemies into thinking it was easier to pay the Tatars off. In the sixteenth century both Russia and the Grand Duchy frequently sent to the Crimea the so-called *kazna* or *pominki*, the payments upon which the favour of the khan depended. The threat from the Crimea depended directly on the regularity and size of such payments; the greater the gift, the greater the likelihood that the Tatar cavalry would not leave the Crimea that year. Conversely, the less that was given, the less chance there was of avoiding an assault. This was a protection racket at a state level.

The situation was aggravated by the fact that Moscow had an interest in the Tatars raiding Lithuania, just as Lithuanian interests were served by raiding Moscow. So, each tried to persuade the Crimea to attack the other. The khans exploited this situation to indulge in more extortion and elicit more bribes. The Russian historian Sergey Solovjov incisively named this situation 'the Crimean auction', in which the highest bidder could secure their borders and cause trouble for their neighbour. But it sometimes happened that the Tatars took money from both sides and then still earned extra income by plundering.

Tatar messages to Moscow, Vilno and Krakow were full of demands for money, furs and rich clothes. And this extortion was absolutely undisguised. The Tatars announced that without bribes and gifts they would not even read the diplomatic letters meant for them. 'What's the use of the "dry messages" for us?' The Crimean princes were very particular. The correspondence of one prince with Moscow is known, wherein he demanded the replacement of the fur hat sent to him as a gift because he thought it to be a woman's one.

One will sometimes read that the *pominki* in the sixteenth century represented a disguised form of tribute paid to the Crimea by Russia in spite of the overthrow of the 'Tatar Yoke' in 1480. This must be refuted. *Pominki* were not on such a large scale, nor so regular, as to be regarded as tribute given by one state to another. Only a few large payments to the Crimea throughout

Tatars (German engraving, sixteenth century)

the whole of the sixteenth century are known. More frequently, Russian diplomats managed to get away with minor gifts which were symbolic rather than expensive (as the incident of the woman's hat presented to the Tatar prince suggests). They often bribed the government officials of the khanate. Russian intelligence gathering in the Crimea functioned successfully, and their network of counterspies was extensive.

How developed were Crimean military forces? In case of emergency the khan could assemble 80,000–100,000 warriors. This was equal to the maximum mobilisation of the Russian state. The number that actually took part in a campaign, however, was usually 20,000–50,000. This was equal to the overall strength of the Russian army serving in times of peace, without special mobilisations. So, the Tatar threat even in ordinary times could match all the Russian armed forces.

The Tatar army was organised on a decimal system. The smallest element was a ten, then a hundred, a thousand and then a horde. The latter denotes a unit numbering 10,000–40,000 warriors with a *murza* at its head. In order to frighten their enemies, the Tatars were known to tie stuffed dummies on their spare horses so that their army might, from a distance, appear two or three times as large as it was in reality.

The main force was light cavalry. The warriors were equipped with sabres and bows (usually with 18–20 arrows), sometimes with light lances (occasionally just poles with fire-hardened tips). Firearms were rarely used. The infantry were fewer in number and for the most part consisted of Turkish janissaries in the service of the Crimean khan. Their role in fighting was modest. Infantrymen were equipped with sabres, daggers, arquebuses and pistols. The artillery arm was insignificant too, though Turkish gunners sometimes took part in besieging fortresses. As mentioned already, steppe armies tended to be slow to adopt firearms because they hindered speed of manoeuvre.

Tatars had almost no armour. Chain armour, iron gauntlets and helmets were only for wealthy warriors, commanders and the khan's guards (*seymany*). Most Tatars were dressed in black sheepskin clothing with the fleece outside. Such a shaggy an army made a formidable impression on their enemies.

There were two types of Tatar campaigns: invasions with a khan or *kalgha* in command, or small forays (so-called *besh-bash*) led by individual princes and *murzy*. In a raid, Tatars advanced in three columns: a main force flanked by right and left wings. The wings broke into small detachments and made plundering raids on villages and the outskirts of towns. In combat, Tatars pressed forwards to attack immediately. The main thrust was usually directed on outflanking the enemy's left. This preference was determined by the fact

A fight between Tatar and Polish troops (Polish engraving, sixteenth century)

that it was easier from horseback to shoot at the rider's left as he passed the enemy's left flank. The tactics of charging home with lances were unknown.

Small Tatar detachments (not more than 3,000–4,000 men) relieved each other to sustain an uninterrupted attack on the enemy line. They shot and dragged warriors from the line with lassos, disrupting the enemy formation. Then the Tatars took to flight. If the adversary was deceived by this manoeuvre and began pursuit, his troops were soon lured into an ambush. If they stood their ground the first attack was followed by a second, a third and so on, requiring them to fight continuously with fresh Tatar forces. The battle ended when the opposing troops wavered and broke into flight. The Tatars themselves called these tactics a 'dance', while the Russians called them 'lava' (since they presented an unpredictable and irresistable stream flowing in all directions), but soon showed that they too had learnt to dance. During sieges Tatars used the usual tactics of constant assault, but they preferred not to get involved with well-fortified fortresses. If they could not set them on fire, starve citizens to death or capture the town with the help of deception or treachery, Tatars ravaged the surrounding countryside.

The main advantage of the Tatar military system was the army's high level of mobility. Every warrior had between two and five spare horses of a special breed, Pakhmat. These horses were small and could manage on little nourishment (they could eat bark and excavate dried-up grass from under snow). They were very sturdy. A day's march, riding high (that is, continuously in the saddle), was around 160 km, and the horses could maintain this rate for three or four months. Before a campaign Tatars fattened up the horses with barley for forty days, but then, immediately before the march, they did not feed them, because hungry animals docilely accepted heavy duty and tiredness more easily. During the march horses were lashed together by their tails. This helped to keep them in good formation. If anybody accidentally stumbled and fell beneath the hoofs, then he was trampled to death. A fatality was not considered reason to stop the march, even for one second.

It is interesting how Tatars fed on the march. The main foodstuffs were made from pea, barley or rye meal (rusks or flats) and from sour curds (*togurt*). Barley or millet meal was dissolved in water or horse's blood (*tolokno* or *tolkan*). A Tatar warrior could ride four days without food or drink and retain his fighting efficiency.

The spare horses were not only transport but also a supply of food. Horse meat was the favourite dish during the march, especially dried. However if a horse died on the march, a Tatar gave up the horse's heart, liver and lungs to his commander. He then cut the meat into steaks 3–5 cm thick, tied them to his current mounts back under the saddle and rode for two or three hours. Then he turned over each piece of meat, moistened it by the horse's sweaty foam and rode for another two or three hours. This dish was considered a delicacy.

The third kind of foodstuffs were those from horse milk. These were fermented milk (*koumiss*), dried milk and dried cheese. Cheese was put into a flask with water and suspended at the saddle. Being shaken during riding the cheese and water formed a peculiar juice – a favourite Tatar drink.

Englishman Giles Fletcher, writing in the sixteenth century, compared the military and psychological qualities of Tatars with that of Russians and Turks:

> [Tatars] condemn death so much as they choose rather to die than to yield to their enemy and are seen, when they are slain, to bite the very weapon when they are past striking or helping of themselves, wherein appeareth how different the Tatar is in his desperate courage from the Russe and Turk.

For the Russe soldier, if he begins once to retire, putteth all his safety in his speedy flight. And if once he be taken by his enemy, he neither defendeth himself nor entreateth for his life, as reckoning straight to die. The Turk commonly when he is past hope of escaping falleth to entreaty and casteth away his weapon, offereth both his hands and holdeth them up, as it were to be tied, hoping to save his life by offering himself bondslave.[1]

Turkish traveller Evliya Cheleby in 1666–7 gave this description of the Crimean Tatars and their role among Muslims:

All are afraid of Tatars . . . They are going all over the world to the un-Muslim countries, which are doomed to get into hell, plundering them and taking prisoners. They capture children and adults, wives and daughters. They torment the prisoners with breaking hearts and binding feet: they feed them by horse's hide, internal organs and intestines. All prisoners with children and kin Tatars send to Islamic lands, where they are honoured to turn to Islam . . . Tatars are merciless people. With the help of God they became the powerful protection of Turkey, and they struggle against all non-Muslims.[2]

The Nogays

The Nogay Horde broke away from the Golden Horde in the late fourteenth and early fifteenth centuries. It became independent in the reign of Prince Nuraddine (1426–40). In the 1550s and 1560s the Nogay Horde itself fragmented into several entities: Great Nogay (ruled by the clan of Prince Ismail), Small Nogay (ruled by the Prince Gazi and so also known as Gazi-ulus) and Altyul'sky Horde (led by Prince Shich-Mamay).

Relations between Russia and Nogay were better than between Russia and Crimea. In 1554 Prince Ismail of Great Nogay became the liegeman of Ivan the Terrible. This was the result of diplomatic negotiations rather than the Russian military threat. Russia was the main market for the horse trade, and horse-breeding was the basis of Nogay's economy. But Small Nogay in 1560 concluded a treaty with the Crimean khanate. Their troops were members of the Crimean and Turkish military expedition against Astrakhan in 1569 and the Crimean campaigns against Moscow in 1571 and 1572.

The Tatars of Great Nogay led a nomadic life on the northern coast of the Caspian Sea, from the delta of the Volga to the Ural river. Small Nogay was based on the right bank of the Volga and on the northern coast of the Sea of Azov (see map 5, p 70). In the second half of the sixteenth century, Nogays actively advanced into the steppe of the northern Caucasus foothills. The population of Great Nogay in the sixteenth century was around 350,000 and of Small Nogay 250,000–300,000.

At the head of a Nogay state was a prince (*biy*). He had something like a government (*karaduvan*), with the hightest officials (*karachi*) subordinated to him. The military leaders were *nuradin* and *kekovat*, the second after the *biy* in the political hierarchy. The Horde was divided into parts (*ulusy*) governed by *murzy*.

The armies of both Great and Small Nogay were around 20,000–60,000 and consisted of cavalry only. In tactics and military organisation they differed little from that of the Crimean Tatars.

The Kazan Tatars

The Kazan khanate appeared between 1437 and 1445 in the Volga region on territory previously belonging to another Turkic state, that of the Volga Bulgars, which had been annihilated by the Mongolian invasion in 1236. The founding ruler of the khanate was Khan Ulug-Mohammed. In the very year of foundation, 1445, the Kazan Tatars defeated the troops of the great prince of Moscow, Vasiliy II, near the town of Suzdal. Since that event, relations between Kazan and Moscow had been hostile and remained so until 1487. That year the Russian troops took Kazan and Great Prince Ivan III established a protectorate over it. Moscow vigilantly ensured that only loyal khans ascended the throne. There was a mighty pro-Moscow faction among the local nobility in Kazan.

In 1505, the Kazan khan Mohammed-Emin incited rebellion, slaughtered the Russian merchants residing in Kazan and launched raids on the eastern border of Russia. In 1518, after Mohammed-Emin's death, Moscow tried to regain its ascendancy in Kazan. A thirty-year-old Khan Shahghali from the kin of the Astrakhan khans was enthroned. This caused the uttermost irritation in the Crimean khanate. In 1521 a military coup was staged in Kazan, Shahghali fled and the throne was taken by the Crimean khan's brother, Sagib-Girei. The raids across the Russian border recommenced.

Thus, after the coups of 1505 and 1521 the status of the Kazan khanate was hard to define. On the one hand, it was a sovereign state carrying out independent foreign policy overtly hostile to Russia. The political patrons of Kazan were the Crimea and Turkey. On the other hand, Kazan's rulers periodically vowed loyalty to Russia and asked for forgiveness 'for the fault', assuring that they did not intend to attack, plunder and capture people and did not understand themselves how it had all happened.

The cause of such duplicity was simple. The Kazan rulers did not want either to offend their high Muslim protectors or to give up the booty brought by the raids on Russian lands. At the same time they feared that one day Russia, unable to contain itself, would gather its strength and retaliate decisively.

Sensible Kazan rulers did not want their relations with Russia to pass the point of no return beyond which a Russian invasion would become inevitable. This explains everything: diplomatic manoeuvres, duplicity of policy and war combined with oaths of loyalty.

In 1535, after one of the recurrent military coups, victory was gained by Khan Safa-Girei, an adherent of war against Russia. From that year Kazan raids terrorised Russian borderlands several times a year. In 1537 the Russian government (during these years Ivan IV was still a child) was compelled to restore the frontier service on the eastern border. The point of no return had been passed. In 1545, Ivan the Terrible launched a long, all-out war which ended in the annihilation of the Kazan khanate by military means in 1552 (as we shall see in detail in Chapter 3).

What was the Kazan khanate like as a military opponent? What military, social and economic potential did it possess? The territory of the khanate exceeded 300,000 sq. km. In the east it bordered the Siberian khanate and reached the Urals. In the southeast and south lay the vast steppes occupied by the Nogay Horde. There were no stable boundaries there since the

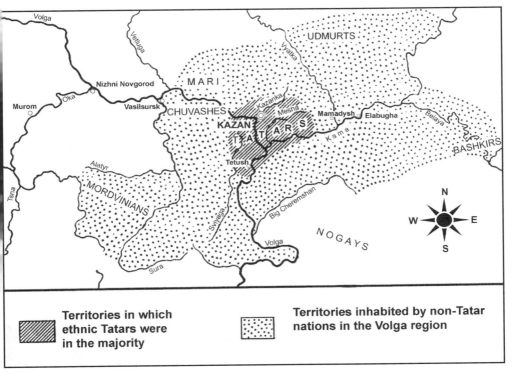

Map 4. Kazan khanate in the mid-sixteenth century

steppe regularly changed hands between the two states. The approximate boundary could be drawn somewhere in the Samara river basin. In the south the khanate's lands went down in a narrow belt to the banks of the Volga river, nearly reaching Sari-Tau (Saratov). The border with Russia went along the Sura river. In the north, the khanate's possessions came to the middle of the Vyatka and the Kama river basins and nearly bordered the taiga zone.[3]

The Kazan khanate occupied an area similar to that of Spain, France or Poland but was five times smaller than Russia. In the mid-sixteenth century the population of the state amounted, according to various sources, to between 200,000 and 500,000 people. The population consisted of Tatars (about one third of the total), Bashkirs, Cheremises, Udmurts (Votjaks), Mari, Chuvashes and others. The allocation of the population over the territory was uneven and depended much on the social and economic structure. The density of the population reached its greatest in the urban centres, the largest of which was the khanate's capital, Kazan itself. The city was surrounded by wooden fortress walls with ten gates in them. It could even boast some stone buildings (some minarets, mosques and the khan's palace). The capital had large suburbs inhabited by merchants and craftsmen. The residences of foreign merchants were grouped together in particular districts: Armenian, Russian and so on.

Kazan was an important point of transit on the Volga trade route. It was also the largest slave market in the region. In 1551, in an attempt to prevent a Russian invasion, the Tatars set free the captives engaged in craft workshops and agricultural work outside Kazan. In total about 60,000 people were released. All of them were Russians captured during raids on the borderlands. And these were only those that had been sold to local inhabitants, within the Kazan khanate. How many people were sold into thraldom to Persia, the Astrakhan khanate, Turkey and further, to other oriental countries, is impossible to count. Perhaps this huge figure (60,000 slaves among a total population of 200,000– 500,000 people) partially explains the cruel ruthlessness shown by Ivan the Terrible while conquering the khanate. Russian warriors had many compatriots to release and to seek revenge for. The more so as the Tatars forced the captives to renounce Christianity and adopt Islam, which in the Middle Ages was regarded as a particular crime.

Kazan and its suburbs were the last remnants of the mighty Volga urban agglomeration of the Golden Horde ruined in 1395 by Timur-i-Lenk (Tamerlane). The rest of the khanate's territory was much less civilised. There were almost no towns there but quite a lot of rural settlements (Russian descriptions of the late sixteenth century give figures of up to 700 of them).

In the steppes near the Volga, bordering with Nogay lands, nomadic horse-breeding prevailed. A significant proportion of the khanate's economy was made up of hunting, fur trading, fishing and home crafts.

The state was headed by the khan. He nominally possessed absolute power but in practice he strongly depended on the nobles' council (*divan*), consisting of members of the noblest families (*karachi*). The *divan* was headed by the big *karachi* (*ulu-karachi*). For discussion of the most important issues an expanded council (*kurultay*) was summoned. It included representatives of the clergy (*sheykhs, mullahs, imams, dervishes, hajis, hafizes, danishmends, sheikh-zade* and *mullah-zade*), military commanders (*oglans*) and landholders (*emirs, bicks* and *murzy*).

In terms of military potential, the khanate was quite weak. The specialised military class was formed of *oglans*, holding estates (though small ones) in return for service. They had Cossacks under their command. The Cossacks were of two kinds: *ichkis* served at the khan's court in the capital and *is'nikis* outside Kazan, in the *ulusy*. The most efficient part of the army was the cavalry, though infantry garrisons protected the cities. The armament and tactics of the Kazan Tatars did not differ much from those of the other Tatar armies. There were, however, three essential distinctions. The Kazan Tatars had artillery, though it consisted only of fortress artillery. They did not have large military formations prepared for long marches and, finally, they had too few good warriors for a field battle. According to a sixteenth-century Polish historian, Matvey Mekhovsky, the whole Kazan army did not exceed 12,000 people. In critical situations, however, 30,000 or 40,000 warriors could be gathered.[4] They showed a good command of defensive tactics while repelling Russian attacks from Kazan, but the khan could not muster large military formations to undertake more ambitious strategic tasks.

The Kazan Tatars raided Russian towns (Murom, Nizhni Novgorod, Kostroma, Galich and Ustjug) using small mobile detachments and never aimed to seize any territories or bring the captured towns under the khanate's authority. The only goals of the campaigns were pillage and the acquisition of new slaves.

The Astrakhan Tatars
The Astrakhan khanate was the last of the Tatar states to appear. The capital of the Great Horde had moved to Astrakhan as early as the 1480s. So, after the Horde's fall it was the Astrakhan khanate that became its political heir. But, owing to the khanate's military weakness, it could not claim to be the real successor of the Great (and earlier Golden) Horde's power over east European lands. The independent Astrakhan khanate had been founded only after the

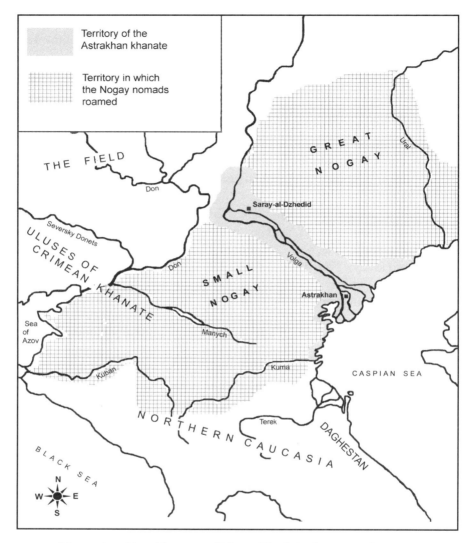

Map 5. Astrakhan khanate and Nogay Horde in the sixteenth century

defeat of the Great Horde by the Crimean khanate in 1502.[5] Astrakhan's policy towards Russia was conciliatory; the khanate had enough problems with the Nogays and the Crimean Tatars as its immediate neighbours. The Astrakhan rulers did not want to get into trouble with their powerful and remote northern neighbour.

Yet, the saying 'if you do not want to busy yourself with politics, politics will busy itself with you' is true in respect of the Astrakhan khans. Astrakhan was not going to fight against Russia. The situation changed after 1521 when Astrakhan started carrying out an obviously friendly policy towards the Crimean Tatars and the Nogays. It was in Astrakhan slave markets that several tens of thousands of Russians, captured during the notorious invasion of 1521 by the Crimean khan Mohammed-Girei, were sold. There are various indications that the Astrakhan Tatars participated in the campaign.

During the first years of Ivan the Terrible's reign, Moscow did not prepare any military operations against Astrakhan but played an intricate diplomatic game, exploiting the ambitions of Astrakhan, the Crimea and the Nogays. The intrigues were aimed at preventing the Tatars from allying with them and at creating a system of counterbalance and containment on the southern borders that played the Tatar states off against each other and, therefore, prevented them troubling Russia. But the effects of such diplomacy were partial and insecure: for example, in 1541, Astrakhan detachments joined the army of the Crimean khan Sagib-Girei to participate in only the second invasion of Russia in the sixteenth century. But this was only a brief episode. History gave the Astrakhan khanate only a quick mention as this state existed on the European map for only fifty-two years (the story of its downfall will be described in the next chapter).

The social and political structure of the Astrakhan khanate did not significantly differ from that of the other Tatar states. There were four ruling clans of *beys-karakcheis*. There was only one large city in the state, Hadzi-Tarhan (Astrakhan to the Russians), with a population of not more than 10,000 people, and some minor settlements in the Volga's estuary. The khanate's economy differed from that of the other Tatar states in that it was based not only on nomadic cattle-breeding but also on transitory urban trade and fishing.

It is difficult to define the number of the non-urban nomadic population but the military forces of the khanate were never substantial and did not exceed some thousand people. In military aspect the main role in Astrakhan's history was played by the Nogays. The structure of the Astrakhan army did not display any important differences to the armies of the Crimean Tatars or the Nogays.

*

OTTOMAN TROOPS IN EASTERN EUROPE

Turkey governed some territories in eastern Europe. The southern towns of the Crimea (Balaklava, Sudak, Kerch, Kapha) formed a special Turkish administrative district, Sadzhack, with Kapha as its capital. Contemporaries called it 'little Istanbul'. Sadzhack occupied around 870 sq. km. Moreover, Turkish troops were deployed in the key points of the steppe part of the Crimea, including Perekop, Arabath, Enikale and Ghezlyov.

The territories of the north coast of the Black Sea, along the lower stretches of the Dnieper and Dniester rivers, formed another Turkish possession, Budzhack. The main fortresses of this area were Kiliya, Bendery, Izmail and Akkerman. On the shores of the Sea of Azov a third group of Turkish strongholds was to be found, including Azik (Azov), Cherckess-Kermen, Taman and Temreon. Besides these major fortresses, these three regions contained many small wooden fortified settlements, known as *palanky*. In the cities lived Turks, Tatars, Armenians, Jews, Mingrelians and Christian descendants of Genoese merchant adventurers.

Turkey deployed only garrisons here. In large strongholds they were Turkish, in smaller ones they were brought up to strength by recruiting from the inhabitants, predominantly Greeks. These garrisons were attributed to the *eyâlet askerleri*, or 'provincial forces' of Turkey. Their infantry was called *yerlikuli piyâdesi*, meaning 'local infantry'. In Turkish military hierarchy they had been downgraded to little more than an infantry militia. Sometimes the sultan sent janissary troops and artillery to Kapha and Ochakov to strengthen the garrison. Garrisons were small in every fortress, several tens or hundreds of warriors at most.[6]

Turkish infantry was equipped with a smoothbore matchlock musket and rifled flintlock muskets and pistols. In addition Turkish weapons included *simşîr* sabres, *yatağan* recurved swords, long daggers and battle-axes. The infantry were well protected by chain mail reinforced with metal plates, composite mail and plate cuirasses and helmets.

In 1512–38 Moldavia, the state in the eastern Europe, was finally brought under Turkey's supervision.[7] The Ottoman Empire had great pretensions, the sultan at one time officially styling himself 'Padishah of Desht-y-Kypchack, Kapha, Crimea and Daghestan'. Desht-y-Kypchack was a medieval name for the steppe north of the Black Sea, known in Russia as *Pole* (the 'Wild Field' or wilderness). Daghestan is in the northern Caucasus by the Caspian Sea. Ivan the Terrible had designs on both the *Pole* and the northern Caucasus and sent Russian troops there.

It seemed Turkey was now an adversary of Russia and, on the face of it, war between them was inescapable. Hence the diplomats of the Vatican and

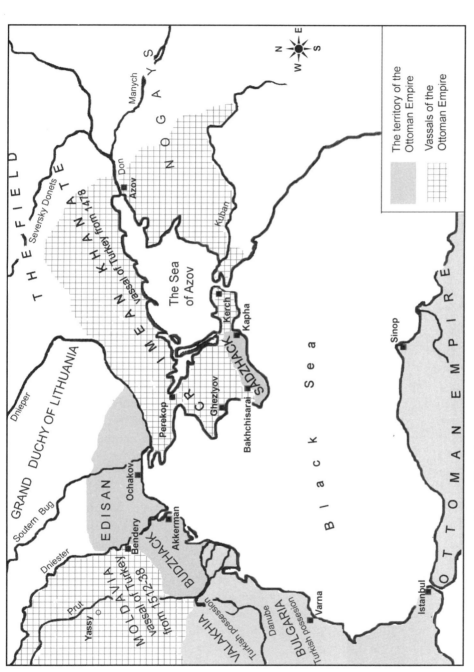

The territory of the Ottoman Empire

Vassals of the Ottoman Empire

Map 6. Turkish possessions in eastern Europe in the sixteenth century

THE FIELD

GRAND DUCHY OF LITHUANIA

Dnieper

Southern Bug

Dniester

Prut

Yassy

MOLDAVIA

Vassal of Turkey from 1512-38

EDISAN

Ochakov

Bendery

Akkerman

BUDZHACK

Turkish possession

VALAKHIA

Danube

BULGARIA

Varna

Turkish possesion

Istanbul

OTTOMAN EMPIRE

Black Sea

Sinop

Kapha

Kerch

Bakhchisaraj

Ghezlyov

Perekop

GREAT

NADZHACK

CRIMEAN KHANATE

Vassal of Turkey from 1478

Seversky Donets

Manych

Don

Azov

NOGAYS

Kuban

The Sea of Azov

N W E S

Holy Roman Empire strongly urged Russia to join the European anti-Islamic league. But Russia was deaf to this appeal. Turkey's policy in respect to Russia was conciliatory. The Sultan didn't persecute Orthodox monasteries in Turkish territory. International trade between Russia and Turkey was very extensive. Russian troops never descended on the lands of Budzhack, and the Russian government always unequivocally dissociated itself from the raids of Don and Dnieper Cossacks against Turkish possessions in eastern Europe. Moscow emphasised that the Cossacks were independent; they were not the subjects of Ivan the Terrible. In their turn, Turkish troops took part in the raids by Crimean Tatars against the Grand Duchy of Lithuania and the Cossacks, but never against Russia. In reality, the sultan indeed has stood behind the khan's back, but the skilful oriental diplomats maintained a useful illusion of Crimean autonomy in foreign policy. There was only one armed conflict between Russia and Turkey. In 1569 Turkish troops besieged Astrakhan (by then in Russian hands) but were crushed and annihilated.

'POSPOLITE RUSZENIE' ('COMMON ARMY') OF THE GRAND DUCHY OF LITHUANIA AND THE MILITARY FORCES OF THE POLISH KINGDOM

The Grand Duchy of Lithuania (GDL) in the sixteenth century was one of the biggest states in Europe. In 1569 there were about four million citizens. The density of population was about eight people per square kilometre. The total area of the GDL in mid century was about 550 sq. km. This was greater than France (450 sq. km) or the Habsburg possessions in the Holy Roman Empire (410 sq. km), but smaller than their Spanish possessions, the European part of the Ottoman Empire or Muscovy. The Polish kingdom at the beginning of the sixteenth century had a population of approximately three million people, a density of 14 per square kilometre).

Where Poland and Lithuania differed most significantly from the other states of eastern Europe was in the large number of towns and townspeople. For example, in the late sixteenth century the population of Gdansk was about 50,000, Krakow 22,000, Lviv 20,000, Poznan 20,000 and Vilno 14,000. In 1578 more than 28 per cent of the inhabitants of Great Poland, 30 per cent of Lesser Poland and 18 per cent of Mazovia lived in cities.[8] The level of urban culture and of the development of Magdeburgian law were exceptional.

The Grand Duchy of Lithuania had been consolidated with Poland by dynastic union since 1385. They founded the unified commonwealth, or

Right: Map of Grand Duchy of Lithuania by Martin Kromer
(Poland, sixteenth century)

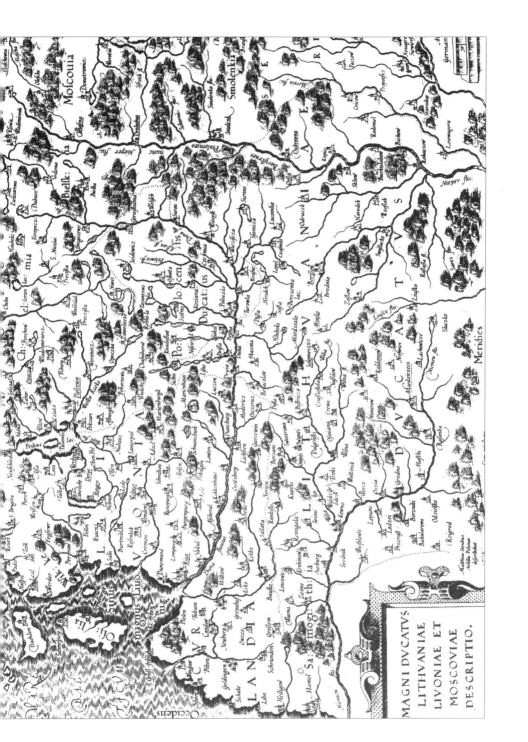

MAGNI DVCATVS
LITHVANIAE ET
LIVONIAE ET
MOSCOVIAE
DESCRIPTIO.

Krakow, the capital of Poland in the sixteenth century

Rzeczpospolita, in 1569. The distinguishing feature of the political system of this state was the weak royal power. Every king was obliged to take into consideration an opinion of the nobles' council (*rada*) and of the nobles' convention (*sejm*). Without support of *rada* and *sejm* a king could not enforce any important decision. In such circumstances, Polish nobles (*magnaty*) and gentry (*shlyachta*) understood their freedom not as the guarantee of private property, but as the potential to receive privileges and benefits from service. Nobles were inclined to believe that they did not serve the king so much as their state and people, the Rzeczpospolita (Republic).[9]

Poland had entered into a military alliance with Lithuania, but both countries had their own armies. Furthermore, the Polish army didn't desire to take part in the wars between the GDL and Russia in the first half of the sixteenth century. As expected, the Polish army was only to defend Poland, and Lithuanian military forces only the GDL. As a result, their military potential was dissipated. In peacetime, Poland maintained troops (about 3,000–5,000 warriors) in a state of readiness only on the southern border (so-

Polish sejm *in 1506 (Polish engraving)*

called *Obrona Potoczna*, or 'Continuous Defence'), to protect the Polish state from the raids of the Tatars.

The backbone of the armed forces of the GDL was the cavalry of the nobility. The noblemen were required to serve in person and also to raise and equip several warriors. The system of service was irregular, the volume of conscription depending upon the king's decree. The mobilisation of the militia of the nobles was called *pospolite ruszenie*.

The mobilisation potential of the GDL and Poland was low. In the sixteenth century the greatest *pospolite ruszenie* in the GDL was assembled in 1567, raising 27,597 warriors. Nuncio Rujery wrote in 1565 that the GDL could theoretically collect 70,000 people at the most, but never gathered them. In practice the maximum was about 40,000. Poland should have been able to collect about 100,000 warriors, but the actual number was no more than 50,000.10 It is a sad fact that in 1563, when the army of Ivan the Terrible had captured fortress Polotsk and Russian cavalry was advancing down the open road to Vilno, capital of the GDL, the great Lithuanian *hetman* Mikolaj Radzivill could collect no more than 2,000 Lithuanian noblemen and 1,400 Poles beneath his banner. The very survival of the Grand Duchy of Lithuania

Vilno, the capital of the Grand Duchy of Lithuania (engraving, seventeenth century)

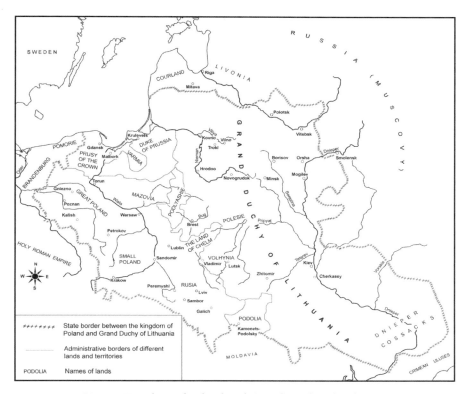

*Map 7. Kingdom of Poland and Grand Duchy of Lithuania
in the first half of the sixteenth century*

was in acute danger and of all her citizens only 2,000 responded to the call to defend the motherland.

The immediate cause of this stubbornness was the gentry's attachment to their own landed property. Lithuanian noblemen had to protect their estates from the assaults of neighbours. Daylight robbery, abduction of peasants, cattle raids and even the capture of estates were commonplace. Under these circumstances every nobleman had his own army for protection of his own property and for aggression against others. In the south of the Duchy, in Volhynia, there was the permanent threat of Tatar and Cossack raids. Therefore, noblemen unwillingly took part in *pospolite ruszenie*.

The commander-in-chief was the king, but actual command could be delegated to his great *hetman*, who was assisted by a field *hetman* (*hetman polny*). *Hetmans* had a headquarters staff, consisting of a field clerk (*pisarz polny*) in charge of the chancellery and finances; a 'warder' or 'guardian' (*strażnik*) in charge of the armed guard, a chief of transport (*oboźny*)

79

responsible for the establishment and maintenance of the camp on campaign; a chief of medical services (*szpitalny*); a provost (*profos*) or head of military justice and a 'head of rear services' (*probantmajster*) who was responsible for logistics.

The commander of a regiment was called a *pułkownik* (equivalent to a colonel). Regiments were divided into several *khorugv* ('banner' or 'ensign') if cavalry and into several companies (*rota*) in the case of infantry. The latter was commanded by a *rotmistrz*, supported by a lieutenant (*porucznik*). One regiment consisted of 5–12 *khorugv* (maximum 40). In each *khorugv* there were up to 200 horsemen in heavy cavalry, or 60–150 in the light cavalry. In action the formation of *khorugv* was the wedge (*klin*) with heavy spears at the edge and light cavalrymen at flanks.

The lowest subdivision of the Polish army was the 'post' (*poczet*), derived from the medieval 'lance' and comprising of twenty-four warriors (so-called *pacholek*, or companions in arms).

The main arm in both the Polish and Lithuanian armies of the sixteenth century was cavalry. The heavy cavalrymen were Polish hussars, who were, in the opinion of contemporaries, the most beautiful cavalry in Europe. The hussars' clothes, armour, armament and style of fighting combined influences from Hungarians, Turks and Serbians.

Undoubtedly, hussars looked very effective: they had metal helmets and cuirasses, glinting in sunlight; long lances decorated with streaming red and white pennons; and, above all, wings on their backs. These wings, made of real feathers fastened to a metal frame, so legend has it, were given to veteran hussars who had fought the Turks like angels struggling against Muslims for the triumph of Christianity. The practical role of the wings is not clear. Some think it was an extra defence against a chop to the back; others that the sight and sound of the winged cavalry with their rustling feathers was intended to horrify their enemies.

Besides his lance, each hussar was equipped with sabre (*szabla*), short sword (*palasz* or *koncerz*), pistols and carbine. In the 1570s and 1580s they generally constituted 85 per cent of all Polish cavalry.

Light cavalry was not popular in Poland (forming only 10–15 per cent of all horsemen in the 1580s), but it was more developed in the Grand Duchy of Lithuania. As in Russia, there were Cossacks, men in chain mail (*pancyrnye kozaki*) and Tatars. They were equipped with lances, sabres, bows, pistols and carbines. Their armour was relatively weak, a hauberk, leather coat, or maybe a kaftan quilted and padded with wool.

Infantry in the sixteenth century were called *draby pieszye*, *haiduks* (in Poland) or *zholners* (the name of mercenaries in both Poland and Lithuania).

Since the end of the fifteenth century there have been two types of infantry. The first was equipped with big shields, spears and swords; the second had bows and arbalests, and later arquebuses, as well as rapiers, sabres and poleaxes.

In each infantry *rota* there were 150–200 soldiers. They were divided into tens, each commanded by *dsiesiętnik*. In the Polish army there were two branches of infantry: pikemen (*kopijniks*) and arquebusiers (men armed with arquebuses). From 1535 they used a special formation, forming a laager of wagons (*tabor*, a train of wagons, or *telegas*) to act as a temporary redoubt. Similar 'mobile fortresses' were in common use in wars in central and eastern Europe in the fifteenth and sixteenth centuries (such as the Czech *wagenburg* and Cossack *tabor*).

Lithuanian warrior (engraving, sixteenth century)

Polish–Lithuanian troops at battle
(engraving, sixteenth century)

Traditionally, the infantry was an auxiliary combat arm, recruited from lowly country folk and the urban poor. But in the second half of the sixteenth century its role became more important. In 1578 the decree of Poland's King Stefan Bathory established the 'chosen infantry' (*wybraniecka infantery*). Initially they were recruited from Transylvanian peasants. They received estates in Poland and wore special a sky-blue uniform according to the Hungarian model. This force became the basis of the famous Polish *haiduks* and played an important role in the war between Stefan Bathory and Ivan the Terrible.

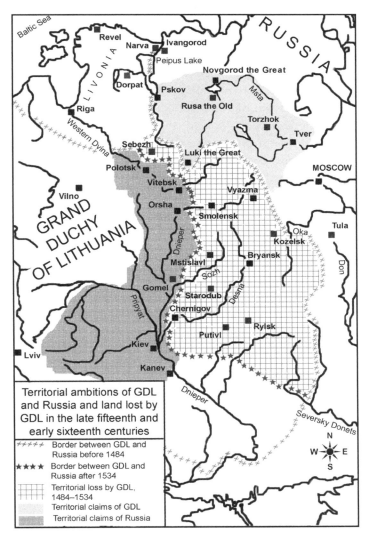

*Map 8. Territorial ambitions of Grand Duchy of Lithuania and
Russia, and lands lost by the
Grand Duchy of Lithuania in the late fifteenth
and early sixteenth centuries*

Artillery (*armata* in Polish) was highly developed and equipped with a wide
variety of bombards, howitzers, mortars and small-bore guns (*tarašnicy*).
The pieces employed included 81-pounder (81-pounder, that is, firing an
81-lb projectile) and 28-pounder mortars (300-mm and 210-mm calibre
respectively) and *kartauns* ranging from heavy 48-pounders (186 mm) and

24-pounders (150 mm), through 12-pounders (120 mm) to light 6-pounders (95 mm). Polish artillery used solid shot (cannonballs) and explosive bombs or shells.

Poland had a navy (*marynarka wojenna*), founded in 1517. It was equipped with galleons and frigates of 400–600 tonnes displacement. It participated in the Denmark–Sweden War of 1563–70, but played only an auxiliary role.[11]

What of relations between Poland, the Grand Duchy of Lithuania and Russia? These have set a peculiar world record for the duration of armed conflict. Officially these countries were at war for almost two hundred years. Starting with the so-called 'First Boundary War' in 1487, these countries knew no peace until the optimistically named 'Eternal Peace' was concluded between Russia and Poland in 1686, though very short-lived ceasefires were contracted occasionally. During this period eleven full-scale wars took place as well as countless minor border clashes.

In five wars with Russia (in 1487–94, 1500–3, 1506–7, 1512–22 and 1534) the Grand Duchy of Lithuania lost a lot of territories: Smolensk, Novgorod-Seversky, Chernigov and the lands near the headwaters of the Oka river. The Russian border approached close to Kiev and Polotsk, and Moscow pressed the GDL along the full length of the frontier (see map 8, p 83). There were no hostilities between Russia and the GDL in 1535–60, the countries having signed an armistice. During the reign of Ivan the Terrible there were two Russo–Lithuanian wars. The first, in 1561–70, ended in a Russian victory, the other, in 1578–82, in defeat for Moscow. Russian troops only fought the Polish army in the second war (apart from insignificant earlier clashes such as at Nevel in 1562).

THE LAST KNIGHTS: LIVONIAN CRUSADES
IN THE SIXTEENTH CENTURY

Because of their '*Drang nach Osten*' strategy ('the drive towards the East'), German knights appeared in the Baltic lands bordering Russia in the late twelfth and early thirteenth centuries. In 1198 the Teutonic Order was founded and the Order of the Sword-Bearers (later renamed the Livonian Order) in 1202. In 1237 the two Orders were formally united. From that moment they were headed by the grandmaster, although until 1520 the Livonian Order retained its own master, who was confirmed in the office by the superior Teutonic master and the Higher Assembly of the Order.

In the second half of the fifteenth and the early sixteenth century, the condition of the Orders started to be rapidly impaired. The ideology of 'armed monks' was losing its vigour by that time, while the opportunities for colonisation had already been exhausted and further expansion turned

Map of Livonia, 1574

Map 9. Livonia in the first half of the sixteenth century

out to be impossible. The flabby structure of the knights' states, constituted as confederations of the Order's own lands, episcopacies and cities endowed with special status, began to fail. The situation was aggravated by internal wars connected both with the ambitions of the Order's last rulers and the spread of the Reformation within the region. The participants in these internal conflicts were remarkably unscrupulous in their search for foreign protectors and, as their contemporaries reported, did not disdain to call for intervention for the sake of the fulfilment of their personal ambitions.

These factors formed the 'Livonian Question', characterised by nineteenth-century historians as the medieval version of the 'Eastern Question' of their own day. Indeed, the similarity was obvious: in both cases the matter concerned the partition of the territory of a weakened state (the role played by the Ottoman Empire in the nineteenth century) by the neighbouring states and, when the process aroused serious disputes between the aggressors, several wars resulted.

In the mid-sixteenth century, Livonia consisted of several historically established areas: Estlandia, Courland, Letlandia and Semigalia. The whole of Livonia was divided into twenty-two districts. The Livonian Order itself had command of 59 per cent of the territory, while 16 per cent belonged to archbishopric of Riga and the remaining 25 per cent was divided between the Dorpat, Courland and Ezel episcopacies and the largest cities. Of the latter, the most significant were Riga (8,000 people), Dorpat (6,000) and Revel (4,000). The cities had lasting contacts with European unions: Revel was linked to Hansa, and Riga had been a member of the Schmalkalden League since 1541. The bishop of Revel did not possess any significant territory of his own.

The population was multi-ethnic. The upper aristocracy of the Order consisted of Germans who were for the most part newcomers from Westphalia. But the number of Livonian knights did not exceed 400–500 people. The much bigger group comprised the so-called vassals, who were of German stock and had been residing in Livonia for ten to twelve generations. Among the townsfolk most burghers were also of German origin and, in general, the German population in the settlements of a fortress city or town amounted to approximately 20 per cent. The peasantry, by contrast, consisted mostly of aboriginal Ests, Livs, Letts, Kurshes and Semigals.

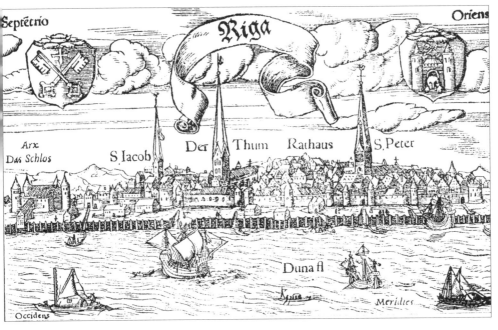

Riga in 1547 (German engraving)

The core of the Order's military organisation was formed by the heavily armed mounted knights followed by the vassal horsemen and the infantrymen (*knechts*). But even during the Livonian Order's heyday the number of knights did not exceed hundreds of people. The Order could provide several thousand people in total, including vassals and *knechts*. That was sufficient for the subjugation and partial extermination of the indigenous Baltic people (Ests, Livs and so on).

Knights' castles rose on the hills and plains of the Baltic as a symbol of the Order's power over the lands. Usually they were quadrangular or pentagonal with stone walls 5–6 m high, a moat 10–15 m wide and a central keep or donjon. There was a permanent garrison of several tens or hundreds of soldiers in a castle, commanded by a *vogt*. Castles held fairly good artillery, not uncommonly including several dozen guns. This allowed even a small garrison to repulse the attacks of the local peasantry and terrify the whole neighbourhood.

So-called 'peasant castles' (*bauernburgen*) were scattered throughout Livonian lands. They were earthen fortifications of different shapes and sizes, sometimes surrounded by a double or triple rampart, perhaps topped by wooden defences. They guarded the property (*myzas*) of Livonian landholders.

Tallinn (Revel) and Riga were the largest fortresses enclosed with mighty walls (those in Tallinn partially surviving today). But the function of the walls was to guard the liberties of the citizens from the Order's appetite. In Riga, the knights' castle was located apart from the city fortifications.

The purposes for which Livonian castles were built was exclusively internal. They played an important part in establishing control over the native population and in confrontations between the Order and bishops or knights and vassals. But the castles did not defend Livonia from the intrusion of external enemies at all. Firstly, there was not any line of border castles which would form a system of frontier defence and the Russian invasion of 1558 demonstrated this lack of protection as every castle fought alone. Secondly, the majority of these castles were wooden or stone fortifications rebuilt from the earlier edifices of the fourteenth and fifteenth centuries. That was sufficient defence against the native peasants and even the bishop's soldiers. But, when the armies of Poland, Lithuania, Russia, Denmark and Sweden entered Livonia with their siege artillery, it became clear that the castles were absolutely unsuitable for military purposes and could not withstand a siege maintained according to the rules of sixteenth-century warfare. They were relics, memorials to the obsolete epoch of the 'last knights', and the military struggle for the Baltic lands, which began in the 1550s, put an end to the Order and to Livonian independence.

Swedish Army and Navy

Until the sixteenth century Sweden had stayed in the 'Danish shadow' being, as Robert Frost has put it, 'a fringe of Europe'.[12] In 1521 the country gained independence and left the Kalmar Union, by which it had been subjugated to Denmark and Norway. The population of Sweden had reached a total of 750,000. Sweden's outlet to the Baltic Sea was blocked by Danish positions on island of Gotland and in Borholm, so the Swedes decided to solve this problem by military means and by the middle of the century had built nineteen battleships for that purpose. Sweden needed new territories in the Baltic. It was not intended that these lands would be obtained at the expense of their former master, Denmark, but rather through conquests in a southern and southeastern direction: towards the Baltic, the Gulf of Finland coast and Karelia. The outpost of Sweden in this region was one of its best fortresses, Vyborg.

Conflict with Russia over these territories was inevitable. The region comprising the Gulf of Finland coast, the Neva river basin and Karelia had officially belonged to the Republic of Novgorod the Great until 1478 and had been inhabited mainly by a Russian Orthodox population which, nevertheless, had peacefully got on with local Finno–Ugric tribes – such as Izoras, Vods and Karelians – who were partially Orthodox and partially pagan in their beliefs. After the subjugation of the Republic of Novgorod in 1478, these lands legally passed to Moscow. There were a number of Russian stone fortresses there – Oresheck, Yam, Karela, Koporje and Ivangorod – which controlled and protected the territory as best they could. But Moscow, with its cavalry of many thousands, lay far away and the local garrisons were small. That's why the area seemed to be defenceless, offering easy pickings, and the first steps of the young Swedish state were directed to incursions into Russian, Baltic and Karelian lands.

The Swedish army of the sixteenth century was based upon an infantry militia armed with arquebuses and crossbows. It was obvious, however, that such an army was suitable only for defensive operations or internal clashes within its own borders. For offensives outside Sweden the king hired mercenaries and these were among his heaviest expenses.[13] The detachments of mercenaries fighting Ivan the Terrible's army in the Baltic rarely included more than 5,000–6,000 men. According to Arvo Viljanti's data, 14,000 infantrymen (11,000 of them Swedish and 3,000 recruited from local Finns) and only 1,500 cavalrymen (about 1,000 Swedes and 500 Finns) fought the Russians in Finland in the 1550s.[14] As we shall see, this was not a sufficient number to beat Ivan the Terrible's warriors, yet the result of the Russian–Swedish conflict in the sixteenth century contradicts this notion.

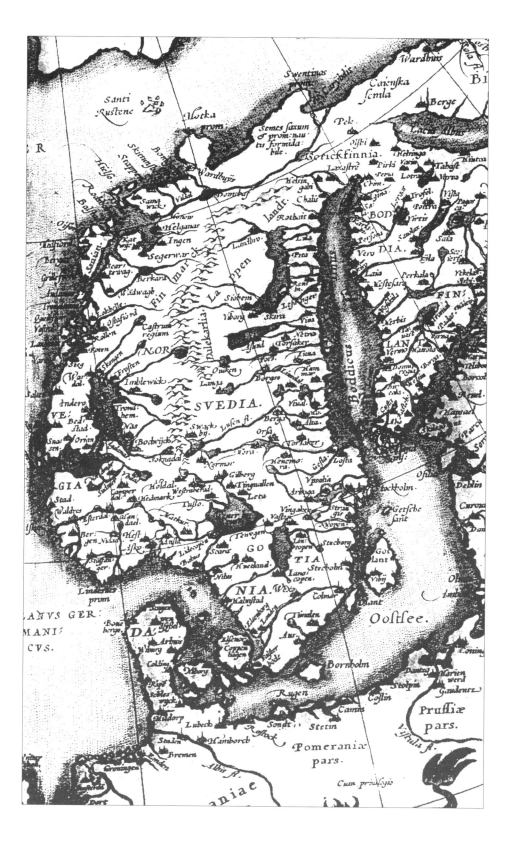

CONCLUSIONS

How should the military potential of the various combatants be estimated? It must be viewed from two angles: the level of military and technical development; and numerical strength.

We have seen that several tactical approaches, several different military techniques and, in a strict sense, several epochs met on the battlefields of the period. The Russian army brought about the decline of the once all-powerful Tatar troops, which, having perfected their martial skills in the times of Chingiz Khan and the Golden Horde, could not evolve in the sixteenth century and were exposed as adherents of an archaic and obsolete form of warfare. At the same time the defeats of both the army of the Grand Duchy of Lithuania and Ivan the Terrible's army demonstrated that the future lay with those armies that accepted the principles of the European 'military revolution', which was to bear fruit in the following century. Those armies consisted of professional soldiers.

The principal technical and tactical characteristics of the armies under consideration are summarised in Appendix III.

Left: Map of Sweden by Abraham Orthely (sixteenth century)

3

The Russian Crusades

Ivan the Terrible Against the Muslims

'EVERYONE KILLED BY A MUSLIM ASCENDS STRAIGHT TO
PARADISE': SIXTEENTH-CENTURY RUSSIAN ORIENTAL DOCTRINE
The attitude of Russia towards Muslim peoples has varied through history.
Actually, it was not Muslims but pagans who conquered Russian lands during
the Mongol–Tatar invasion in the thirteenth century; Islam became the general
religion of the Golden Horde only in the fourteenth century. However, the fact
that the conquerors were pagans initially held some advantages: Mongol–
Tatars were mostly tolerant towards the Orthodox Church; the Russian
Orthodox clergy was exempt from paying tribute; and there was even the
Orthodox eparchy in the capital of the Golden Horde!

The adoption of Islam by the Golden Horde led to some tension between
Russia and Great Tataria.* It is certain, however, that Tatar rulers had no
intention of converting Russia to Islam; they tried to avoid religious matters.
They did not build mosques in Russian cities, nor did they force Russian
princes to convert. Although there were instances of conversion to Islam, the
converts were mainly captives taken to the Horde who either remained to live
there or were sold further east, to Asia or Turkey.

The Tatars' religious tolerance was driven by common sense: they did
not want anti-Horde rebel movements inspired by the idea of defending
Christianity against Islam. In Russian lands, by contrast, the supporters of
the struggle against the Tatars played the religious card and emphasised that
the war against the Horde was essentially a war for the defence, and ultimate
triumph, of the Orthodox Church. The princes who wanted to get rid of the
control of the khans realised that it was possible to receive public backing
only if the confrontation took the form of the defence of the Christian faith,
rather than antagonism between ambitious rulers.

---

* Great Tataria is the correct name, as no state called the Golden Horde has ever
actually existed, this being coined by later historians. The Tatars called their state
Great Tataria and Russian chronicles mention it simply as the Horde.

These tendencies gained momentum as Tatar power in eastern Europe weakened. In the thirteenth century the Tatars conducted seventeen devastating raids into Russian lands, in return suffering only two military expeditions by Russian princes which can be regarded as counterattacks. In the fourteenth century the ratio was twenty-eight to nine, and by the fifteenth century it was twenty-six to twelve (according to Yuri Seleznev's calculation).[1]

Yet, the weaker the Tatar threat became, the stronger the anti-Muslim ideology in Russia became. According to the Orthodox ideologists, the military triumph over the Tatars, their defeat and subjugation, the gaining of power and greatness by humiliating and annihilating the former overlords was the historic revenge, the ultimate victory of Russia over the Horde. The Tatar khanates of the fifteenth and sixteenth centuries were identified with the already-nonexistent Golden Horde; the Horde's 'successor states' – the khanates of the Crimea, Kazan and Astrakhan – now had to take the punishment for the guilt of Batu, Uzbek and Tokhtamysh, the real conquerors of the Russian lands in the thirteenth and fourteenth centuries.

Victories over the Tatars came to be regarded as pleasing to God, and warriors who died in these battles were promised absolution and a place in heaven. In the fifteenth- and sixteenth-century chronicles, former battles of the Russians with the Tatars (the battle of Kulikovo 1380, for example) began to be presented as miracles where the Lord had given deliverance unto the Russians through his angelic host attacking the Tatars from heaven and destroying them with swords. The battle of Kulikovo became symbolic and was often compared to Armageddon: having defeated the Muslims at Kulikovo *Pole* (Field), the Russians saved the world, as though this was the final battle between good and evil before the Day of Judgement.

The rapid development of this ideology started at the end of the fifteenth century, and Bishop Vassian Rylo of Rostov can be considered as one of its creators. In 1480, in his letter to Grand Prince Ivan III, he compared Russia to New Israel – the new 'chosen people' – and the khan to Pharaoh. The Russians should free themselves from Tatar captivity as the Jews had freed themselves from the land of Egypt. Then the deeds of Russian rulers would be equal to the deeds of the kings of Israel in the Bible and Russia, New Israel, could exalt itself above the nations and show the entire world the way to the Kingdom of Heaven.

During the reign of Ivan the Terrible, the ideology of the Holy War against the Tatars was championed by the senior hierarchs of the Orthodox Church: Metropolitan Macarius, archbishops Theodosius and Pimen of Novgorod and others. Before the campaigns against the Tatars, in their customary addresses to the tsar and his warriors, the hierarchs promised paradise to those killed in battle. In addition, the tsar's speeches praised the feats of arms that brought glory to the Orthodox Church and shame to the Muslims. 'Saracens' were declared to be the cause of distress to the Orthodox Church: temples were neglected, Christians were taken captive or killed. In the speeches of the church ideologists, supporters of the struggle against the Tatars, the tsar was presented as a 'good shepherd' (John 10:14) who 'gives his life as a ransom for many' (Mark 10:45).

What was the main stimulus for the aggression against Muslim states during the reign of Ivan the Terrible? Was it the 'Holy War' ideology championed by the Orthodox hierarchs? Yet, the Russians got along together with the Muslims in the Russian army (Tatars from Kasimov, Temnikov and other Tatar enclaves in Muscovy). Indeed, Russia has never fought religious wars, though it has used religious rhetoric to justify its aggression.

Was it revenge that drove Russians in their campaigns on the khanates of Kazan, Astrakhan and the Crimea, revenge for long centuries of the Tatar yoke, for hundreds of thousands of countrymen killed and made slaves? There is no denying the element of revenge. All Russian sixteenth-century texts tell us about the joy of freeing the captives and meting out retribution and punishment to the Tatars. Yet it should be noted that the wrongs done to the Russians by the Tatars of Kazan, the Crimea and especially Astrakhan could not be compared to those of the Golden Horde period. However, the Russians punished Kazan and Astrakhan for all the grief done by Chingiz Khan's empire and the Golden Horde. What pushed the Russian state in its *Drang nach Osten* was the historical instinct – the intense feeling that it was necessary to get rid of the historical complex of the enslaved country that the Tatars had instilled in the Russian minds since 1237. That is why the Russians sought to avenge themselves on those identified with descendants of the Golden Horde. From the Russian point of view, it was retribution and restoration of historical justice. From the point of view of those who lived in Kazan, Astrakhan and the Crimea, it was aggression. Tragedies caused by mutual misunderstanding have been, and will be, numerous in history.

This was the ideological context of the eastern policy of Ivan the Terrible. His first target was the khanate of Kazan.[2]

'STREAMS OF BLOOD INSTEAD OF STREETS':
THE RUSSIAN CONQUEST OF THE KHANATE OF KAZAN
AS REVENGE FOR CENTURIES OF SLAVERY

'The Kazan War' began during the reign of Grand Prince Ivan IV on 2 April 1545 and lasted seven years and six months, ending on 2 October 1552. In actual fact, the fighting did not end in 1552; the peoples of the Volga region continued guerrilla operations and Ivan the Terrible sent punitive expeditions to the former lands of the khanate of Kazan long after that date. It was in 1552, however, that the capital of the khanate of Kazan was captured, the administrative structure ruined, the khan overthrown and the Tatar army destroyed. That was the end of the Kazan Tatar statehood; the khanate of Kazan was wiped from the face of the earth.

In April 1545, during the spring tide, the Russian army set off from the towns of Nizhni Novgorod and Vyatka. The troops joined at the mouth of the Kazanka river and ravaged Tatar settlements on the banks of the Kama, Vyatka and Sviyaga rivers and around Kazan. Several Tatar noblemen were killed and Murtaza-murza was captured. Khan Safa-Girei, outraged by Russian success, accused his princes of complicity with Moscow. Several suspected traitors were executed. As a result, the nobility fled from Kazan to the grand prince of Moscow and other lands.

Nobles disaffected with Safa-Girei decided to organise a coup. On 29 June 1545, two Tatar noblemen, Kadysh and Chyura Narykov, addressed Moscow on behalf of the conspirators asking that troops be sent and promising to arrest the khan and his Crimean clique. Russia guaranteed full support. However, on 17 January 1546, it became known that the coup had succeeded without Russian troops. Safa-Girei had been banished, and his supporters killed. After long talks with the boyars, on 13 June 1546 Khan Shahghali, Moscow's puppet, ascended to the throne. He remained in power only one month before the citizens of Kazan revolted against him and reinstated Safa-Girei.

It was only a few months later, on 6 December, that Tatar nobles again asked Moscow to send troops to once more dethrone the khan they were already tired of. In February 1547, troops under Prince Alexander Gorbaty and Prince Semen Mikulinsky were despatched from Nizhni Novgorod, bound for Kazan territory. This campaign was in response to the letter of Atachik, commander of the Cheremises, in which he proposed to join forces with the Russian commanders downriver from Vasilsursk for a joint attack on Kazan. However, none of the troops reached Kazan.

That autumn it was decided at state level to launch a large-scale campaign aimed at the conquest of the khanate of Kazan. The campaign lasted from 17 November 1547 to 7 March 1548. It was the first campaign in which the young tsar, Ivan IV, took part; he was seventeen years old. He marched with the main force as far as the point where the Rabotka river, a small tributary, flowed into the Volga. Attempting to cross the Volga, which had begun to thaw, cannon and *pischals* fell through the ice. It was impossible to cross the river and a lot of people drowned, failing to see the holes made in the ice as this was covered in a layer of water. The tsar decided to return to Moscow with the main force, sending a detachment under the command of Prince Dmitry Belsky and a Tatar, Prince Shahghali, to continue against Kazan. They won the battle of Arsk Field, forced the khan to flee into the city and besieged it for a week.

In October 1548, the Kazan Tatars attempted a counterattack. The army of Arak-bahadir attacked the outskirts of the town of Galich. However, *voevode* Zakharij Yakovlya intercepted him on the Gusevskoye Field by the Yezevka river. The Tatars were defeated and Arak was killed. At the end of 1548, Alexey Basmanov-Pleshcheev from Murom raided the Kazan lands.

On 25 March, news of the death of Khan Safa-Girei reached Moscow and the Russians immediately began preparing to use force to ensure the succession of their own candidate to the throne of the Kazan khanate. The troops gathered in Nizhni Novgorod. The prospective puppet khan, Prince Shahghali, under supervision of Feydor Nagoy, was also sent to that city. In July 1549, the tsar took counsel with Metropolitan Macarius and the boyars and it was again decided to launch a large-scale campaign against the khanate of Kazan under the command of the tsar himself. It lasted from November 1549 to February 1550. Once more, the weather spoiled everything: it rained every day and it was so warm that the ice on the smaller rivers melted, making it impossible to approach the city.

The failures of 1547–8 and 1549–50 reflected poor strategy within the Russian army. Long autumn and winter marches to Kazan exhausted the soldiers. The beginning of military operations coincided with the season of bad roads and spring high water. It became obvious that the operational principles of the war against Kazan should be changed.

At the end of the campaign of 1549–50 it was decided to build a fortified base on the Sviyaga river. In spring 1551, in Uglich district (*uezd*), a troop of noblemen under clerk Ivan Vyrodkov prepared parts for the wooden walls of the future fortress Sviyazhsk. In April, these parts were transported on rafts downriver to the mouth of the Sviyaga, to Mount Kruglaya, 20 km from Kazan. On 24 May, the Russians began assembling the fortress walls. The fortress became the nearest military base to Kazan.

Even before the fortress of Sviyazhsk had been fully constructed, isolated Russian armed parties started attacking Kazan territory along the Volga, from boats. On 18 May, Prince Peter Serebryany, whose unit had partially scattered and lagged behind in the fog over the Volga, suddenly attacked the outskirts of Kazan and even managed to free some of the Russians held captive in the city.

Serebryany's success and the new Russian fortress that had miraculously appeared close to Kazan profoundly impressed the local people. Talks began with representatives of the Cheremises, Chuvashes, Mordvinians and the Tatars of the so-called 'High Side' region (Gornaya Storona) about siding with Ivan the Terrible. They swore allegiance to the Russian tsar and promised to regard Sviyazhsk as their capital city instead of Kazan. Ivan the Terrible gave them his charter with the golden seal and granted them exemption from taxes for three years.

In June, at Ivan the Terrible's order, troops of the Chuvashes, Cheremises and Mordvinians crossed the Volga and attacked Kazan. The tsar planned to make his new subjects do all the work of defeating the Tatars. The ensuing battle took place on the Arsk Field close to the walls of Kazan. The defenders used the fortress artillery to scatter the Chuvashes and Cheremises. Ivan's hopes of winning an easy victory and capturing the city were disappointed.

This failure did not stop Ivan the Terrible. All summer he received the vows of Tatar troops that had deserted from Kazan and decided to enter his service. The tsar offered them his best food and gave liberal presents. A Russian chronicler noted that nobody had been paid such generous salaries as the Tatars. Troops of Russian noblemen blocked all the water routes on the Volga, Kama and Vyatka; Kazan was besieged.

Armed clashes began inside the city. Arsk Tatars (*Arskiye lyudi*) were ready to surrender the city but the Crimean Tatars, who constituted the most militarily efficient part, were against it. As a result, the Kazan and Crimean Tatars began to massacre each other right in the khan's palace. In the end, those in favour of surrender won; the Crimean Tatars decided to flee from the city to avoid arrest and extradition. Leaving behind their wives and children, a group of 300 officers and Tatar princes escaped from the city. They soon ran into the Russian cordon and, fighting them off, fled along the Kama and the Vyatka. They were finally defeated by men from Vyatka under Bahteyar Zuzin and the Cossack atamans Fedka Pavlov and Severga. Forty-six men were captured and Ivan the Terrible ordered them to be executed for the 'hardness of their hearts'.

The Kazan Tatars sent a delegation to Ivan the Terrible asking him to depose Khan Utamesh and his mother Soyembika, the ruling regent, and to give them Khan Shahghali as a new khan. He would have been Moscow's puppet but at least the outward appearance of independence would have been retained: the ruler would have been a Tatar, even though placed on the throne by Ivan the Terrible.

Russia did not agree to the proposal and placed the condition that all the Russian captives should be released, the rest of the Crimean Tatars and their families arrested, and Soyembika and Khan Utamesh handed over to the Russians. The territory of the khanate should be divided, and one part, the

High Side, passed to Sviyazhsk. The delegation headed by the *murza* Yenbars agreed to all conditions. On 6 August 1551, the tsar's diplomat, Alexey Adashev, informed Shahghali that he was the new khan. On 11 August, the deposed Soyembika, Khan Utamesh and several families of Crimean Tatars were brought from Kazan and sent on Moscow. On 14 August, Shahghali entered Kazan and occupied the throne. After difficult talks (the Tatars did not want to surrender the High Side), the new khan and the Kazan noblemen pledged allegiance to Ivan IV. On 16 August 1551, Prince Yury Golitsin, Ivan Khabarov and clerk Ivan Vyrodkov inaugurated Shahghali as khan of Kazan. The mass liberation of captives began – 60,000 of them according to Russian chronicles – and a chronicler compared this event to the exodus of Jews under Moses.

By September, complaints against Shahghali had begun, both from Russian *voevodes* and Kazan Tatars. The new khan was in deadlock. It was impossible for him to disobey Ivan the Terrible's orders to return captives and hand over the High Side. Yet it was also impossible for him to obey those orders, since the loss of slaves caused disaffection amongst their Tatar masters and ceding the High Side humiliated and irritated the Tatar noblemen. Shahghali tried to serve two masters, giving Moscow and Kazan mutually exclusive promises.

The end was dismal. In October 1551, a Tatar delegation came to Moscow requesting the return of all the tax revenue from the High Side, if not the High Side territory itself, to Kazan. The delegation was arrested and it was declared that it would be kept hostage in Moscow until the last Russian captive had been released. Shahghali replied that he could not return all the captives because the Tatars had got used to Russian slave labour and might rebel. A conspiracy soon followed: Tatar princes attempted to make an alliance with the Nogays, but Shahghali intercepted their correspondence, invited the conspirators to dinner and had them killed. Russian *streltsy* guarding the khan's palace killed the other conspirators who remained in the courtyard outside. In all, more than seventy people were killed. It is noteworthy that one party of the survivors fled to the Nogays while the other went to Ivan the Terrible with complaints against Shahghali and begging to be accepted into Russian service.

In 1551, ambassador Alexey Adashev arrived in Kazan for talks with Shahghali. Shahghali declared that he could neither guarantee the return of Russian captives nor make the Tatars give up their demand to return the High Side. He would, therefore, remain khan a little longer, try to execute as many as possible of the Tatars opposed Ivan IV and then flee to Moscow.

Shahghali had a peculiar way of exterminating Moscow's enemies. In January 1552 the Kazan Tatars made an official complaint that Shahghali executed innocent noblemen, robbed their property and raped their wives and daughters. The delegation asked Ivan to depose the odious Shahghali, who, believing in his own impunity, committed bloody crimes. In February 1552, the tsar sent Alexey Adashev to Kazan with orders to depose Shahghali. This raised the difficult question of who should take his place, a Russian governor or a new puppet khan. If the latter, who should be the new candidate?

On 6 March 1552, Shahghali fled from Kazan. He had pretended to go fishing (escorted by 500 Russian *streltsy*). Only eighty-four Tatar noblemen followed him; nobody else wanted to follow the man hated by all Tatars. Shahghali left his wife to the mercy of fate in Kazan. Ivan the Terrible ordered Prince Semen Mikulinsky to occupy Kazan. However, all Prince Mikulinsky could do was evacuate Shahghali's wife from the city. The prince was not allowed into the city; when he approached, the Tatars closed the gates and began taking up arms. The reason was an ingenious rumour that Mikulinsky led a punitive expedition and had orders to kill the Kazan citizens as revenge for disobedience to Ivan the Terrible. Mikulinsky, who had no such orders, stayed for some time before the walls, trying to come to an agreement with the local nobility. The talks were a failure. The prince turned back, bringing an unhappy message: Kazan was disloyal, it did not obey Russian authority and the Tatars refuse to negotiate.

In April 1552, yet again the decision was made to send a large-scale expedition to finally destroy the khanate of Kazan. Furthermore, from the Volga region came alarming reports that Russian troops and those of their allies were being attacked. A Nogay prince, Yadegar, had arrived in Kazan and been proclaimed as the new khan. It became clear that the situation demanded harsh measures. On 16 June 1552, Ivan the Terrible, at the head of the army, left Moscow on what was to be the final expedition against Kazan.

The march to the Volga was not easy. Andrey Kurbsky in his autobiography gave this description:

And in that time he [the tsar] sent us with 13,000 men through the land of Ryazan and then through the land of Meshchera where the Mordvinian people dwell . . . And after about five weeks of hunger and dire distress we arrived at the River Sura at the mouth of the little river Barysh, and he [the tsar] arrived there too on the same day with the main army. And on that day we ate our fill of dry bread with much relish and thanksgiving, buying some at a very dear price, borrowing some from our fellows, both friends and comrades. For we had had none for about nine days, and the Lord God fed us and the army now with fishes, now with other animals, for in those barren steppes there are very many fishes in the rivers.[3]

On 13 August, the tsar arrived in Sviyazhsk. On 23 August, soldiers began preparations for the siege, constructing wooden siege towers and building earthworks reinforced by paling. Then siege weapons were mounted. At that time the first clashes occurred; the tension had been too much for the Tatars and they made the first sortie. Their cavalry attacked a *streltsy* infantry unit near Kaban Lake, but Tatar bows were no match for Russian firearms, which halted the attack. The Tatars fled in disarray, pursued to the very gates of the city by the cavalry of Yury Shemyakin and Fyodor Troyekurov.

On 26 August, Ivan the Terrible decided the direction of the main attack. He gave orders for the building of 'big castles', instead of ordinary siege fortifications, in front of the Tsarsky (Khansky), Arsky, Atalykovy and Tyumensky gates. Realising what this meant, the Tatars again made a sortie and fought desperately. A chronicler supplies this description of the battle by the gates:

> Both Christians and Tatars fought fiercely and long; the walls and the gates were constantly bombarded from cannon; *streltsy* fired their hand gonnes [guns], and from the city they fired from cannons and gonnes; and the battle was big and severe; because the boom of artillery, crashing of hand gonnes, men's shouts and clatter of swords and spears not a single word could be heard even near; and it was great thunder and blasts of fire from cannons and gonnes and smoke.[4]

The Tatars did not succeed in driving the Russians from their positions and, on 27 August, Peter and Mikhail Morozov began to mount siege artillery. Kazan was subjected to artillery bombardment, guns pounding the walls while the howitzers and mortars threw exploding and incendiary shells in an arching trajectory to land within. Prince Kurbsky gave the following description of that artillery duel:

> Now when they [the Russian troops] had well and truly set the trenches in order, and when the soldiers and their commanders had dug themselves into the earth, thinking themselves to be safe from the firing from the city and from sorties, then they dragged up to near the fortress and the town the large and the medium guns, with which they fire upwards; I remember that in all there were about one hundred and fifty large and medium guns behind all the trenches, placed on all sides of the fortress and town. And the smallest distance between them was one and a half sazhen [3.2 m]. And apart from that there were many field guns near the tsar's tents. Now when they began to fire from all directions at the walls of the fortress, they had already silenced the large guns in the citadel, that is to say they did not allow

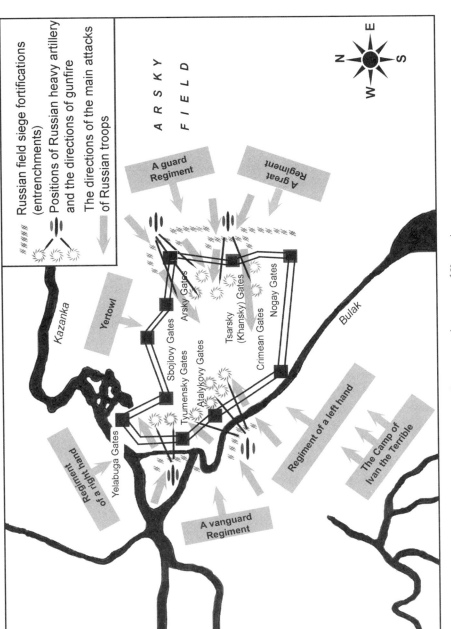

Russian field siege fortifications (entrenchments)

Positions of Russian heavy artillery and the directions of gunfire

The directions of the main attacks of Russian troops

A R S K Y
F I E L D

N
W — E
S

A guard Regiment

A great Regiment

Kazanka

Yertowl

Sbojlovy Gates

Arsky Gates

Tsarsky (Khansky) Gates

Nogay Gates

Crimean Gates

Tyumensky Gates

Atalykovy Gates

Bulak

Regiment of a left hand

The Camp of Ivan the Terrible

Regiment of a right hand

Yelabuga Gates

A vanguard Regiment

Map 10. The siege and capture of Kazan in 1552

the enemy to shoot from their heavy pieces at the Christian army; they were unable to silence only the harquebuses and muskets, with which the Tatars caused much damage to the Christian army in men and horses.[5]

On 28 August, the situation changed. The Tatars tried to sandwich the Russian troops between the walls of Kazan, from where they constantly made sorties, and Tatar forces outside the city that now concentrated and struck Ivan the Terrible from the rear. The Tatars were pushed back and scattered in the woods only after the screening reconnaissance force (*peredovoy polk*), vanguard (*storozhevoy*) and centre units, along with units under command of the prince's *voevodes*, had been sent against them.

The following day, the Russian army was divided. Units under the command of Peter Shchenyatev, Andrey Kurbsky, Yury Pronsky and Fyodor Troyekurov built siege fortifications on the opposite bank of the Kazanka river, in front of Kazan, and began constant bombardment of the city. The Russians used cannons, arquebuses and bows and the Tatars responded with the same weapons. The other part of the Russian army covered the Arsk Field, from where the previous relief attempt had been made. The Tatars came out of the woods and assumed formation but did not dare to attack. The enemy units faced each other all day but did not fight. Ivan the Terrible ordered the building of siege towers on Arsk Field, parallel with the city walls. Thus, by 30 August, Kazan had been completely encircled.

The tsar did not want to storm the city while enemy units remained in the woods to his rear. On 30 August, he sent the units under Alexander Gorbaty and Peter Serebryany, along with Mordvinian allies, to clear his rear area. The Tatars were defeated at the Kiliri river and then *streltsy* and Cossacks combed the woods, eliminating small enemy groups and doing what in the twenty-first century is called 'mopping-up'. They captured 340 Tatars. Ivan the Terrible had them led in front of the city walls and promised to release them all if the city capitulated. Khan Yadegar refused to surrender and Ivan the Terrible ordered the captives tortured to death in full view of the city. However, according to Kurbsky, the Tatars themselves shot the captives from the walls.

And when they [Russian soldiers] brought the prisoners whom they had captured alive to our tsar, he ordered them to be led out in front of the trenches and be bound to stakes, so they might beg and warn their comrades within the fortress to hand over the city of Kazan to the Christian tsar . . . But having listened to these words in silence, the Tatars began to shoot from the walls of the fortress, not so much on our men, as on their own men, saying: 'We would rather see you killed from our Mussulman hands, than slaughtered by the uncircumcised Giaours!' And other blasphemous words they belched forth with much fury so that all of us who were watching were amazed.[6]

The Russian tsar did not want to take chances storming the city walls; he wanted to be sure of his success. Captive Tatars had spoken of an underground passage that led to a secret source of water. Alexey Adashev and a German engineer – history is silent about his name, Russian chronicles call him 'Razmysl', meaning 'wise man' – received orders to destroy the underground passage by digging a mine under it. On 4 September, Vasily Serebryany, with great precautions, filled the mine with eleven powder barrels and at dawn detonated the explosive. 'Razmysl' did more than had been expected: not only was the underground gallery destroyed but part of the city wall collapsed and burning splinters showered the city, starting fires.

Ivan the Terrible ordered the city to be bombarded night and day, 'lest the enemy sleep'. Stone cannonballs brought down Arsky Gate, making a breach. Incendiary shells rained down upon the residential quarters. Kazan was burning ever more fiercely and there was no time to extinguish the fires. The Tatars, deprived of their water supply, were in a state of panic. People tried to dig wells inside the city but the only result was putrid water that caused diseases. As a last resort, the Tatars tried to use magic against the Russian army. Kurbsky gave a description of how Tatar magicians aimed to harm the Russian troops:

> But it is worth briefly recalling how the Tatars worked magic against the Christian army and brought on great rains. Soon after the investment of the fortress, when the sun began to rise, both very old men and women would come out on to the citadel in full view of us, and would shout out satanic words, waving their clothes at our army and turning round in an indecorous manner.[7]

On 6 September the Russian forces under the command of Alexander Gorbaty and Zakharij Yakovlya, together with the Kasimov Tatar and Mordvinian allies, attacked a temporary wooden fortress built by the Tatars in the Russian rear, on the Arsk side. The fortress stood between two marshes and all approaches were barricaded by felled trees, making it impossible to build siege works and apply the usual methodical tactics. So the fortress was simply stormed by infantry, the commanders leading the soldiers from the front. After a bloody battle, the fortification was captured and the Russian units proceeded to the settlement which lay on the Arsk side, burned it down and moved further on. The territory up to 150 km from Kazan was mopped up. In villages, many Russian slaves were freed and many Tatars were captured.

Now that there was no threat of a strike from the rear, Ivan the Terrible gave orders to prepare for the decisive storming of Kazan itself. Clerk Ivan Vyrodkov erected a siege tower opposite the main gates (Tsarsky/Khansky) and opened fire over the walls from cannons and handguns. The Russians began slowly but steadily moving belfrys (wheeled siege towers) towards the walls, up against the moat. On 30 September, Ivan the Terrible gave the order for mines beneath the outer earthworks (*taras*) to be detonated and the resultant explosions killed a great number of Tatars. The Russians stormed the city gates (Tsarsky, Arsky, Atalykovy and Tyumensky), scaled the walls and started fighting hand-to-hand. 'The fight was furious and terrible', a chronicler noted. In several places, as *voevode* Mikhail Vorotynsky reported, the Russians managed to enter the city. Yet Ivan, unsure of success because some troops were not yet ready to take part in the storming, ordered a retreat. The Russians withdrew, setting fire to the city wall. One Russian unit established itself in the Arsky Gate, providing a base for a future assault.

On 2 October, at the first light of dawn, the German engineer detonated the next mine and a large part of the city wall collapsed. Russians began storming the city from all directions. Here is the description of the storm by Prince Kurbsky:

> Let each man tell of his own deeds; I will briefly and truthfully narrate what I had before my own eyes at that time and what I did. I allocated my 12,000 troops to their various commanders and we ran up to the walls of the fortress, to that great tower which stood on a hill in front of the gates. When we were still quite far off from the walls, we were not fired at from a single musket or bow; but when we got near, then for the first time fire was directed on us from the walls and from the towers. The arrows fell so thickly, that they were like heavy rain, and so incalculably great was the number of stones that the sky could not be seen! And when we had fought our way up to the wall with great difficulty and suffering, they began to pour boiling water on us and to hurl whole beams at us. None the less God helped us by giving us bravery and strength and forgetfulness of death, and in truth with cheerful heart and with joy we fought the Mussulmans for Orthodox Christianity; and within about half an hour we drove them away from the embrasures with arrows and musket fire. Furthermore, the guns from behind our trenches helped us, firing at them; for they now stood openly at that great tower and on the walls of the fortress, not concealing themselves as before, but fighting fiercely with us, face to face and hand to hand. And we might straightway have killed them all, but, although many of us took part in the assault, few came right up to the walls of the fortress: some went back and many lay on the ground pretending to be killed or wounded.[8]

The Russians quickly drove the Tatars out from their fortified positions and street fighting began; in the crowd, soldiers could not use swords and had to attack with knives. In one clash Tatar and Russian spears got interlocked and opposing groups of soldiers stood for hours not willing to yield and not being able to overcome each other.

Some Russian soldiers were carried away with plundering and even managed to return to their camp with loot two or three times. They were soon punished. Kurbsky supplied the following description of the episode:

> And when the Mussulmans saw that few of the Christian troops remained – for practically all of them fell on to the spoil, and many, so they say, went back two or three times to the camps with loot and returned again, while the brave soldiers fought on without ceasing – when the Mussulmans saw that these brave soldiers were exhausted they began to press strongly and to attack them. Now when the looters I have mentioned saw that our troops, while resisting the Mussulmans, were of necessity retreating little by little, they immediately took to flight in such a way that many of them were unable to get through the gates; but a great number rushed over the wall without their loot, while others even threw away their loot crying: 'They are killing! They are killing!' But thanks to the grace of God the brave of heart were not stricken.[9]

Eventually the Tatars were pushed back to the khan's palace. Their troops wavered then tried to muster the strength for a sudden counterattack and escape from the city. In order to divert the Russian troops the khan and his camarilla sacrificed their harems, as Kurbsky describes:

> And when they saw that they could no longer help themselves, they took to one side their wives and their children clad in their fair multi-coloured garments, some ten thousands in number, and they stood on one side of the khan's great court hoping that the Christian troops would be seduced by their beauty and would spare their lives.[10]

The khan decided to flee in the direction of the Yelabuga Gate. The escaping Tatars successfully swept aside those of Kurbsky's and Peter Shchenyatev's troops that attempted to block them, then tried to hide in the woods. However, it was not an organised breakthrough and their flight was rather disorderly. Fleeing Tatars were pursued and many were killed. Khan Yadegar was lucky. Realising that the breakthrough was impossible, he had taken up a defensive position on a nearby hill, but his followers demanded negotiations and handed him over to the Russians.

Ivan the Terrible, in the image and likeness of St George, defeating Kazan Khan Yadegar (picture from the Russian historical tale 'Kazanskaja istoriya', 'The History of Kazan', seventeenth century)

Thus, on 2 October 1552, Kazan surrendered. Yadegar was brought to Moscow and baptised under the name Simeon. The road was cleared of dead bodies and Ivan the Terrible, accompanied by the former khan, Yadegar, entered the city. Russian priests sanctified the city and on 4 October, among ruins, the tsar took part in the construction of Kazan's first Russian Orthodox church.

The army of the khanate of Kazan was eliminated. Ivan the Terrible ordered the execution of all the city's adult male defenders as traitors because they had recognised Shahghali as their ruler and then betrayed him. Almost all Tatar officers and many noblemen were killed. The loss was irreplaceable. According to contemporary records, the city and the surrounding area were strewn with dead bodies and in some streets the blood was deep enough to cover the hooves of horses. A Russian chronicler proudly noted that, whereas every Tatar had previously owned a Russian slave, now every soldier brought home several Tatar slaves. Kurbsky rapturously describes the great spoils and the riches of the conquered land:

> in that land there are great plains, which are most fertile and which abound in
> all kinds of fruits; also the courts of the princes and magnates are extremely
> fine and indeed amazing, and the villages are frequent. As for grain, there
> are so many kinds, that it would indeed be hard to believe, were one to tell
> of them all – it would be like the multitude of the stars in the sky. There are,
> too, countless herds of different kinds of cattle and there is valuable profit
> to be had especially from the various wild beasts which are in that land; for
> costly martens breed there and squirrels and other animals which can be
> used for clothing and for food. Furthermore, there are a great number of
> sables and also many kinds of honey – I know not where beneath the sun
> there are more . . . And at that time there was great rejoicing in the Christian
> army and we sang our thanks to God, and in our army all forms of livestock
> were cheaper – one could buy a cow for ten Moscow *den'gi* and a large ox
> for ten squirrel skins.[11]

The Russians had finally mastered the inferiority complex caused by the Tatar yoke. Russia had subjugated a Tatar state, though the guerrilla war in remote parts of the former khanate went on for many years. Now it was to be the turn of the khanate of Astrakhan.

*

RUSSIAN 'DRANG NACH OSTEN':
THE MUSCOVITE ARMY ON THE SHORES OF THE CASPIAN SEA

The resolve and uncompromising stance of Russia and its ruler, Ivan the Terrible, during the war against the khanate of Kazan in 1545–52 impressed the neighbouring Tatar states. At the end of 1549 or in early 1550, a force of Cossacks unexpectedly attacked Astrakhan and captured it. The Cossacks soon departed but the fact that they had easily taken Astrakhan left the Tatars with an uneasy feeling. What would happen next time when, instead of just Cossacks, they were faced with the main forces of the Russian tsar, his noble cavalry, *streltsy* and artillery? The answer to that question was both obvious and frightening. Astrakhan would stand no chance.

In 1551, not waiting for the same fate as was then befalling Kazan, Yamghurchi, Astrakhan's ruler, turned to Moscow and asked for the establishment of a Russian protectorate over his khanate. He hoped that the khanate of Astrakhan would enjoy special status if it joined Russia voluntarily. In addition, the khan of Astrakhan might perhaps become deputy ruler of Kazan following its capture by Ivan the Terrible. Yamghurchi was in conflict with the local nobility and not all recognised him. The khan thought that the Russian army would support him if Ivan were his overlord.[12]

In the thirteenth and fourteenth centuries, Russian princes, forgetting about the evils they brought to their own people, invited Tatar armies to help them in their feudal conflicts. History now repeated itself, farcically, in reverse. A Tatar khan wanted to become a Russian subject, hoping to have riches and power. Yamghurchi's case shows that the Tatars became hostages of their rulers, who were ready to betray their own people. Shahghali betrayed the Tatar people in Kazan. Yamghurchi betrayed them in Astrakhan.

In 1552, Ivan the Terrible's ambassador, Sevastyan Avraamov, arrived in Astrakhan to receive oaths of loyalty from the Astrakhan citizens. But Yamghurchi had already changed his mind. Ambassadors from Turkey and the Crimea suggested that Astrakhan should be included into the sphere of Turkish policy in the Caspian region. Having been subjected to humiliation, the Russian ambassador was exiled to an island in the Caspian Sea. In Astrakhan, Yamghurchi massacred some of his relatives and other Tatar noblemen who were opposed to this policy.

In October 1553, a deputation from Prince Ismail of the Nogays arrived in Moscow. The Nogays proposed that Russia should aid the Nogays to forcibly dethrone Khan Yamghurchi and replace him with a Nogay prince, Derbish-Ghali, who would be obedient to Moscow. This agreed with the plans of Ivan the Terrible and planning began for joint military action by Russia and the

Nogays. Prince Ismail was to provide for the Russian passage down the Volga to Astrakhan and would himself attack another Nogay prince, Prince Yusuf, who was disloyal to Ivan IV.

Russian diplomats accused Yamghurchi of breaching old agreements with Russia and assaulting the Russian ambassador, Sevastyan Avraamov. Even a historical justification was provided when Moscow declared that Astrakhan had originally been a Russian city, Tmutarakan, the legendary ancient capital of southern Russia. Then the Tatars of the Great Horde, it was alleged, had captured Tmutarakan and made it their new capital (the exisiting one, Saray, having fallen into neglect), renaming it Astrakhan. This was pure fiction; Russian Tmutarakan had been on the shore of the Sea of Azov, not the Caspian Sea. Yet, in the Russian and Nogay political game of 1553, it was sufficient to justify and legitimise Moscow's action.

The Russian army, under *voevodes* Yury Shemyakin, Mikhail Golovin and Ignaty Veshnyakov, moved down the Volga. Their forces included units of noble cavalry, *streltsy* and units from the Vyatka region. On 29 August 1554, the boats reached the place where the Volga and the Don are very close to each other (known as Perevoloka, the place where the Volgo–Don canal was later constructed). This place was considered the northern border of the khanate of Astrakhan. Here, near Black Island, a clash took place with boats under the command of Salman and the Tatars were defeated. Some prisoners were taken and these revealed that Yanghurchi was 5 km from Astrakhan with a small army, there was a garrison in the city and that the majority of Tatars had stayed in their home *ulusy* instead of gathering to defend the khanate.

On 2 July, troops under Yury Pronsky approached Astrakhan by river. The boats divided into two groups and blockaded the city upstream and downstream. When the Russians disembarked and started to march towards the city in battle formation, the Tatars surrendered without a fight. The only military action was chasing fleeing Tatars.

Meanwhile, troops under Alexander Vyazemsky attacked the army of Yamghurchi but, again, there was no battle. Yamghurchi escaped when he learned that Astrakhan had been captured and that his men had scattered, fleeing in boats, on horseback or on foot, having abandoned the artillery.

In Astrakhan, the backing of Russian arms ensured the enthronement of Derbish-Ghali, Yamghurchi's second cousin, who was not discouraged by the fact that he fought against his kin. Russians meanwhile swept the islands in the Volga delta for any of Yamghurchi's forces that were still able to offer resistance. As an exotic trophy, the Russians captured a boat carrying the khan's harem. Yamghurchi himself fled with twenty men to the Turkish stronghold of Azov on the Sea of Azov. From 7 July the Tatars started entering *en masse* into Russian service or that of Derbish-Ghali, Moscow's protégé. By 29 July, the process of annexing the khanate of Astrakhan to Moscow was complete and Russian troops departed, having left a garrison of Cossacks under the command of Peter Turgenev. Every year Astrakhan had to pay a tribute of 1,200 roubles, 10,000 horses, 20,000 sheep and 30,000 sturgeons. At the same time, Muscovite fishermen had the right to fish anywhere in the Volga, its delta or the Caspian Sea. It is possible the numbers in Russian sources are exaggerated; Tatar sources mention 3,000 fish.

In spite of this success, the situation around Astrakhan remained difficult. Whereas the Kazan Tatars had no support and had to limit themselves to guerrilla warfare, the Astrakhan Tatars tried to avail themselves of the dissension among the Nogay princes who roamed nearby and presented a somewhat severe threat. In March 1555, Yamghurchi approached Astrakhan with the Nogay army of Prince Yusuf, which included Crimean Tatar troops. It soon became clear, though, that the Nogays stood no chance against the Russian garrison's artillery. The Nogay cavalry, unaccustomed to assaulting fortifications defended by artillery, pranced for some time before the walls, suffered heavy losses and retreated. In May 1555, the attack was repeated but this time matters did not proceed so far as an attack on the city itself as the Nogay cavalry of Prince Ismail, loyal to Moscow, rebuffed the attackers.

In that same month, disturbing news came from Astrakhan. The commander of the Cossack garrison, Peter Turgenev, left the city for Moscow since the one-year period of his stay in Astrakhan had expired and the khan 'let him go home'. This left no Russian military presence in the city. It was Turgenev's mistake, but perhaps he had been eager to take his men away from the city for fear of treachery on Derbish-Ghali's part. On the Volga, a unit of *streltsy* under command of Gregory Kaftyrev came across the boats carrying Turgenev's Cossacks. Kaftyrev ordered Turgenev's men to turn back and led his men to Astrakhan, having dispatched messengers to Moscow with the alarming news.

When Kaftyrev and Turgenev reached Astrakhan, the city was empty; the khan and the citizens had thought that it was a punitive expedition. The aid that the khan of the Crimea had sent to Derbish-Ghali was not great: Prince Chegilek and three other princes with cannon and muskets. Therefore, the unlucky Astrakhan ruler preferred to begin negotiations with the Russians. After talks with the ambassador, Leonty Mansurov, the khan surrendered, returned to Astrakhan and again swore an oath of loyalty as a vassal of Ivan the Terrible (or, as a chronicle has it, 'recognised himself a slave of the Russian sovereign'). Meanwhile, the Nogay Prince Ismail defeated the Nogays of Prince Yusuf. Mansurov took up residence in a separate fort that consisted of earthworks strengthened by reed stems while Derbish-Ghali lived in another. A kind of diarchy was thus established in the Volga delta.

In November 1555, a deputation from Prince Ismail arrived in Moscow with another report of secret contacts between Astrakhan and the Crimea. Ismail was asked to depose the khan of Astrakhan and introduce direct rule through a governor after the pattern of Kazan. Ismail's Nogays pledged an oath of loyalty to Ivan the Terrible, the usual formula of which was 'we go where the tsar sends us; we are friends of the Russian tsar's friends and enemies of his enemies'. On 15 February 1556, a delegation led by Andrey Tishkov set out from Moscow to the Nogays to confirm that Ivan the Terrible had graciously accepted the Nogays as Russian subjects.

Derbish-Ghali soon proved his reputation as a rebel. On 1 March 1556, the Nogay envoy, Bichura, brought news that the khan had violated his oath to Ivan the Terrible by ousting ambassador Leonty Mansurov in league with the Crimean Tatars and the Nogays under the command of Prince Yusuf. Mansurov entrenched himself in a small fortress in the Volga delta, fended off the Astrakhan Tatars, then marched north in an attempt to break through. He managed to escape with 500 men but not all of them returned home, many dying of starvation.

Ismail moved his Nogays towards Astrakhan. Ivan the Terrible sent fifty Cossacks armed with arquebuses under the command of Ulanka and 500 Cossacks under Ataman Lyapun Filimonov. The Cossacks marched to Astrakhan using skis; it was the first known Russian ski march. A few days later, in May 1556, *streltsy* under Ivan Cheremisov and Timofey Teterin, Cossacks under Mikhail Kolupayev and troops from Vyatka under command of Fyodor Pisemsky were sent down the Volga river.

In September 1556 a message was received from these troops announcing that Astrakhan had been captured. Derbish-Ghali had again escaped without fighting and the citizens resorted to their tested trick of fleeing from the city and hiding on the delta islands until the situation calmed down. The Russians occupied the fortress and strengthened it against a possible attack. Then they took to boats, sailed into the sea and attacked the fleet of Derbish-Ghali that waited at the distance of five days' voyage from Astrakhan. Tatar ships were boarded and the fleet defeated. Derbish-Ghali and his retinue managed to escape to the shore.

On 1 December 1556, a Nogay embassy came to Moscow with the news that Ismail's and Yusuf's Nogays had made peace and wanted to become Russian subjects. Derbish-Ghali, realising the futility of further struggle, left his companions and went on pilgrimage to the holy city of Mecca. Unlike the Kazan Tatars, who continued their guerrilla war for years, the Astrakhan

Tatars did not want to, or could not, organise large-scale resistance. After the conflicting groups of Nogays had been reconciled and Derbish-Ghali had fled, the Astrakhan Tatars started to return home and take the oath of loyalty to Russia. Now the city and the rest of the territory of the former khanate was governed by a deputy of Ivan the Terrible. The khanate of Astrakhan ceased to exist. Now it was time to turn attention to the Crimea.

'DESTROY THE TATARS UTTERLY!': THE RUSSIAN ADVANCE ON THE CRIMEAN KHANATE IN 1550s

The khanate of the Crimea was the next target of Ivan the Terrible. If it had been conquered, there would have been no more remnants of the Golden Horde in Europe. There would have been no Tatar state independent of Russia.

The military potential of this new enemy was much greater than that of the khanates of Kazan and Astrakhan. Both Russia and the Crimea were able to mobilise approximately the same number of troops but the structure of their military forces was different. Russian infantry, firearms and artillery counterbalanced the advantage of the Crimeans in cavalry. However, the Crimea had one definite strength. The Russian army had yet to be transported to the khanate's border, whereas the Crimeans could, even with small forces, seal off the entrance to the peninsula at the Perekop, the narrow isthmus linking the Crimea with the continent.

At first glance, it may have appeared impossible for the army of Ivan the Terrible to invade the Crimea. The idea of breaking through the Perekop isthmus was hardly feasible, or at best it would be extremely difficult. However, the Crimea can in fact be accessed through the system of shallow lakes, coves and inlets between the eastern shore of the peninsula and the Sea of Azov, the area known as Syvash. Unfortunately, the Russian army of the sixteenth century did not have the military engineering skills to cross many kilometres of marshland and shallow coves with their artillery and ammunition.

Yet this apparent strength was simultaneously a weakness. While it was difficult to get into the peninsula, it was equally difficult to get out. The Crimean army could be bottled up within the peninsula if the nearby mainland regions, the territories or *ulusy* subordinate to the khanate, were occupied. The main pastures were there and, if they were destroyed, the horse-breeding was at risk. Therefore, a permanent military base near these *ulusy* would lock the Tatars within the Crimea. The Tatar army would not leave the peninsula, not only for fear of an encounter with Russian troops but also primarily because this would leave the Crimea unprotected against Russian invasion.

This was precisely the strategy that Ivan the Terrible applied against the khanate of the Crimea. In June 1555, troops under the command of Ivan

Sheremetyev and Lev Saltykov moved towards the eastern *ulusy*. They marched along the Muravskaya Road, the route used by the Tatars for their plundering raids on Russian lands. As it happened, 60,000 troops under the command of the khan himself set out from the Crimea at the same time. Fortunately, Russian intelligence worked well and all the movements of the Tatar troops and their intentions soon became known. The main Russian forces, under the personal command of Ivan IV, blocked the approaches to the khan's possible targets, the fortresses in Tula and Kashira. The troops under Sheremetyev and Saltykov – 4,000 noble cavalry, 13,000 Cossacks, plus *streltsy* and auxiliary units – outflanked the Tatars and attacked their supply wagons and reserve horses from the rear. They captured, if the Russian chronicle is to be trusted, 60,000 horses, 200 Arabian horses and eighty camels.

The khan quickly made the decision to withdraw, but Sheremetyev's force was on his line of retreat. On 3 July, in the locality of Sudbishchi, the Russian troops met the vanguard of retreating Tatars and defeated three Crimean units. Sheremetyev's detachment was not, however, strong enough to stop all 60,000 Tatars troops and he desperately called for reinforcements. But when they came it was only a meagre 500 men. Moreover, Sheremetyev had sent 6,000 men to accompany the captured supply train to Ryasan and Mtsensk. Therefore, he had to fall back.

The forces were too unequal; 11,000 Russian troops could not match 60,000 Tatars (perhaps the numbers were smaller if the previous losses are taken into account). Sheremetyev stood his ground until 4 July, defeated the Tatar vanguard units and drew back at the approach of the main Tatar forces headed by the khan. The unit of Alexey Basmanov was especially brave at the battle. It held its position in an oak wood and fought off repeated attacks of the khan's troops. The khan outflanked Basmanov's unit, pushed back other Russian troops that were under the general command of Sheremetyev and broke through into the Crimea. Russian losses were severe: 320 noblemen, about 2,000 *streltsy* and 5,000 militiamen.

Despite the casualties and the failure to prevent the khan's withdrawal, the battle of Sudbishchi was a great psychological boost for the Russians. It was the first time that the Crimean Tatars had been virtually encircled and put on the defensive. The loss of the supply train had a bad impact on the Tatars. Although Sheremetyev's unit sustained severe losses and retreated, it caused no small damage to the enemy in a field battle, which was a first in the wars between Russia and the khanate of the Crimea.

The battle was an enormous humiliation for the Tatars. In his report to the Turkish sultan, Devlet-Girei described the battle of Sudbishchi as his great victory where he had killed and captured about 60,000 *giaours* (as the Muslims called Christians), whereas Sheremetyev's force had only numbered 11,000 men in total. In the Crimea a 'damned *giaour*' by the name of Shirmerd or Shiremed, who had become legendary as a redoubtable enemy of the Crimean Khan, was actively discussed. Unable to accept that the Russians could produce such heroes, and supposing Shirmerd to be an Armenian name, the Tatars decided that he was an Armenian from Persia converted to Russian Orthodoxy. In fact it was a corruption of Ivan Sheremetyev's name.[13] Thus he became a symbolic figure in Russian–Crimean relations.

After the battle of Sudbishchi, the Russians embarked upon an offensive policy against the Crimea and attacked the territory of the khanate the following year. The main striking force consisted of the Don Cossacks in Russian service, peoples from the northern Caucasia (Circassians and Kabardins) and the Lithuanians of Dmitry Vishnevetsky, the prince of the Grand Duchy of Lithuania who entered Russian service in 1556. The *ulusy* of the khanate of the Crimea were subjected to attacks from two sides: the northeast, from the Don, across the Sea of Azov and the Kerch Straits; and the southwest, from the Dnieper along the Black Sea coast.

In June 1556, a Russian nobleman, Matvey Rzevsky, reported from the Dnieper region that 'Lithuanians', by which he meant Cossack atamans from the towns of Cherkassy, Mlyn and Kanev, had joined him in attacking the Turkish fortresses of Islam-Kermen and Ochakov and devastated the *ulusy* near the Dnieper delta. The Tatars and Turks had suffered heavy losses and Ochakov was on fire. Meanwhile, Ataman Mikhail Cherkashenin with the Don Cossacks passed down the Mius river in light boats (*strugs*), entered the Kerch Straits and completely devastated the suburbs of Kerch. It was the first time that the Russians had conducted military actions on the territory of the khanate of the Crimea.[14]

In the autumn and winter of 1556, increasingly encouraging news was coming from the Crimean seat of war. Prince Dmitry Vishnevetsky founded a fortress on Khortitsa Island in the Dnieper, which might serve as a forward base for the Russian advance on the Crimea, as Sviyazhsk had served against Kazan. The Lithuanian prince stormed Islam-Kermen, burned it and removed all the captured artillery to the new stronghold. The eastern border of the khanate was attacked by the Circassian of Pyatigorsk, new allies of Ivan the Terrible. They captured two Tatar towns, Temryuk and Toman. Nogay Prince Tokhtamysh, who had escaped from the Crimea after his coup attempt against Devlet-Girei failed, came to Russia. The news of a coup attempt was received in Moscow with glee as it signalled a split among the Crimean aristocracy of the kind seen in Kazan and Astrakhan. Ivan the Terrible hoped that this split would increase, that the abortive coup of Tokhtamysh had been only

Above left: *Ivan the Terrible in the so-called 'Copenhagen portrait' (sixteenth century). It is generally accepted that this medieval image bears the closest resemblance to the true appearance of Tsar Ivan*

Above middle: *This portrait of Ivan the Terrible (from the seventeenth-century manuscript 'Titulyarnik') shows how Russians imagined 'the terrible and cruel tsar' one hundred years after his death*

Above right: *This stylised image of Ivan the Terrible (from a German engraving) was typical of German propagandistic literature of the sixteenth century*

Left: *Fyodor Ivanovich, son of Ivan the Terrible, is believed to have been mentally retarded, and it was possible that he suffered from Down's syndrome, but he was kind and calm in comparison with his father. There was nothing he liked better in life than to ring the bells of the Kremlin cathedrals. This picture produced towards the end of sixteenth century was among the first Russian portrait paintings (so-called* parsuna)

Above: Tatar warriors of the sixteenth century, in a reconstruction by M. Gorelick. (Reproduced with permission of the Russian historical journal Rodina)

Left: Russian warriors of the sixteenth century, from a painting by Oleg Fedorov. (Reproduced with permission of the Rodina)

Below: Lithuanian nobles, from a nineteenth-century picture

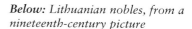

Above: Polish hussars (from an early seventeenth-century painting). Hussars were the most beautiful cavalry in eastern Europe, and were famed for the huge 'wings' worn on their backs, giving them a very striking appearance. Although they were generally the elite of the Polish army, Hussars were used rarely in the wars against Russia in the sixteenth century

Below: Polish knights (from a painting in the Tournament Hall of the King's Castle of Wawel, 1534–1535). Knights (Rycerstvo) in medieval Poland had a special code of honour, but as a military force they were antiquated and swept away by 'military revolution'

Above left: The tsar's throne (1551) in the Cathedral of Assumption in the Moscow Kremlin. The gold-plated throne stands at 6.5 m and is covered in patterned carvings. At the base are reliefs depicting the legendary campaign of Prince Vladimir Monomakh, prince of Ancient Russia, receiving the tsar's regalia from the Byzantine Emperor Konstantin Monomakh. It was an apotheosis of the messianic idea of continuity between the Orthodox Byzantine Empire and 'last Orthodox Kingdom in the World' – Holy Rus

Above right: Russians believed that the main Russian Crown – the so-called 'Monomakh's cap' – originated in Byzantium and was presented by Konstantim Monomakh to Prince Vladimir Monomakh in the twelfth century. In fact, this precious cap descended from the Golden Horde (fourteenth century) and was adapted into a crown by Russian jewellers

Right: The throne of Ivan the Terrible. The throne was made in western Europe from ivory, wood, soft fabrics and iron, and elaborately crafted by highly skilled artisans using techniques of carving, casting and gilding. The proportions are just 138 x 64 x 64 cm. Among the bas-reliefs adorning it are scenes depicting King David, who was Ivan the Terrible's favourite biblical figure

Above: The Russian tsar, from a painting by S. Ivanov. In this nineteenth-century painting, the young Russian tsar is shown leaving the Faceted Palace (Granovitaya Palata) and entering the Cathedral Square in the Moscow Kremlin. Boyars supported the tsar, and strelitsas stood guard over his safety

Right: A sixteenth-century Moscow torture chamber (from a painting by Appolinary Vasnetsov, 1912). Family members came to take away the bodies of relatives who had died in prison

Below: The Russian icon 'The militant church' (Cerkov' voinstvuyuschaya), 1550s. Here you can see the army of Orthodox righteous men with the tsar at the head, reaching the New Zion, Heavenly Town of God. It was believed that this was produced in response to the victory of Kazan (1552). Before the decisive campaign metropolitan Macarius promised Paradise to all warriors killed by Tatars near Kazan. The icon was an allegory of this idea

Above: The siege of the Russian fortress (from a painting by Appolinary Vasnetsov, 1918). Armed citizens gathered in the central square near the church to defend their town

Below: The capturing of Kazan (from an engraving of a watercolour by A. Kivshenko, 1881). Following his defeat (in 1552), Kazan Khan Yadegar kneels before Ivan the Terrible

Above: The Lublin Union in 1569 (from a painting by the nineteenth-century Polish artist Jan Matejko). Note the two groups in the picture. The Poles (left) celebrate victory, while the Lithuanians (right) cry bitter tears, suggesting the union between Poland and Lithuania was unequal. In the centre stands King Sigismund II Augustus with a crucifix in his hand, attempting to reconcile the parties

Below left: Tatar raid on the Russian fortress of Pronsk. This painting, from a typical Russian chronicle of the 1570s, shows the fortifications of the town and depicts the typical armour and clothing of the period. The Tartars (to the left) of the picture however are depicted as Russians, in Russian armour and with Russian bows – a stylisation that was typical of this period

Below middle: Lithuanian ambassadors in Moscow (from a Russian chronicle, 1570s). The painter depicts three events simultaneously: negotiations between Russian and Lithuanian diplomats (top left), the briefing of a Russian diplomat by the tsar (top right), and the departure of Lithuanian envoys (bottom right).

Below right: The siege of Marienburg, the Livonian fortress that was captured in 1560 (from a Russian chronicle, 1570s). Note the heavy artillery and siege fortifications

Right: This fragment from 'The Defence of Pskov' by the Russian painter Karl Brullov (1839–43) reflects the Russian myth of the defence of Pskov as a Holy War of Orthodoxy against European Catholics and Protestants. In it, Orthodox clergymen – armed only with crosses, gonfalons and icons – are rushing to attack the invaders

Below: Stefan Bathory at Pskov: Russian noblemen are depicted handing over the keys of the town and bowing before the Polish king. Painted by the Polish artist Jan Matejko, it reflects the Polish national myth regarding the Pskovsky siege. In reality Pskov never fell to the Poles, as the conflict ended with negotiations before the siege was concluded

Above: A marble bust produced by the Russian anthropologist Michael Gerasimov in 1964, using Ivan the Terrible's cranium. Note Ivan's famous hawk nose which was regarded as evidence of his connection to the Byzantine dynasty of the Paleologues

Above: The king of Rzeczpospolita, Stefan Bathory, was a military leader and political figure who was capable of blocking Ivan's offensive into Europe. (Portrait by an anonymous sixteenth-century painter)

Below: The fortifications at Pskov were famous because this Russian stronghold was never captured by foreign enemies. In the sixteenth century Pskov had thirty-seven towers and forty-eight gates. The walls were 6–7 m high and 4–6 m thick. In Russia only Moscow and Smolensk had fortification systems of equal stature during that period

Above: Ivangorod from the Estonian side of the Narva. In the foreground are the ruins of the Well Tower (Kolodeznaya), while in the background to the right is the Victuals Tower (Proviatskaya) and to the left is the Portal Tower. This most western Russian fortress in the Baltic stood at the 'border of two worlds' – Russia and Europe. Ivangorod was built by Italian architects in 1492 and often had to be reconstructed

Right: Fortifications of the Pskovo-Pechersky monastery, built in the 1560s. In 1581 these walls alone successfully halted the best European mercenaries from Scotland and Germany. The monastery was defended by ordinary Russian monks, who took up arms for the first time in their lives

Below: Underground church in the Pskovo-Pechersky monastery (modern photograph), which is embedded in the rock. There are a great number of underground vaults and caves containing cells, graves and some chapels

Left: A chapel and cross at Savkina Gorka – the outpost of Voronach, a Russian fortress near Pskov. Stefan Bathory's troops passed by here en route to Pskov in 1581

Below: Fortification towers of the Russian fortress Izborsk, situated to the west of Pskov. From left to right are the Talawskaya Tower, the chapel and the Fortress Tower (Bashnya Vyshka). In 1569 a Lithuanian detachment captured Izborsk by trickery – they had disguised themselves as Russian oprichniki, and scared garrison troops opened the gates. From then on, Ivan the Terrible suspected the whole population of Pskovsky and Novgorodsky region of treason

Left: The so-called Thick-Margaret Gun Tower (turret), with the Great Sea gates and Olevuste Church in the background. Revel's fortifications consisted of more than thirty towers and they were never captured by enemies. During the Livonian War Russian troops stormed Revel many times – the main fighting being in 1570 and 1577 – but were unable to penetrate the fortifications

Left: Revel (modern-day Tallinn). In the foreground is the Virgin's Tower (fifteenth to sixteenth centuries) and in the background is the Dome Cathedral (reconstructed in the seventeenth century). According to legend, city prostitutes were held prisoner inside this tower. They could go free only if by some miracle they became virgins again

Left: Dorpat (modern-day Tartu). The ruins of the bishop's Cathedral were dedicated to the apostles Peter and Paul. It was destroyed by Russian troops during the Livonian War in 1558

Left: A modern view of the Livonian knights' castle (fifteenth to sixteenth centuries) situated in Riga, now the capital of Latvia. Citizens of Riga did not like crusaders so their castle was outside the town. According to legend, a witch lived in the castle and was a magical guardian of the town. When Riga was under attack, it was said that the witch turned into a magpie and attacked the adversaries. Russian troops were unable to take Riga during the Livonian War

Right: The City Hall and House of the Blackheads situated in the old town of Riga, Latvia. Riga was an independent city during the Livonian War. Its citizens defended the town from Russian troops and refused to allow the Polish–Lithuanian government to conclude a treaty of union. Riga only submitted to Stefan Bathory at the end of the war, in the 1580s

Right: Modern reconstruction of the fortress of the Livonian Order at Fellin (modern-day Viljandi). The castle was one of the biggest, mightiest and most important strongholds in Livonia and was where the commanders resided

Right: Modern photograph showing the ruins of Fellin

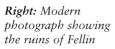

Above: *Founded in 753, Old Ladoga is Russia's oldest fortress and the former residence of Prince Rurik, founder of the Russian state in 862. In the sixteenth century the fortifications were rebuilt and earth bastions added*

Above: *Ruins of the Higher Castle of Vilno. In the sixteenth century Vilno, which was surrounded by a high wall with towers, was under threat from Russian invasion during the Livonian War, although in fact Russian troops never approached it*

Below: *Fortress of Narva, the famous Livonian castle and Baltic port. Narva was taken by Russian troops on 11 May 1558. During the Livonian War the navigation of the Narva river was a matter of dispute between Russia, Sweden, Denmark and Poland*

Below: *'The Cattle Driving Tower' in the Swedish fortress Vyborg (later named 'Thick Katerina'). Ivan's troops stopped here in 1556 during their assault on Vyborg. The battle put an end to the Russian advance on Finland in the sixteenth century*

Above: Wawel, the ancient residence of the Polish kings in Krakow. This was where the Polish government made foreign policy decisions regarding the war against Livonia and Russia and where the struggle for the Polish Crown during the Interregnum in the 1570s took place. The Polish kings Sigismund II Augustus and Stefan Bathory are interred in the Cathedral

Below: The Cathedral of Trinity or Cathedral of the Protection of the Mother of God (Chram Pokrova-na-Rvu), *more commonly now known as St Basil Cathedral. It was built in 1555–61, to commemorate the capture of the khanate of Kazan (1552). According to legend, Ivan the Terrible admired the beauty of the cathedral so much that he ordered that the architects be blinded so they could never construct such a masterpiece again*

Below: Livonian cannon 'Revel's Lion', made by a local master, Karsten Middeldorp, in 1559. The cannon depicts a stylised image of Tsar Ivan the Terrible. Middeldorp would never have seen Ivan in person, but, as British historian Sergey Bogatyrev points out, the cannon is a unique portrait of Tsar Ivan produced in his lifetime. The gun is currently located at The Russian Military Museum of Artillery in St Petersburg

Above: The sixteenth century Pokrovsky Tower, where the most severe hand-to-hand fighting took place between Russians, Poles, Lithuanians and Hungarians during the siege of Pskov. Bathory's troops broke the wall near this tower and rushed into the city but they were halted by Russian troops. It remains an important site of commemoration for Russians today.

Below: A view of inside the Pokrovsky Tower. You can see the numerous casemates and embrasures for guns and pischales.

Above: The battle of Pskov (1581) was the final conflict of the Livonian War. The Russians displayed great courage and halted the Europeans under the walls of Pskov fortress. This conspicuous Polish failure encouraged their king, Stefan Bathory, to end the war. From a Russian nineteenth-century engraving

a beginning and that the same fate would befall the Crimea as Kazan and Astrakhan. Talks between Russia and the Crimea in which the khan asked for peace also gave birth to hope.

In May 1557, Dmitri Vishnevetsky reported that the Crimean khan had besieged his fortress on Khortitsa Island for twenty-four days before being forced to return to his own land 'with reproach and dishonour'. Vishnevetsky argued, and with good proof, that as long as the fortress on Khortitsa was manned with troops loyal to Ivan the Terrible, there was no access for the Crimeans to Russian territory. Building upon his success, the Lithuanian prince began the systematic destruction of the Tatar nomad camps around the mouth of the Dnieper.

It is not now easy to discern the reasoning of Ivan the Terrible but the fact is that the Tsar gave no support to Vishnevetsky. The prince received neither troops nor ammunition nor food. In October 1557, the Tatars forced him to leave Khortitsa and he took his men to occupy Cherkassy and Kanev. He asked Moscow what he was to do next and whether the tsar desired to spread his borders to include these towns of the GDL in his domain. The tsar responded that this was not his desire, that peace with Sigismund II Augustus (king of Poland and grand duke of Lithuania) was more important and ordered Vishnevetsky to return the towns. Vishnevetsky had no choice but return to Russia, where he was given the town of Belev and surrounding villages.

In January 1558, Vishnevetsky received orders to advance to the River Psiyol, a tributary of the Dnieper. He was accompanied by Kabardins and Circassians under Kanklych Kanukov, Ignatiy Zabolotsky and Shyryay Kobyakov with troops of Russian noblemen and Danila Chulkov with Cossacks and *streltsy*. Vishnevetsky took up position 6–10 km from the Perekop and expected that the Tatar army would attack him at any moment. Yet the khan did not attack, preferring to 'withstand the siege', as defectors informed the Russians.

That same year, the Russians founded a new outpost, Pselsky Town on the River Psiyol. This fortress was in a key position. The Russians, if the khan's army left the Crimea, could strike it in the flank or invade the unprotected territory of the khanate behind it. Throughout 1558 there were clashes in the outlying *ulusy* between the Don, Dnieper and Lithuanian Cossacks and the Crimean Tatars, who suffered considerable losses.

In February 1559, Vishnevetsky was sent to the Seversky Donets river to build a fleet, enter the Sea of Azov through the mouth of the Don and attack the coast of the Crimea as far as Kerch. To replace Vishnevetsky in the Dnieper, Ivan the Terrible sent Russian *voevodes* Danila Adashev, Ignatiy Zabolotsky and Shyryay Kobyakov. Thus Ivan now intended to implement his plan to strike the Crimea from two directions, the northeast and the southwest. This strategy proved successful.

Vishnevetsky defeated the Tatars at Azov, near the small town of Aidar. Ataman Mikhail Cherkashenin mopped up the territory along the Seversky Donets. Danila Adashev besieged Ochakov, ravaged adjacent *ulusy* and then put out to sea and won a few minor battles with the Turkish fleet. Meanwhile the devastation of *ulusy* continued and stopped only 15 km from the Perekop. Adashev returned with many captives, but Ivan the Terrible released all the Turks among them because 'he was friends with the sultan'. The 1559 campaign was the most successful campaign of Ivan the Terrible in the war against the Crimea.

In February 1560, Dmitry Vishnevetsky and Ivan Cheremisov were sent to the Caucasus to make the Circassians and Kabardins Russian subjects; separate clans of these peoples had already, of their own free will, taken an oath of loyalty to the Russian tsar and were taking part in the war against the Crimea. Vishnevetsky and Cheremisov had to make arrangements for conversion of the peoples of the northern Caucasus and then make them attack the khanate of the Crimea from the east.

Against the *ulusy* of the Crimea, the tsar sent the Astrakhan Tatars under the command of Tibay-murza, Ismail's son. To aid him, Ivan the Terrible sent the state Cossacks, equipped with firearms, to the Don. The Nogays passed along the Azov and Black Sea coasts, threatened to attack the Perekop, destroyed Tatar-razed *ulusy* and attacked the Turkish fortresses of Ochakov and Akkerman. The khan again merely withstood the siege and did not dare venture outside the Perekop fortifications.

In the autumn of 1561, Dmitry Vishnevetsky was again in the Dnieper region devastating the *ulusy* of the Crimeans. However, the campaign started to show signs of losing momentum. Effectively it came down to looting the Crimean *ulusy*, besieging Turkish fortresses on the Black Sea and making plundering sea raids on the Crimean coast, mainly around Kerch and along the west coast of the peninsula. The military achievements should have been consolidated and developed. It was time to storm the Perekop or invade the peninsula by other means. Yet the Russians were not strong enough to do anything more than looting and massacring, doing the same as the Tatars had done.

Why did Ivan the Terrible not build on his successes in the war against the Crimea? Undoubtedly, among the reasons was the fact that in the Crimea there was no opposition to the khan's rule, let alone pro-Russian opposition. It had been rather easy to place the puppet khan Shahghali on the Kazan throne as the Kazan aristocracy largely sympathised with Russia. Astrakhan's fall had been mostly the result of the intrigues of the Nogays, who were divided into those who supported Russia and those who were against her.

Russian secret agents gave out large sums as bribes to Tatar officials, especially members of the diplomatic service. Tatars readily accepted the bribes, declared that they would serve both Ivan the Terrible and the khan, swore loyalty to the tsar and promised to work well for 'the salary'. However, they sold only information that was far from being top secret and their services, at best, amounted to 'influencing' the khan and other aristocrats to reduce their military zeal against Russia. Searches for a candidate for the role of a puppet khan who could challenge Devlet-Gerei proved fruitless. None of the more or less significant Tatars took the Russian side.

In the early 1560s, however, Ivan the Terrible's policy towards the khanate of the Crimea took a sharp change of course.

4
From Offence to Defence

The Military Policy of Ivan the Terrible Against the Muslims in the 1560s and 1570s

HOW THE KHAN OF THE CRIMEA TURNED FROM AN ENEMY
INTO RUSSIA'S BEST FRIEND: THE DIPLOMACY OF
IVAN THE TERRIBLE UP TO 1569

The tsar realised that Russia was not strong enough to defeat the Crimea. At the same time, the truce agreed with the Grand Duchy of Lithuania (GDL) was expiring. Ivan the Terrible wanted to kill two birds with one stone. He suggested to King Sigismund that Russia and the GDL should form a military alliance against the Crimea in the name of the unity of Christian nations against Islamic countries. This offered the prospect of achieving military superiority over the Crimea and turning Lithuania, a potential rival, into an ally.

In 1554, just after the establishment of the Russian protectorate over Astrakhan, an envoy, Fyodor Voksherin, was sent to Vilna to conduct preliminary talks on the possibility of Russia and Lithuania making a league to 'free Christianity from the hands of the Muslims'. Sigismund congratulated Ivan the Terrible and wished him success in his struggle against Islam. In 1555 Lithuanian diplomats, who negotiated the prolongation of the truce agreement, supported the idea of unity of the Orthodox Church, again in the name of saving Christianity from the 'hands of the Muslims'.

However, the talks brought no constructive results. A little earlier, on 30 January 1554, Polish ambassador Skumin Tishkevich had set out for the Crimea. He assured the Tatars that soon the king would send the khan large sums of money and presents and he asked for peace. Sigismund chose to pay the Crimeans and talk to the Moscow diplomats about an anti-Muslim league, while extraditing to the Tatars the Dnieper Cossacks who devastated their *ulusy*.

Meanwhile, Devlet-Girei tried to instigate dissent between Moscow and Vilna and to receive money from both. In 1557, the khan openly offered to make a military alliance with Sigismund against Moscow. As the Tatars would be fighting with Sigismund's enemy, Devlet-Girei asked the king for money. Sigismund excused himself, saying that he had a truce agreement with Moscow. He said that the military success of the Crimea pleased him and he would have fought against the Russians himself except that the truce agreement had been prolonged and he had to keep his word.

The situation changed a little after 1557. In the winter of 1557/8, the territories of the GDL suffered from a devastating raid by the Crimean Tatars. In February or March 1558, Russian ambassadors Roman Alferyev and Ivan Tyutev delivered a proposal for a league against the Tatars and a number of Lithuanian magnates (Konstantin Ostrozhsky among them) were ready for a serious discussion. On the whole, Vilna was in favour of the Russian proposal but the aristocrats were suspicious of Ivan the Terrible. They feared he might take advantage of the war with the Crimea to attack Lithuania. The general feeling was that both the king and the tsar had a common interest in the war against the khan and that together they should be able to drive him from the Crimea; but, on the other hand, the Turkish sultan might come to the khan's defence and avenge him. Moreover, the Russian tsar was guileful and not to be trusted.

The prospect of an anti-Muslim Russian–Lithuanian league was discussed in June and July 1558 with ambassador Jan Volchek. However, he had brought from King Sigismund nothing but noncommittal answers and a diffuse exposition on the oppression of Christians by Muslims, about the collapse of the Byzantine Empire because of dissent among the Christians and about the necessity of unity before the Muslim threat.

Russian diplomatic efforts failed. It remains unknown how serious was the desire to make a military alliance with Lithuania, or to what extent it was a stratagem to prolong the truce agreement once again. This military alliance would have disrupted the balance of power between the three states. Lithuania realised it, feared the excessive increase of Russian power and preferred to keep the Crimea as a counterbalance to the ambition of Ivan the Terrible.[1]

In 1562, Sigismund complained to the khan of the Crimea that Moscow wanted to conquer the territory of Livonia, occupied by Poland–Lithuania since the previous year. In May 1561, Lithuanian ambassador Yury Bykovsky arrived in Bakhchisarai and informed Devlet-Girei that King Sigismund called for help and asked him to attack Russia. The king officially endorsed the punitive measures by the Tatars against the Dnieper Cossacks who attacked the Crimea. On 22 September 1562, Sigismund issued orders prohibiting his troops on the southern border and the Lithuanian Cossacks from attacking the Tatars of Belgorod and the Perekop because they were now the king's allies.

In this new situation, Moscow rejected the idea of a league of Christian states against Islam (especially because by 1561 the war with Lithuania was in full swing). Ivan the Terrible decided to turn the khan of the Crimea into his ally, sacrificing the GDL to him. In March 1563, Moscow began preparations to send ambassador Athanasius Nagoy to the Crimea with a proposal for a military and political alliance between Russia and the khanate of the Crimea against Lithuania.

It is evident from the instructions to Nagoy that Moscow did not actually consider the prospect of making an alliance with the khan. Perhaps the main intention was to achieve peace on the southern border and frighten Sigismund. If Devlet-Girei made a few looting raids on the southern lands of the GDL, the king's imagination would do the rest and he would realise what might happen to Poland and Lithuania when Moscow and the Crimea acted together. The king would become more amenable and it would be easier to obtain favourable peace terms and bring the Livonian War to a victorious conclusion.

The tsar in his message to the khan acknowledged that his southern policy of the 1550s had been an error, and its initiators, Ivan Sheremetyev (the hero of the battle of Sudbishchi), Alexey Adashev and Ivan Viskovaty (heads of the Russian foreign office), were proclaimed traitors who attempted to sow discord between the tsar and the khan. Moreover, in order to please the khan, the tsar made an unprecedented decision. In 1562 he ordered the demolition of Pselsky Town. The strategic position of this town had hitherto practically paralysed any military activity by the Crimeans. This decision of the Russian tsar utterly amazed the khan's headquarters, so Russian ambassador Athanasius Nagoy had to explain that the town's location was unfavourable for agriculture and 'our sovereign does not need new towns. By the mercies of God, he has plenty of old ones'.[2]

Nagoy's instructions gave the impression that Moscow realised the perversity of a league with the Tatars against Lithuania, a Christian state. Although this league was important to Ivan the Terrible, the constructive proposals about joint operations against Sigismund were lost among trifling conditions. Nagoy therefore had to make sure that the khan was the first to confirm the text of the treaty by oath and was the first to send a major delegation. In other words, the peace initiative should appear to come from the Crimea whereas the Russian tsar only agreed to the request of 'his cousin'. Nagoy had to make sure that golden seals (symbolising the equality of contracting parties) were attached to the documents; in no circumstances could the seals be red, red *nishan* being an overlord's symbol. Nagoy also discussed a special tribute to the Crimea, so-called *pominki*. Nagoy bickered about minor conditions, gave generous promises and miserly gifts. He was haughty and aggressive; he would not sit at the same table with ambassadors of other countries, refused to pay taxes and was excessively frugal.

As a result – as happened all too often with Russian diplomatic missions – form had superiority over content and immediate gain overshadowed long-term profits. Moscow wasted time, let Devlet-Girei become increasingly suspicious and waver, and lost the diplomatic game to the Lithuanians who were also courting Crimea's friendship. Nagoy is hardly to blame for this failure, as he had followed strict instructions from Moscow. History does not deal with things that might have happened, yet if the Russian tsar had acted differently it would have been possible to make an alliance with the khan. The effectiveness of such an alliance had been proved by the events of the late fifteenth century when the Crimea and Moscow destroyed the Great Horde, the former superpower of eastern Europe! Ivan IV in his messages to Devlet-Girei constantly stressed that a new epoch was beginning in the relations between Russia and the Crimea and that he wanted to be good friends with the khan, as his grandfather Ivan III had been with Mengli-Girei.

On 25 June 1563, Devlet-Girei gave audience to Athanasius Nagoy and discussed the peace agreement and the alliance against Lithuania. The khan received the Muscovite proposals with suspicion. He feared that the Russians, though they were now fighting the Lithuanians, might the next day make peace and join against the Tatars, so he deemed it advisable not to commit himself. Nagoy reported back that in Bakhchisarai they suspected Ivan IV of deception. During the talks the khan made it clear that the fate of any peace agreement depended on cash payments from Moscow. Talks of alliance would be possible only once Russia had paid at least as much as Lithuania. The Crimean diplomats made Nagoy understand that 'the Tatar likes those who give more money and gifts. The Tatar is friends with those who pay more'.[3]

Nagoy found himself in a difficult situation. At the beginning, he had proudly declared that 'our sovereign does not buy friends'. Now the ambassador realised the futility of this position and tried to convince the khan that the tsar would pay once a major delegation had been sent to Moscow. The immediate effect of this promise was seen on 23 July when thirty-six wagons of Lithuanian money arrived in the Crimea. The khan had taken advantage of the situation and demanded double pay from Lithuania, threatening to make an alliance with Ivan IV if it was not forthcoming.

In September 1563, Moscow received an official document from Devlet-Girei that clearly demonstrated the position of the Crimea. The khan listed the gifts that should be given to Tatar aristocrats: falcons with falconers, caps of precious fur, fur coats and so on. Devlet-Girei stressed that Sigismund sent gifts regularly so the Russian ruler had yet to prove that he was worthy to be a friend of 'the great ruler of the Great Horde'.[4] Moreover, ambassador Yan-Magmet brought similar documents from Tatar princes, *murzy* and members of the royal family, each demanding gifts for his contribution in influencing the khan towards peace. Apart from fur hats and coats, the average bribe was between 100 and 230 roubles.

In the autumn of 1563, Lithuanian ambassador Yury Bykovsky arrived in the Crimea. He informed the khan that a truce had been established with Russia until 6 December but proposed to muster troops and attack Russia before 21 November. Bykovsky argued that the Russian army was at Polotsk and the borders were left unprotected. The Crimeans were to attack the regions of Smolensk and Novgorod-Seversky.

However, Russian diplomats in the Crimea were more ingenious and on 14 November 1563 the khan promised to make an agreement with Russia and together launch a campaign against Sigismund, adding that Murat, a *murza*, was about to lead a delegation to Moscow. Yet within a week these promising negotiations had failed. Crimean noblemen bombarded the khan and the diplomats with demands that the Russians pay more for the agreement. Devlet-Girei even quarrelled with his son whose demands he thought to be excessive.

On 23 December 1563, the khan abandoned all his promises, including those about the anti-Lithuanian alliance, and rejected the terms of Ivan the Terrible. He insisted the tsar should be the first one to confirm the text of the treaty by his oath; only then might the khan consider the prospect of peaceful relations with Moscow. To witness Ivan IV taking his oath, Ashibash Faruh was sent to Moscow.

On 2 January 1564, the khan confirmed by oath the text of the Russian–Crimean treaty, in its 'Crimean' version. This version contained the article about joint military action against Lithuania but also stipulated that Russia should pay great sums of money and send rich presents. After the tsar had taken his oath, the same document was to return to the Crimea where the Tatar aristocrats would take their oaths, after which the treaty would be ratified.

On 26 February, Moscow received Ashibash Frukh. After a consultation with boyars, the tsar decided to take his oath on the Crimean version of the treaty and did it on 9 March in the presence of the Crimean ambassador. However, another Russian envoy, Grigory Zlobin, was to deliver to the Crimea the old version of the treaty, the same as Nagoy already had, and make the *murzy* take their oaths on this version. Thus, Ivan's oath was only a trick. The Russian tsar was adamant in his intention to make the agreement on Russian terms.

Talks in the Crimea failed. On 25 July it became known that the sultan had ordered the khan of the Crimea to prepare for the campaign against Astrakhan. On 28 June, Nagoy was informed about a serious disagreement between the khan and the Crimean noblemen about the size of the Russian payment. Princes and *murzy* insisted that the main condition of the peace agreement with Russia should be a 'great sum of money'.⁵ On 4 August the Tatars declared that they were in two minds because King Sigismund had launched a campaign against Russia and promised to pay good money if the Crimea joined him. On 5 August, Nagoy flatly refused to pay excessive sums. Russia was willing to pay, but much less. As early as 6 August the khan launched a punitive expedition against Russia.

On 31 September 1564, Tatar troops turned up near Ryasan and it was rumoured that Devlet-Girei himself was at their head. *Voevode* Alexey Basmanov was in charge of the defence of Ryasan and the city withstood the siege. During the siege, the Tatars handed Basmanov a letter for Ivan IV stating that the condition for peace was an annual payment of enormous sums of money. An alliance against Lithuania was not even mentioned. Devlet-Girei had made his choice.

In autumn 1566, the idea of an alliance between Russia and the khanate of the Crimea was suddenly revived. The Tatars made a large-scale raid against the Grand Duchy of Lithuania. Fifteen towns in the Dnieper region were pillaged. Devlet-Girei joyously informed Ivan the Terrible that this campaign should unite Russia and the Crimea against their common enemies, the GDL and Poland. The khan invited Russian ambassadors, wanted to be friends, to make an alliance and wanted Russian money too.

Moscow's reaction to the Tatar ambassador Yelyushka, which arrived on 15 January 1567, was rather cold. The ambassador was presented with a list of complaints: Devlet-Girei acted against 'righteousness', unlawfully detained ambassadors, attacked Russian borders and in every other way demonstrated his evil intents. Yet the tsar agreed that peace should be made and proposed to exchange ambassadors once more.

Why should it be then that Ivan IV, in February 1567, virtually rejected Devlet-Girei's proposal of a league against Lithuania? Was it political foresight – an understanding that the Tatars were not to be trusted? Or did Russian diplomacy once again fall pray to its own standard formulas and prove unable to react to an unusual offer from the khan of the Crimea? The response of Ivan IV was based wholly on emotion instead of the political situation. In his letter, the tsar complained that Devlet-Girei had spoiled 'the good work' begun in 1563, because of 'a quarrel of evil men' and 'righteousness' had been violated, which was already irrelevant in 1567. The tsar called the campaign against Lithuania 'a good thing' but then returned to reiterating the same conditions, already rejected by Bakhchisarai, and demanded that the khan should ratify the Russian version of the treaty brought to him by Nagoy way back in 1563. Only after this might the tsar, perhaps, send money and presents.[6]

Ivan IV did not suggest anything new and did not take advantage of the situation to defeat Lithuania. In April 1567, Nagoy found out that a pro-Lithuanian party was urging the khan to begin a war with Russia and spreading false rumours in the Crimea about the illness and death of Ivan IV. Turkey came to the defence of Lithuania. In March, Sigismund sent an official complaint to the sultan about the actions of Devlet-Girei. As a result, relations between Russia and the Crimea deteriorated again, and relations between Lithuania and the Crimea improved. The competition for the Crimea's support was not over yet.

On 29 November, the tsar and boyars discussed the Crimean question. It was decided that the diplomatic actions in dealing with the Crimea had been successful and the tsar rewarded the diplomats, Athanasius Nagoy, Fyodor Pisemsky and Luka Novoseltsev. The main thing that the tsar and the boyars realised was that the khan was afraid of Russia, did not want to break diplomatic relations even if Russia did meet his demands and did not dare to launch large-scale military operations against Russia. At this discussion, Athanasius Nagoy was quoted, with great pleasure, reporting that the Crimean Tatars said that princes and *murzy* should not be overjoyed as Russians had sent fur coats to Kazan too. So it was concluded that the Crimea treated Russia as a powerful, rapidly expanding state. The tsar had conquered Kazan and Astrakhan and now threatened to capture Kiev, after which he would build new fortresses on the Dnieper and that would mean the beginning of extremely hard times for the Muslims.

To what extent did this position correspond with reality? Indeed, Russian diplomatic tactics were rather successful. Russia managed to sow discord between the khan and the Lithuanian king, and delayed large payments while giving only insubstantial presents. There were no big raids by the Crimeans on the southern borders in those years, which gave Ivan IV a free hand in Livonia.

However, this success was mainly due to the firm stance that Russia took in 1563, when the diplomatic mission with Athanasius Nagoy was sent. In those four years practically nothing changed in the Crimean policy of Moscow; the same adherence to rigid ritual, the same stubborn determination to achieve peace on the terms of 1563 and refusal to respond to concessions. Indicative is the fact that instructions for diplomats in the Crimea remained essentially unaltered from 1563 to 1567, regardless of the change in political situation in eastern Europe. And the change was not small.

Russia did not achieve its strategic aim of making the Crimea permanently hostile to Lithuania. It is doubtful whether this was achievable; the money

Sigismund paid did not save him from Tatar raids but there was no way to make Devlet-Girei an ally but paying money. However, Russia twice missed its opportunity, in 1564 and 1567, to make at least a temporary alliance against Lithuania and weaken the king. Moreover, Russia, in assessing the political situation, did not consider Turkey and the increasing influence of the sultan on the foreign policy of Devlet-Girei. Sigismund had more foresight and in 1568 signed a peace treaty with Sultan Selim. Soon the Sultan sent a document to Devlet-Girei instructing him to make peace with the Grand Duchy of Lithuania. This lowered the tension on the southern borders of Lithuania and Poland and gave these two states a free hand to act against Russia. Russia also failed to heed the protests of the Crimea and Turkey against its advance on the Terek river.

All spring and summer in Bakhchisarai prospects of the joint Turkish–Crimean campaign against Astrakhan were discussed. On 20 July 1568, ships full of troops started to arrive in Kapha. Between the end of December 1568 and January 1569, there were talks in Moscow with the Crimean delegate Devlet-Kildei. The Tatars informed Russia about the imminent attack on Astrakhan and said that the khan had to obey the sultan and take part in the campaign. There would be no friendship during the war between Ivan IV and Devlet-Girei.

The Crimea had its selfish aims in sending this delegation; it was not a friendly warning but an attempt to threaten invasion and make demands for territorial concessions. However, the prospect of Turkish invasion did not impress Ivan IV. It was decided to send to the Crimea a minor nobleman, Ivan Chebukov, in order to maintain diplomatic relations. He was to give no presents but to deliver a letter to the khan saying in direct terms that Devlet-Girei 'has wicked things in mind' and informed Russia not out of good will, nor even the desire to extort money, but because he wanted Astrakhan for himself before it was conquered by the Turks.

THE FIRST WAR BETWEEN RUSSIA AND TURKEY: 1569
Until the 1560s Russia and Turkey were at peace with each other. Ivan the Terrible gave strict orders to *voevodes* to release Turks captured by accident during the clashes with the Crimea. The Sublime Porte in its turn ignored the calls of the Crimean, Kazan and Astrakhan khanates to attack Russia and protect Muslims from the tsar. The tsar, during talks with western countries about the prospect of Russia joining an anti-Muslim alliance, refused to promise that the Russian army would fight Turkey, as desired by the Europeans. Russia considered the Crimea to be its main Muslim threat, not Turkey.

The situation changed in 1567 when Turkey decided to advance on northern Caucasia, the Volga region and the territory by the Sea of Azov. Here the interests of Turkey and Russia inevitably clashed. Talks gave no results, as Turkish diplomats were even more haughty and stubborn than their Russian counterparts. The Turks could accept only one solution: Russia must surrender Astrakhan and give up northern Caucasia, leaving all those peoples that had sworn allegiance to Ivan the Terrible to their fate. Only then might the Turks change their mind and not invade. Needless to say, these conditions were unacceptable to Moscow and the prospect of war did not frighten Ivan the Terrible.

The Turks had been preparing the Astrakhan campaign for several years, transporting troops and artillery to the Crimea. In the spring of 1569, 17,000 troops and 100 cannon were based in Kapha. The infantry of the janissary corps constituted the main part of the Turkish army, and the sultan expected his vassal, the khan of the Crimea, to provide cavalry. In the summer of 1569, the Turko–Crimean army left the peninsula and headed towards Russia. Its objective was Astrakhan.

On 15 August, the Turks rowed up the Don in large galleys to Perevoloka. Here the Turks were joined by 40,000 Crimean Tatars and large numbers of Nogays who were quick to change their allegiance as soon as 'new masters' appeared in the region.

For two weeks the Turks tried to carry their cannon-bearing galleys overland along the portage. If they had succeeded, the Turkish fleet would have gone down the Volga and entered the Caspian Sea. The Russians would not have been able to stop the big Turkish galleys there. However, the ships and their guns had to return to Azov. Unrest among the janissaries began as they were discouraged by the vast almost-uninhabited country with big rivers, where an army has to cover long distances before it could even meet the enemy. As a result, 5,000 troops who refused to fight were also sent back to Azov. The Russians had not fired a single shot and the number of Turkish troops had been reduced by one third, which resulted in failure of the Turkish expedition.

The Russians followed the Turkish troops but did not attack them. By the portage a small fleet under the command of Prince Peter Serebryany was on guard. When Serebryany knew about the approach of the huge Turko–Tatar army, he moved upstream to Kazan. Astrakhan was left to the mercy of fate and had to rely on the heroism and military skill of its garrison.

On 16 September, the Turks approached Astrakhan. The Turkish commanders were at a loss after their engineers reported that conventional means were useless because the water table in the delta was very high, making the digging of mines and trenches impossible. The commanders made a strange decision to occupy the old Tatar fort not far from Astrakhan and spend the winter there.

The half-hearted actions by the Turks emboldened the Russians. The small fleet under Serebryany moved to Astrakhan. The Russian garrison even took the guns from the city walls and bombarded the Turkish camp. The damage was insignificant as the distance was too great but the event lowered morale among the Turkish troops.

The janissaries refused to spend winter near Astrakhan. They did not understand the plans of their commanders who tried to explain to them that they were preparing for a siege of many month and aiming to take the city by starvation. It sounded like mockery as the Turkish troops were dying of infectious disease and there were big problems with supplies. The janissaries demanded that they should be returned home.

In their haste to get back home, the Turks decided not to return to the portage and marched to Azov by the shortest route, across the vast arid plains of northern Caucasia. Almost the whole army died of thirst and starvation during this march and only a pathetic remainder of the Turkish army reached Azov.

Thus, in the first Turko–Russian War of 1569 Russia won a decisive victory without even engaging in significant military action and it was to be more than 100 years before the Turks dared another invasion, the so-called Chigirin campaigns of 1676–81.

A TRAITOR AND A WAR HERO: THE TRAGEDY AND GRANDEUR OF THE MOSCOW BATTLES IN 1571–1572

The year 1571 was a dark one for Russian history. The country was on the verge of collapse. It seemed that the moment would come soon when Russia would be thrown back several centuries into the past and the hard times of the Tatar yoke would be restored. Brooding darkness hung over Muscovy. But suddenly, like a bent tree, Russia sprang back up and not only dispelled that gloom but managed to solve the 'Tatar problem' for at least the next thirty years.

Heroes and scoundrels hold sway of destinies in such troubled times. Here we meet two figures: one a traitor who contributed to the ruining of Moscow and other Russian cities in 1571, the other a hero who saved Moscow in 1572. Paradoxically, Ivan the Terrible ordered the execution of the latter and intended to grant mercy to the former.

The defeat of the Turkish and Tatar forces near Astrakhan in 1569 prompted the Crimea to seek peace with Russia. On 15 January 1570, Devlet-Girei summoned Athanasius Nagoy to his court and offered to renew negotiations concerning peace and friendship between the two countries. But on 16 March, while the negotiations were still in process, a new Lithuanian ambassador arrived in Bakhchisarai with a new suggestion from the Lithuanian king. The latter proposed a considerable sum of money in exchange for the khan's guarantees not to attack the Grand Duchy of Lithuania and to begin a war with Russia instead. The khan started bargaining again, hoping that Russia was ready to pay more for its safety than Lithuania. This was a new round of the so-called 'Crimean auction', where both Lithuania and Russia tried to win the khan's favour.

Russia did not undertake any resolute actions. On 8 December 1570, a Tatar messenger, Bor Cherkashenin, was received in Moscow. He delivered a letter from Devlet-Girei in which the khan accused Ivan the Terrible of breaking the peace talks. The Crimean ruler proposed an exchange of detained ambassadors. The Russians should promise to release a Tatar diplomat, Yan-Bolduy, while the Tatars promised to free the Russian ambassadors, Athanasius Nagoy and Fyodor Pisemsky. Cherkashenin said: 'A sovereign treats his ambassadors as fitted arrows and now we feel as if we have lost our arrow.' The khan threatened a new war: 'Unless we can be on good terms with you I shall try to take revenge on you for our shame and then you will have only God to blame for what will happen to you.'[7]

The threats did not impress Russian diplomats. On 1 January 1571, Bor Cherkashenin had to leave Moscow. The negotiations had achieved nothing. Perhaps the serenity of the Russian government was due to certain measures undertaken not long before, which included organising a 'watch service' on Russia's southern border. In January and February, a council of 'experts' on guarding the southern boundaries took place in Moscow. These 'experts' normally did their military service in the *Pole* (wilderness or steppe, that is, in the field). Prince Mikhail Vorotynsky headed the council. A whole system of 'watch service' was worked out. The plan was quite an elaborate one and included all the details such as the location of watch-towers and patrol routes.

Previously the southern defence line had run along the Oka river. That's why it was called 'Oka border' (*oksky rubez*) or 'river-bank' (*bereg*). Every spring (by 1 March) and autumn (by 1 September) the lists of *voevodes* serving 'on the bank against the Crimeans' were drawn up. There were five units placed along the Oka in the towns of Aleksin, Serpukhov, Kaluga, Kolomna and Kashira. On receiving news of Tatar attacks the regiments set out from their positions towards the enemy. The supplementary forces, sometimes led by the tsar and his personal regiment, were mobilised from Moscow.

Under Ivan the Terrible, Russia began building strongholds at key positions, thus moving its border southward. Michailov was founded in 1551, Shatsk in 1553, Dedilov in 1554, Bolkhov in 1555, Orel and Yepifan' in 1566 and Dankov in 1568. This meant bringing the frontier fortresses further southwards, beyond the *oksky rubez*. This step proved to be successful: the Tatars could not burn these towns down and were delayed on their way to the Oka river.

Prince Mikhail Vorotynsky devised the whole way to protect the Russian state from the raids of the nomads. According to the plan, four fortresses (*storozi*) were built where an attack was most probable. Each stronghold had a permanent garrison commanded by an officer called a *stoyalaya golova*. Every garrison was responsible for a certain territory and regularly sent scouts to search the area. In fact, these strongholds were the first Russian frontier posts. In spring 1571, Prince Mikhail Tyufyakin and Matvey Rzevsky, installed crosses with their names and the date of erection carved upon them on the banks of the upper Mius and Orel rivers. Those were the first Russian boundary signposts. Thus, Russia actually marked its southern boundaries officially. However, the signposts were placed too far in the *Pole*, 300–400 km away from the nearest Russian fortification lines. That was a clear claim on the disputed territories, which drove the khan to fury.[8]

In the spring of 1571, the Crimean khan Devlet-Girei advanced on Russia with his army of 40,000. The army consisted of Crimean Tatars, Tatars of the Great Nogay Horde and the Small Nogay Horde as well as small detachments from northern Caucasia. The army was ordered to pillage territory around the town of Kozelsk, which was meant to frighten the Russian tsar and make him more pliable and generous at the 'Crimean auction'.

Russian troops headed by Prince Ivan Belsky took up positions on the bank of the Oka river and blocked the khan's way. Russia at that time had an army of about 20,000, but in the autumn of 1570 half of that number had been sent to besiege Revel in Livonia. It is not known whether those troops had time to return to Moscow. (Ivan the Terrible stated later that the Oka river was defended by only 6,000 men). The Russian troops on the Oka river were soon joined by three small regiments headed by *oprichniki*, Vladimir Yakovlev, Mikhail Cherkassky and Fedor Trubetskoy.

It was rumoured that Mikhail Cherkassky's father, Temryuk Cherkassky, headed one of the khan's Caucasian detachments. Cherkassky's family originated from Kabarda, a region in northern Caucasia, and Mikhail had moved to Russia only in 1560 when the tsar married his sister Maria Cherkasskaya (Ivan' s second wife). On hearing the rumour about his father, the tsar fell into a fit of rage and ordered the execution of the innocent Mikhail

Cherkassky. The Russian army then became dispirited by the execution of one of its commanders.

Devlet-Girei did not dare attempt to break the Russian defence. His plan was to go through the area around Bolhov town to the densely populated Kozelsk region and ravage these lands. The fortresses of the area did not have strong military forces to defend them. Small town garrisons could not withstand an army of thousands of warriors. But on his way in that direction, on the Zlynsky Field, Devlet-Girei was approached by a Russian nobleman Kudeyar Tishinkov, who promised to lead the Tatars to Moscow by a route that outflanked the Russian army. Seeing the khan's hesitations, Tishinkov grabbed his horse's bridle and exclaimed: 'If you don't take Moscow, impale me before its walls!' There was a serious argument but Devlet-Girei believed the traitor and made for Moscow.

So the Tatars took the Russian troops in the rear. They passed Kozelsk region and (by the Svinaya road) skirted around Serpukhov, where the Russian troops awaited them. Tishinkov showed the way. When Devlet-Girei started advancing upon the Russian rear, Ivan the Terrible left the army and fled to Rostov the Great with his *oprichniki*. The Tatars divided their forces, the main part moving towards Moscow through Kaluga while the rest attacked the Russian positions near Serpukhov and beat *oprichnik* Jakov Volynsky's regiment.

The capital stood unprotected. Prince Ivan Belsky was forced to hurry back to Moscow but arrived there only one day before the enemy, on 23 May. Perhaps because of his haste, Belsky did misread the situation and made a fatal mistake. Instead of taking up positions outside Moscow, Belsky led the troops into the city where they would be under protection of the fortifications. But the Crimeans decided not to bother about taking the city by assault and street fighting. Devlet-Girei camped near Kolomensky village and gave an order to raze the neighbouring villages and monasteries. On 24 May the Tatars set Moscow on fire.

At the outbreak of the fire all the churches started ringing their bells. During three hours of a horrible conflagration Moscow was burnt to ashes. The most serious destruction was caused by the explosions of a powder magazine in the Kremlin and Kitay-Gorod area. A considerable part of the Kremlin wall next to Frolovsky Gate (near the modern Spasskaya Tower, by Red Square) was demolished by the explosion. Streets were jammed with wild crowds of people rushing about in confused attempts to save their lives. People clambered on each other's shoulders and heads trying to escape. Those who managed to get on top trampled to death those who were on the bottom. Trying to make their way in this horrible throng, people were stabbing each other with knives, killing their neighbours in their panic. As the fire spread, human yelling grad-ually ceased as did the bell ringing as church bells cracked from the heat.

As many as 120,000 people died in the fire, including virtually all the Russian army (only 300 men survived) and its commander, Prince Ivan Belsky. He arrived home to learn his family's fate, went down to the cellar where they were hiding and never came out, having been suffocated by the smoke.

It took two months to clear Moscow of debris after the fire. There was a lesson to learn. The tsar banned the building of houses outside the fortress walls to prevent the enemy from burning the city. The walls of Moscow were covered with turf and now looked yellowish-green and shaggy. Grass and turf were expected to stop fire from spreading. The best merchants and craftsmen were forcibly moved to Moscow from other cities to repopulate the capital. More than one hundred families were driven from Novgorod the Great alone. This measure affected at provincial trading centres. The economy of the capital was reconstructed quickly at the expense of regional economies. Furthermore, upon his homeward journey Devlet-Girei plundered his way through the lands of Kashira and Ryasan, devastating thirty-six towns and capturing more than sixty thousand people. Russia had not known devastation on this scale since the years of the Tatar yoke. Ten days after the tragedy the courtiers were afraid to tell Ivan the Terrible about it.

The effect of the sudden defeat was enormous and news about the fall of Muscovy's capital spread across Europe with lightning speed. The news was discussed even in faraway England, not to mention Russia's nearest neighbours, Germany, Poland and Lithuania. It is interesting to examine the estimation of the Tatar victory of 1571 in oriental sources. A Turkish historian, Pechevily, called it 'the most important' Crimean victory over Russia. Crimeans themselves reported that Devlet-Girei had been honoured with the nickname 'He who has taken the capital'. Seyid-Muhammed-Riza said that from 1571 Ivan IV was obliged to pay an annual general tribute (tish).[9]

In June 1571 Crimean ambassador Devlet-Kildei visited Moscow. Negotiations took place between 13 and 17 June. The ambassador raised a categorical claim for the immediate transfer of Kazan and Astrakhan to the Crimean dominion. In the ambassador's speeches the khan was portrayed as a peacemaker trying hard not to let angry Turks invade Russia. The khan presented Ivan with a knife decorated with gold. The tsar did not accept the gift but the hint was absolutely clear.[10]

Devlet-Girei understood that he had won, above all, a moral victory over his antagonist. He had showed what a real monarch should have been. In his letter the khan shamed Ivan IV and reproached him for his panicked flight and shameful abandonment of his capital to God's mercy. Devlet-Girei named himself 'a Moscow sovereign' but in the Russian tsar he only saw 'shame and low-noble birth' as the sovereign should stand protecting his boundaries and not hide in remote monasteries. 'And your people's sins are on your neck', Devlet-Girei pronounced, having beaten his opponent completely. Considering that wartime catastrophes of such a kind were regarded in the Christian world as undoubted proof of divine retribution, the psychological effect of the khan's letter upon the tsar should not be underestimated. The defeat was evidence of divine disgrace.

The tsar put on a theatrical performance. According to the report of the Piskaryevsky chronicle, he received the ambassador dressed in a rough sheepskin coat crying: 'Look what the khan has done to me! I am a beggar now; I have nothing to give him!' As a sign of good will, demonstrating readiness to make concessions, Ivan ordered the destruction of the town of Sunzensky, Russia's stronghold in northern Caucasia. Russia left northern Caucasia for 250 years. On 17 June 1571, during negotiations for the Bratoshino settlement, Ivan IV agreed to transfer Astrakhan to the Crimea but only on condition that a peace treaty was signed between Russia and the Crimea.

Easy victory turned Devlet-Girei's head. He remembered the strength of the Golden Horde khans and decided he was powerful enough to demand absolute submission from Russia. He even distributed Russian towns (some of which had not been won yet) between his nobles. In 1572 Devlet-Girei undertook a new invasion. This time his aim was to gain complete control of Russia.

At that time Kudeyar Tishinkov was living in the Crimea. He was happily married and was fully content with his life. Nevertheless, after a while, Tishinkov fell out with the khan and decided to return to Russia. He wrote a letter to Ivan the Terrible pleading for forgiveness. The tsar promised forgiveness because he needed a 'repenting sinner' to demonstrate the effectiveness of his policy of terror. We don't know anything further about the fate of Tishinkov.[11]

When news of the new offensive reached him, Ivan the Terrible took to his heels again. This time he found shelter in Novgorod the Great, very far from Moscow. He tried to justify his actions by saying that he had information that Sweden was about to invade Novgorod. There was a certain advantage in Ivan's flight; at least he did not hinder his commanders in defending the capital.

Prince Mikhail Vorotynsky took command of the Russian army. There is a legend that Vorotynsky, on the eve of the decisive battle, vowed to die within one year of it, if only he was granted a victory the next day. The prince kept his word. He defeated the Tatars in a battle near Molodi on 2 August

1572. Soon after, Vorotynsky was executed as a traitor on Ivan the Terrible's order. Contemporaries reported that the tsar felt insulted when, after the victorious battle, Russian officers glorified Prince Vorotynsky first and only then drank to the tsar's health. To Ivan's mind, that was conclusive evidence of Vorotynsky's treason.

THE BATTLE OF MOLODI 1572

Devlet-Girei decided to build on his success of 1571. He had all the necessary prerequisites for this since the Russians had not rebuilt the fortifications, destroyed by the fire, around their capital. Inspired by the triumph of the Crimeans, rebels in the Kazan lands stirred to activity and began a guerrilla war. The Nogay Horde, loyal to Russia not long before, sided with the Crimea. Some peoples of northern Caucasia, the Adyghes among them, also supported the khan. Devlet-Girei advanced against Russia with a large Crimean Tatar army (estimates range from 40,000 to 60,000). In addition there were thousands of Nogays of the Great and Small Nogay Hordes, the Circassians, the Adyghes and Turks (the last servicing the artillery).

Devlet-Girei had a minimum and maximum plan. The minimum was the conquest of Kazan, Astrakhan and Volga region, while the main objective was to establish control over the trade route along the Volga river. The khan was so sure of his success that scores of Tatar merchants followed his supply train with licenses to do business in the Volga region that was soon to belong to the Crimea. Almost all of these merchants would find themselves in Russian captivity instead of markets. The maximum plan envisaged the conquest of Moscow and making the Russian state dependant on the Crimea, as the Russian lands had been dependent on the Golden Horde.

The catastrophe of 1571 had taught Russian commanders a good lesson. In autumn 1571, Moscow had issued orders to burn hundreds of kilometres of the steppe between the towns of Novosil, Dankov, Orel and Putivl, along the main routes of Tatar invasions. Now the enemy's advance was complicated because many thousands of horses (80,000–120,000, not including horses of the supply train and those of allies such as the Adyghes and other peoples from northern Caucasia) were without food.

Along the Oka river, between the fortresses of Kolomna, Serpukhov and Kaluga two lines of stockade, 1–1.2 m high, were built. Behind the stockade trenches were dug for *streltsy*. Moreover, men with arquebuses and artillery were positioned near fords and places where the Tatar army could cross the river. Thus, the main line of defence was constructed along the Oka river with emphasis on firearms and artillery near fords. This was the first time that Russia confidently relied on its technical superiority in a field battle.

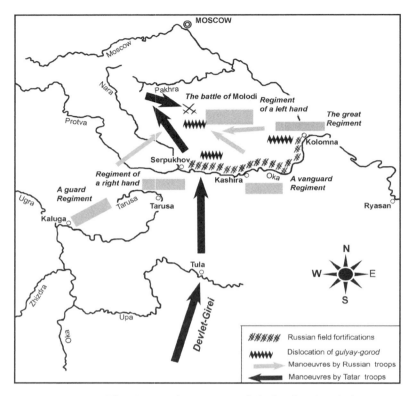

Map 11. The Tatar raids in 1572 and the battle of Molodi

However, the Russian army was considerably smaller than the Tatar one. The Russian supreme commander, Prince Mikhail Vorotynsky, commanded 12,000 noble cavalry, 2,035 *streltsy* and 3,800 Cossacks. The number of armed peasants brought by nobles is unknown. Altogether the Russian army hardly amounted to more than 30,000 or 40,000. Moreover the Tatars were ready for a concentrated strike, whereas the Russian army was stretched along the line of defence.

Vorotynsky, with 8,255 troops and the most of the artillery, positioned himself in Kolomna. Here a *gulyay-gorod* ('walking town', a mobile fortification) several kilometres long was made of wooden screens, 2–3 m high, mounted on wheels. Vorotynsky relied on this *gulyay-gorod* if the Tatars crossed the Oka. Nikita Odoyevsky commanded the right flank (3,590 men) and was positioned in the town of Tarusa. The left flank, led by *voevode* Prince Andrey Repnin (1,650 men), was positioned on the Lopasna river. The vanguard (*storozhevoy*) of 2,063 men, led by its *voevode* Prince Ivan Shuysky, garrisoned the town of Kashira. Thus, the main forces blocked the path of the

Tatars if they approached from Ryasan and the rest of the troops blocked the approaches from the towns of Tula and Serpukhov. The route Devlet-Girei had taken in 1571 was blocked by the guard regiment (*peredovoy polk*) of some 4,475 warriors, commanded by Prince Dmitry Khvorostinin.[12]

On 23 July 1572, the Tatar army crossed the Russian border. At first Devlet-Girei intended to strike at Tula but then decided not to besiege the town and simply passed it by. On 26 July, the Tatars attempted to cross the Oka river at Senkin Crossing near the town of Serpukhov. Ivan Shuysky's vanguard made a counterattack and pushed the Tatars back from the ford. The Tatars started to move in formation along the bank of the Oka. On the other bank, the Russians moved forward the *gulyay-gorod*. Devlet-Girei commanded his Turkish gunners to bombard the *gulyay-gorod*, but this did not do much damage. The Russians did not return fire, saving their ammunition for the moment the Tatars tried to cross the river again.

The situation changed rapidly on the night of 27/28 July 1572 when a Nogay unit led by Tereberdey-murza defeated 200 Russian noble cavalrymen guarding the Senkin Crossing and captured it. The Nogays crossed the river and sped, unimpeded, deep into Russian territory. At dawn, the Nogays found themselves on the roads near Moscow. Tereberdey-murza was perplexed. His detachment was too small to attack Russian fortresses or big units. Looting was useless as he was deep in Russian territory and it was impossible to return from here encumbered by captives and cattle. His unit had to remain mobile if he wanted to break back through the Russian positions. As a result, his cavalry unit wandered aimlessly near Moscow, playing for time and waiting for the main forces.

The Tatar vanguard commanded by Divei-murza began crossing the river. In the morning, the Tatars were attacked by the Russian guard regiment led by Dmitry Khvorostinin. Of course, 2,390 noble cavalry and 535 *streltsy* could not stop the Tatar army of 60,000. The Russian advanced detachment was crushed in a few minutes and Khvorostinin ordered his troops to retreat. Near the Nara river the Tatars' path was blocked by the left flank detachment led by Prince Nikita Odoyevsky. The detachment fought to the bitter end but could not stop the enemy. As a result, by the afternoon of 28 July the Tatars were on the Serpukhovskaya Road leading to Moscow.

On the same day, at the village of Molodi, cavalry led by Khvorostinin thoroughly defeated the Tatar rear guard which was caught unawares. Khan Devlet-Girei was immensely surprised when he saw his warriors fleeing from Russians past his tent. The Tatar commanders explained to their ruler, carried away by his victorious advance, how dangerous it was to find themselves between two enemy groups. The khan now regretted that he had placed his sons in command of the rearguard, hoping to keep them safe, for it was they who were attacked first and had to flee.

It was the khan's sons who demanded he halt the advance. They argued that the Russians had defeated them here at Molodi but there were even more Russian troops in Moscow. So it was necessary to deal with the troops in their rear (by that time the Russians had concentrated their main forces under the command of Mikhail Vorotynsky near Molodi) and only then go on to Moscow.

The khan hesitated, but the events that followed forced his hand. The khan sent 2,000 Crimean and Nogay cavalry against Vorotynsky's 2,000 horsemen. Khvorostinin retreated, luring the Tatars into the line of fire from the *gulyay-gorod*, which had already moved near Molodi. The guns of the mobile fortress started firing at point-blank range into the Tatar cavalry, inflicting severe losses. Devlet-Girei knew now that his sons had been right and assault on Moscow was out of the question as long as Vorotynsky's troops were at Molodi.

On 29 July it was quiet. The Tatars occupied a position 30 km from Moscow, on the Pakhra river, and were preparing for a decisive battle. Tereberdey-murza, who had been wandering with his horsemen near Moscow, was unfortunate to find them here. Tereberdey-murza was to be killed the next day during an assault on the Russian positions.

On 30 July the Tatars began an assault. The battle plan was simple. The whole army of Devlet-Girei attacked the *gulyay-gorod* while the Russian troops defended and made counterattacks from the flanks. The fight went on all day and the outcome was not comforting to the Tatars. The *gulyay-gorod* had withstood the attack. Thousands of Tatars had died from the fire of hand-guns and cannon. As well as Tereberdey-murza, three princes, commanders of troops from northern Caucasia, were killed. During one of the Russian counterattacks Divei-murza, the commander-in-chief of the Tatar army, was captured. By evening the khan had a great deal to ponder.

Even so, the Russian victory of 30 July could very soon have turned into a defeat. Russian troops that fought in the field had suffered heavy losses. Now they had to take cover in the *gulyay-gorod*. During the battle, the Russians lost their supply train and now in the mobile fortress, crowded by troops, there was a shortage of food. Using their numerical superiority, the Tatars surrounded the fortification and cut it off from the Rozhay river. Thirst was even worse than hunger. Horsemen started to kill their horses, which suffered without water. *Voevode* Vorotynsky began to think that defeat was imminent.

If the Tatars had besieged the *gulyay-gorod* a few more days, that would have been the end of the Russian army. Pure chance saved the situation.

Muscovite *voevode* Yury Tokmakov sent a letter to Vorotynsky informing him that the Danish Prince Magnus, king of Livonia and vassal of Ivan the Terrible, was marching to his rescue with 40,000 troops from Novgorod. It was a lie and there were no reinforcements coming to his relief but Tokmakov wanted to encourage Vorotynsky.

The result was unexpected. Tatar scouts intercepted the messenger with the letter. Devlet-Girei believed that the troops were coming and commanded the *gulyay-gorod* to be taken by assault before Prince Magnus arrived. On 2 August the Tatars launched a massive assault on the Russian defences.

Witnesses to the battle of 2 August mentioned a great number of severed hands lying before the *gulyay-gorod*. The Tatars, advancing in an endless stream, grabbed parts of the walls and tried to topple them down. The Russians hacked their hands off with axes and shot at point-blank with handguns and cannon. There was a risk that the Tatars, when the heaps of dead bodies were high enough, might climb over the walls.

The Tatars could not continue intensive assaults and keep the *gulyay-gorod* surrounded. Their troops had been greatly depleted in the battles of 28 and 30 July, and on 2 August their numbers were severely reduced further. By the evening, taking advantage of the fact that the Tatar troops were concentrated on one side of the fortifications, Prince Vorotynsky secretly, under cover of a shallow depression in the ground, led the cavalry out of the *gulyay-gorod* and into the rear of the Tatars. The defences were left under the command of Prince Khvorostinin who, when Vorotynsky sent him a signal, ordered all the cannon and handguns to fire at the enemy in a concentrated volley and to make a sortie. The main force in this counterattack were German mercenaries. At the same time, Vorotynsky's cavalry attacked the Tatars from behind.

The Tatars could not withstand this double blow, their retreat very soon turned into a stampede. Khan Devlet-Girei was running headlong like an ordinary soldier. Fleeing Tatars were pursued and killed. Among the dead were the son and grandson of Devlet-Girei and scores of *murzy*. The Tatar army of 60,000 was destroyed. The khan remembered his feeling during the flight for the rest of his life and never again launched campaigns against Russia.

After the battle of Molodi there was no confrontation between Russians and Tatars for several decades. Russia gave up its plans of expansion into the Crimea while the khanate of the Crimea in turn desisted from large-scale raids into Russian territory until the 1590s. The Tatars did not demand the return of Kazan or Astrakhan, and if Tatar diplomats did mention it they did not mean it. After the battle of Molodi, relations between Russia and the Crimea experienced a calm and peaceful period that lasted till the end of Ivan the Terrible's reign.

IVAN THE TERRIBLE'S LAST ATTEMPT AT A MILITARY ALLIANCE
BETWEEN THE RUSSIANS AND TATARS

On 13 October 1576, Moscow received Tatar ambassadors who informed him of a great victory of the khan over the Polish–Lithuanian Commonwealth. Ivan the Terrible, with obvious pleasure, listened to a story of the Tatars burning the Dnieper region and of their victorious raid through Lithuania to the Polish border. The khan again proposed to make a political and military alliance against the Polish–Lithuanian Commonwealth, on the same terms as offered in 1563.

Russia agreed to resume talks about the peace treaty and sent Yelizar Rzevsky as messenger. He carried a letter in which Ivan the Terrible approved campaigns against the Grand Duchy of Lithuania, thus virtually siding with the khan, and expressed his readiness for talks. Russia reiterated its indispensable condition that the first step should be taken by the Crimea; the khan should send ambassadors as though asking Ivan the Terrible for peace, while the tsar would only agree to the khan's entreaty.

On 2 February 1577, however, the Boyar Duma decided not to wait for the arrival of the Crimean embassy and started preparations for sending a major Russian delegation to the Crimea with Vladimir Mosalsky and Armenin Shapilov. The Russian diplomats were to wait in the town of Borovsk until they received word that Tatar ambassadors had set out for Moscow. This time the Tatar delegation was expected eagerly. Boyars even suggested sending a large sum of money and gifts to the Crimea. This topic had been taboo not long before.

Even so, this attempt to make an alliance failed, this time due to circumstances beyond Russia's control. Devlet-Girei died. The policy of the new khan was still unknown, but he had made some radical pronouncements about Russia. So, in June 1577, it was decided to send a single messenger, S. Kobelev, with letters and gifts instead of a large delegation. The messenger was to inform the khan that Ivan the Terrible was ready to begin talks about a military alliance. An ambassador, Halil Chelibay, who arrived in Moscow in December 1577, brought the response that Khan Mohammed-Girei suggested that Russia and the Crimea return to negotiating the peace agreement on terms close to those of the early 1560s. But the new king of Poland and Lithuania, Stefan Bathory, did not wait for Russia and the Crimea to realise all the advantages of their alliance against Lithuania. Bathory complained to Turkey, being virtually the latter's protégé. The sultan advised the khan to restrain his ardour and leave the Lithuanian lands alone. The Lithuanian nobility hoped that in June 1578 the Tatars would launch a campaign against Moscow. About that time, a

Polish ambassador returned from the Crimea and much hope was pinned on Stefan Bathory's policy towards Turkey and the Crimea.

Unsurprisingly though, the Crimea openly played a double game. A Tatar ambassador stated that the khan was free to be friends with Moscow. Lithuania treated it as absurd (*absurda et similia powiada*). In the autumn of 1578, Crimean ambassador Kuremsha arrived in Moscow. He described a successful campaign against the Polish–Lithuanian Commonwealth in which the Tatars had captured thirty towns and defeated the king's army in open battle. The khan promised that, if the treaty with Russia was concluded, he would fight more against Poland and Lithuania. Ivan the Terrible had been expecting the ambassadors from Bakhchisarai to come with a draft treaty.

Kuremsha did not bring such a draft. Instead, he handed a letter, rather sharp in tone, from Mohammed-Girei. The khan again demanded the return of Kazan and Astrakhan, reminding Ivan the Terrible about his promise to return the latter, and threatened war between the Crimea and Russia. On 10 September 1578, Russian diplomats handed Kuremsha a letter of reply that contained refusals to all paragraphs except the one about the need to make a peace agreement. The letter firmly stated that if the khan wanted peace he should give up his claims to Kazan and Astrakhan. The tsar named as a top priority the need to reach a peace agreement that could be signed by the major Russian delegation led by Mosalsky and Shapilov. The instructions for the delegation were prepared in September and October 1578.

Moscow needed only the guarantee of non-aggression from the Crimeans. By making a treaty Russia hoped to obtain legal international recognition on a number of important issues. In the text of the agreement Ivan IV is mentioned several times with the title tsar, to which 'of the whole of Russia' was added. The Tatars should promise not to attack towns on the Russian border, but especially those taken from Lithuania a short time before (which had also been mentioned in letters of 1563–4). Thus Moscow hoped to achieve international recognition of the fact that those towns belonged to Ivan the Terrible's Russia. The text contained a noteworthy passage in which Russia assumed an obligation not to attack Tatar lands and also promised that Livonians would not take part in such attacks. If the agreement had been made, the Crimea would have become the second state (the Kingdom of Denmark being the first) that recognised Livonia as part of Russia.

Yet in 1578 agreement was not reached; the negotiating parties did not trust each other and each pursued its own objective. Russia was not disposed to pay money for peace; Russia had not paid in the more troubled years of 1560–70, and after 1572 Ivan the Terrible was quite confident in his dealings with the Tatars. Even if the Crimea demanded money, it realised that, after the battle of Molodi, Russia was not to be bullied by military threat. But military threat was the only argument the Tatar diplomats knew. As a result, the negotiations failed.

CONCLUSIONS

The confrontation between Russia and the Muslim Orient continued beyond the end of Ivan the Terrible's reign. What were the results of his military policy in this direction?

- On the whole his anti-Muslim policy may be considered successful. Russia destroyed two enemy states (the Kazan and Astrakhan khanates) and, in the end, turned out to be the winner in the military confrontation with the Crimea.
- During Ivan's reign, the total balance of victories and defeats in wars against the Tatars was in favour of Russia.
- His reign saw the creation of an effective defence system in the south of Russia that later, in the 1580–90s, after Ivan the Terrible's death, made it possible for Russia to expand into the *Pole*, the steppe no-man's land between Russia and the khanate of the Crimea. In 1585, Ivan's successor repeated and further developed his tactic of moving the boundary southward by creating complexes of strategic fortresses. Eight new strongholds in the *Pole* were designed, the first to be founded being Livni and Voronezh (both in 1586).
- Russian diplomatic policy in the sixteenth century was successful on the whole. Russia did not succeed in making a military and political alliance with the Crimea that might have made it possible for Russia to defeat Europe in the Livonian War. However, Russian diplomats prevented the Crimea, the Grand Duchy of Lithuania and Poland (the Polish–Lithuanian Commonwealth) from making an anti-Russian alliance. The unstable balance of power in eastern Europe – with Russia, the Crimea and Poland/ the Polish–Lithuanian Commonwealth as the main players – persisted after Ivan the Terrible's death.
- The conquest of Kazan and Astrakhan was a tragedy for the peoples of these Tatar states who suffered heavy losses. They had to pay for the sins of the Golden Horde that had disappeared long before. The Tatars served a useful purpose in allowing Russia to overcome its inferiority complex caused by the Tatar–Mongol yoke.
- It should be noted that, after the conquest, Ivan the Terrible was more tolerant towards the Muslim peoples. Tatar and Russian units fought alongside each other in the Russian army; Tatar princes and *murzy* held

command positions in the army and received land and money from the tsar. Ivan the Terrible did not demand that the Tatars converted to Christianity. The russification of the Muslim peoples began much later, in the eighteenth and nineteenth centuries in the Russian Empire. During Ivan the Terrible's reign, when a Tatar entered his service he became the tsar's subject like any other Russian nobleman, and sometimes could even enjoy more privileges.

5

Ivan's Baltic Wars

THE BALTIC QUESTION IN THE MIDDLE
OF THE SIXTEENTH CENTURY

Few seas, except the Mediterranean perhaps, can match the Baltic for the number of bloody wars that have raged on its shores. The Baltic ones have experienced the Viking era and the Northern Crusades. Then followed the wars of the fifteenth to seventeenth centuries for supremacy in the Baltic (*Dominium maris Baltici*), for control of the trading routes between Sweden, Denmark, Poland, German military (or crusading) Orders, different duchies and towns, the Hanseatic League and Russia.[1] The Great Northern War of 1700–21 should also be mentioned, the war in which the Swedish Empire perished and the Russian Empire was born. Of course the naval battles of the two World Wars in the twentieth century are not to be forgotten either.

The military policy of Ivan the Terrible forms a distinct period in the history of the Baltic shores. In the sixteenth century a combination of several factors made redistribution of these territories inevitable. The era of domination by the knights of the Teutonic and Livonian Orders, which lasted from the thirteenth to the fifteenth century, was coming to an end. The northern crusading Orders had degenerated both militarily, politically and ideologically. They were preoccupied by internal disputes between masters and bishops and had lost their former glory and influence.

The Reformation dealt a shattering blow to the German Orders in the Baltic. The Reformation encouraged towns, which had previously had separatist tendencies, to become independent from the Orders. Being trading centres, towns and cities were the economic base of the region, and the military Orders were mainly reliant on the towns and cities, so the downfall of the Orders was only a matter of time.

From the late fifteenth century the position of the Hanseatic League in the Baltic region became gradually weaker. The Hanseatic League was giving way to new and expansionist states such as Denmark, Sweden, Russia and Poland.

These states had been there for some time but in the late fifteenth and early sixteenth centuries they appeared on the Baltic scene in a new guise.

Sweden became independent in 1523, when the Kalmar Union disintegrated, and it now wanted to occupy a suitable place in the Baltic region. Denmark, in its turn, was seeking to find compensation for its loss of influence on Sweden. The attention of the both countries was attracted by Livonia, which was easy prey.

In 1525 Prussia became a vassal of Poland. The duke of Prussia, Albert Hohenzollern, had sworn fealty to the Polish king, Sigismund I the Old.* Next on Sigismund's list was the Livonian Order, a junior branch of the Teutonic Knights. The aggressive Polish policy was supported by the Grand Duchy of Lithuania, an old enemy of the Teutonic Knights. Both the Polish and the Lithuanians sought the destruction of the Teutonic Order and the weakening of the Livonian Order. This was seen as revenge for all the knights had done, for thousands of raids in Lithuanian and Polish lands from the thirteenth to the sixteenth centuries and for political intrigues that prevented these countries from making profitable agreements with Europe. These lands might offer consolation for all the evils the Orders had done to the peoples of eastern Europe.[2]

Russia played a special role in instigating the conflict as it was interested in gaining control over the Livonian towns that were trading posts. In modern histories, one often comes across the opinion that Russia wanted to gain access to the Baltic. This view is based on a misconception; in fact, in the sixteenth century, Russia already had access to the Baltic. Russia possessed the coast of the Gulf of Finland from the mouth of the Neva river to the mouth of the Narova river, roughly the same territory that belonged to the Russian Federation in the early twenty-first century (though it now has part of the northern coast too, from St Petersburg to Vyborg). However this coast was not suitable for sea trade. There were neither ports nor trading posts, nor ships nor the necessary infrastructure. But neighbouring Livonia possessed all these as it was the intermediary for trade between Russia and Europe. Russia wanted to profit from the sea trade and the decision was obvious: gain control of the Livonian trade. It could be achieved by making the Livonians pay tribute, if they agreed to pay rather than letting the Russians use their infrastructure. Or it could be had by invasion and conquest of the territory of the Livonian Order and the capture of that infrastructure. Because, in the sixteenth century, Russia was unable to build its own trade infrastructure, it

---

* Sigismund I the Old (Zygmunt I Stary to the Polish; 1467–1548) of the Jagiellon dynasty reigned as king of Poland and grand duke of Lithuania from 1506 to 1548.

Russian freight ship (engraving, 1598)

wanted to capture one that already existed and worked well, and happened to belong to a state that was, to all appearances, weak and unprotected.[3]

All these desires and expectations of the Baltic states implied one thing: the Livonian Order had to cease to exist and its territory, towns, money and other riches had to serve other nations. All neighbours regarded Livonia as potential prey. In the sixteenth century this prompted a number of Baltic wars, the first of which was the military dispute between Russia and Sweden for the coast of the Gulf of Finland.

THE FIRST WAR BETWEEN RUSSIA AND SWEDEN, 1555–1557

Conflict between Russia and Sweden had been brewing a long time. The spheres of influence of these two states in the Neva basin, on the coast of the Gulf of Finland and Lake Ladoga were still regulated mainly by the Treaty of Oresheck of 1323, signed between Sweden and the republic of Novgorod the Great. After the republic of Novgorod became part of Russia in 1478, negotiations with the Swedes were conducted exclusively by the governors of Novgorod, who regularly prolonged the peace treaty (usually for a long time, about sixty years). From the 1530s, however, the Swedes began to seek ways to expand their territory and sharply increased their activity near the Russian borders.

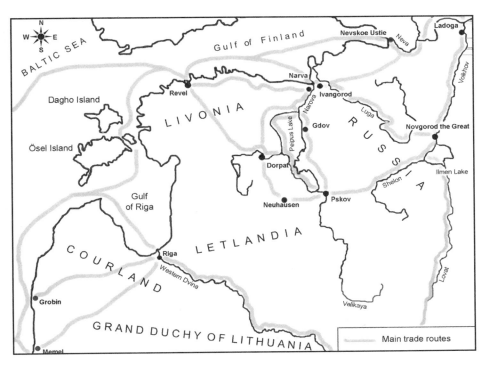

Map 12. Trade routes in the Baltic in the sixteenth century

Twenty years of armed clashes occurred between the Swedes, Finns and Russians in Karelia and around the Russian fortress of Oresheck. Situated at the head of the Neva river on an island in Lake Ladoga, the fortress held a key strategic position blocking access from the Baltic Sea to the lake. From the lake it was possible, along the Volkhov river, to reach Novgorod and then, via the river system, practically anywhere in Russia.

When Sweden became independent from Denmark, Gustav I became king. Swedish diplomacy then faced one more problem. King Gustav needed recognition of his status by other states. So he refused to negotiate with the governors of Novgorod and demanded that his ambassadors should be received by the Russian tsar. If the tsar agreed, it would mean that he recognised Gustav as his equal. The events that followed are described in a Russian chronicle.

> In 1555 many people near the border quarrelled, both sides started to kill and rob, and the Germans started to come and burn villages and kill noblemen, and in their lands they arrested many Russian merchants and put them into prison, and one Russian nobleman was impaled through his throat.[4]

Fortress Oresheck, Noteburg in Sweden (German engraving, seventeenth century)

Although no war had been declared, more and more Swedish units crossed the Russian border, seized land, captured villages, looted and burned settlements. In September 1555 a Swedish unit led by Jakob Bagge attacked the Russian fortress of Oresheck. The Swedes besieged the fortress for three weeks, using their fleet and artillery. The Russian garrison, under the command of Peter Petrov, put up a stubborn defence and even made sorties, humiliating the Swedes. A party under Semen Sheremetyev helped the besieged by attacking separate Swedish units on the left bank of the Neva river. Finally the Swedes had to raise the siege and depart. According to a chronicle, the losses on each side were not great, from five to twenty men in some encounters. Thus the first clashes of the war were rather small scale.

Since minor battles of this kind were of little use and could not solve the problem, in December 1555 Ivan the Terrible launched a major campaign against the fortress of Vyborg, sending troops under the command of Peter Shchenyatev and Dmitry Paletsky. To scare the Swedes, the Russian army included Astrakhan Tatar troops. In January, Russian troops pillaged the northern shore of the Gulf of Finland near Vyborg and captured a few small settlements. The Swedes, who did not possess large forces, did not attempt to defend their remote settlements; instead they prepared for a decisive battle and took up positions 5 km from Vyborg among cliffs and rocks.

The Russian troops surrounded Vyborg and started to bombard it methodically with cannon. The Swedes could not even make a sortie as all their troops, as soon as they left the fortress, came under fire from artillery and handguns. Not many of those who ventured outside the fortress walls returned alive, mainly those who were the quickest fleeing. The Russian troops camped around Vyborg. They intended to devastate the surroundings, gradually expanding the extent of the operation. Eventually they scoured the territory up to 100 km in each direction from Vyborg.

It soon became clear, however, that it was going to be far from easy to capture the fortress, its fortifications being of the most advanced kind. Although the garrison suffered heavy losses from bombardment, it defended itself quite efficiently. An assault promised to be difficult and bloody, so the *voevodes* decided against this method. It was much more interesting to pillage the defenceless surroundings. Russian troops moved from Vyborg along the Vuoksi river, which had many Swedish and Finnish settlements along its banks. Most of the people from these settlements were captured and enslaved, causing a fall in prices on the slave market; a slave girl, for example, cost only fifteen kopeks! The Russian troops left Vyborg, raided Finnish lands on the Karelian Isthmus, reached the Russian border and then went on to Karelia with a great amount of booty.

In June 1556, Knut, master of the Swedish town of Abo, arrived in Moscow. He brought with him a proposal to begin peace talks. In February 1557 in Moscow, the heads of the Russian diplomatic service, Alexey Adashev and Ivan Viskovaty, conducted rather difficult talks with a Swedish delegation and concluded them triumphantly. Gustav agreed to the humiliating condition that Swedish ambassadors could sign peace treaties only with governors of Novgorod the Great. Swedish ambassadors should not come to Moscow and the tsar would not grant them an audience, which would have done too much honour to the Swedes. The border between Sweden and Russia was established on Russian terms. Ivan IV ordered the governors of Novgorod to ratify the treaty on these terms. The war between Russia and Sweden ended in victory for the Russian tsar.[5]

*

THE STRUGGLE FOR LIVONIA IN THE MIDDLE
OF THE SIXTEENTH CENTURY

Poland was the first state, way back in 1422, to express the idea of annexing Livonia. However the destiny of the Order was decided in 1525, when the last grandmaster of the Teutonic Order, Albert Hohenzollern, knelt down in the central square of Krakow and pledged his loyalty to King Sigismund I.

The Polish to this day remember this event as the greatest triumph of their people. The place where the knees of the haughty knight touched the Polish pavement is marked by a flat stone. One of the famous works by Jan Matejko, a Polish painter of the nineteenth century, is called *The Prussian Tribute* and depicts the moment that Albert received the Duchy of Prussia as a fief from the Polish king. The Germans who occupied Krakow in 1939 were hunting for this painting, which they regarded as a symbol of the humiliation of Germans. But Polish patriots saved the painting and in 1945, after the Germans had been driven out, *The Prussian Tribute* was exhibited with ceremony in Krakow's famous picture-gallery, Sukiennice, near the actual site of the event.

The final annexation of Prussia in 1525 was a decisive event in the Polish advance into the Baltic region. From the moment Albert accepted that he was Sigismund's vassal, redistribution of spheres of influence in the region began. Prussian rulers occupied a special position, suggesting that the Livonian Order, which – regardless of the facts – they still considered a junior branch of the Teutonic Order, should also be subject to Krakow.

Albert could not influence Livonia militarily, as he now lacked any significant military forces, but he still had the right to appoint his men to certain key posts. In 1530, Wilhelm of Brandenburg, a younger brother of Albert (son of Sophia, daughter of Casimir IV Jagiellon and sister of Sigismund I the Old) was made coadjutor of the archbishop of Riga without taking into account the opinion of the master of the Livonian Order.* Wilhelm wanted riches, honour and power in abundance. So he started to intrigue, to interfere with matters of the Order, to capture lands by deceit and guile. At the same time he did not refrain from using force; several times the troops of the bishop burned the villages of his political opponents.

The main threat to the Order came from the fact that Wilhelm had influential relatives. When the authorities tried to bring him to his senses, he turned for help to his kin, to Albert and Sigismund; in other words he called for Polish, Lithuanian and Prussian intervention in Livonia. The first time he called for such help was in 1533. In 1539, when Wilhelm became archbishop of Riga, his confrontation with the Order received fresh impetus.

---

* The coadjutor is second after the diocesan bishop in the church hierarchy.

Sigismund II Augustus (engraving, sixteenth century)

All this ended badly for the Livonian Order. Poland took a long time to decide to annex Livonia but at last it did so. The final discussion on annexation took place in 1552 during secret meetings held in Krupishki and Breitenstein between the king of Poland, Sigismund II Augustus, and Albert of Prussia. In August 1554 a secret Polish–Prussian memorandum was prepared, outlining a plan for the subjugation of Livonia. Poland was to offer the Order protection from foreign (primarily Russian) aggression on the condition that the master recognised the king of Poland as his suzerain. Thus, under the pretence of rescuing the Livonians – the easternmost Christians – from the barbarians of Muscovy, the 'voluntary' joining of the Baltic region to Poland and Lithuania would have been achieved.[6]

However, Sigismund and Wilhelm had to hurry. In 1551 a thirty-year truce between Livonia and Moscow was running out. Diplomats intended to prolong the truce for fifty years. From 28 April to 1 June 1554 negotiations were conducted in the Russian capital, during which the Livonians had an unpleasant surprise. They were subjected to a whole array of accusations, each one being a potential *casus belli*: violation of former agreements; persecution of Orthodox communities in Livonia; desecration of Orthodox temples; restriction of Russian trade with Europe caused by unfavourable mediation and the detention of craftsmen and certain kinds of goods; an insult to the governor of Novgorod and even the invasion by Livonians from the town of Neuhausen into territory that belonged to the Russian town of Pskov. Muscovite diplomats said that the only way for Livonia to make up for its faults was to pay the so-called *Yuryevskaya* tribute for many years in advance and carry out other Russian demands.*

The Livonians tried to object. They declared right away that they were ready to return churches, if Orthodox priests could prove their claim was just. The Novgorod ambassador was lying; nobody had done him any wrong. He had been received properly but got drunk and started a brawl. Men that came with him had smashed the windows of respectable burghers and attempted to break in and rape German women. As to the trade restraints, the Livonians had only been acting according to orders of the emperor, so any complaints should be forwarded to the Holy Roman Empire. With regard to the trade mediation, trade could not be done without Lithuanian agents, and the rule applied to all foreign merchants, not only Russian ones, because towns lived off transit trade.

The demand that caused the most objections was paying the *Yuryevskaya* tribute. If the diplomats recognised the demands of the Russian tsar as just,

---

* Yuryev is the ancient Russian name of the Livonian town Dorpat; today it is the Estonian town Tarty.

Russian merchant (German engraving, sixteenth century)

that would mean not only financial loss but also that the Order became a vassal of Moscovy according to the time-honoured rule that 'if you pay him, he is your lord'. Ivan used whatever excuse he could find to justify his conquest of neighbouring lands, and these arguments seemed compelling to contemporaries and for generations to come. The *Yuryevskaya* tribute was first mentioned in documents in 1463. The interesting thing is, every time the peace was prolonged, three peace treaties were drawn up, the first between Livonia and Novgorod the Great, another between Livonia and Pskov and the last between the bishop of Dorpat (Yuryev) and Pskov. The tribute was mentioned only in the latter treaty and concerned only Dorpat. The bishop ignored the requirement to pay the tribute and the Russians did not insist upon it, until 1554.

The origin of this tribute was unclear and this gave rise to several legends. According to one, the Livonians payed the Russians six Livonian *solids* a year for each tree with honey bees. As time went by the population increased, the woods turned into fields and the tribute was forgotten. Ivan the Terrible, according to this explanation, misinterpreted it by turning the payment for each tree with honey bees into a charge per person.

Balthazar Ryussov, a Livonian chronicler, cited another legend. On a plot of waste land between Neuhausen and Pskov, local people collected honey from several hundred trees. Dorpat and Pskov contested the right to impose tribute on the honey gatherers, which resulted in constant clashes. Finally, the towns came to an agreement according to which the Russians received five *poods* (approximately 80 kg) of honey every year. With time the matter became forgotten, until in 1554 it was revived by Ivan the Terrible, but in a new interpretation. Instead of the Dorpat region, it was now applied to the whole of Livonia, and instead of a few *poods* of honey Moscow now demanded one mark per person plus payment of the arrears accrued over the previous years. The total sum was rather impressive.

According to yet other sources this tribute originated as funds allotted for the support of Orthodox churches in Dorpat. In 1554 the Russians demanded that Livonia must restore St Nicholas Church in Dorpat, closed in 1548, and pay off all the arrears of money, going back many years, for the support of Orthodox churches. Again, all Livonia was to pay. Indeed, the tributary relations of Dorpat and surrounding territories with Russian dukes were very complicated and went back to the thirteenth and fourteenth centuries. The parties changed their agreements several times, imposing or cancelling the tribute. It was very difficult to disentangle all these international legal relations going back hundreds of years, hence numerous legends, the bewilderment of Livonian ambassadors and the insistence of Russian diplomats who realised perfectly that in this situation they could demand whatever they liked from Livonia.

In all Russia demanded 6,000 marks (about 1,000 ducats or 60,000 thalers). Interestingly, when Dorpat was captured in 1558, the house of a single nobleman, Fabian Tisenhausen, was found to contain 80,000 thalers, more than was needed to prevent the war! But the Livonians did not want to pay and signed up to the obligation to collect money only after a Russian diplomat, Ivan Viskovaty, unambiguously warned that the tsar would come personally to collect the tribute.[7]

A version of the agreement was first prepared in Moscow and then finalised on 15 June 1554 by the governor of Novgorod the Great, Dmitry Paletsky. The document contained a paragraph about a fifteen-year truce on condition that Livonia paid the stipulated tribute within three years, restored Russian churches damaged during the Reformation; Russian merchants were granted free trade both in Livonia and, through Livonian ports, with Hansa (except trade in military equipment); all foreigners were given the right of free passage through Livonia to Moscow and back; and any alliance between Poland and Lithuania against Russia was banned.

Once Poland and Prussia knew about the Russian–Lithuanian agreement of 1554, they increased their efforts to capture Livonia. They counted on a civil war in Livonia during which one of the warring parties would turn for help to Poland, legitimising intervention. In 1556 a rebellion started in Livonia, instigated by Poland. The rebellion was raised by a commander, Kasper von Münster, who had Archbishop Wilhelm behind him. Von Münster should have become a coadjutor of master Heinrich von Galen, who preferred the candidature of commander Johann Wilhelm von Fürstenberg. Von Münster thought that he had been ignored and decided to take revenge.

As a means of vengeance he chose treason. On 10 May 1556, the rebels officially applied to Sigismund for intervention by Polish troops. Now Krakow had a pretext for the invasion of Livonia. However, the actions of the archbishop of Riga met opposition, firstly from his subordinates, the bishops of Livonia and the town of Riga. On 8 June Riga declared that it did not obey the rebellious archbishop; on 16 June all the bishops of the Order joined Riga.

Coadjutor von Fürstenberg did not hesitate to use force against the rebels. Riga provided funds for hiring mercenaries. Knights pillaged the rebel castle of Kremon and, on 21 June, burned down the castle of Ronneburg. On 28–29 June the troops of the Order besieged the castle of Kokenhusen, the centre of the rebellion. The rebels were defeated. Wilhelm of Brandenburg was removed from the post of archbishop of Riga and put under arrest in the castle of

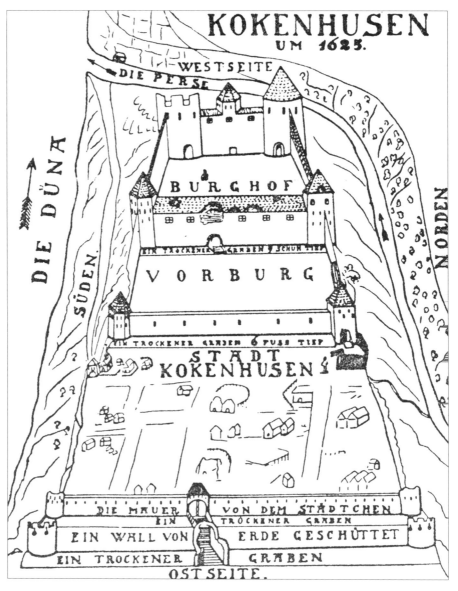

The castle of Kokenhusen (engraving, 1625)

Smilten, where he spent one year. His coadjutor, Christopher of Mecklenburg, was put into prison.[8]

The destiny of Livonia was in the hands of Poland. The Livonians, tense with apprehension, waited to see whether the king would support the bishop or not. Yet, after their allies had been suppressed in June 1556, Prussia and

Poland did not dare to start an open intervention. Polish troops drew close to the borders of the Order but contented themselves with mere muscle flexing.

In the summer of 1557, 20,000 Lithuanian troops, including 4,000 royal infantry and 2,000 cavalry, headed by royal marshal (*marszałek*) Jan Malezky, marched from Vilno to Anykščiai (Onikszty) and concentrated at the border of the Order's territory. Meanwhile, Prussian troops under Albert, who planned to join Sigismund at Birzhi and Salaty, moved from the castle of Ragnit to the Livonian border.

On 2 August 1557, Sigismund offered the Order peace on the condition that Livonia restored all the damage it had done to Lithuania and Poland and gave back all the property of the bishop of Riga. Under threat of invasion, the new Livonian government (master Heinrich von Galen had died and been replaced by Johann Wilhelm von Fürstenberg) said that it was ready for talks on any terms.

On 5 September 1557 Sigismund and Fürstenberg signed the Pozvol peace treaty, which contained a number of agreements. The first was between the master and the archbishop of Riga. Wilhelm was restored to his post of archbishop of Riga, Christopher of Mecklenburgh became his coadjutor and the Order was to pay the bishop 60,000 thalers to cover war expenses. The decision of the *landtag* of the town of Wolmar was cancelled. The Order was also to recompense all the harm it caused to the bishopric of Riga during the so-called 'War of Coadjutors'. Thus the rebels, who had been defeated in battle, turned out to be the victors in the end.

The second agreement was between the master and the king of Poland. Von Fürstenberg humbly begged forgiveness for the insults he had inflicted on Wilhelm, Sigismund's relative. Lithuanian merchants received the right of free trade in Livonia. This humiliating agreement became the cause of rumours that, after the Pozvol treaty, Livonia became subject to the Polish crown. Moreover, on 14 September 1557, von Fürstenberg signed a separate treaty of alliance with Sigismund against Russia. This treaty was to come into effect after twelve years, upon the expiry of the 1554 agreement between the Livonian Order and Russia, which excluded any possibility of a military alliance between Livonia and Poland. The parties also agreed not to let qualified craftsmen and strategic goods into Russia.[9]

After the Pozvol peace treaty the way to the Livonian War was open. No matter what the reservations might have been, the treaty violated the 1554 agreements between Russia and Livonia. Then Livonia had accepted the obligation not to make alliances with other countries without Moscow's knowledge; and now there was Pozvol. Unfortunately, it was usual in the sixteenth century that monarchs and diplomats lacked the skill, or rather desire, to find a peaceful solution to such problems. The war for spheres of influence in the Baltic region was inexorably drawing near. The events of 1556–7, the War of Coadjutors and the Pozvol treaty that might have prevented the division of Livonia, are now remembered only by historians. The Russian invasion of 1558 overshadowed all those events and thwarted anything that Albert and Sigismund had been planning with regard to Livonia. Subsequent events took place in a quite different context.

Master of the Livonian Order von Galen questioned the treaty of 1554. He declared that the ambassadors had exceeded their authority and that the leaders of the Order were not, therefore, obliged to implement this treaty. Livonia was not collecting the tribute. Livonia intended to live in peace until the three years given for the collection of the tribute had expired and then hope for the best.

In 1556 a cellarer from Novgorod, Terpigorev, arrived at Dorpat to discuss the size of the tribute. The chancellor of the bishop of Dorpat, Jurgen Holzschuher, during these talks proposed to make no categorical pronouncements, recognise the treaty nominally and at the same time ask the German emperor to declare the tribute unlawful; thus the dispute would have been transformed into a conflict between Russia and the Holy Roman Empire. Jurgen Holzschuher argued that the emperor was definitely able to show the Muscovites their proper place. This statement did not impress Terpigorev. 'My sovereign does not care about the emperor!' he said. The ambassador compared this agreement about the treaty with a calf that would bring, when it had grown up, a lot of meat, as well as much gain to the tsar. Terpigorev was overconfident.

In 1557 the three-year term for collecting the *Yuryevskaya* tribute ran out, but Moscow did not receive the money. Instead, Livonian ambassadors Gerhard Fleming, Valentin Melchior and Heinrich Winter went to Moscow and attempted to revise the agreement of 1554. In December 1557, rather tricky talks took place. The diplomats managed to reduce the size of the tribute to 18,000 roubles, in addition to which Yuryev was to pay an annual tribute of 1,000 Hungarian gold coins. The tsar agreed but demanded the money right on the spot, which, of course, the diplomats did not have on them. They attempted to borrow the stipulated sum from Muscovite merchants who were willing to lend the money as they feared that the tsar, in case he did not receive payment, might start a war in the Baltic, which would mean the end of trade – Russian, Hanseatic and Livonian – in the region. But Ivan the Terrible forbade the merchants to lend the money. The attitude of ambassadors who tried to extricate themselves by paying money that did not belong to them filled him with rage. The result of his fury was quite predictable; the Tsar went

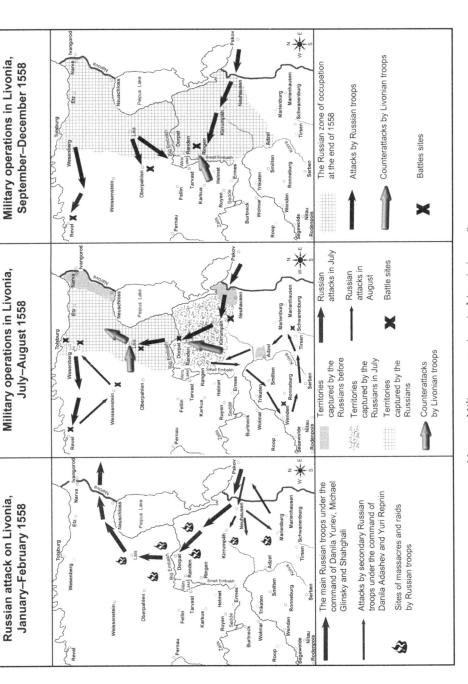

Map 13. Military operations in Livonia in 1558

to collect the tribute personally. Before the ambassadors departed they were invited to dinner, where they were served empty dishes.

At the end of January 1558, 8,000 Russian troops crossed the Livonian border. The aim of the raid was to make the defaulters pay up, to threaten the Order and make it understand that tribute is better than a devastating war. A contemporary of the events, Balthazar Ryussov, recorded: 'The Muscovite began this war not with the intention to conquer towns, fortresses and lands of the Livonians, he only wanted to prove to them that he is not joking, wanted to make them keep their word.'

The troops took a semicircular route from the border in the Pskov area to the border of the lands around Narva, to the west of Lake Peipus, mostly via the territory of the bishopric of Dorpat, the lands from which the money was mainly wrung. This raid was somewhat unusual. The Muscovites raided the lands of the Order. They did not capture towns or castles but made only token sieges, burned and pillaged suburbs, and devastated the surroundings. In short, it was primarily a threat and a flexing of muscles combined with plundering. In fourteen days 4,000 households, villages and estates were burned.

The knights of the Order put up no resistance to the Russian troops. They knew very well about Russian power. It is not true that Muscovy only knew how to fight with the steppe armies, nor that the Livonian knights were an unknown enemy. Wars between Livonia and Novgorod the Great, Livonia and Pskov had been frequent from the fourteenth to early sixteenth centuries, the last great conflict, the First Livonian War, taking place in 1500–1503. And in most cases victory had gone to Russia. The irrational fear of Russians existed in ordinary Livonians at the genetic level.

Russia considered the war in Livonia as a minor, short, local conflict. Russia was convinced that the Order would not persevere in their vain attempts to resist and would quickly collect the money to pay the tribute. In early 1558, none of the potential allies, neither Poland nor Lithuania, nor the Holy Roman Empire, attempted to defend the Order from invasion by Russian troops. All the previous agreements remained on paper.

Livonia was left to its own resources. On 13 March 1558, the *landtag* of Wolmar started to discuss whether they were going to pay the Russian tsar or not; and if they were going to, where they could get the money from. It was decided to collect money from the rural and urban populations as an indemnity from the former and as loans from the latter. The town of Pernau even sacrificed part of its church plates. Riga, Revel and Dorpat collected 60,000 thalers. At the end of April 1558, another delegation, headed by Gotthard Fürstenberg and Johann Taube, set off for Moscow. The diplomats were taking the tribute to Moscow.

During the journey, however, the 60,000 thalers mysteriously turned into 40,000. Where the other 20,000 were, nobody knew. Furthermore, while the ambassadors were on the way to Moscow, the question of tribute lost its urgency. The Russians had taken the Livonian fortress of Narva and the situation changed abruptly.

Narva, from the early Middle Ages, was regarded as a boundary between the civilised West and the barbarian East, which, in the opinion of the Europeans, included Muscovy. On the other bank of the river, right opposite Narva, the Russian frontier fortress of Ivangorod was founded in 1492. The two towns were in constant dispute and mutual antipathy was building up. The war provided an opportunity to give vent to all previously contained resentments and to remain unpunished. In March, clashes began between citizens of Narva and Ivangorod, which quickly escalated into genuine military action. Exchanges of fire over the river became an artillery duel between two fortresses. Every day, about 300 stone cannonballs, each 6.5 *poods* (approximately 106 kg) in weight, were propelled into Narva. Narva had no money for defence. Burgomaster Joachim Krumhausen confiscated goods worth 8,000 marks from merchants, but he did not have time to spend the money.

Seeing that the matter had taken a bad turn, the merchants of Narva, trying to preserve their business from destruction, began negotiations in April 1558, first with the *voevode* of Novgorod and then with Moscow. The ambassadors announced that Narva was ready to reject Livonia and swear allegiance to the Russian tsar. Ivan the Terrible received this suggestion favourably.

On 11 May there was a fire in Narva. According to most sources, the house of a barber, Kordt Ulken, was the first to start burning and the fire then spread to neighbouring buildings. Instead of trying to extinguish the fire, people took cover in the castle. Those who were too late for the castle hid in the moat. Infantry soldiers, thinking an assault had begun, gathered on the central square and took positions by the gates. They waited for some time, saw no enemy and then took cover from the flames and smoke in the castle.

According to Russian chronicles, Russian *voevodes*, when they saw the flames, demanded that their troops be let in to help extinguish the fire; Russians regarded Narva as their own so it was their obligation! But the Livonians did not let the foreign troops into the town so the Russians had to break in. They swam the Narova river holding onto doors, logs and other things that happened to be at hand and were borne across 'as if carried by an angel' (in the words of one Russian chronicle). Troops under Alexey Basmanov and Danila Adashev entered through Russian (Vodyanyye) Gate and Ivan Buturlin led his troops through Kolyvansky Gate. Besides extinguishing the fire, the Muscovites started bombarding the castle from Livonian cannon they found abandoned on the town walls. The German soldiers could not fire back as a cannon on the Tower of Herman burst and rendered the whole artillery position unserviceable.[10] The garrison of the castle appealed for help from the coadjutor, Gotthard Kettler, whom the Order had placed in charge of the defence of Narva. His troops made camp 3–5 km from the fortress. Kettler pensively watched Narva burning and did nothing.

The castle had three barrels of beer, a little rye flour, a lot of lard and butter, and gunpowder that would have lasted for half an hour. With these resources any opposition was futile. Talks about surrender began. The Livonians gloomily watched the end of the talks; a Russian *voevode* demanded water, washed, solemnly kissed an icon and swore that he would let the garrison go and keep all other promises. The Russians said that anybody might leave the town and take as much of their belongings as they could carry in their hands. To those who preferred to stay the tsar promised to build new houses. At night people began to come out of the castle. Knights, ordinary soldiers and citizens who did not want to stay in occupied Narva joined Kettler's troops and set off towards the castle of Wesenberg.

Capturing Narva opened new prospects for Ivan the Terrible's campaign, more tempting than just extorting tribute. The events of the first half of 1558 showed that the Order did not pose a serious military threat and was easy prey. Moreover, the willingness with which some of Narva's citizens had become Russian subjects raised hopes that their example would be followed by others. From this moment on, Russia began a war of annexation and started to occupy Livonian towns and lands. On 6 June, the troops that had captured Narva occupied Neuschloss (Syrensk in Russian sources). Thus Moscow controlled the eastern part of the district of Allentaken. Russians also advanced into the southeastern part of Odinpe, that is the long-suffering bishopric of Dorpat. In June the castles of Etz (Adezh to Russians) and Neuhausen were taken. These were the first Russian acquisitions in Livonia.

These events decided the fate of the master von Fürstenberg. After the fall of Neuhausen, he commanded his troops to retreat without engaging the enemy. The master was accused of cowardice and incompetence, and Gotthard Kettler, his coadjutor, was placed in command of the troops regardless of the fact that he had behaved no better at Narva.

In July 1558, troops under the joint command of Peter Shuysky and Andrey Kurbsky moved along the route of the winter campaign of 1558, over the territory of Odinpe and the bishopric of Dorpat around the Lake Peipus. But this time the Russians besieged and captured towns, not merely devastating and pillaging the area around them. Kirrumpäh, Dorpat, Randen, Ringen and others were taken by Russian troops. By August 1558 the Russians had seized almost total control of the territories of Odinpe, Wirland and Allentaken. Now they directed their assault on Letland, towards Wenden and Schwanenburg.

Russian *voevodes* stuck to a tested strategy: first a cavalry raid, devastation of nearby towns and destruction of the Order's units in field battles. Then these Russian troops retired and, along the route they had opened up, the main forces moved, capturing towns and castles and making the population subjects of Ivan IV.

The last talks between Russia and Livonia, in May 1558, had failed. Ivan the Terrible did not even meet the ambassadors who brought part of the tribute. He said that he had captured more in Livonia than the money they had brought. Having achieved nothing, the ambassadors returned to Livonia, where the money was promptly taken by the master, who said that it had been collected for the Order anyway.

King Sigismund was taking his time and did not assist the Order as he should have according to the treaty of Pozvol. But in 1558 Denmark took its first steps towards occupying the territory of the Order. The commander of Revel, Franz von Segenhagen Genant Astel, left for Denmark, handing command of the fortress to the *vogt* ('protector', military officer) of the bishop of Ösel, Christopher von Münchhausen. On 5 July 1558, King Christian III of Denmark sent a letter to von Münchhausen addressing him as Danish royal governor of Livonia and instructing him to mount the Danish royal emblem in Revel. On 25 July 1558, von Münchhausen declared that Revel should become subject to the Danish crown. However, this view was not shared by the citizens, who preferred to become Swedish subjects. Gotthard Kettler, who was brought to Revel for recuperation, ousted von Münchhausen and returned the town to the Order.

About that time, the archbishop of Ösel and Courland, Johann von Münchhausen, offered to sell the lands under his control to the Danish crown. On 18 September it was agreed that the king would pay 20,000 thalers immediately and 15,000 thalers per month for the next six months. During this time he would have to help Livonia against Ivan the Terrible. Thus Denmark joined the struggle for Livonia, having demanded, like Poland, land in return for protection.

The weak point of the agreement of 18 September 1558 between Denmark and Livonia was that the realisation of the right of Denmark to the lands of northern Estlandia was fully dependent upon the goodwill of Ivan the Terrible, for this territory was already under control of his army. The fate of this land was to be decided by talks between Denmark and Russia, so, on 23 December 1558, a delegation sent by Christian III and headed by Klaus Urne and Peter Bille set off from Riga for Moscow.

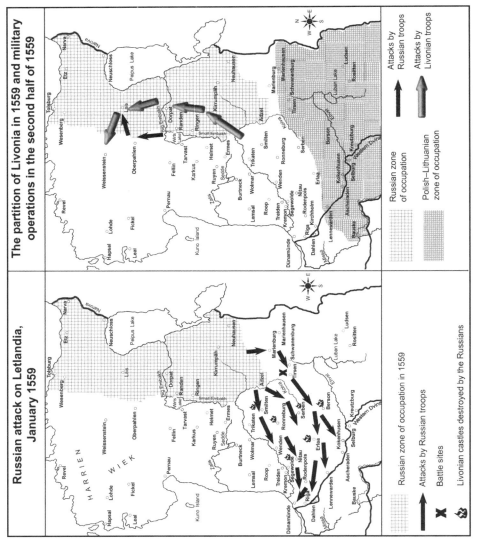

Map 14. Military operations in Livonia in 1559

In September 1558, 1,200 German mercenary infantry (*landsknechts*) and 100 cannon arrived in Livonia from Germany. Perhaps this was the cause of the slowdown in the Russian advance in September and October 1558, when their military actions were less successful than previously. Only two new strategic points were occupied – the castles of Tolsburg (in September) and Kinevel (in October). The attempt to conquer Revel failed, although Livonian troops were defeated in open battle before the fortress walls. *Voevode* Peter Zabolotsky could not consolidate his grip on Oberpahlen and burned the town instead.

In October the troops of the Order under Kettler made their first successful counterattack. In November, after six weeks of siege, Kettler recaptured his first castle, Ringen, and moved on to Dorpat. This counterattack revealed that the Russian army in Livonia was weak and, in order to block Kettler's advance, troops were redeployed from Wesenberg, Dorpat and even from from Vyshgorod and Krasny in Russian territory. On 8 November 1558, Kettler was severely injured in a battle at a bridge in Elve and the troops of the Order retreated to Wenden.

Thus, in the second half of 1558 the Livonians gained some small measure of revenge. Obviously, it was due to the fact that the Order offered resistance that the campaign became more violent. In November 1558, Ivan the Terrible wrote to the master, the archbishop, bishops and all the people of Livonia. The tsar declared that the Livonians had not met their obligation, so he would punish them for their unrighteousness and violation of their holy oath, and all blame for what would happen was on those who had sinned before God and committed perjury.

On 17 January 1559, 50,000 Russian troops crossed the Livonian border in seven different places. A force of 10,000 troops moved towards Schwanenburg and Sesswegen, Riga being their final goal. This group was under the command of Nikita Yuryev and at its core were 600 men armed with arquebuses. It is noteworthy that these firearms had been bought not long before from Livonian merchants who were not overscrupulous when it came to making profit.

The January campaign of 1559 seems to have been designed as a repeat of that of the previous January, but it was more violent. Military action was aimed at the destruction of castles, villages, towns and enemy troops. A broad strip of land between the rivers Koiva and Evsta, up to the Western Dvina, was ravaged. The Russians did not waste their time on well-protected castles (Riga, Wenden, Ascheraden, Kokenhusen and others), pillaging nearby territory instead. But castles with weaker defences (Smilten, Serben, Schujen, Erlaa, Sunzel, Rodenpois and others) were taken by assault and burned.

According to Russian sources, eleven Livonian castles were abandoned by their fleeing garrisons. Seven towns near Riga were pillaged; ships that did not have time to escape from port were sunk. Unlike the campaign of the spring and summer of 1558, the Russians did not now attempt to consolidate their grip on the captured positions, instead waging a war of extermination. All attempts by the Livonian troops to put up some opposition failed. In a battle at Tirsen the Livonian army was defeated. On 17 February the Russian troops left Livonia.

The January campaigns of 1558 and 1559 had a lot in common with Tatar raids (there were many Tatar units in the Russian army). The campaigns were aimed not at the long-term conquest and consolidation of territory but at intimidating the population, defeating the army, undermining the economic centres, disrupting the local administration and general pillaging and marauding. The Livonians had not previously seen a strategy like this. It was not without reason that Europeans began comparing the Russian style of waging war with the Turkish and general Asian style.

THE FIRST PARTITION OF LIVONIA, 1559

In 1559, Livonia requested the assistance of different European countries. The Revel officials negotiated with Denmark, Solomon Henning and Rombert Hildesheim went to Sweden and Kettler turned to the Holy Roman Empire, the nominal suzerain of the Order. The Hanseatic League was asked for money to hire an army. All turned a deaf ear to the Livonians. The only ones willing to help were the Crimean Tatars who sent a delegation with a constructive offer of a military alliance against Moscow.

In the Empire, the Reichstag in Augsburg discussed the Livonian question in January. Livonian ambassadors were present and officially applied to the Empire for assistance. It was decided to ask towns for a loan of 100,000 *guldens* (guilders) for hiring troops and to intercede with Ivan the Terrible and urge him to stop military operations in Livonia. However the financial problem remained unsolved; the money was not collected.

Also in January, a Livonian delegation was sent to King Sigismund. The diplomats reminded him about the obligations the Polish crown had undertaken and asked him to adhere to the terms of the agreement of Pozvol. Seeing that the king was wavering, the Order suggested a compromise. The king could make it appear as though the master of the Order had hired the Polish troops. Thus, officially, the king's army would not take part in the conflict; the soldiers would be mercenaries and the king would not be responsible for them. But, after two months of talks, Sigismund did not agree even to this. On 14 March, the diplomats received the final refusal, the main reason for which was the king's unwillingness to violate the truce with Ivan the Terrible. Even so, Sigismund realised that Ivan the Terrible needed peace on their mutual border and wanted to prolong the truce, so the king started some diplomatic blackmail.

In 1559, Moscow was ready, in exchange for eternal peace with Lithuania and an alliance against the Crimea, to give up claims on Russian lands that were part of the Grand Duchy of Lithuania. This proposal was expressed by Alexey Adashev, head of the Russian diplomatic service, during talks with Lithuanian ambassador Vasily Tishkevich in Moscow in March 1559. The conditions of the peace laid down by the Lithuanians were the return of Smolensk, Novgorod-Seversky, Chernigov, Starodub, Bryansk and Vyazma. The Lithuanian diplomats cited a fable: 'A snake lived in the yard of a certain man, ate his wife and children and wanted to live in his house. And this world is the same: it will eat the wife and children and will eat the man himself'. The enraged Russian diplomat called the response of the Lithuanians 'rotten seeds' that 'can't even be dreamt of'. But Sigismund's ambassadors persisted: Smolensk and Novgorod-Seversky were the necessary conditions for peace. The Boyar Duma reached a decision that, since the Livonians refused to compromise, Russia would adhere to the truce agreement while it lasted, but would not prolong it.

On 10 March the Lithuanian ambassadors made a statement accusing Ivan the Terrible of violating peace with Christian states and assaulting Wilhelm, archbishop of Riga, Sigismund's relative. They made it clear that Sigismund's intentions were more than serious and the prospect of a new war between Russia and Livonia would not stop him. The Russian diplomats met Tishkevich's declaration in silence. And they had a good reason to be silent. After a relatively small punitive raid against the weak Order, Russia suddenly faced the prospect of a large-scale war with European countries! On 16 March the Lithuanian ambassadors were expelled from Moscow. Ivan the Terrible gave orders not to give mead to the diplomats and, when parting, said that Russia would adhere to the truce agreement while it lasted and then see what happened.

For all this display of sang-froid, the Russians were impressed with this *démarche* by Poland and Lithuania. Russia felt that it should diminish the intensity of pressure on Livonia and heed the opinion of other countries, especially those that were going to divide Livonia among themselves. Denmark, where Frederick II had just ascended the throne following the death of Christian III on 1 January, was one of those countries. The delegation of Klaus Urne, in March, 1559, brought to Moscow the draft of an agreement on the partition of Livonia between the Russian and Danish crowns. Russia was willing agree to Danish demands and give up some of the former possessions of the Order, but Denmark had to guarantee the capitulation of Livonia and make the master of the Order and the archbishop come to Moscow and humbly beg for investiture. It seems that so much hope was placed on the partition of Livonia between Ivan IV and Frederick II of Denmark that, in his final speech, Alexey Adashev declared that Russia favoured the request by the Danish diplomats to make a truce with Livonia, to last from 1 May to 1 November 1559. It was a grave mistake, as it turned out later.

This truce, made under the prompting of the Danish ambassadors, turned out to be disadvantageous to both King Frederick and Ivan the Terrible. Instead of getting ready to capitulate, the Order used the truce to prepare resistance and to find protectors among the neighbouring countries. In May 1559 Archbishop Wilhelm sent Sigismund a letter expressing his willingness to become a subject of the Polish crown after the Prussian pattern, on the condition that Livonia remained a nominal subject of the Holy Roman Empire at the same time. Soon Kettler joined the talks, demanded that Sigismund put into effect the conditions of the peace agreement of Pozvol and offered in exchange to make the Order a vassal of the king of Poland.

In Vilna on 31 August 1559, the First Vilna Pact was made between Sigismund II Augustus and Gotthard Kettler, who was soon (21 September) to become the new master of the Livonian Order. The king of Poland took the lands of Livonia under his protection. On 15 September, Archbishop Wilhelm of Riga joined the agreement. Sigismund was to render the Livonians military assistance against Russia, if needed, and, not later than 11 November, to send a delegation to Ivan IV with a demand to stop the war in Livonia. In return, the king received the lands of the Order on the middle reaches of the Western Dvina, and the castles of Dinaburg, Selburg, Ludsen, Rositten and Bauske were given to him as security. Thus the southeast of Letland, the part bordering on Russia, passed under the control of Sigismund, making conflict between Poland, Lithuania and Russia almost inevitable.

At almost the same time, Denmark received its share of Livonian land. In 1559 a conflict broke out between King Frederick II of Denmark and his younger brother, Duke Magnus, who contested the land of Holstein. Frederick II decided to appease Magnus with faraway Livonia and in September 1559, under the agreement of Neubourg, he bought Ösel for 30,000 thalers. The lands of the bishopric of Courland also passed to Denmark. Duke Magnus officially gave up claims on Holstein, received the title of bishop of Ösel and Courland and began preparations to set off to his new domain. Now Denmark had a legitimate pretext for moving its troops into the lands of the Order.

Duke Magnus

Meanwhile, in the autumn of 1559, the Livonians, who had received the support of Poland, launched a counterattack which disturbed the headquarters in Moscow. The knights directed their strike at the former Dorpat, which was now Russian Yuryev, their aim being no less than the capital of the Muscovite territories in Livonia. Again, as in the autumn of 1558, it turned out that there were not enough Russian troops near the city. At the very least Moscow had to urgently manoeuvre units from Pskov, Krasny and other Russian fortresses on the border. At the end of November, the Livonian troops attacked Yuryev itself, bombarding and attempting to storm it for ten days before raising the siege. After these events, orders from Moscow look panicky. Even troops from central Russia were hurriedly moved into Livonia; setting off unprepared, when it was cold and roads were impassable, their march was slow.

Since military action had not solved the problem, it might have seemed that it was now time for diplomats to play their part. Yet Russia pursued a course of aggravating the confrontation with the Grand Duchy of Lithunia. On 7 December, during talks with Alexey Adashev, Fedor Sukin and Ivan Viskovaty, the Lithuanian ambassador Andrey Khoruzhy expressed the desire of the nobility to solve the conflict peacefully. Adashev responded that the Boyar Duma had the same desire, but the king had invaded Livonia, which belonged to Ivan the Terrible, so, unless the king went, bloodshed was inevitable. The talks failed again.

THE FALL OF THE NORTHERN CRUSADERS: THE END OF THE ORDER, 1560–1561

Russia, without enquiring into the root of the diplomatic collision late in 1559 (which was without reservation a mistake of Ivan the Terrible) was attempting to alter the situation in its favour by traditional means. In January and February 1560, further forces, arriving from central Russia, invaded Livonia. The first thrust was directed at the town of Marienburg (Alyst in Russian sources). After capturing it, the troops made a devastating raid over a broad strip of Letland and Jerwen from Fellin to Wenden, hitherto untouched by the war, then withdrew towards Pskov. This campaign was again aimed at devastation and pillaging and the Russians, besides killing many people, returned with plenty of captives, cattle and other plunder.

All the while, the number of those who wanted to take part in the partition of Livonia grew. In April 1560, troops of the nineteen-year-old Danish Duke Magnus landed at Arensburg to begin implementing the Neubourg agreement of 1559. The situation of the Danes was not an easy one though and they had to fight a minor engagement with the Order. Heinrich Wolf von Lüdinhausen, *vogt* of the castle of Zonenborg on the island of Ösel, attacked the army of Magnus and Kettler sent him aid. The worries of the master were quite easy to understand; the nobility of Wiek regarded the arrival of the Danes as a turning point in the war. Chronicler Balthazar Ryussov recorded that 'many Livonians had strong hope that good times shall come'.[11]

The balance of power in Livonia strongly depended on Denmark. If it decided to play an independent role, as it had before, or was simply neutral towards Russia, it would mean that several forces would compete for possession of the former territory of the Order. If Denmark joined Poland and Lithuania, then there was hope of making an anti-Russian coalition. So Sigismund several times appealed to Frederick II to at least prohibit trade with Russia through Narva. Denmark did not want to spoil its relations with Poland, but neither did it wish to lose profit from the sea trade. So, the Danes complied with the wishes of Poland, ostensibly. On 12 May 1560, trade relations between

	Russian zone of occupation		Polish–Lithuanian zone of occupation		Attacks by Livonian troops
	Danish zone of occupation		Attacks by Russian troops	**X**	Battle sites

Map 15. Military operations in Livonia in 1560

Denmark and Russia were officially banned, though in practice the ban was not effectively enforced.

As a result of the evasive attitude of Denmark, Magnus' domain in Estlandia was under threat of invasion by Russian troops. As it turned out, part of the lands in Harrien and Wirland that passed to Denmark had been given out to Russian minor nobility. The aggravation of relations with Ivan the Terrible, inevitable in the event of a league between Denmark and Poland, could lead to war. The outcome of such a conflict, taking into consideration the distance between the Danish mainland and the seat of war, was quite predictable: Magnus would lose Estlandia. The situation of the Danish prince in Livonia was very precarious. His units were constantly clashing with Russian, Swedish, Polish and Lithuanian troops. So in 1560 Denmark chose to be consistently neutral towards Russia. On 16 June 1560, Frederick II asked Moscow 'for the sake of friendship' not to attack Magnus' duchy.

Sweden, another participant in the Baltic conflict, became more active too. Protestant regions of Livonia, which did not want to be subject to the Catholic king of Poland, began separate talks with Sweden. Sweden had become Protestant by that time and the Protestants of Revel hoped to find in the Swedes their spiritual brothers. In September 1560, the citizens of Revel and nobility of Harrien appealed to Sweden for assistance. The Swedes promised money, troops and protection if Revel became subject to the Swedish crown. The town was also promised it would retain all its privileges. After some time, Revel's citizens and the noblemen of northern Estlandia declared their secession from the Order and, in June 1561, the knights (4 June) and citizens (6 June) signed an agreement making them subjects of the Swedish crown.

Once Sweden claimed part of the Livonian lands, it had to determine its attitude towards the other contestants: Denmark, Russia, Poland and Lithuania. Only their attitude towards the Danes was clear; they were enemies by definition. Stockholm did not want to quarrel with Poland, nor with Russia. Moreover, both countries were good trade partners. So Sweden refrained from engaging in military action in the region and hoped to find diplomatic solutions to controversial issues.

While the Baltic states were increasingly active, the Holy Roman Empire remained politically impotent. In August 1560, the question of financial aid to the Order was raised again. In September 1560, the Reichstag of Speyer decided to apply for support for Livonia to England, Poland, Denmark, Sweden and the cities of the Hanseatic League. A ban on the export of arms and ammunition to Russia was also suggested. But these measures were not implemented and the calls received no response. On 1 November 1560, the emperor issued a decree forbidding Narva to sell munitions to Livonia. The inability of the Empire to give its Baltic province any substantial support when this support was needed was to a large extent caused by the reluctance of the cities of the Hanseatic League. The war was a source of profit for them so they did not want its termination.

As Denmark and Sweden were neutral, the main Russian enemies were Poland and the Grand Duchy of Lithuania. Sigismund, in his letter of 8 December 1559, informed Ivan the Terrible that he had made the master and the archbishop his subjects at their request and by the Emperor's consent. Sigismund was making himself out to be a believer in applying the principles of Christianity in politics and a defender of Christendom from Russian schismatics. Ivan the Terrible was accused of selling captive Christians to Muslim countries and violating the truce with Livonia. The tsar was commanded to stop the war in Livonia immediately.

In response, Ivan the Terrible gave orders to continue military action in Livonia and instructed Russian diplomats to prepare arguments in support of the right of Russia to capture the territory of the Order. The first instance of this argumentation is found in the letter of 24 January 1560 from Ivan IV to Emperor Ferdinand. The tsar enumerated the 'sins' of the Livonians. They had despised the word of the Lord and accepted the teaching of Luther, that is to say they had became Protestants. An Eastern Orthodox tsar looked rather strange as a fighter against Protestantism but such subtleties did not bother Ivan the Terrible. Ivan IV maintained that Livonia was originally Russian land. Yuryev had been built by Russian princes in ancient times and the Livonians then had promised to pay Russia a tribute. In Riga and Revel Russian Orthodox churches had been consecrated, trade fairs had been organised and fortifications had been built. The Livonians had sworn allegiance but had then broken their oath. They had turned Orthodox churches into stables and places for the collection of human excrement. Ivan the Terrible had admonished the renegades but it had been futile for their hearts had hardened. So the Livonians were receiving punishment by fire and sword, not because of the tsar's wish but of their own accord. What was happening in Livonia was testing justice (*justitiae revisio*).

In May 1560, troops under Andrey Kurbsky defeated the army of the master of the Order near Weissenstein and devastated Harrien. In July and August, Fellin, Ruyen, Tarvast and Oberpahlen (abandoned by the Germans before the Russians had approached) were taken. In Fellin, which was occupied on 21 August, the former master, von Fürstenberg, was captured, the most prominent Livonian official that had been seized by the Russians.

In the spring and summer of 1560, an intensive exchange of correspondence took place between Kettler and the government of the Grand Duchy of Lithuania. The master begged, demanded and pleaded for troops to be moved into territories not yet occupied by the Russians. Poland and Lithuania took their time. Only on 19 July 1560 did isolated Lithuanian units cross the Western Dvina and then they did not engage the Russian troops in battle. Lithuania had a force of only 800–2,500 troops, divided into separate detachments. As a result, the Livonians did not receive any practical aid and had to fight alone. Not until October 1560, after long correspondence between Sigismund, Kettler and Lithuanian noblemen, was the decision finally made to move Lithuanian troops into Ermes, Helmet, Trikaten, Karkus and Wolmar. Kettler's appeals to occupy Weissenstein and Fellin, important strategic positions, had lost their relevance as they had since been captured by the Russians.[12]

On 2 August 1560, near Ermes, a battle took place that turned out to be the last large battle in eastern Europe in which the northern crusading orders were involved. The Livonian army was destroyed by Muscovite troops. The commander of the army and practically all military leaders of the Order (commanders Werner Böll, Heinrich von Galen, Christopher Sieberg and Reinhold Sass) died in captivity. This result actually made Master Kettler glad and benefited him personally, as the military leaders with their 'code of chivalry' had irked him and prevented him from secularising the ecclesiastical state.

At that moment Russia made an unexpected move. On 18 August, at the conference of the tsar with the metropolitan, a new scenario was planned. A delegation consisting of Fedor Sukin and clergyman Grigory Shapkin was to go to Lithuania to arrange a marriage between Ivan the Terrible and one of Sigismund's daughters, either Anna Jagiellonka or Katarzyna Jagiellonka. The marriage was to be accompanied by the conclusion of eternal peace between the two states. Both the marriage ceremony and the concluding of peace were, by all means, to take place in Moscow, Ivan the Terrible being the host and the Jagiellons being guests.

On 27 October, Sukin sent a report that appeared promising. The idea of Ivan the Terrible as a prospective son-in-law was an unexpected one to Sigismund. The Polish and Lithuanian nobles came up with the excuse that because of the war in Livonia it was impossible to talk about anything but its termination.

Then the discussion of the bridal candidates began. The Russians preferred the younger sister, Katarzyna, but the Polish nobles argued that it was impossible to marry the younger sister before the elder one, Anna. On 12 October Sigismund agreed to Katarzyna marrying Ivan IV and to send high-ranking ambassadors for further discussion. Russian diplomats were even shown the bride, although secretly. As she visited a church (kostel), Sukin and Shapkin were secretly placed in a nearby house from which they could see the royal cortege 'and the princess . . . Katarzyna turned and looked at the house where we were hiding, but we do not know whether she saw us or not'. Thus, in October 1560, the marriage proposal was not rejected and details were to be discussed.

On 4 December 1560, a delegation comprising Jan Shimkov and Jan Gayka was sent to Moscow. The marriage was possible under the following terms: Russian troops should be withdrawn from Livonia, eternal peace should be concluded and the marriage ceremony should take place not in Moscow but on the border between the two states. On 11 February, during the continuing discussions, Lithuanian diplomats even made the usual territorial claims on

Map 16. *The partition of Livonia between Poland, Grand Duchy of Lithuania, Russia, Sweden and Denmark after 1561*

Novgorod the Great, Novgorod-Seversky, Smolensk and other towns. It is difficult to tell whether Sigismund knowingly made demands that could not be fulfilled or really hoped to get something. Whatever the case, the Lithuanian demands were absolutely unacceptable to Moscow. The attempts to prolong the truce between Lithuania and Russia were also futile as Russia refused to stop military action in Livonia before Lithuanian troops were withdrawn from there. On 18 February, the ambassadors, having achieved nothing, left Moscow.

On 30 May, Sigismund demanded from the Order that Riga, Pernau and other towns should pass to the Polish crown and insisted that the Polish sovereign should become commander-in-chief of all the troops fighting in Livonia against the Russians, regardless of whose money the soldiers had been hired with. This virtually deprived the Order of its own army, which had, in any case, already been defeated. Prince Mikolaj Radzivill was to become head of Livonia. In August and September, Radzivill made a tour of the Order's castles and talked about the terms of their passage under the king's rule.

On 28 November 1561, the Second Vilna Pact officially recognised the abolition of the Livonian Order. All its possessions formally passed under the jurisdiction of Lithuania and Poland. The last master recognised himself as a vassal of Sigismund II Augustus and was granted the duchies of Courland and Semigalia as his fief. Archbishop Wilhelm and the coadjutor of the Order each received a small landed property that was to provide for their maintenance, and their former lands passed to Sigismund.

On 5 March 1562, the master, archbishop and Livonian noblemen took the oath of loyalty to Radzivill. This date is considered to be the end of the Livonian Order. Strictly speaking, the Livonian War with the Livonian Order was over. The Order was no more. But the struggle for the partition of Livonia was just beginning. And the seat of war was about to expand radically.

6

The Dispute Over Russian Lands
Ivan's Policy towards Poland and Lithuania in the Third Quarter of the Sixteenth Century

THE WAR BETWEEN RUSSIA AND
THE GRAND DUCHY OF LITHUANIA, 1561–1570

The demise of the Livonian Order did not solve the problem of the partition of Livonia. Four zones of occupation (Polish–Lithuanian, Russian, Swedish and Danish) of the Baltic lands had formed as a consequence of the military operations. None of the parties recognised the conquests of the others. So there was a new difficult period of Baltic wars ahead. The states who were victors in the war of 1556–61 were to become participants in a new conflict. The 1560s were marked by two lines of confrontation: the first between Russia and Lithuania, and the second between Denmark and Sweden. As a result, a new state, Rzeczpospolita, appeared on the political map, while the Swedes, hoping to make the Baltic Sea its own internal lake, began to extend their empire over its coast.

Military conflict between Russia and Lithuania began in August 1561 on the territory of Livonia. Before the truce had expired a Lithuanian unit attacked the fortress of Tarvast. The town was besieged, taken and its garrison was captured. On 1 September Russian *voevodes* were robbed and set free, in disgrace. A Muscovite relief force, under Vasiliy Glinsky and Peter Serebryany, caught up with the Lithuanian unit and defeated it near Pernau. Tarvast was burned down by order of the tsar.

In November 1562, Moscow decided to start preparations for a large-scale campaign against Polotsk, one of the largest towns of the Grand Duchy of Lithuania (GDL). A number of factors determined the choice of target. Polotsk was the main fortress on the route between the Russian border and Vilno, the capital of the GDL. If the fortress was captured, Russian cavalry could move freely along the Vilno highway, which opened up the possibility of conquering the whole of Lithuania. Moreover, a glance at the map shows that the zone of the sixteenth-century clashes between Muscovy and Lithuania gradually shifted from the southern border (the province of Chernigov and Novgorod-

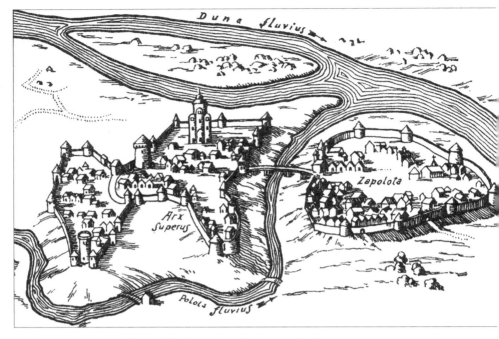

Polotsk in the sixteenth century (Polish engraving)

Seversky) towards the north, to Smolensk and Orsha. By the 1560s, large-scale wars had settled the border dispute everywhere except in the region of Polotsk and Sebezh.

Another reason for choosing Polotsk was ideological. Way back in 1513, Russia offered to recognise the Holy Roman Empire's right to invade the Prussian lands occupied by the Jagiellons if the empire recognised the right of Russia to capture Kiev, Polotsk and Vitebsk. Almost every Muscovite demand for the return of 'originally Russian' territories captured by the GDL included Polotsk. Before the Livonian War there had been no attempts to put these demands into practice, suggesting they were seen mainly as a means of putting diplomatic pressure on Lithuania. That's why the assault of 1563 on Polotsk created a great political impact.[1] It made the Poles and Lithuanians think that the Russian tsar had passed from words to deeds and that, after Polotsk, Kiev and Vilno would follow.

On 30 November 1562, troops set off from Moscow. The army marched through Mozhaysk and Toropets towards Luki the Great. It contained 10,017 noblemen, 5,003 Cossacks and 5,579 Tatars, Meshchera and Mordvinians. Including other troops the total number of warriors was about 30,300. The number of armed serfs accompanying the noblemen is unknown, but the

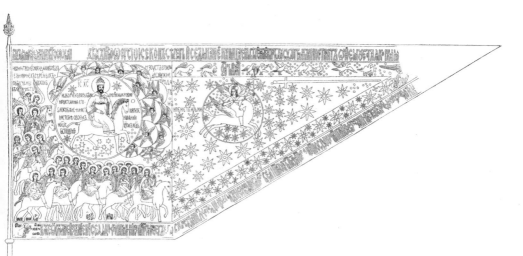

The Russian banner of the Polotsk raid with holy symbols, 1563

figure for the cavalry should be at least doubled. It was one of Russia's largest foreign campaigns in the sixteenth century.[2]

Sigismund II did not expect the attack. The forces of the Grand Duchy were unable to stop the invasion. The king confined himself to promising moral support in this severe test, but the *hetman* of Lithuania, Mikolaj Radzivill, started mustering troops but it was impossible for them to reach Polotsk in time. When the siege began there were only 2,000 Lithuanian and 400 Polish troops. The town's garrison was left to the mercy of destiny. The thousands of people who took cover behind the town walls made the task of Stanislav Dovojna, *voevode* of Polotsk, even more difficult. If the siege was long, the supplies might not last till Radzivill came.

Ivan the Terrible sent a messenger to Polotsk with an invitation to surrender and become his subjects under their own terms. The citizens killed the messenger. On 30 January 1563, the tsar personally inspected the site of the coming battle and, on 31 January, troops started to take up positions around the fortress in preparation for a siege and assault. The original plan was to attack the fortress crossing the frozen Polota river as the defences facing the river were weaker. But it turned out that the ice was too thin and it was too risky to send infantry and cavalry across the river under gunfire. So the troops were positioned opposite the walls of Polotsk. They received orders to build fortifications of gabions (wicker baskets filled with earth), behind which siege artillery was installed.

The first attempt to storm the fortress took place on 5 February. *Streltsy* under Ivan Golokhvastov set fire to a fortress tower by the Western Dvina river, captured it and penetrated behind the stockade. However, they did not manage to keep their position and had to retreat. The town was bombarded into the evening by light artillery, as the large siege guns had not been installed yet. However, even this bombardment was enough and the citizens offered to negotiate a surrender.

The negotiations that took place from 6 to 8 February failed. Russian *voevodes* had moved the siege towers to the town walls and readied the heavy guns. On 8 February the negotiations were broken off and artillery fire commenced. According to contemporary reports, the thunder of the guns was so great that it was as if heaven crashed down on Polotsk. Large cannonballs breached the walls and destroyed buildings behind them. A big fire started in this suburb and 3,000 households burned down. Accounts differ as to the reason for the fire. Some attributed it to the Russian bombardment; others said that the fire had been started at Dovojna's command because he had decided to withdraw his troops into the castle. Whatever the cause of the fire, when it started, the Russians began their second assault. Russian noblemen, led by princes Dmitry Ovchina and Dmitry Khvorostinin, entered the burning streets and drove the Polish garrison into the castle but did not manage to take the castle by assault.

Thus, by 9 February Polotsk was partially captured. Between 11,000 and 24,000 people, including both residents and those from the surrounding country who had taken cover in the town before the siege, surrendered to the Russian troops. The fortress walls were poor protection against the Russian guns and it would have been sheer lunacy for civilians to stay in the war zone under bombardment.

From 9 to 11 February the heavy guns and siege towers moved towards the castle walls, concentrating on the place where the fire had been. The bombardment went on for several days and nights without a break. The guns were sufficiently close and powerful that some cannonballs crossed the space enclosed by the castle and hit the opposite wall. Citizens hid from the bombardment in cellars. The garrison was occupied by extinguishing fires instead of fighting. Even so there were too many fires and soon the whole castle was in flames. Forty sections of fortified wall out of the 204 that made up the castle's defence were destroyed by gunfire. It became clear that the fall of the castle was just a matter of time.

The defenders of Polotsk were brave, even making sorties aimed at destroying Russian siege engines. The sorties were futile and each one left the number of defenders further depleted. On the morning of 15 February 1563, the town gate opened and a procession of Orthodox priests, with Bishop Arseny at the head, emerged. Polotsk offered to surrender. Talks went on until

Kurtze Abschrifft vnd

Verzeichnus / des grossen vnd gewalti-
gen Feldtzugs / so der Moscheobiter für
Polotzko in Littawen / den 31.
Januarij / dieses LXIII.
Jars gebracht hat.

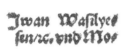 Iwan Wasilye-
sen 2c. vnd Mos-  witz Großfürst in Reuß
schraw.

German leaflet on the Russian capture of Polotsk in 1563. The anonymous author
describes the destruction of the 'flourishing European city' of Polotsk, an event that
was considered Ivan the Terrible's first great offensive on Christendom. However, it is
unlikely that the author had ever been to Polotsk or had first-hand knowledge of its
capture: thus he portrays the typical progaganda image of a generic European town
suffering at the hands of the barbarous Muscovites

evening and Ivan the Terrible promised not to harm the town's defenders. When agreement was reached, 3,907 men and 7,253 women came out of Polotsk to meet the Russian troops.

The tsar kept his word, partially. The heroic Polish garrison was allowed to leave under arms and with banners flying. Cavalry officers received rich presents from Ivan the Terrible: sable fur coats with linings of precious fabric. There was no repression against the citizens, whether Orthodox or Catholic, but later some of them were brought to Moscow as captives. Rumours spread over Lithuania that a Tatar unit had entered Polotsk and massacred a group of Bernardine monks, and also that those Jews of Polotsk who refused to convert were drowned in the river. Whether this was true or not is unknown, but at that time stories about severe punishments inflicted upon Polotsk by the Russian tsar made the rounds.

The conquest of Polotsk was the greatest Russian success on the Lithuanian front. As it turned out, Polotsk became the westernmost point of Russian advance in the sixteenth century. Rumours circulated in Poland and Lithuania that, following his victory at Polotsk, Ivan the Terrible prepared a silver coffin for King Sigismund.

The Grand Duchy of Lithuania was shocked by the loss of Polotsk to the point of being unable to organise an adequate counterattack. The assembly (*sejm*) of Lithuanian gentry that took place in Vilno in May and June decided to draft the militia (*pospolite ruszenie*) by 1 August 1563. Quotas were established as to the number of fully equipped men that Lithuanian nobles should provide from a certain amount of property. Failure to provide the required number of armed men might entail the confiscation of land. However, despite such strict measures, the mobilisation proceeded slowly. Few, if any, wanted to fight, even though the country was in extreme danger.

In June and July, troops of the GDL attacked Russian positions. But it was not the Lithuanian nobles, who were supposed to form the Duchy's main strength, that took part in these local clashes, but Circassians of Kanev (that is, Ukrainians from around the town of Kanev) and Tatars of Belgorod (from the Dniester region). Led by Prince Dmitry Vishnevetsky, a defector who had once served Ivan the Terrible, the Lithuanian troops invaded lands near Chernigov, Novgorod-Seversky and Putivl. All these Lithuanian attacks were repulsed.

On 5 December 1563 a high-powered delegation headed by Yuri Khodkevich, Grigory Volovich and Mikhael Garaburda arrived in Moscow. These ambassadors were instructed to demand the return of Polotsk and to discuss conditions of 'eternal peace'. They were also to lay stress on Christian values and argue that it did not befit Christian rulers to shed the blood of their brothers in faith instead of making war on the infidel Tatars and Turks.

On 11 December, the boyar Vasilij Yuryev read out a list of places that belonged to the ancestral lands of Russia's Rjurikovichi dynasty, but as a result of 'adversities had passed from our forefathers to the Jagiellons who were Catholics'. Sigismund was asked to give up those lands. The territory from Smolensk to the Berezina river, Kiev, Brest, the lands of Podolia and Volhynia to the Polish border were Old Russian territories. These lands had been the ancestral lands of the Rjurikovichi since the time of Prince Vladimir (980–1015) and his son Yaroslav the Wise (1019–54). This territory passed to the Lithuanian princes as a result of aggression after the invasion of Khan Batu, who captured many Russian towns.[3]

It was the first time that Moscow had made such extensive and detailed territorial claims on Lithuania, which was undoubtedly a result of euphoria after the victory at Polotsk. The Russian conditions of eternal peace were no less impressive: Sigismund was to recognise Ivan's royal title of tsar and withdraw troops from Livonia without conditions. Lithuanian scribe Mikhail Garaburda, hearing this, noted before debates: 'Let's first discuss the minor issues and then the important ones.' By 'minor issues' he meant the capture of Polotsk.

Lithuanian demands were mainly concerned with relatively recent territorial losses. The ambassadors informed the Russians that the king wanted to receive Novgorod the Great, Pskov, Smolensk, Polotsk, Toropets, Luki the Great and Novgorod-Seversky. Except for the lands of Novgorod the Great and Pskov, the main talking point was lands lost by the Grand Duchy in Russian–Lithuanian wars in the first half of the sixteenth century.

The talks failed. The boyars told the ambassadors that the tsar would give up neither Polotsk nor Smolensk. The Lithuanians were presented with a new list of territorial claims that gives an idea of how Ivan the Terrible wanted to see the territory of Russia. The Dnieper river was to become the axis of the new territories and Kiev was to become their centre. But these demands were only a trick intended to threaten the Lithuanian delegation and make it more tractable. The ambassadors were invited to sign a truce on the condition that Lithuania recognised the legitimacy of the Russian conquest of Polotsk and Livonia. In case the ambassadors should decline, they were asked to stay in Moscow until a new delegation arrived from Vilno with instructions about 'eternal peace' and the handing over of Kiev to Russia.

Since in such a case the chances were that the ambassadors might die in Moscow of old age, they went back on their word; the king would recognise his loss of Polotsk during the whole time that the truce lasted but offered to consider the border of the Polotsk lands as passing along the Western Dvina river. In Livonia, however, Sigismund had suggested, as a basis for the truce agreement, recognition of the borders as they were at the commencement of the talks. Lithuania offered a truce lasting until 1 July 1564, while Russia offered a truce of ten to fifteen years but on condition that Moscow received Polotsk and all the Livonian lands to the northeast of the Western Dvina river. Sigismund's diplomats refused to discuss this offer. On 4 January the Lithuanian ambassadors, having achieved no results, left Moscow.

On 23 January 1564, from Polotsk, large bodies of Russian troops marched deep into the territory of the Grand Duchy of Lithuania. The thrust was aimed at Orsha, Minsk, Novogrudok and the surroundings of Drutsk. Their commander, Prince Peter Shuysky, did not have orders to capture territory, the aim of the campaign once more being intimidation, looting and devastation. From Smolensk, troops under Vasily Serebryany moved to join Shuysky. Estimates of the number of Russian troops ranged from 20,000 to 50,000.

The main Lithuanian forces, 10,000 troops commanded by Mikolaj Radzivill and Grzegorz Khodkevich, were concentrated near Lukoml. Here, on 26 January, the Lithuanians received reports that the Muscovites had launched an attack. The Lithuanians assumed battle formation near the Ula river and carried out reconnaissance. Shuysky did not expect to encounter any significant number of Lithuanian troops here. Radzivill attacked the Russian positions before night fell. According to a Muscovite chronicle: 'The Tsar and Grand Prince's *voevodes* did not have time to don their armour, nor to bring their troops into a battle formation'. The chronicle blamed the *voevodes* for not following the tsar's orders during the march as they went unarmed, all their armour and weapons carried on sledges. The Russians put up fierce, yet ineffective, resistance.

The Russian commander, Shuysky, fell in the battle. Estimates of the casualties differ greatly. Russian chronicles relate that Shuysky's troops scattered and fled and only 150 men were killed. Lithuanian sources report that 20,000 Russians were killed or captured. The former report must have understated the number, while the latter obviously exaggerated it.[4]

What is the significance of the battle of the Ula, which is considered by the Lithuanians almost as retaliation for Polotsk? It is not to be denied that the Russian army was defeated, Shuysky killed and the Russian January campaign aimed at the inner territory of the GDL thwarted. In the wider sense, however, it was no disaster: a battle was lost but not the war, and the balance of successes was not in favour of Lithuania. The victory at the Ula did not retrieve Polotsk, nor did it prevent future Russian attacks. This battle did not in any way influence the course of the war that went on along the whole

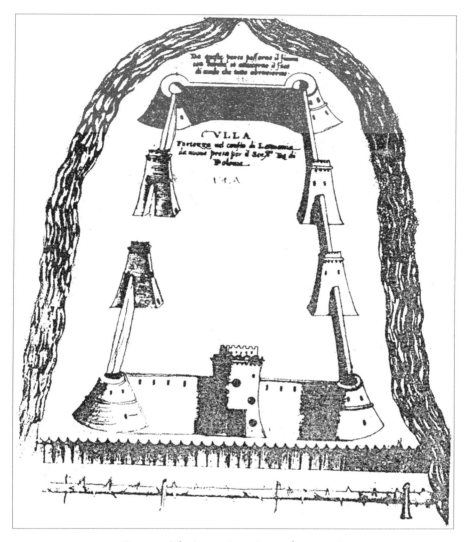

Fortress Ula (engraving, sixteenth century)

Russian–Lithuanian border and in which mainly local noblemen and town garrisons took part, supported by units sent by the central governments.

In September Lithuania at last made an attempt to recapture Polotsk, but the three-week siege was a half-hearted enterprise and brought no results. That same month, Sigismund's troops had more success in the Baltic region when Lithuanian and Livonian units under Gotthard Kettler took Pernau back from the Swedes. In October, though, the Russians occupied the Lithuanian fortress of Ozerishche.

Copey des Brieffes:

Welchen der Lyttaw,

ische Haubtman gen Warschaw, dem Herrn
Radiuill zugeschickt, darinn er vormeldet, wie es jme
in eroberung der Schlacht, so er mit dem Muscowit.
ter gethan, ergangen, Mit erklerung, was für
statliche Beutten sein Kriegßvolck die Lttrawen, daruon ·
gebracht vnnd bekommen haben,

Geschehen den 26. Januarij, dieses) 5 6 4 Jars.

*German leaflet on the battle of Ula. This triumph was considered the second great
victory by Lithuanian troops over the Moscovites in the sixteenth century – the first
being the battle of Orsha in 1514. Polish and Lithuanian propaganda exaggerated the
idea that they were the last shield of Christendom against barbarians from Moscovy.
This leaflet describing the glorious victory is an example of such propaganda*

On the whole, after the events of 1563–64, the Russian–Lithuanian War
followed the pattern of the Smolensk War of 1512–22. In both cases Russia
dealt the enemy a heavy blow by capturing a large town (Smolensk in 1514
and Polotsk in 1563). And in both, initial success was followed by defeat (the
battle of Orsha in 1514 and the battle of the Ula in 1564), after which the

war turned into a series of frequent, but small-scale, border clashes against a backdrop of difficult truce talks lasting several years.

It was some two years later, on 20 October 1566, that Russian troops crossed the Dvina and founded a fortress in the mouth of the Ula. On 28 October, a unit from Polotsk attacked a newly built Lithuanian fortress near Voronach. In response, the Lithuanians attacked the district of Polotsk. Lithuanian Cossacks from the towns of Drissa and Kobets robbed those who passed along the Nevel road near Polotsk.

New truce talks with the Russian embassy headed by Fyodor Umny-Kolychev took place from 24 July to 19 August 1567 in Hrodno. The talks were very difficult. Lithuania wanted to consolidate the status quo, each party keeping what it had at that moment, but with one reservation: when the truce was over the king would have the right to try to regain the lost territories. Russia, on the other hand, thought that the war had ended in a Muscovite victory so it had the right to demand new territorial concessions from the 'defeated' GDL. The talks were destined to failure.

In fact, both parties wanted peace; Russia needed to secure its success while Poland and Lithuania wanted to prevent any worsening of their situation. The total balance of successes was in favour of Russia, despite a number of defeats. The war demonstrated the inability of Lithuania to offer resistance. Lithuanian magnates complained to the king that it was impossible for them to make their subjects go to war and that Russia was too strong for the GDL. The motto of this defeatist party of the nobility was the phrase Mikolaj Radzivill addressed to King Sigismund: 'Fighting with Russia is like attacking the sun with a mattock'.

In this situation the nobility of the GDL, unable to mobilise forces for defence, agreed to the final merging of Poland and Lithuania into a single state, the Polish–Lithuanian Commonwealth (Rzeczpospolita). In January 1569 at Lublin, the *sejm* with representatives from both Poland and Lithuania started discussing the terms of the merger of the two states. It was decided that the two states were to have a common administration, a common monetary system and a common army. And from now on the two states were to pursue the same foreign policy. Previously, the two states had not always cooperated with each other on foreign policy and had experienced conflicts. Lithuania had not always supported Poland in its struggle against the Teutonic Order, while Poland often left the Lithuanians alone against the Russian threat. Now Lithuania hoped that the Polish army could be used in the war against Muscovy.

Without the Polish army, Lithuania would, in the opinion of many, have been no more. It would not have survived against Ivan the Terrible. This opinion is a little exaggerated, however. Before the merger, the Grand Duchy of Lithuania was, indeed, in a difficult situation; but was the situation catastrophic? Lithuania, by all appearances, was losing the war against Russia, but it was not the first war that the GDL had lost to Russia in the sixteenth century. Each defeat had entailed territorial losses but there had never been any question of a loss of statehood by Lithuania. And this question did not arise in 1569 either.

The fears of town dwellers and nobles (*szlachta*) that the Russian tsar would assault Vilno and Kiev were excessive. As far as can be seen, Russia would have contented itself with Polotsk and the Jagiellons' renunciation of their claims to Livonia, which Ivan IV had been trying to achieve at talks since December 1563. Russian diplomats demanded Kiev and other Russian towns at each meeting with Lithuanian ambassadors, but these demands were intended as threats and never, during the whole of the sixteenth century, was there any attempt to turn these threats into reality. From the capture of Polotsk in 1563 up to 1569, the Russian army conducted no major campaign into the territory of the Grand Duchy of Lithuania. Russian troops merely ravaged the territories near the border and did not take any big towns, as they did not have orders to do more.

Unfortunately, Livonia turned out to be a stumbling block. The Polish kings, as previously mentioned, wanted to make Livonia their colony and were not willing to give up this plan. Thus, Livonia became a small card in the political game of the Baltic wars. Neither Poland nor Lithuania alone could have held its positions in Livonia and oust the Russians and Swedes from there. The implementation of the 'Polish Baltic' project demanded the merger of the two states, and, as it was believed at that time, Poland virtually absorbed Lithuania.

Lithuania was caught between two fires. On one side there was Russia, which had already in the sixteenth century captured much of the Lithuanian territory near the border and, to all appearances, was set to continue its progress. Perhaps Lithuanian fears of losing their independence to Russian conquest were exaggerated and that Moscow would actually have been unable to defeat and subjugate the whole of the GDL. But these fears were widespread among the population, especially the elite, *szlachta* and magnates. To them the Russian threat was no illusion. The noblemen strongly believed that alone Lithuania would not be able to defend itself against the threat from the east. That is why, although the actions of the crown caused indignation, the noblemen were attracted to it and sought its protection.

On the other side was the fact that, in the event of a merger, Lithuania would play a subordinate role. Polish culture was in every respect more developed,

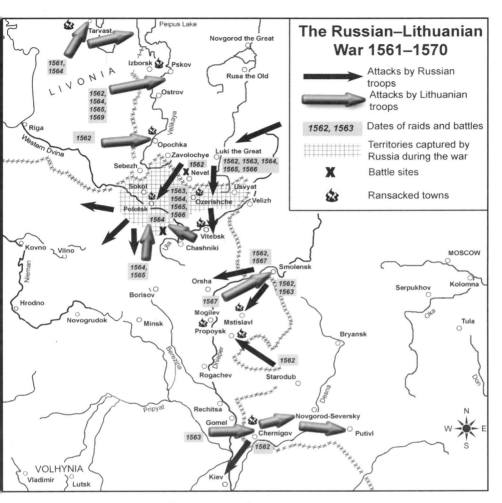

Map 17. The Russian–Lithuanian War 1561–1570

and, moreover, it had experience of spreading over newly acquired territories. One of its strong points was its considerable tolerance; it is not without reason that early modern Poland was called a 'state without fires'. Polish culture spread not by violence; it attracted people and was adopted by free will. It was clear to everybody that in the united state the etiquette, the system of values, political, religious and cultural life would be determined by Poland.

As a result of the Union of Lublin, the military potential of Russia's enemies sharply increased, although the process of merging Poland and Lithuania took decades. The war of 1561–70 with Lithuania was the last Russian victory in the west during the sixteenth century.

On 10 May 1570, Moscow received the first delegation from Rzeczpospolita headed by Jan Skrotoshin. The dialogue took the usual turn: the Lithuanians (Vilno and the Lithuanian diplomatic service were made responsible for relations between Russia and Rzeczpospolita) demanded Novgorod the Great, Pskov, Smolensk, Polotsk, Ozerishche and other towns captured from Lithuania not long before. The boyars in their turn read out a list of Russian claims that included Kiev and nearby towns on the Dnieper, Volhynia, Brest, Lviv and about ten other major towns.

Since the territorial dispute turned out to be insoluble, the talks that took place from 18 to 20 June settled on a compromise: a three-year truce without defining the borders of Livonia in documents and thus avoiding formal statement of the right of each party to Livonian lands. The border between Russian and Polish Livonia was to pass along the Western Dvina river. The parties agreed to leave open the question of the partition of Livonia. On 24 June 1570 the parties signed the agreement which put an end to the war between Russia and Lithuania.

The results of the war were favourable to Ivan IV. By taking Polotsk he had continued the capture of major Lithuanian towns begun by his father (Vasiliy III had taken Smolensk), concluded a truce and achieved a temporary recognition of the Russian conquests in Livonia.

THE VICTORY OF RUSSIAN DIPLOMACY:
THE LEGITIMISATION BY EUROPEAN COUNTRIES OF
THE RUSSIAN MILITARY USURPATION IN LIVONIA

Whereas there was nothing new in Russian–Lithuanian relations in 1561–1562, contacts between Russia and Denmark developed. Denmark realised that Russia was ready to recognise its new acquisitions in Livonia and thus make them legitimate. Neither Poland nor Sweden would have done it. Small Danish units that invaded Livonia were unable to compete with Russian noblemen who, without permission, attacked villages, looted them, captured villagers and imposed tributes promising protection. Since Russian troops were stronger, villagers preferred to surrender to them rather than the Danes; the Russians might punish but they also might provide real protection, if necessary.

In March 1562, King Frederick II of Denmark addressed Ivan the Terrible and proposed peace negotiations. The negotiations began in July 1562. During the negotiations, the parties radically disagreed about the status of Livonia. The Danes acted on the premise that the land was partitioned, so it should be partitioned to the end; it remained only to agree to whom each part belonged. Moscow, on the other hand, considered the whole of Livonia as a

Polish sejm *of 1570 (Polish engraving, sixteenth century)*

single and indivisible estate in the tsar's possession. Lands occupied by foreign troops were, therefore, either illegally captured (by Lithuania and Poland) or granted by the Russian tsar for a limited period to another ruler (to the Danish Duke Magnus for example). So talks about partition might take place but, in any case, the part that would pass to the Danish crown would do so not as its property but vouchsafed by the (retractable) goodwill of the tsar of Muscovy.

On 16 July 1562, Danish ambassadors presented a list of Livonian lands that they wanted to secure for the crown by agreement. Russian diplomats used their favourite policy, making tiny concessions only after long debates and then reluctantly, giving the strong impression the Russian tsar was not going to give any more. This policy was calculated to exhaust the patience of the foreign ambassadors.

On 27 July 1562, the negotiations entered a new phase. The Russian party apparently decided that the Danish ambassadors were exhausted enough by petty bargaining and declared that Russia was going to agree to concede almost all the territories that the king of Denmark desired (except two estates, known as Kolki). But this was on condition that the peace treaty would state Riga, Pernau and other Livonian towns not yet captured by Moscow as belonging to Russia. The Danes replied that they did not dare to sign such a treaty. Then began a debate over the period of the truce, entailing a battle of wits. The Russians suggested that all common enemies should be mentioned by name in the treaty, insisting that an eternal truce was otherwise impossible. Without this condition only a truce of two to five years was acceptable. The Danish ambassadors countered that nobody needed an eternal truce and Denmark would be quite content with the period of a hundred years. Gradually the parties lowered their demands; the Danes were ready to agree to fifty years while the Russians were willing to accept five or six years.[5]

The underlying reason for such behaviour on the part of the Muscovite diplomats was quite simple. They strived to either make Denmark an ally against Poland and Lithuania or at least make sure that it guaranteed not to involve itself in the conflict on the side of those countries by providing funds or mercenaries and such like. To this Copenhagen was ready to agree, in general. But on 2 August, during the signing ceremony, there was a new conflict: the Danes discovered that the Russians had included in the document towns that were currently in the hands of Poland and Lithuania. Alexey Basmanov made an indignant protest, saying that Denmark desired the partition of Livonia too, so Denmark should take northern Estlandia, while the rest passed to Russia. The towns and granges that passed to Denmark were mentioned by name, so those passing to Russia were to be mentioned in the like manner.

The ambassadors refused to sign the Russian version of the treaty. Ivan IV gave the ambassadors time to think it over and told his boyars to break the negotiations if the towns were not mentioned by name. On 2 August the parties attempted to reach a compromise. The Danes said that they were ready to include a clause in the treaty to the effect that Russian acquisitions in Livonia were not of their concern, that this was a matter that concerned only the Russian tsar and the kings of Poland and Sweden. The tsar said that he would not mind if Frederick captured the Polish towns of Gdansk, Torun, Hwoynitsa and the Swedish towns of Stockholm, Vyborg, Abo and the others. The tsar also promised to hand over to Denmark the territories bordering on northern Estonia that Russia was going to conquer. The Danes in their turn, when they captured the towns listed in the treaty as Russian, would have to hand them over to Russia. Ivan IV was especially interested in possessing Riga and Wenden.

The Russian tsar's confirmation of his oath before foreign diplomats

The solution was found on 4 August and it demonstrates how little treaties meant in the sixteenth century. The boyars suggested preparing two versions of the treaty, a Danish one, where the right of Ivan IV to Livonia would be mentioned only in general terms, and a Russian one, with a detailed list of towns. Should a document kept in a Moscow archive make any difference to Frederick? The delighted Danish diplomats confirmed that it really made no difference and agreed to this variant. On 7 August 1562 Ivan IV confirmed the documents by an oath.[6]

The results of the Moscow talks of 1562 were beneficial to both sides. Denmark's achievement was that its rights on that part of Livonia that it already possessed de facto were affirmed by an international treaty. Copenhagen received from Russia, the main threat in the region, guarantees of the inviolability of its frontiers. Denmark also reached agreements about direct sea trade with Russia. All this was, without doubt, advantageous to Frederick II.

The main benefit to Moscow was Denmark's promise not to interfere militarily in the Livonian conflict or give support to the enemies of Russia. There is no telling how serious Ivan IV was about listing in the treaty the Livonian towns that were to be captured. The persistence with which the Russian party insisted on including this paragraph in the treaty seems to be evidence of the importance of this issue. On the other hand, Moscow's diplomats can not have failed to realise that the oath of monarchs, who confirmed different versions of the treaty, could not be relied on. Even so, somehow or other, the result was the first international document that declared Livonia to be the legitimate possession of the tsar.

In mid-September 1562 a delegation headed by Anton Romodanovsky set off for Denmark to ratify the treaty. The talks in Copenhagen were held 3–6 December 1562 and the dispute over the possession of Kolki turned out to be a stumbling block. The Russian diplomats showed weakness and, when the Danes threatened the dissolution of the treaty, gave up Kolki to Denmark under the Danish terms. On 6 December 1562, King Frederick ratified the treaty with Moscow. The treaty with Denmark opened the gate to implementation of the 'Russian Livonia' project, and the loss of two towns was no calamity.[7]

The diplomatic activity of the early 1560s freed the hands of Russia and Denmark to launch a new round of Baltic wars. At the same time, these events convinced Poland, Lithuania and Sweden that the destiny of the Baltic region was to be decided only by the sword. In 1561–2, military activities were sluggish but did not stop for a single month and, from 1563, grew more active. Russia invaded the territory of the Grand Duchy of Lithuania while a naval war started between Sweden and Denmark.

IVAN THE TERRIBLE AND THE WAR BETWEEN DENMARK AND SWEDEN 1563–1570

On 24 May 1562, Erik XIV of Sweden commanded his admirals, Jacob Bagge and Jonson Bong, to block the trade route through Narva. The trade of European countries with Russia through Narva angered the monarch and caused financial losses to Swedish merchants.

Swedish ships cruising near Narva did not stop the Baltic trade, though. Merchants from the Hanseatic League, England, Holland and Scotland took their cargo to Revel, which belonged to Sweden. Denmark and Lübeck were indignant at the barefaced impudence with which Stockholm deflected the trade routes in its favour. They declared that the sea should be free and everyone should have the right to choose where to sail and with whom to trade. The argument quickly turned into a military conflict between Denmark and Sweden, a war for control of the Baltic Sea which went on from 1563 to 1570 and ended in favour of neither of the participants.[8]

While this Danish–Swedish war (the so-called Northern Seven Years War) went on, Russia played its own diplomatic game. In 1567, Moscow conceived the idea of dividing Livonia into small duchies, the rulers of which would take oaths of allegiance to the monarchs of Poland, Sweden, Denmark and Russia. Thus the spheres of influence would be divided peacefully. At first Ivan the Terrible made an offer to the former master of the Livonian Order, Johann Wilhelm von Fürstenberg (who was in Russian captivity), by which he would found a vassal Livonian kingdom, but he refused. A similar offer was then made to Gotthard Kettler, who already held Courland and Semigalia as Sigismund's vassal. But the last master of Livonia also rejected the tsar's offer. The only one who agreed was the Danish Duke Magnus, who regarded this offer as a chance to provide himself with a state of his own, albeit formally subject to Moscow. His previous role, as the virtual deputy of the king of Denmark in the Danish occupation zone of Livonia, no longer satisfied him. The words 'Be master of your destiny: the crown of Livonia is waiting for you!' were music to his ears.

On 27 January 1570, the ambassadors of Magnus returned from Moscow to Arensburg, the capital of Danish Livonia. They brought with them an agreement in which Ivan IV promised to hand over to Magnus all his conquests in Livonia. After Magnus' death the lands were to pass down to his descendants and, in case there were none, they were to pass to the Danish crown. The Russian population was to be evicted from Livonia, and the sole right to the commercial activity in Livonia was to be given to the Danes and Livonians. In return, Magnus was to swear allegiance to the Russian tsar.

Poland closely watched the union between Magnus and Ivan IV. The royal diplomats had lively discussions on what the phrase 'Magnus, the vassal of Ivan IV' might mean. Was it an indication that the Baltic region was being divided between Denmark and Russia? The army of Magnus now acted in Livonia in cooperation with Russian troops. On 21 August, their combined forces attacked Revel, although they did not manage to take the town by assault and a long siege proved fruitless when the Swedes delivered supplies to the town by sea. On 16 March 1571, the Danish–Russian troops retreated from Revel.

The forging of closer relations between Russia and Denmark, on the one hand, and between Sweden and Poland on the other, was caused by the position of these states regarding the sea blockade of Narva. The Swedes and the Poles wanted to stop the trade through Narva, whereas Denmark and Russia were interested in this trade. While the *sejm* at Lublin of 1569 was in session, Sigismund II issued a manifesto calling all monarchs to make efforts to stop the Narva trade and hired a squadron of fourteen ships under Jan Munkeben.

A war of privateers, pirates commissioned by states to attack enemy ships, began on the sea. Danish privateers hunted Swedish ships, whereas Polish and Swedish buccaneers captured all vessels that headed for Russian Narva. Ivan IV had no sea fleet, though much later he hired Danish privateers who have passed into history as 'the corsairs of Ivan IV'.

HOW THE RUSSIAN TSAR NARROWLY FAILED
TO BECOME A EUROPEAN MONARCH: MUSCOVY AND
THE POLISH INTERREGNUM OF 1572–1576

In 1572, King Sigismund II Augustus of the Polish–Lithuanian Commonwealth died, ushering Poland and Lithuania into an interregnum, full of turbulent political events, which was to last until 1576. Ivan the Terrible offered his candidature for the Polish crown, hoping to become the ruler of the Polish–Lithuanian Commonwealth without firing a single shot and to resolve the problem of the Baltic region in his favour. However, Poland preferred a French prince, Henry Valois, and Polish noblemen made him accept the so-called Henrician Articles (*Artykuly Henrykowskie*), the terms under which he received the crown. These conditions were so strict that they left practically nothing of the royal power. King Henry had no legislative power: he could neither declare war nor make peace, could not cancel or introduce taxes, and could not even marry without permission of the council of the Polish noblemen.

The Polish aristocracy rejoiced; they liked the new king. Henry, however, did not share their glee and after a few months fled his new kingdom. It was perhaps the only case when a monarch fled from his subjects, having no desire to rule them. His flight occurred when King Charles IX of France died; Henry quickly forgot about Poland, a country that he considered wild and barbarous, and sped to Paris to occupy the French throne so dear to his heart.

The outraged Poles and Lithuanians were left without a monarch and had to start a second election campaign. The country was split: one part of the nobility supported the candidature of the Holy Roman Emperor Maximilian; another part was in favour of a little-known prince of Transylvania, Stefan Bathory. There were some who supported Ivan the Terrible, who offered his candidature again, and especially his son Fyodor. Fyodor was feeble-minded, which attracted the Polish *szlachta* to whom a weak king could be made to do whatever they wanted and so was the model ruler. However, the reputation of Fyodor's father, Ivan the Terrible, gave the Poles and the Lithuanians pause as he was not the man to have his son pushed around by the nobles.

The fact that, in 1576, Russia and the Holy Roman Empire managed to coordinate their efforts was the cause of extreme danger to the Polish–

Henry Valois, king of Rzeczpospolita

Lithuanian Commonwealth. Ivan the Terrible realised that Maximilian was a more likely candidate for the Polish crown, while the Russian tsar had more supporters in Orthodox regions of the Grand Duchy of Lithuania.[9] So a plan for the division of eastern Europe between Germany and Russia was formulated. Poland was to pass over to Germany while the lands of the GDL were

Emperor Maximilian II

to go to Russia. The dividing line bore a remarkable resemblance to that of the Molotov–Ribbentrop Pact of 23 August 1939, according to which Poland fell under the German sphere of influence while western Ukraine, western Byelorussia and the Baltic region were assigned to the sphere of influence of the USSR. After that Germany invaded Poland, beginning the Second World War and the Red Army occupied Lithuania, Latvia, Estonia and western Ukraine, while western Byelorussia was annexed. This scenario might have been acted out more than 350 years earlier, in 1576.

However, in 1576 Stefan Bathory was elected king, but he had to suppress a number of rebellions against him, the largest being that in Gdansk, which did not recognise the new king. Stefan was lucky in one respect. In October of that year his main political rival, Maximilian II, suddenly died and his son Ernest was a weak politician who failed to become leader of the pro-German party of Polish nobility. Ivan the Terrible lost an ally and the 'Maximilian–Ivan the Terrible Pact' remained only an idea.

Although the interregnum was a time of anarchy and instability, the Russian tsar's participation in the elections was beneficial to the Polish–Lithuanian Commonwealth; while Ivan the Terrible had a chance to take the throne peacefully, he did not make war. From 1571 to 1576 there was generally peace on the Russian–Lithuanian border and in the occupied Livonian territory. Though there were isolated clashes and both sides made looting raids, there was no war on a state level and neither army conducted large-scale military operations.

When Bathory was elected, the situation changed. It was only after some time that Ivan the Terrible accepted that he had lost the elections. For a long time he considered Bathory as a parody of a king rather than a true monarch. The first delegation from Bathory that came to Moscow, in October 1576, was received with animosity. Boyars from the start began asking unpleasant questions about the background of Stefan Bathory, about his relations with other monarchs and whether these monarchs considered him their peer, and what were the relations of the new Polish king with Turkey (the sultan had supported Stefan in his claim to the throne).

Ivan the Terrible felt slighted by the letter delivered from the Polish king. The tsar was especially offended by the fact that Stefan became king not by right of birth but by election. Ivan the Terrible inquired: was it right that an ordinary prince, a former subject of the king of Hungary, was elected king by mere mortals? There was no royal blood in Bathory's veins. He was immeasurably lower than real hereditary monarchs like the German emperor, the Turkish sultan and the king of France. And of course he was lower than Ivan the Terrible who was descended, as he believed, from the Roman emperor

Caesar Augustus. Inevitably, the talks failed. Ivan gave orders to make ready for a major campaign to conquer Livonia completely.

THE LAST VICTORY: IVAN THE TERRIBLE'S TRIUMPHANT RAID ON LIVONIA, 1577

The tsar himself headed the campaign. On 8 June 1577 Ivan IV set off from Novgorod the Great and reached Pskov on 15 June. Some problems with allies, with Danish Duke Magnus for one, prevented Russia from beginning the campaign immediately. Denmark was displeased by the policy of Moscow and thought that Russia was a useless partner. Ivan the Terrible in his turn considered Magnus as his subject, vassal, and did not think it necessary to take him into consideration. The duke was summoned to Pskov to a kind of trial in which he barely managed to clear himself of accusations of treason and breach of the tsar's orders.

In fact, there were good reasons for these accusations. In 1576 Magnus conducted secret talks with the Lithuanian 'governor of Livonia', Grzegorz Khodkevich. Lithuania attempted to split the Russian–Danish union and the attempt was successful. Magnus felt he was not getting his fair share from Russia and was humiliated. In Pskov he was made to sign an agreement that considerably reduced Danish possessions in Livonia. Now its centre was the town of Wenden and it stretched a small distance to the north to the Aa river. The Russian government made the mistake of putting excessive pressure on Magnus. Ivan the Terrible virtually made him throw himself into the arms of his enemies. Poland and Lithuania did not miss their chance.

However, Magnus would not commit his betrayal until later in 1577 and for now the Russian and Danish troops were to march across Livonia together. On 13 July, 30,000 troops headed by the tsar and his son, another Ivan, set off for Livonia. They were accompanied by the troops of Simeon Bekbulatovich. At the same time, Magnus' troops invaded the Lithuanian occupation zone of Livonia from the north.

Khodkevich had only 4,000 warriors at his disposal, so all he could do was retreat. Stefan, who in 1577 was besieging rebellious Gdansk, did not give aid. Garrisons in Livonian fortresses numbered tens or, at best, hundreds of men. It was obvious that they would not withstand siege and assault. The fortresses surrendered one after another, their garrisons preferring captivity to certain death. On 16 July, Marienhausen surrendered; the fortress was defended only by twenty-five men. On 24 July, the governor of the fortress of Ludsen, when he saw Muscovite troops nearing the walls, expressed his ardent desire to enter Russian service and gave orders to open the gate. On 27 July the fortress

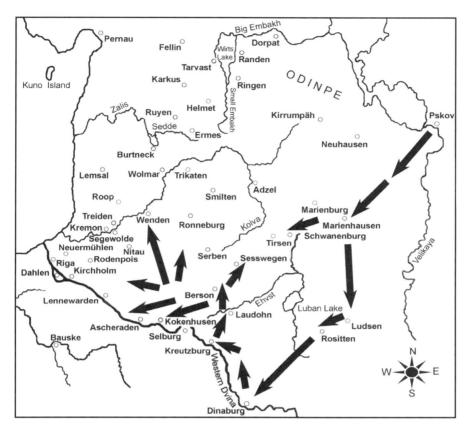

Map 18. The raid by Ivan the Terrible's army in Livonia in 1577

of Rositten fell and Dinaburg capitulated on 9 August. Ivan IV 'graciously' accepted the garrisons of all these fortresses into Russian service.

On 8 August 1577 the governor of Wolmar, Alexander Polubensky, reported to the Polish–Lithuanian Commonwealth about the catastrophic defeat being suffered in Livonia. The castles were unprepared for defence and undermanned; the Livonians and the troops of Kettler, the duke of Courland, were poor fighters. If the royal army did not come to the rescue, Livonia would be captured as Polotsk had been. The royal army did not come. On 12 August the hooves of the Russian tsar's horse trod the banks of the Western Dvina, where the castles of Kreutzburg and Laudohn were captured. Sesswegen surrendered to Russian troops on 20 August, followed closely by Schwanenburg (21 August) and Beran (22 August).

The progress of the Russian and Danish troops in the Baltic was not without its reverses. Seeing that the conquest of Livonia could not be prevented and that Poland and Lithuania had abandoned it to its fate, the Livonians had to choose between surrendering to Russia or Denmark. Naturally, the choice was made in favour of Denmark as the Danes, being brothers in the Protestant faith, were closer in culture and lifestyle. Moreover, Magnus was reputed to be a less bloody ruler than Ivan the Terrible. As a result, the end of August brought Ivan IV, then near Kokenhusen, an unpleasant surprise. He discovered that a number of Livonian towns, Wenden and Kokenhusen among them, had pledged allegiance to Magnus and were now his subjects. Magnus sent a letter saying that it was his valiant troops who had captured eighteen Livonian towns. So these towns became part of the Livonian kingdom of which the Danish prince was the ruler.

This virtual rebellion by Magnus was only half the trouble. There was nothing surprising in the Livonians preferring the Danes to the Russians. What enraged the tsar was that Magnus had stolen his victory with the result that it was Denmark that benefited from the success of the Russian troops in Livonia. Ivan the Terrible replied to Magnus, demanding in the strongest terms that he stick to the Pskov agreement of 1577. If not, the Danish prince should go while the going was good, either to Ösel, which belonged to the Danish crown, or to Copenhagen.[10]

The Livonian citizens who had sworn allegiance to Magnus paid for their trust. A unit led by Peter Tatev took Kokenhusen and carried out a massacre there as punishment for betraying Russia by pledging allegiance to the Danish duke. On 1 September, Wolmar, captured by Bogdan Belsky, suffered the same fate. On 5 September, Wenden fell and mass executions took place here as well. Rheinhold Heidenstein, a contemporary of the events, described the capture of the fortress of Ascheraden, near Wenden, as follows:

> A great number of people of both sexes and of every social class gathered in Ascheraden, especially there were many women and girls; Landmarschall, a man respectable because of his age and high positions he had held, was also present. The Moscow Prince killed each and all capable of carrying arms and the less bellicose sex, women and girls, were passed over to the Tatars to be raped; then he headed for Wenden. The citizens, frightened by rumours of the felonious deed of the Moscow Tsar, locked the gates. Magnus, who came forward to intercede for the citizens, begged humbly for mercy, grovelling at the Tsar's feet, but was scolded by the Tsar who even hit him in the face. Realising that Magnus' influence would not help them as he was in danger himself, and seeing that they were surrounded and deceived by the perfidious enemy, the citizens, affected by anger, fear and despair, placed gunpowder under their homes and this explosion killed a great number of people of both

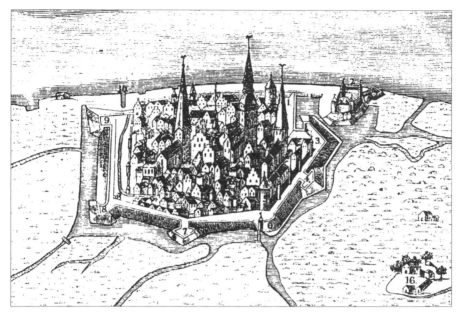

Riga (engraving of 1621)

sexes, of all ages and social classes and all the flower of the Livonian nobility that had remained up to that moment.[11]

Thus, Magnus did not manage to gain control of the majority of Livonian territory, and punitive measures by Russian troops alienated him from the local population. Perhaps it was this misfortune that spurred Magnus to take the side of Stefan Bathory.

The tsar did not know anything about the duke's intentions yet. Ivan the Terrible rejoiced; he now possessed almost all of Livonia to the north of the Western Dvina and the larger part of Estlandia (except Riga, Revel, Swedish and Danish possessions). The campaign of 1577 had achieved complete success.

In autumn 1577 Russia started to suffer defeats, which should have alarmed Ivan the Terrible but he did not take them seriously. In November Lithuanian troops captured Dinaburg and Wenden. Here is the description of these events by Heidenstein:

About that time Dinaburg was returned to the king, recaptured by Boris Sava and Wilhelm Platter. These watchful commanders, observant of minute detail, having noticed that the Moscovite garrison suffered from a shortage of provisions, pretending friendship and military solidarity, sent them some food and drink, including a cask of vodka, the drink favoured by the Moscovites for want of a good wine. When the Moscovites got drunk, the Lithuanians, who foresaw this event, at night leaned ladders against the ramparts, the only protection of the fortress, scaled them, got inside and drove the Moscovites, who barely had gathered their wits after sleep and drinking, out of the fortress and captured it. Some time later Wenden was recaptured in the like manner. Under Matthias Dembinski there was a Latvian carpenter whose sister was among the Russians; using the freedom of passage granted to peasants he often came to Wenden under the pretext of visiting his sister. Once, seizing an opportunity, he made a wax imprint of the keys to the town, made duplicate keys and gave them to Dembinski. At a prearranged time, when the Moscovites celebrated by the town gate, Dembinski approached with his hastily gathered unit and, when on one side ladders were lent to the wall and on the other side Latvians that were in Wenden came running, one of them opened the gate and let the Poles in.[12]

RUSSIAN OBSTINACY AGAINST POLISH PRIDE: THE DIPLOMATIC STRUGGLE BETWEEN RUSSIA AND RZECZPOSPOLITA IN THE 1570S

Ivan the Terrible hoped that Stefan, who had a lot of internal problems, would sue for peace. And it looked like his hopes were about to come true. On 1 January 1578 a huge Lithuanian delegation, 470 men with 528 horses, set out from Orsha, headed by Stanislaw Kryski. The talks began as soon as the ambassadors arrived in Moscow, on 16 January.

There were difficulties right from the start. Russian diplomats made very scornful comments about the new Polish king. Stefan Bathory was of humble birth, he stood in dubious relations with the Turks and he had become king not by right of birth but by election. So Stefan had to remember his inferior status and gladly accept Ivan IV's will. It was not becoming for Ivan the Terrible to deal with Stefan personally, because of the difference in rank, but the Russian tsar was ready to condescend and agree to begin talks for the sake of peace among Christians. The Lithuanian diplomats wanted to make an objection to such impolite words. They argued that all Christendom liked Stefan Bathory, that he fought for the true faith in battles with Muslims, that his ancestors were valiant people widely known for their virtues. The king was not at all a pretender; he occupied the throne by God's will, having been chosen by the people. The ambassadors soon realised that their arguments were ignored.

Credit should be given to Stanislaw Kryski who assumed a constructive position. He said that the fundamental questions of relations between countries and peoples were issues for discussion by special delegations. Whereas his aim was only to conclude a truce and nothing more. The Lithuanians tried to put through a variant of the peace agreement of 1561, with pre-war borders. In answer, Russia demanded the Livonian territory up to the Western Dvina and Polotsk with surrounding lands. Finally, it was decided to discuss the division of the Baltic region at special talks at the end of which 'eternal peace' was to be concluded. Meanwhile only a truce of three to five years' duration could be at issue. It was not necessary to discuss redivision of land, it was enough to affirm the status quo. On 30 January 1578 this truce agreement was signed.

The Russian tsar thought events were developing after the scenario of the early sixteenth century when Russia captured one town after another from the Grand Duchy of Lithuania then achieved a truce guaranteeing the status quo. After ten years or so it was difficult for the Lithuanians to get the rus-sified towns back from Russia; that is how Novgorod-Seversky, Smolensk and others had become Russian forever. The same policy was being pursued in regard to Polotsk and the eastern part of Livonia; the Lithuanians had concluded a truce in 1570; now, in 1578, it was extended. Events seemed to be unfolding in favour of Ivan the Terrible.

The tsar did not realise that the international situation had changed dramatically by the late sixteenth century. So the truce signed in January 1578 in Moscow was doomed. The Lithuanian ambassadors had played a cunning trick. The Russian and the Lithuanian versions of the agreement turned out to be different. The Russian version contained a paragraph about the 'non-invasion' of Stefan into Livonia and Courland and about the right of Ivan IV to Riga, Kokenhusen and Dinaburg. Thus the Russian version of the truce agreement of 1578 annulled the First and the Second Vilno Pacts according to which Livonia and Courland passed over to the GDL. Meanwhile, the Livonian ambassadors, in their version of the document, did not mention Livonia at all. The document of the agreement contained only the description of the borders between Russia and Lithuania according to which Polotsk, for the time being and until the truce expired, remained Russian. As a result, each negotiating party had different knowledge of the results of Kryski's mission. Ivan the Terrible thought he was the winner; he had reached an agreement with the Polish–Lithuanian Commonwealth which recognised his conquest of the lands of Polotsk and Livonia. Stefan, on the other hand, received from Kryski a quite passable document which put off returning Polotsk till some time in the future and did not mention Livonia at all. Therefore all Russian conquests in the Baltic region turned out to be illegitimate.[13]

It was not without reason that Stefan even hurried the Russian tsar to ratify this surprisingly favourable truce agreement. On 12 March the Lithuanian messenger, Peter Garaburda, received a document that he was to deliver to Russia reminding Ivan that Stefan was ready to accept Russian ambassadors for the ratification of the agreement. On 30 April 1578 a diplomatic mission headed by Mikhail Karpov and Peter Golovin set off for Vilno to ratify the agreement. The diplomats received no new instructions regarding Livonia, but had orders not to start arguments over the tricky questions (the tsar's title and form of address) but only ratify the Russian version of the agreement, that was thought to be the only true one.

The delegation of Karpov and Golovin was a complete failure.[14] While it was on its way to Lithuania, the political situation changed. Whereas in March 1578 Stefan sought peace, in April he started preparations for a campaign against Russia; the three-month session of the Warsaw *sejm* (January–March 1578), which made the decision to start war against Russia and recapture Polotsk and Livonia, was over. Karpov and Golovin arrived in Lithuania on 2 June 1578. The diplomats had to spend more than six months traipsing round different towns, Slonim, Lviv and others. The ambassadors wanted to meet Stefan but when they arrived in a town they would be told that the king had just left but was sure to meet them in the next town. On 4 September, while in Lublin, Karpov died. In correspondence between Polish noblemen there is a comment: 'One of the Moscow ambassadors died in Lublin, I wish it had been the Moscow Prince'. On 10 November 1578 the ambassadors woke up to the boom of a gun salute. When they asked what the cause for celebration was, they received the reply: 'We've beaten the Russians near Wenden and now are giving praise to God.'

During the course of the year the Russians had suffered repeated defeats at Wenden. The Russian attack on Wenden was conceived as a response to the loss of this town and Dinaburg in November 1577. In February 1578 the Russians made their first assault. For weeks the troops remained at the fortress walls, achieved no results and retreated. On 27 June the troops again set off for Wenden but for unknown reasons (the documents say 'the *voevodes* have been delayed') never reached their destination. In October a third siege of Wenden took place, lasting just five days. At first the Russians had some luck and their artillery breached the wall. But then large bodies of troops came to relieve the garrison: the Lithuanians under Andrzey Sapieha, the Poles under Matthias Dembinski, the Livonians under Nikolay Korff and the Swedes under Georg Boye. The relieving forces made a successful cavalry charge and the Russian troops wavered, the Tatars being first to flee. The Russians retreated into their camp, which was stormed and taken the next morning. The Russians lost more than thirty guns and several high-ranking commanders.

The diplomats in Moscow refused to believe reports of the debacle at Wenden. They were amazed; there was truce between Russia and the Polish–Lithuanian Commonwealth so the battle could not have happened! But they were presented with inflated reports of the losses suffered by Ivan the

Terrible's army: 60,000 Tatars, 4,000 *streltsy*, 12,000 auxiliary troops. The actual losses were smaller, but the fact remained that the Russian army had not been defeated so utterly by the Lithuanians since the battle of the Ula.

Soon after the failed talks the Russian ambassadors were expelled first from Krakow and then from the territory of the Polish–Lithuanian Commonwealth. King Stefan refused to ratify the agreement concluded by ambassador Stanislaw Kryski. On 15 July 1579 the Russian diplomats returned home. Their mission, which had lasted more than a year, had failed.

The failure of Karpov and Golovin's diplomatic mission was not the worst trouble. This failure might have been foreseen, for the diplomats were too late even before they crossed the border of the Polish–Lithuanian Commonwealth. On 5 May 1578, Peter Garaburda, messenger of Stefan Bathory, crossed the Russian border carrying a letter with new claims from the Polish king. Nevertheless, on 16 May the delegation of Karpov and Golovin set out for Rzeczpospolita. From 10 May to 25 August, Garaburda was delayed in various Russian towns. As it happened, while Karpov and Golovin followed King Stefan all over Lithuania and Poland in a vain attempt to get an audience, Garaburda moved from town to town and waited to be called to the tsar's palace in Moscow.

It was not until 31 August 1578 that Peter Garaburda was received by Ivan IV, in the town of Alexandrov (Alexandrovskaya Sloboda). Garaburda boldly read out Stefan's letter of 20 March that he had carried all this time. The letter said that the truce was impossible until the Livonian dispute had been settled. To this end Krakow and Vilno waited for a Russian delegation that was to negotiate on the territory of Rzeczpospolita, and the terms of surrendering the Livonian lands captured by Russia. This amounted to a demand for capitulation. If the tsar, instead of delaying Garaburda, had displayed an interest in the letter he was carrying, Karpov and Golovin would not have been sent on their pointless mission. When the Russian ambassadors crossed the Russian–Lithuanian border they were ignorant of the fact that King Stefan had already made up his mind to quarrel with Russia.

The reaction of Ivan IV was rather unusual; he ignored Stefan's ultimatum. Garaburda was kept in diplomatic quarters for six months and only on 22 December was the decision made to let him return to Lithuania. On 11 January 1579 the Lithuanian diplomat was handed a document that contained an invitation for new ambassadors from Rzeczpospolita to come to Russia and conclude the peace agreement! In the covering letter addressed to Bathory, Ivan the Terrible expressed his outrage (when a year had passed) and bewilderment at the claims of the Polish king. The tsar had concluded peace with ambassador Stanislaw Kryski and confirmed the documents by kissing the cross, so Garaburda's mission was out of place. Let regular ambassadors come and they could talk everything over; and as a sign of Ivan's goodwill he included a writ of protection that would guarantee free passage to the new delegation. By this time Moscow had still not heard anything from Golovin's mission.

On 9 June 1579, Filon Kmita reported from Orsha that a messenger, Wenclaw Lopatinski, was carrying an important statement from the Polish king. Ivan IV decided that it was expedient to make the diplomat arrive later and Lopatinski was detained in Dorogobuzh. Ivan the Terrible was waiting to hear from Golovin's delegation, lost somewhere in Rzeczpospolita. The lesson of the Garaburda incident had been learnt though. A nobleman, Baim Voyeykov, and a clergyman, Ivan Streshnev, were commanded to coax Stefan's letter out of Lopatinski, who was under arrest in Dorogobuzh, and pass it to Moscow. Lopatinsky at first refused to give up the documents, saying that he was to deliver them personally, but ceased to be stubborn when he was told that he would never leave Russia unless he gave up Stefan's letter.

The content of Bathory's letter was extremely unpleasant. He refused to observe the truce and declared that he would do what a Christian ruler should. It was virtually a declaration of war.

7

The Military Disaster of Ivan the Terrible

THE WAR AGAINST STEFAN BATHORY ('MOSCOW WAR'), 1579–1781
Bathory's preparations for war were in full swing. In June 1577 a special tax for defence of the borders against the Muscovites and Tatars was introduced. Those who were to take part in the 'Moscow War', as the new campaign was called at Polish court, were granted financial privileges by special decree of Bathory as early as 1577. Stefan laid emphasis on mercenary troops rather than armed *szlachta* of the *pospolite ruszenie* that had no obvious advantage over the Russian noble cavalry. So Bathory decided to call professional soldiers to his colours. Christopher Rozrazhevsky and Ernst Weyer were sent to the German lands to hire soldiers. In addition, Stefan's brother Christopher, prince of Transylvania, sent the king several Hungarian infantry and cavalry units. As it turned out later, the Polish king had made the right decision: the mercenary army proved much stronger than the Muscovite troops of armed noblemen. This was the main factor that determined the Russian defeats in 1579–81.

Bathory decided to direct his first attack at Polotsk as this fortress blocked the way to Livonia and Pskov. By capturing Polotsk, Bathory could take control of a large stretch of the Western Dvina, which would give the opportunity to transport troops and supplies to Livonia more quickly and with less expense by water. Moreover, the loss of Polotsk in 1563 was the heaviest defeat the Grand Duchy of Lithuania (GDL) suffered in the second half of the sixteenth century, so the recapture of this town was sure to give a huge boost to morale and earn the king undying fame.

On 30 June 1579, 40,000 royal troops began their march to Russia. The armed noblemen of the GDL, led by crown *hetman* Mikolaj Radzivill, constituted the core of the army. His son Krzysztof commanded troops of mercenary infantry (*zholners*); Polish knights were led by Mikolaj Mielecki, the *voevode* of Podolia; and Christopher Rozrazhevsky led German mercenaries. Near Polotsk they were joined by Prussian infantry and cavalry from Podolia.

Russia did not expect Bathory's advance. The Russian army was, by the tsar's order, preparing for a campaign to the far side of the Western Dvina, in Courland. On 7 July *voevodes* Dmitry Khilkov and Mikhail Beznin crossed the Western Dvina and made a reconnaissance in force. They pushed through a cordon of 150 Courland warriors, crossed the river at Kokenhusen, raided the nearby territory and devastated the lands of Selburg. They might have continued their raid, as all battle-worthy Lithuanian troops had left Livonia with their commander, Krzysztof Radzivill, to take part in the Polotsk campaign. But, as troops started to be manoeuvred towards Polotsk to fend off Bathory, Khilkov and Beznin received an order to return quickly and could not exploit their success.

The Russian reinforcements came too late. On 1 August, units led by Feydor Sheremetyev, Peter Sheydyakov and Feydor Mstislavsky set off from the area around Pskov to relieve Polotsk. As they reached the line formed by the towns Nevel, Ostrov and Sokol, their cavalry clashed with troops led by Krzysztof Radzivill and Jan Hlebowicz. The Russians stopped and took up a defensive position. The Russian commanders were afraid of running into superior enemy forces and did not press on to relieve Polotsk, instead restricting themselves to sending small parties to disrupt the enemy's communications and attack their supply trains. Meanwhile, the Lithuanians took Kozyan (on 28 July), Krasny (31 July) and Sitna (4 August). These were forts in the Polotsk area and Bathory's army soon had Polotsk hemmed in on three sides.

The town was besieged according to all the rules of the military art. Bathory's troops built entrenchments and started to bring siege weapons closer to the town walls. At the same time mines were dug under towers. It was planned to fill the mines with explosive and blow the fortifications up, defenders and all. The town was under constant artillery bombardment. Since ordinary cannonballs bounced off the oak stockade, the Hungarians used heated shot. As described earlier, the balls were heated in fires and wrapped in wet grass to prevent them igniting the powder charge prematurely, but these also proved of little use on this occasion.

The heated shot having failed, the king called for volunteers to set the walls on fire with torches. A number of units were formed of the volunteers but almost all of them were killed as they came under fire from bows, cannons and arquebuses as they tried to reach the walls. Moreover, the defenders dropped huge logs from the walls that rolled down the slope and smashed anyone in their path. All the people of Polotsk, including women and children, extinguished fires and brought boiling water to the top of the walls to be rained down on their attackers. Some brave people were lowered on ropes outside the wall and hung there, under enemy gunfire, quenching with water

Polotsk (Polish engraving, 1570s)

The siege of Polotsk in 1579 (Polish engraving)

those torches thrown at the bottom of the wall. The weather was on the side of the defenders, continuous rains soaking the wood so Bathory's troops could not burn Polotsk.

The rain also made life very uncomfortable for Bathory's troops as they camped in the open field. Rheinhold Heidenstein's contemporary account gave the following description of the situation:

> Because of heavy continuous rains the roads became impassable to the extent that pack horses, stuck in mud and not being able to get out, mostly died of starvation, and all the roads were covered by dead horses. The rains soaked the soil so much, rich and moist as it is, and drenched everything else, that even under the skin tents of magnates there was no place to lie down. The consequence was that the price of supplies, hay especially, rose extremely; the fact unheard of, especially in Poland, a measure of oats was bought for

10 thalers, so it was fed only to nobler horses; on the other hand, there were those among the Poles and Hungarians who had no scruples against eating the meat of the dead horses themselves; and this new and unusual food was not as amazing as the fact that those who ate it did not notice that it caused them any illness. In this predicament the Germans suffered most because they were accustomed to make war in lands with many towns.[1]

None of the almost-incessant assaults that went on from 11 to 29 August had any success. Hungarian and German mercenaries and Polish infantry proved the best fighters. At the same time, these troops could poorly withstand the bad weather and the shortage of supplies, so the king feared that they might refuse to fight. The Lithuanian noble troops, even with the support of the Polish troops, would hardly be enough to take Polotsk. Bathory had to choose between a retreat and a decisive assault. He chose assault.

On 29 August, during a dry spell, the besieging troops managed to set the wall on fire in several places. The defenders fought the fires all day but could not prevent heavy damage to the fortifications. There was unrest in the town; there were those who thought it was time to surrender. Ten people scaled down the walls using ropes and ran towards the besiegers. Unfortunately for them they happened to reach the Hungarians. The Hungarians had decided not to take prisoners because a voluntary surrender would have denied them the chance to pillage the town without restraint and thus reward themselves for suffering and losses incurred during the assault. So the Hungarians killed the defectors. Heidenstein explained their motives:

> The rumour of ancient treasures of this famous town, and especially those kept in the Church of St Sophia, of silver statues, rich gifts of princes of Old Russia, that, as people said, were kept there, raised the soldiers' hopes for big booty; inspired by hope, they calmly endured adversities in order to take the fortress.[2]

In the evening the Poles and Hungarians attempted to enter the town through the breach where part of the wall had burned down. But the defenders had dug a ditch on the inside of the wall, right in front of the breach, and mounted artillery there. The attackers were met by gunfire and fled back. The king and his retainers, Chancellor Jan Zamojski and the commander of the Polish army, Mikolaj Mielecki, personally brought troops up to the walls to cover the retreat of the attackers and prevent the town's garrison from making a sortie. Bathory displayed remarkable courage as he commanded troops while under fire from the walls and towers of Polotsk.

On 30 August the Hungarians managed to capture and burn down a tower near the breach. Taking the opportunity presented by a whole stretch of the wall being damaged and without protection, Bathory's soldiers succeeded in bringing the siege fortifications as far as the moat. This made the fortress extremely vulnerable. As a result there was dissent among the besieged. The soldiers decided to end all resistance and surrender the town whereas Bishop Cyprian and the *voevodes* insisted on fighting to the end. Cyprian even commanded that fire be set to the powder magazine so that the garrison would die rather than surrender, but the ordinary soldiers prevented the explosion. Cyprian and his supporters locked themselves up in the Church of St Sophia and refused to come out.

Polotsk capitulated on 1 September 1579. The Russians ended their resistance on condition that they could either go to Russia or enter the king's service. As many as 6,000 people surrendered. On entering the town, Bathory's troops were disappointed. There was not the rich loot they had hoped for. There were only dead bodies, damaged cannon, abandoned ammunition, scorched earth, crows and empty houses. The most valuable thing in Polotsk was a big library, but the mercenaries ignored it. Disgruntled soldiers gave vent to their displeasure, which resulted in quarrels. Mass brawls began among the Poles and Hungarians when dividing the meagre spoils. The king was able to stop this disgrace only after he handed out rich presents from his own funds.

The capture of Polotsk was not the end of Bathory's campaign. Lithuanian Cossacks burned castles along the Western Dvina to within 7 km of the Ula. There were attacks on the Russian fortresses of Sokol, Nisha, Turovlya. The largest battle took place near Sokol, where Mikolaj Mielecki and Mikolaj and Krzysztof Radzivill stopped the picked troops of Russian noblemen, Don Cossacks and *streltsy* under the command of Feydor Sheremetyev, Andrey Paletsky and Vasily Krivoborsky. These troops were marching to recapture Polotsk but could not break through Bathory's battle lines and turned back.

The tactics of the army of the Polish–Lithuanian Commonwealth were simple: they set castles on fire and then destroyed the fleeing garrisons. On 4 September the fortress of Turovlya fell. On 25 September Sokol was taken by assault. The Muscovites had surrounded Sokol with earthworks and the battle took place mainly in these trenches. In the battles near the walls of Sokol and Turovlya more than 4,000 Russians died, among them Boris Shein, Andrey Paletsky, Mikhail Lykov and Vasily Krivoborsky. The German mercenaries, who were carried away by massacring civilians and did not see that they were cut off from the main body of troops, were surrounded and suffered heavy casualties, including more than 500 killed.

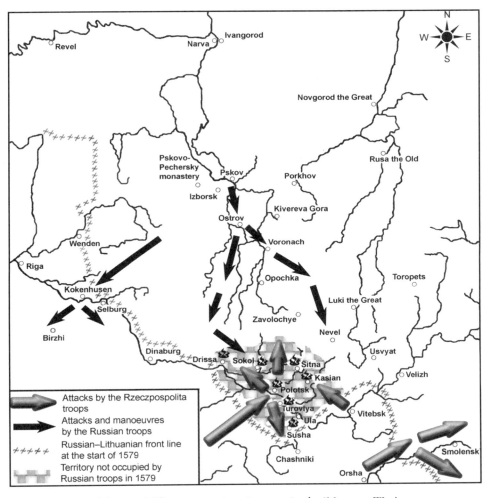

Map 19. Military operations in 1579 in the 'Moscow War'

On 6 October the *voevode* of Polotsk, Mikolaj Dorogostajski-Monivid, took Susha. The town surrendered voluntarily and its garrison of 6,000 men was allowed to leave carrying arms. At the same time the head of Orsha, Filon Kmita, commanding Lithuanian knights and Cossacks, devastated the territory around Smolensk, burned down hundreds of small villages and the suburbs of Smolensk, and drove away a lot of cattle. Konstantin Ostrozhsky and Mikhail Vishnevetsky crossed the Dnieper, besieged Chernigov and burned it down.

The Polish–Lithuanian Commonwealth rejoiced. The new king brought them glory by defeating the arch enemy, the Muscovites. Polish poets and writers competed with each other in praising their beloved monarch. Jan Yanushevsky created a panegyric on the capture of Polotsk by King Stefan. He extolled the Polish victory as the greatest triumph in history. The over-enthusiastic author wrote that the king had 'tamed the furious Bucephalus', 'managed to navigate his ship between Scylla and Charybdis and bring her into port'. Stefan was like Alexander the Great, Caesar and Charlemagne put together. Thus the Polotsk victory of 1579 was equated with the great feats of antiquity and the Middle Ages.

In Russia, spirits were low after the loss of the city. What disconcerted most was the fact that some troops surrendered without a fight. Ivan the Terrible found a handy explanation for all his military defeats: traitors. The tsar's mistrust and suspicion sharply increased. He was convinced that Polotsk might have continued its defence had it not been surrendered by traitors. The slow advance of the Russian relief army had been caused by a conflict between the tsar and one of the *voevodes*; when Prince Ivan Mstislavsky suggested moving faster, Ivan the Terrible accused him of treason, and said that the duke wanted to lure the troops into a trap. The tsar shouted at the *voevode*: 'You, old dog, are still full of the Lithuanian spirit' (the ancestors of Mstislavsky came from Lithuania). Ivan the Terrible beat the military commander who wanted to save Polotsk with a stick in front of the boyars.

Apart from the misfortunes at Polotsk, Russia had new problems in the Baltic region. The Swedes took the opportunity to boost their activity. On 18 July the Swedish fleet attacked Narva and Ivangorod and set the suburbs ablaze with gunfire. On 27 September troops under Heinrich Horn besieged Narva. The siege lasted two weeks and was raised only when troops led by Dmitry Khilkov came to relieve the fortress.

Ivan the Terrible attempted to make up tactically what he had lost strategically. The tsar moved his troops into Lithuania, looting and terrorising civilians. In autumn 1579, *voevodes* Vasiliy Khilkov and Mikhail Beznin went into Lithuania from Pskov. Troops under Ivan Fustov raided Livonia and Courland. A Russian chronicler reported that the troops went as far as Vilna, but it must have been an exaggeration. In autumn 1579 there were only local engagements and the main scene of military activity was around the borders between the lands of Polotsk and Pskov.

Thanks to the efforts of Stefan Bathory and Chancellor Jan Zamojski, by spring 1580 Rzeczpospolita had reformed and strengthened its army. The most efficient units were, as before, the Hungarian infantry. Their numbers had been severely depleted at Polotsk but, on Zamojski's initiative, new troops were levied and the number of Hungarian units considerably increased. These units were to act together with mercenary mounted troops commanded by

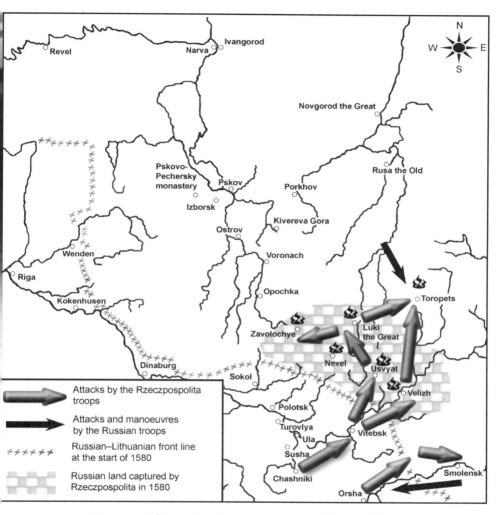

Map 20. Military operations in 1580 in the 'Moscow War'

Jürgen Fahrensbach. Moreover, this time the pick of the Rzeczpospolita cavalry fought under the colours of King Stefan. The main components of these troops were armoured Polish hussars and the lighter cavalry consisting of Lithuanian Cossacks carrying carbines and pistols. In 1580 Rzeczpospolita invaded Russia.

The first fortress to be besieged was Velizh. A peculiar incident happened before its walls. Polish and Lithuanian commanders argued about whose troops were to take the fortress. The dispute was settled only when Jan Zamojski led the troops towards the fortress himself. The march was difficult:

a 12 km path had to be cut in the forest to allow passage for cavalry and artillery. The defenders of the fortress surrounded it with abatis (*zasyekas*), barricades of felled trees, as Heidenstein described:

> [the Russians] hacked trees under one side, felled them on the other side, entangled the tree trunks and felled more trees on top and so surrounded themselves by *zasyekas* thousands of paces long and more secure than any wall; the sunlight barely penetrated into the forest and even during the day it aroused in those who entered it fear like during the night.[3]

Zamojski sent infantry to cut passages through the abatis, while Lithuanian Cossacks were sent to the enemy's rear. The Cossacks were to cross the Western Dvina river and cut the road between Velizh and Luki the Great. Because of the abatis, it was no surprise attack. The Russians, knowing about the approach of the enemy, burned the suburbs of Velizh and sheltered the civilian population behind the fortress walls.

The leading part in storming Velizh was played by the Hungarian infantry under Johann Bornemissza and the Polish units under Nikolay Urovetsky. In a few days they built siege fortifications and started bombarding the fortress, the Hungarians shooting heated shot. As it happened, a technical trick of the defenders of the fortress turned against them. They had covered the stockade with turf so that the heated balls would not set the wooden wall on fire. But it turned out that cannonballs penetrated the layer of turf and split into small shards which were impossible to extract from the wood. Thus, the effect of the heated balls was enhanced. When two of the towers started burning, the defenders decided to surrender as it became clear that further resistance was useless. On 6 August, Velizh fell.

In his letter, which he sent to Ivan the Terrible early in August 1580, Bathory declared Novgorod the Great, Pskov, Smolensk, Novgorod-Seversky, Luki the Great and Livonia to be lands that originally belonged to the Grand Duchy of Lithuania. Actions of the troops of Rzeczpospolita on this territory could not, therefore, be considered as aggression, war or breach of the truce since the Polish and Lithuanian troops simply marched through their own lands. The king called himself a 'protector of the peace of Christendom' and Ivan the Terrible its disrupter.

On 15 August, a second fortress on the way to Luki the Great, the fortress of Usvyat, was besieged. The siege was conducted by the Lithuanian unit under Yury Sokolinsky and the ubiquitous Hungarian infantry. The siege was not long; the fortress surrendered on the following day, 16 August.

On 26 August, the whole army of King Stefan Bathory approached the walls of Luki the Great, the key Russian fortress on the western border. The

Leaflet declaring King Stefan's challenge to the Muscovy tyrant (1580). Polish
propaganda focused its attention on the confrontation between King Stefan and
Ivan the Terrible. It represented the Polish monarch as protector of the cultural and
spiritual values of Christendom. Through such leaflets aimed at the Russian people,
the Polish king promoted the idea of freedom, democracy (in its medieval form) and
the triumph of Polish Crown over the barbaric despotism of Ivan the Terrible's rule

citizens burned the suburb, although it was protected, and took cover in
the castle. Green shaggy towers and walls stood on the high hill before the
invaders; all the defences of Luki the Great were covered by turf after the
pattern of Velizh.

Meanwhile, on 14 August 1580, a high-ranking Russian delegation headed by Ivan Sitsky, Roman Pivov and clergyman Druzhina Petelin crossed the Lithuanian border. It headed through the front line area towards Luki the Great, where the king promised to receive the diplomats. The diplomats, who had to make their way through enemy troops, had a nightmarish feeling and a sensation of approaching disaster. Once they had to let a unit from Podolia pass, and, when the diplomats moved through the royal guard regiment, *haiduks* started to shoot from their arquebuses and wadding fell on the ambassadors. The Muscovites got into a jam on the road, became mixed up among the troops and only got out of the aggressive mob with difficulty. When the diplomats complained about the lack of respect shown for their diplomatic status, they were told that they might, if they wanted, cut a road for themselves through the wood parallel to the road used by the royal troops.

At their first royal audience, on 29 August, the Russian diplomats bravely declared that the king was to return to his land and humbly wait there for the arrival of diplomats from Moscow. The only reaction to this statement was sardonic smiles. The ambassadors were sent back to their diplomatic quarters where they spent several days waiting for the invitation to another audience. On 1 September, before the very eyes of the shocked diplomats, the bombardment of Luki the Great began.

Sitsky attempted to stop the assault. He refused to resume talks until the military action was stopped. But the Poles and Lithuanians were carried away by their success and either mocked or ignored his refusal, for the Russians were doomed, or so they thought. Seeing that his *démarche* had no effect, on 3 September Duke Sitsky said that he was ready to resume talks. His subsequent behaviour, however, was strange. It demonstrates the extent to which a Russian diplomat's freedom to take decisions was restricted by instructions that often became obsolete before he even reached his destination. The Muscovite diplomats, with the boom of cannon bombarding Luki the Great in the background, demanded the return of Polotsk and other Russian towns captured by Bathory and the withdrawal of Polish and Lithuanian troops from Livonia and Courland. In exchange, Russia offered a number of fortresses in Livonia. The king refused to negotiate these terms and the further talks were delegated to Lithuanian noblemen. They said that the aim of the war was the return of all the lands lost by Rzeczpospolita and the revision of borders in eastern Europe. Sitsky flatly refused to discuss the issue.[4] As the diplomatic efforts failed, it was the turn of guns to have their say.

What did the capture of Luki the Great look like? It began with clashes near the fortress walls. The German mercenaries intercepted a Russian unit that ventured outside the fortress. The Hungarians were ambushed by Russian troops and their commander, Johann Bornemissza, barely managed to escape half naked. The Russians grabbed him by his clothes but he dropped off part of them and fled.

Voevodes Fyodor Lyko-Obolensky, Mikhail Kashin and Ivan Voyeykov were in charge of the defence of the town. A unit under the command of Dmitry Khilkov and Dementy Cheremisin was ready to advance from the direction of Toropets to relieve the besieged town. The besieged defended actively and made frequent sorties. Meanwhile the siege fortification on all sides of the town had been erected and the guns had been mounted.

The artillery duel demonstrated that the defenders had been right: the thick layer of turf made cannonballs absolutely ineffective (in Velizh the turf layer cannot have been thick enough). So Bathory's gunners aimed at the embrasures of the towers. Two turrets were set on fire but the wet turf prevented the fire from spreading and it soon went out. Seeing the fire, the Hungarians started an assault but were stopped by the Russian sortie. Having suffered losses, both the Hungarians and Russians returned to their positions.

During the night the attackers undermined a tower and in the morning detonated the powder charge. The tower itself withstood the explosion but the turf protection fell off. All day the Poles and Hungarians attempted to set the tower and the walls next to it on fire, and also to kill as many as possible of the defenders who bravely extinguished the fire. This took up the whole of the second day of the siege.

Early on the third day it became clear that Bathory's cannon were getting the upper hand; many Russian guns were damaged and the attackers were able to approach the walls. Now the state of the turf was to the attacker's advantage as it allowed the walls to be climbed, using spades and hooks, much more easily. Even so, the assault of the Hungarian infantry was repelled and the attackers suffered heavy losses. The next day Polish soldiers managed to get to the bottom of the wall, clear part of it of turf and build a huge fire out of resinous wood. The tower would not catch fire but filled with acrid smoke, forcing the defenders to leave it.

Zamojski invited the besieged to negotiate terms of surrender. The garrison readily sent their envoys because talks meant a respite from battle. What happened on the night of 5/6 September is unclear. Heidenstein related that towards dawn, when the king had approached the walls for the decisive talks, a large crowd of camp followers, who had not taken part in the assaults, scaled the wall to pillage the town. At the same time, the Hungarians made a violent charge and entered the town. Heidenstein, attempting to justify this treachery, related that the Hungarians were outraged by the marauders and hurried to capture the town before it was looted by those who had not taken part in the siege. But then the outrage of the Hungarians was directed on the citizens rather than the camp followers. The mercenaries did not stop the marauders; as soon as they were in the town they started massacring the citizens.

Stefan let the town be plundered. For several hours the troops were allowed to do whatever they wanted, plundering and raping at will. The army of the 'most beautiful civilisation in Europe', as the Poles called their Rzeczpospolita, massacred more than 7,000 civilians, including women and children. Contemporaries reported that human blood running in rivers along the streets covered the hooves of the Polish cavalry marching through the town. An end was brought to the sacking in a most unpleasant way for the soldiers, as fires that had been started caused the powder magazines to explode. Thus a measure of justice was done, with many Polish marauders being killed by the explosions.

Once Luki the Great was captured, Bathory sent several units to conduct a reconnaissance in force near Toropets, where Khilkov stood with his troops. Again mercenaries were sent to fight: the Hungarian cavalry under Georgy Barbely, the Germans under Jürgen Fahrensbach and the Polish cavalry under Jan Zbarazhsky. As the enemy advanced, the Russians started to retreat to Toropets, leaving behind small parties of 1,000–4,000 warriors to hinder the enemy's advance. The retreat very soon turned into a flight, especially after a large Russian unit was defeated near the town. The citizens of Toropets burned the suburbs and prepared to withstand a siege.

Meanwhile Filon Kmita attempted a repeat of the raid he had made at Smolensk but was beaten, abandoned his artillery, killed the Russian captives he had taken in previous battles and hurriedly retreated to Orsha. Meanwhile, Dnieper Cossacks under Ivan Orishovsky attacked the outskirts of Starodub and devastated them.

Bathory's next target was Nevel. It was already besieged by Lithuanian troops under Mikolaj Dorogostaysky, though so far without success. Bathory sent the Hungarians under Bornemissza to Nevel and planned to set off for that town himself on 30 September 1580. But the town fell before the king had time to break camp. The Hungarian soldiers again proved their worthiness. They employed the same trick of mining the walls and igniting the fortifications by torches and building fires. It was enough to make the besieged surrender.

After Nevel it was the turn of Ozerishche and Zavolochye. Ozerishche, situated 50 km from Nevel, offered no resistance and voluntarily surrendered as soon as the enemy troops approached. The garrison of Zavolochye, the

Warhaffte vnd gründ-
liche Zeitung / Welcher maffen die Kön:
May zu Poln etc. bewogen den Krieg kegen dem
Erbfeind dem Moscowiter vorzunemen/ Wie sie kegen
demselben hiebeuor wie auch in diesem jegtlauffenden
1580 Jare im monat Augusto gesieget / vnd
was ferner dabey zu hoffen vnd zuuers-
mutten.

Getruckt zu Dantzigk / durch Jacobum Rhodum.
M. D. LXXX.

This leaflet on the capture of Luki the Great (1580) describes the famous victory of the Polish–Lithuanian army over the old Russian town. It elaborately praises King Stefan as the protector and saviour of Christendom against the Moscovites

fortress that stood on an island, hoped to withstand the siege by sitting it out behind the walls. The Russians did not even respond to the enemy's shots. The fortress towered above the water and was silent. The only sign of its

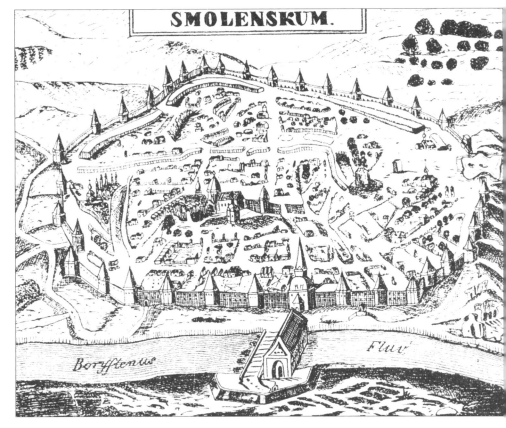

Smolensk (engraving of 1627)

determination not to give up was the execution of two captured foragers. The Russians killed them on the wall before the Lithuanian army and threw the bodies down.

The walls of Zavolochye were only coated with clay and had no turf covering. The clay could help against incendiary arrows and torches but it was no protection against cannonballs. Zamojsky positioned his troops on a nearby island. Nikolay Urovetsky with his men built a raft big enough to transport a large unit to the fortress walls. Zamojski told the soldiers to collect all the wool in the camp (mainly from horse cloths), fill bags with it and attach the bags to wooden poles. Specially assigned men were to carry these poles with bags in front of the attacking Lithuanian unit. As soon as Zamojski's soldiers were at the walls they would be out of reach of the Russian guns, which did not cover the bottom of the walls. Russian arquebuses might become deadly at close range but the wool bags, in which the bullets would lodge, should protect the soldiers from serious harm.

The assault failed. Only part of the Lithuanian unit had time to board the raft before the soldiers who held the ropes dropped them and fled for cover as the Russians started shooting. The defenders destroyed those who remained on the raft and tried to capture it, but the current carried it to the shore, where the attackers picked it up again. It was only with difficulty that Zamojsky managed to convince the soldiers to repeat the attack as the Lithuanians, demoralised by the death of their comrades, refused to step on the raft. Nikolay Urovetsky saved the situation when he bravely brought the raft close to the walls, landed and fortified his position on the island. Meanwhile the Hungarians attacked the fortress over the bridge they had constructed and were halted only by the palisade itself. At this moment the besieged made a sortie and cut down the attackers with poleaxes. Again, the assault failed.

Bathory sent a reinforcement of 900 Polish horsemen and 1,000 Hungarian infantry. Zamojski took a large boat from the local monks who used it to drop fishing nets and ordered the sides to be made higher and covered with untreated ox hides. The result was a vessel capable of carrying about eighty men. The storming party was picked from the best Polish noblemen who dismounted from their horses, the Germans and the Hungarians. The fortress was attacked simultaneously from the raft, from the converted boat and a number of small boats. Zavolochye fell, its garrison surrendered. Bathory's campaign against Luki the Great was over.

'HOW WE SHOULD FINISH THE WAR?': DIPLOMATIC DISPUTES BETWEEN RUSSIA AND RZECZPOSPOLITA IN 1581

The war, however, was not over for Russia; in the Baltic region and in Karelia the Swedes pressed their advance. In November 1580 the fortress of Karela, the main Russian fortress in Karelia, was taken by troops under Pontus Delagardi. During the assault and the massacre that followed, 2,000 Russians were killed. In northern Estlandia the Swedes besieged the fortress of Padis. The besieged, suffering from starvation, ate all their horses, dogs, cats, hay, straw, skins; there were even some who secretly tasted human flesh. In December 1580 the exhausted garrison could not withstand the second assault and surrendered.

The beginning of 1581 was marked not only by diplomatic activity but also by heated military action. In February, troops led by Martin Kurz and Gabriel Golubok captured the town of Holm. Filon Kmita, who became commandant of Luki the Great, burned down Rusa the Old and destroyed its saltworks.

The enemy advanced in Livonia too, where Duke Magnus fought together with the Poles and the Lithuanians against the Muscovites. The castle of Smilten was captured and the territory around Livonian Yuryev devastated. Early in 1581 the Swedish troops of Pontus Delagardi also invaded Livonia. In March, after a long bombardment, Wesenberg surrendered to the Swedes.

Russia responded by separate small counterattacks, initiated by local *voevodes*. In March 1581, troops from Mozhaysk made a successful raid on the territories around Dubrovna, Orsha, Mogilev and Shklov. The troops returned with booty and captives towards Smolensk.

From 18 January to 18 February ambassador Sitsky and his delegation negotiated in Warsaw with Stefan Bathory and the royal council. There were no results. The parties did not understand each other and spoke of different things. On 18 February the Sitsky delegation left Warsaw empty handed. In March the tsar discussed the issue with the Boyar Council and it was decided to make a number of concessions to Bathory. In his letter of 17 March 1581 Ivan IV expressed his agreement to send his senior ambassadors to Rzeczpospolita with offers of peace. It looked like the tsar was about to accept the idea that he had lost this war.

This top-level Russian delegation was to be headed by Eustaphy Pushkin and Fyodor Pisemsky. Their instructions contained several options for concessions which Russia was ready to accept in order to stop the war. Eternal peace was ruled out as the tsar hoped to regain the lost territories in the future. Russia intended to get only a temporary ceasefire. According to the first option, the diplomats were to offer, in exchange for a truce, to recognise the right of the Polish–Lithuanian Commonwealth to fifteen Livonian towns. If Stefan refused, the diplomats were to add three more towns and the fortresses of Usvyat and Ozerishche, but only if the king agreed to return Luki the Great, Nevel, Zavolochye, Velizh and Holm. Then, in each round of talks the diplomats were allowed to add a few towns. They were to refuse point-blank to give up Yuryev, Lais, Kirrumpäh, Adzel, Marienburg, Neuschloss and Narva. However, if the negotiation stalled, the diplomats were to return to their quarters, wait three or four days and then offer to exchange Livonian Yuryev and nearby towns for Luki the Great, Nevel, Zavolochye, Velizh and Holm. As the final offer for this first option, Russia would keep in Livonia only Livonian Neuhausen, Neuschloss, Etz (Adezh) and Narva.

According to the second option, if the negotiations were in danger of breaking down, the diplomats were to offer a short truce, six months to two years, maintaining the status quo or at least a ceasefire during the negotiations. The third option was for the ambassadors to suggest a truce on condition that Holm was returned to Russia, while Russia would give up Luki the Great,

Ozerishche, Zavolochye, Velizh, Nevel, Usvyat and eight towns in Livonia to Rzeczpospolita. If the Polish–Lithuanian party started haggling, the Russians were to concede one town at a time in the following order: Ludsen, Rositten, Walk, Wolmar, Ronneburg, Trikaten, Hapsal, Kirrumpäh, Fellin, Weissenstein, Tarvast and Porkhol.[5]

Ivan the Terrible used the same negotiating tactics that had been tested in 1571 when Devlet-Girei demanded Astrakhan. The tsar did not deny the possibility of withdrawing Russian troops from Livonia but instructed his diplomats to say that it was 'an important issue' which could not be decided quickly and without making a proper agreement.

On 9 May 1581, Pushkin and Pisemsky started their journey. On 24 May 1581 the delegation arrived in Vilna and on 26 May talks with Stefan and delegates of the *rada* began, lasting until 4 June. From the very beginning Pushkin and his diplomats were dictated to in very hard terms. The Polish–Lithuanian diplomats said that if the instruction given to the Russian ambassadors did not include surrender of the whole of Livonia, there could be no negotiations and the ambassadors might go home. In the face of such intransigence, the attempts to bargain according to their instructions, slowly giving up towns one at a time, failed. Rzeczpospolita demanded not only Livonia but also Pskov, Smolensk, Novgorod-Seversky and money to cover all the expenses of the Polish–Lithuanian army; Russia was being asked to pay the Poles and Lithuanians for the job of conquering Russian territory.

These claims were, however, reduced to Sebezh and 400,000 Hungarian zlotys to pay the army. If it was too hard for the Russians to part with Sebezh, then, as an alternative, it might be burned down, and Stefan, in his turn, would order the burning of Drissa. As to the titles, the Lithuanians suggested a compromise: they would recognise 'of Smolensk' in the title of Ivan the Terrible if the Muscovites recognised 'of Livonia' in Bathory's title. Pushkin flatly rejected the last item and, since the negotiations on every other issue failed, it was decided on 2 June to send a messenger to Moscow for further instructions. At the same time, an ambassador from Bathory, Krzysztof Derzhek, set off for Moscow to notify the Russian tsar with the demands of Rzeczpospolita.

The talks in Moscow between Derzhek and the boyars began on 21 June. At the council of the tsar and the Boyar Duma it was decided to give up one more portion of Russian and former Livonian towns in exchange for keeping a part of Livonia. Pushkin was instructed to make an offer of eternal peace on the condition that not only Livonia and the territories of Polotsk and Luki the Great would be divided, but also the lands in the region of the middle Dniepr.

A feast in the tsar's court with foreign ambassadors

If Stefan did not agree to the general redrawing of borders, then the diplomats were to conclude a seven-year truce agreement with division of only Livonia and the region of Polotsk and Luki the Great. It is noteworthy that, unlike the previous instructions, this set did not make the Russian diplomats offer towns as bargaining chips. Pushkin was to offer either peace or a truce on the Russian terms. If the king did not agree, the tsar was willing to continue the war.

On 30 June 1581 Derzhek was allowed to return home. The letter from Ivan the Terrible that he was carrying did not look like a letter from a monarch who wanted peace. The main idea of the epistle was to contrast the true Christian ruler, Ivan IV, with Stefan Bathory who had become king 'not according to the Christian custom' and who acted in a manner that did not behove a Christian ruler. Bathory was 'worse than a Muslim monarch' because he was guilty of shedding the blood of Christians. If Russia agreed to the terms of the king and gave him Livonia, the border towns and money to boot, Rzeczpospolita would become strong enough to conquer Russia and was sure to attack it. So why, asked Ivan the Terrible in his wrath, should he make peace? He compared Bathory with a barbarian, with legendary tsars (caesars) of antiquity, persecutors of Christians.[6]

Derzhek delivered Ivan's letter to Stefan on 15 June 1581 and ambassador Pushkin arrived at Bathory's court on 18 July. He offered to let the king keep all he had conquered in the border region between Polotsk and Luki the Great in exchange for thirty-six towns in Livonia. Then the tsar would be ready to conclude a truce of six or seven years. The king responded that he would fight to conquer not only Livonia but also the whole of Russia. It looked like the tsar's promise of a half-century war between Russia and Rzeczpospolita was going to come true. There was no possibility of peace between the two states in the foreseeable future. Pushkin's delegation was sent back to Russia. On 25 August, near Orsha, messenger Matvey Prevozsky caught up with the Muscovites. He carried Bathory's sharp response to the tsar's insulting missive. The Polish king took up the gauntlet.

Ivan IV received Prevozsky in Staritsa on 8 September 1581. The messenger handed the Polish king's letter to the tsar who read its uncompromising contents. The tsar had good reason to be offended. In his letter Stefan 'made holy war' against the Muscovite. The king said that all the world knew the 'pagan' deeds of Ivan IV. Bathory, as a Christian, felt obliged to save the Muscovite tsar from his sinful ways. The king compared Ivan the Terrible, 'fallen into the bog of sins and ignorance', to 'a beast without understanding, an ass or an ox' that fell in a mire by accident. However, as Stefan commented, even an ass could get out of the mire, whereas Ivan Vasilievich because of his 'abominations' was unable to 'receive his sight' and 'pull out the beam that is in his eye'.

Furthermore, Bathory ridiculed Ivan the Terrible's quoting of Holy Scripture – 'You seem to be an upright man and psalms are always in your mouth' – but contrasted his actual deeds to the Christian values professed by Moscow. The tsar, he said, did not 'understand the rights of God and the Christians'. The Russian tsars could do nothing but lie, betray, kill and rob. Bathory claimed that Ivan the Terrible and his family came from 'the dough of tyrants' and illustrated this statement by the supposedly-true story of Ivan III inviting delegates from Novgorod for talks and perfidiously killing them. The king compared the 'acquisition of Novgorod' to 'the Devil's guile'; 'Satan, too, treated Adam and Eve to an apple'. Ivan the Terrible was called 'Pharaoh of Moscow', whose heart was too hardened to be truly Christian. The king asserted that 'God tolerated you so long' that the tsar got into his head that this would always be so. But now the day of reckoning was close by!

Stefan declared that Moscow was far from Christendom. The Muscovites did not take part in Christian church councils. The Muscovites communicated mainly with the Muslim world – with the Tatars, Nogays and other infidels and pagans. There was no other country, the king stated, not even a pagan one, where rulers humiliated foreign diplomats as Russia did. The letter also contained a few personal invectives that overshadowed the usual insults of Ivan the Terrible. Bathory reproached the tsar, asking if his previous communication contained his sober words or drunken delirium. In another place: 'Oh, you purposeless man, all your words are delirium!' At the end of the letter Bathory challenged Ivan IV to a duel, a personal trial by combat to decide who was right and appeal to the judgement of God. If the tsar refused to take the challenge, was he really so sure of his righteousness?[7]

On 15 September, without the usual invitation to dinner, Ivan let Prevozsky return home, bearing the tsar's 'terrible answer'. But the messenger was detained before he reached the border and had to stay in Mozhaysk until 18 February 1582, while Russia waited for Dmitry Eletsky and Roman Alferyev to return from Yam Zapolsky, where they had gone to conclude a truce. When, on 11 February, Eletsky returned with the news that the talks had been a success, the 'terrible' letter was taken from Prevozsky and he was given a letter with a noncommittal reply to take to Bathory instead; it was explained to him that there was no need for a letter with angry words now that 'the work had turned out good'. Unfortunately the 'terrible' letter has been lost and we will never know what words made it so dreadful.

'THE RUSSIAN PARIS AGAINST THE WHOLE OF EUROPE': STEFAN BATHORY'S SIEGE OF PSKOV, 1581

Stefan Bathory prepared very thoroughly for the campaign of 1581 against Pskov. The campaigns of 1579 and 1580 proved that the best troops, which decided the outcome of every big battle, were mercenaries from Hungary and Germany. So special attention was paid to the recruitment in Hungary, which was carried out by Stefan's brother, Christopher of Transylvania. The successful German commander, Jürgen Fahrensbach, recruited German mercenaries who had served in Holland for Rzeczpospolita. Nikolay Urovetsky was entrusted with choosing the best Polish warriors for the royal infantry. The army also included a unit of Prussian soldiers under Bartholomäus Buttler, a group of Prussian volunteers and a unit of Germans from Lübeck.

On 8 August, Stefan's army set off from Zavolochye and moved towards Voronach. On 17 August troops led by Stanislaw Tarnovsky and Nikolay Urovetsky and Hungarian troops besieged the fortress of Ostrov, the last barrier on the way to Pskov. An attack sector was allocated each to the Hungarians and to the Poles, and the construction of siege fortifications began. The town surrendered after three days when the well-aimed shots of the Hungarian gunners breached the wall. The population readily swore loyalty to the conquerors lest the Luki the Great massacre be repeated. The peasants

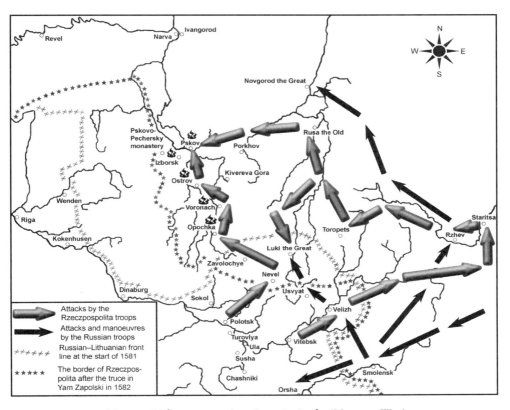

Map 21. Military operations in 1581 in the 'Moscow War'

that gathered outside the town walls expressed their desire to become Stefan's subjects so loudly that Zamojski thought that a new battle had begun and came galloping up with his cavalry.

On 25 August Stefan's army approached Pskov, but the vanguard and scouts had already been there. The town had prepared to withstand the assault. The citizens made additional wooden fortifications, two wooden walls with earth filling between, built wooden towers on the stone walls and placed artillery there. However, there were not enough guns. In 1580 Ivan the Terrible had decided that Pskov would not be able to defend itself against an assault in any case and ordered some of the guns to be dismounted from the walls. Luckily, the tsar's officials had dismounted only a fraction of heavy guns and not carried them far from the town before they were lost, because of some negligence, in Ilmen Lake, and the disarmament of Pskov was left at that. Now Pskov was hastily fortified again.

The ratio of attackers to defenders during the siege of Pskov remains a controversial issue. Russian authors, extolling the feat of the Russians, often quote 100,000 enemy troops against a garrison of 17,000. By contrast, the Europeans, explaining their failure, mention 57,000 Russian troops against 30,000 men in Bathory's army. The numbers are undoubtedly exaggerated as the whole Pskov population in the late sixteenth century hardly exceeded 20,000, and it is not likely that Bathory managed to collect more than 30,000 troops. So, the forces were approximately equal.

Ivan Shuysky, Andrey Khvorostinin and other *voevodes* were in charge of the defence of Pskov. They had at their disposal 7,000 infantry troops, Cossack units and noble cavalry. All adult male citizens took up arms. Women and children helped to build fortifications and carry ammunition and supplies. The defence of the town united its whole population.

On 2 September Bathory's army began the construction of siege fortifications, consisting mainly of entrenchments. At this point the main weakness of Bathory's army became obvious. Each mercenary unit fought separately (each national unit had a commander, and even a judge, of the respective nationality). The main rivals were the Poles and Hungarians, each trying to be the first to enter the town. To all his appeals to coordinate their actions Bathory received the same reply: 'Every cat hunts by itself'.

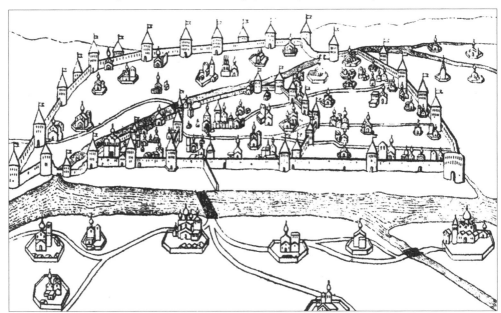

Fortress Pskov (from a Russian icon)

On 8 September the Hungarian gunners managed to make a great breach in the wall near the Svinussky Tower. The Hungarians were bursting to go into action while the Poles discussed whether the entrenchments should be completed first. Both Hungarians and Poles wanted to be first to enter the town, hoping to gain an advantage when it came to the sharing out of booty. While the argument went on, fifty German and French mercenaries were sent to carry out reconnaissance. They entered the breach and found that behind the stone wall the Russians had erected a wooden one and dug a ditch. There was a clash with the defenders and a French officer was killed. The Polish unit under Prokopy Penyonzhek and Andrey Orzhekhovsky hurried to the site of the battle. This unit captured the Svinussky Tower and raised the royal banner on it. The Hungarians, piqued by the success of their rivals, attacked without orders, captured the neighbouring Pokrovsky Tower and flew the Hungarian banner.

While Bathory's troops competed to see who would fly more banners, the defenders led by Ivan Shuysky, the commander of the garrison, gathered near the breach. Wounded, on horseback, he called upon his warriors to throw the aggressor out of Pskov. The bishop and priests walked in front of the Russian troops, carrying holy icons and relics. The defenders had arquebuses and cannons whereas the Poles and Hungarians responded only by throwing javelins. The Pskov troops attacked and the enemy abandoned the Svinussky Tower. More than forty Polish noblemen were killed. The Hungarians remained in the Pokrovsky Tower until nightfall and then gave up their position under cover of darkness. A Russian source, *The Tale of the Attack of Stefan Bathory on the Town of Pskov*, quotes the losses on both sides in the attempted storming: the Russians lost 863 killed and 1,626 wounded, the enemy 5,000 killed and 10,000 wounded. The numbers are evidently exaggerated but there is no doubt the battle was violent and bloody.

The failure of the assault depressed Bathory. It became clear that the capture of this town would not be quick and easy. Hetman Jan Zamojski suggested sending the armed noblemen home and leaving only mercenaries by the town walls. The king refused as it would have meant that the army of Rzeczpospolita recognised its inefficiency. Royal secretary Ioann Petrovski made the following commentary in his diary: 'God help us! It seems to me that we are about to attack the sun with a mattock'. The secretary compared Pskov to Paris ('What a big city, like Paris!') and stated that it had been some time since the royal army besieged a town like this.

Stefan's advisers suggested a reasonable plan to take the nearby small fortresses of Porkhov and Gdov, cut off Pskov from Russia and take the town by starvation. But this time it was Bathory's turn, after Ivan the

Terrible, to exhibit pride and arrogance; he declared that it would have been unworthy of their great campaign and that the towns of Muscovy should be taken beautifully.

Preparations for a new attempt at storming began. It was decided to dig mines under the walls. The Poles again lost in this unofficial competition with the Hungarians; two Polish mines met hard rock. The Hungarians managed to get around the rocky obstacle and brought the mines to the surface, covering the exits with intertwined twigs. But they did not succeed further as on 24 and 27 September the Russians completed countermines and blew up the enemy right in their tunnels. Russian sources quote nine destroyed mines.

Stefan was also much bothered by Russian units that tried to get access into Pskov by the Velikaya river on boats and from the surrounding forests on carts. The king, therefore, had to divert many troops, including the best German mercenaries at that, from their main task to place them as guards in the most vulnerable places. The ring of the siege turned out to be incomplete and small groups numbering scores of troops continually managed to enter the town. Many such units were scattered but the result was that Russian troops started to accumulate on the outer side of the siege ring. There was a risk of the besieging troops being trapped between Pskov on the inside and Russian units on the outside.

Meanwhile, events in the Baltic region made any further extension of the siege senseless and dangerous. Heidenstein made a caustic remark that 'the Swedish king extracted profit out of the victories of others'. The garrison of Narva, before the battles began, had decided to protect Pskov. Now the Swedes commanded by Pontus Delagardi easily captured Narva. Italian mercenaries commanded by Geronimo Canol played a special role. It was their assault that proved decisive. After Narva, Yam, Koporje and Weissenstein fell and Pernau was besieged. Bathory was in danger of losing Livonia, and not to Ivan the Terrible but to Sweden, a former ally!

Stefan gave orders to stir up the activity of the royal forces in Livonia lest the whole of Livonia should become Swedish. But he did not have enough troops. The main body of the royal army constituted the troops of Duke Magnus, who had betrayed Ivan IV not long before, with which he conquered the fortress of Kirrumpäh. Other forces also had their successes: Thomas von Emden took Salis, while Matthias Dembinski took Lennewarden and Ascheraden by storm with Scottish soldiers and infantry from Riga. Dembinski then used these men, along with Polish troops, to besiege Kokenhusen.

Another exploit, later glorified by Polish poets, was the raid of a unit under Krzysztof Radzivill into inner Russia. The original aim of the operation was revenge for the Russian assault on the Mogilev and Shklov areas, but it became much more significant. Radzivill acted together with a unit under Filon Kmita and Garaburda. At Toropets they defeated 3,000 troops under Mikhail Nozdrovaty and Peter Baryatinsky who headed towards the Lithuanian border. Then the Lithuanians moved to Rzhev and Yam Zubtsovsky and found themselves near Staritsa. The war might have been ended by a single stroke as Ivan the Terrible was in Staritsa with only 700 guards. Radzivill did not dare to assault Staritsa, but if he had attacked and been successful he might have captured or killed the Russian tsar, guaranteeing Rzeczpospolita's victory in the war. But the Lithuanian nobleman was confused by the information from captives who told that Staritsa was protected by a large Russian army. The Lithuanian troops went towards Dubna, raided the territory around Toropets, Rusa the Old and Opochka and joined the main body of troops.

Although the raid had few practical results, which were limited to a number clashes with Muscovite troops, robbery and a few captives, it was a huge morale boost. 'Our cavalry reached the Volga!' shouted Polish poets, vying with each other. One sixteenth-century poet, Jan Kochanowski, dedicated his poem *Jezda do Moskwy* (Raid to Moscow) to Krzysztof Radzivill's feat. Radzivill had several hundred more kilometres to go before reaching Moscow but this hyperbole presented the Polish military leaders to advantage and earned prestige for Stefan Bathory and his generals.

Let us now return to the siege of Pskov. Ivan IV was in no hurry to relieve the besieged. He relied on Russia's main ally in all times: 'General Frost'. The tsar was convinced that as soon as winter came, the Europeans, used to comfort, would flee from Russia. His calculations proved to be right: with the first light frosts the troops of the Polish–Lithuanian Commonwealth camped outside Pskov started to grow demoralised. Cases of desertion became more numerous, the deserters often fleeing into the besieged city. There they found houses that were warmer than their own tents in the open field, exposed to winds. The Lithuanians gave their king an ultimatum: either he immediately concluded a truce or the Lithuanian troops left the army. They were not going to spend the winter near Pskov.

There were not enough warm clothes so soldiers began to take them from each other by force, and the Hungarians were the most violent. The mercenaries constantly demanded money and could not stand the absence of women, who, on Jan Zamojski's order, were forbidden to enter the military camp. When two Italians bought a woman from the Cossacks, the camp began to stir and the commanders seriously feared a sexual mutiny.

Attempts to deal with the breach of discipline only aggravated Bathory's troops. Zamojski gave orders to put those *szlachta* nobles who were caught drinking in the pillory and to beat with a cane those who littered and soiled in the camp. Noble descent was no protection against corporal punishment, which angered the nobles. The troops hated Zamojski and he paid them back in their own coin: in order to humiliate the 'filthy army' the *hetman* chose offensive passwords. Heidenstein described this measure of the chancellor as follows:

> Setting a password as is the military custom, Zamojski mainly chose words that censured the laziness, cowardice and idleness of those who wanted to return home soon; and praised persistence, steadfastness, qualities worthy of a nobleman; two or three words contained admonishment to change from dejection to patience, if somebody was not bright and cheerful enough.[8]

As a reaction, leaflets started circulating about the camp ridiculing Zamojski as scholastic. On 20 October, the angry troops from the Grand Duchy of Lithuania, who constituted a considerable part of Bathory's army, gave their king another ultimatum; he had eighteen days to win or to make peace. The king decided to win.

The next major assault took place on 29–30 October. The attack was directed at the breach, protected now by palisades. The Hungarians again proved the best fighters. They managed to scale the wall and partly demolish it, but boiling water, tar and large timbers with iron weights on the end were used against them. The Russians swung the timbers suspended by chains and rammed the crowded enemy troops. The assault was repulsed.

The siege of the Pskovo-Pechersky monastery near Pskov also failed, which dampened the troops' spirits. The king had sent his best troops, the German unit under Jürgen Fahrensbach, but the monks took up arms and defeated the professional German warriors. The king then sent the Hungarians under the command of Johann Bornemissza himself to reinforce and renew the attack. But to no avail; the joint assault of the Germans and the Hungarians, supported by the fire of the Scottish soldiers, was a spectacular flop.

In the monastery, the monks ardently thanked God who had wrought this great salvation. Bathory's camp was gloomy. The attackers could not accept the idea that God himself helped the besieged, yet they had no rational explanation why professional European soldiers with military training were regularly defeated by peaceful clerics, many of whom took up arms for the first time.

Zamojski, using information from defectors, made a plan. It was obvious that it was impossible to take the town by assault. A long siege to starve the town was the only way out. The spies reported that provisions in Pskov would last until spring, to May approximately. Consequently, the troops would have

IOHANNES DE ZAMOSCIO CANCELLARIVS, ET SVMM
DVX, EXERCITVV   REGNI POLONIAE.

Jan Zamojski

to remain near the town for more than six months. It was impossible to keep the army in camp: there was no food. So he suggested dismissing part of the troops; the Polish and Lithuanian noblemen might be sent home till spring, while others might be sent to loot the lands around Pskov.

It was necessary to attack the Pskovo-Pechersky monastery immediately and the nearby fortresses of Gdov, Porkhov and Rusa the Old. Zamojski planned to capture them and garrison a large part of his troops for the winter. From there it would be possible to make raids into Russian territory in the direction of Novgorod the Great, Tver and Moscow. It is obvious that

Zamojski intended to remain in Russian territory a long while. It was not an invasion but an occupation, an attempt to conquer the country.

However the mood of the ordinary soldiers of Rzeczpospolita did not allow these projects to be realised. On 2 November the decision was made to begin breaking camp. The soldiers, suspecting that they might be left without money, demanded that the commanders should mortgage their estates to guarantee payment. Bathory saved the situation on 10 November by guaranteeing the wages of the soldiers, pledging the crown lands. The mercenaries stayed near Pskov. On 1 December only Stefan, the Polish noblemen and some of the Lithuanians left the camp. The Germans, French, Italians, Scots, Hungarians, Poles and the remainder of the Lithuanians decided to overwinter near Pskov. These Europeans received the main blow of 'General Frost'.

Heidenstein described the impression that the Russian climate made on the invaders:

> The frosts were so strong that, as soon one left the tent, the frost injured all his members, especially those that were not covered: nose, ears, face; and the man died. The terrified Europeans said that only the Arctic Ocean could be colder.

They thought that it was so cold in the Pskov region that some animals that were red or black in other lands turned white here – hares and wolves for example. A third of the troops caught cold or had pneumonia. Many had their hands and feet injured by frost. And the only cure in the field hospital in those days was amputation. The camp was filled with the cries and groans of delirious soldiers who looked for their severed hands and feet.

Numerous small clashes (the siege saw thirty-one assaults by Bathory troops and forty-six sorties made by the defenders) failed to bring any result for either side. The exhausted soldiers grew inclined to mysticism. The siege of Pskov gave rise to many fantastic legends among the European mercenaries, such as that of Stanislaw Zholkevsky, who rode his horse before the walls and was shot at by 500 cannon at point blank, and each one missed; or the legend about a 'remarkable operation' that resulted in blowing up the Russian headquarters. The cunning conquerors sent a bomb disguised as a coffer into Pskov, knowing for certain that the Russians would not be able to resist the temptation to see what was inside. This infernal machine was designed by Jan Ostrometsky. Heidenstein described this bomb as follows:

> [Ostrometsky] put into an iron box twelve musket barrels, deliberately made thin so that they burst more easily; he filled them and the box with the finest powder; and in the middle he placed, cocked ready, that part of the musket that by means of a wheel and a flint attached to it produces sparks to ignite

the powder; this box was placed into a wooden box; then to the spring that [if released] usually turns the wheel and produces sparks he attached two laces – one from the bottom of the wooden box, the other from the lid of the iron box; so that if someone lifted the iron box from the wooden one or opened the lid of the iron box, the spring would be released, and the powder would detonate and all present would be hit by the shards of the barrels and the iron box. Ostrometsky thought that if this box were sent to Shuysky, the latter would be tempted to open it and would be deceived.

Heidenstein narrated that the Muscovites in the headquarters building, like small children, all gathered around the box and started to open it. Shuysky, according to the narrator,

> was occupied at the moment by some matters but immediately, without due examination, ordered others who had gathered for conference to open the box; there were many who had been attracted there by the novelty of the matter as well as by natural human curiosity. The most daring among those present and a rival of Shuysky, another *voevode*, Andrey Khvorostinin . . . pushing one foot against the wooden box was trying to lift the iron box. At this moment the spring was released, powder ignited, the iron box and barrels burst, and not only all present were torn to pieces but even part of the roof was damaged by the fire and the explosion of the iron barrels.[9]

The explosion was so strong that the roof of the headquarters building, sent flying above the town walls, could be seen from Bathory's camp. There is only one discrepancy in the narrative: the Russian boyars and *voevodes* who, according to Heidenstein, became victims of this terror attack, were alive and prospering years later. According to Russian sources, the 'infernal machine' was disabled in time.

The siege of Pskov continued until the Yam Zapolsky treaty with Rzeczpospolita. The news that the war was over was brought to Pskov by Alexander Khrushchev on 17 January 1582. Zamojski invited him to breakfast but the messenger hurried on into the town to tell the citizens that they had withstood the siege. He rode to the Pokrovsky Tower and shouted that the war had ended. Happy citizens carried him along the wall, started to kiss his feet, called him archangel and messenger of peace. The besieged started to fraternise with the former aggressors. The Russians invited the Europeans as guests into the town they had not managed to take by force. On 4 February Bathory's army withdrew from the walls of Pskov.

Rzeczpospolita and Moscow assessed the outcome of the Pskov campaign. Stefan and Zamojski thought that victory was theirs for Moscow had signed the peace agreement. In the nineteenth century, Jan Matejko, a Polish painter who created a number of canvases representing key moments of Polish history, depicted Russian boyars laying the keys to Pskov at Bathory's feet. In reality there was no such episode; the artist exaggerated the truth and invented an image of the fall of Pskov.

In Russia the defence of Pskov became one of the symbols of heroism and the fortitude of the Russian spirit. The Russian painter Karl Bryullov embodied this idea in his painting *Defence of Pskov*, in which monks with icons raised over their heads and ordinary citizens who took up arms throw the enemy out of the breach in the wall.

HOW THE POPE AND THE GERMAN EMPEROR RECONCILED
RUSSIA WITH RZECZPOSPOLITA

In the final stages of the Baltic wars of the second half of the sixteenth century, the Holy Roman Empire, which lost its province of Livonia, played the decisive role. Maximilian II died in 1576 and Rudolf II, a cunning and cautious politician, became the new emperor. However, he did not quarrel with Russia and did not try to play political games with her, as Maximilian had.

Moscow, which lost all its unstable allies during the Baltic wars, relied as before on the support of Vienna. This became especially obvious in the late 1570s and the early 1580s when a succession of Russian ambassadors started to ask the emperor to mediate peace between Ivan IV and Stefan Bathory. In 1577–8, ambassador Zhdan Kvashnin visited the 'Centre of Christendom' with this mission. On 12 March 1580 the Russian messenger Afanasy Rezanov set off for Vienna with a letter in which Ivan the Terrible agreed to join the anti-Turkish league and aid the Empire militarily, if only the emperor 'restrained' this odious Bathory. Even before the messenger returned, the tsar decided to send another ambassador, Istoma Shevrigin, on 25 August 1580. Ivan the Terrible presented the emperor with a scheme for a broad coalition that would include Russia, the Holy Roman Empire and even the Vatican. Then the Turks, unable to withstand this great force, would flee with disgrace from Europe. There was only one problem: the attack of King Stefan, who was the sultan's ally by the way, on Russia. As a result the true Christian ruler, Ivan IV, instead of punishing the infidels with fire and sword, had to fight with his fellow Christians. Let the emperor, as the leader of the Christian world, help to put an end to this scandal!

Ivan the Terrible calculated correctly. Since the end of the fifteenth century the Vatican and the Holy Roman Empire had sought alliance with Russia in order to make it Catholic and use its military power against Turkey. But Ivan III and Vasiliy III rejected their numerous offers. And now the Russian tsar himself was seeking alliance, offered to fight against the Turks and wanted to be close friends with the Catholic German emperor! Could it mean that Russia in the last hundred years had finally realised the necessity of uniting with the Roman Catholic Church?

So the emperor's court and the Vatican considered the suggestions brought by Istoma Shevrigin very seriously. Nobody was going to offend or restrain Bathory since a Catholic king was in any case closer to Christendom than Ivan the Terrible, the leader of the Orthodox schismatics. Still, both the emperor and the pope agreed that the Polish monarch might have directed his energy on something more useful. If only he would use his talents against the Turks . . . But now he was fighting with Ivan the Terrible, who, although an enemy of Europe, was far from being the main enemy. Moreover, the Russian tsar was making hints that he was ready to correct his ways according to Western norms.

It was decided to respond to the call of Ivan the Terrible to intervene in the conflict between Russia and Rzeczpospolita. In September 1581 the main player in the negotiations became the papal legate, Antonio Possevino. His task was to inform the Russian party of Bathory's conditions, the main one being the concession of the whole of Livonia. At the same time, Possevino was to make sure that Stefan did not make unreasonable demands.

The mediation of Possevino was very important to Ivan IV. This way the tsar attempted to regain his authority, to demonstrate that he sought reconciliation with the king only to please Christendom, to meet the wishes of the pope and the emperor. The head of the Russian delegation, Prince Dmitry Yeletsky, received instructions that specified three options for the terms of the peace agreement.

The first option implied the division of Livonia. The larger part of Livonia was to be conceded to Rzeczpospolita but Stefan was to return to Ivan IV the territories captured in the Pskov region. The Sebezh issue was to be suspended: Russia was to burn down the town of Sebezh, Russia's stronghold in the region, while Lithuania was to destroy Drissa. Russia was ready to sign a truce agreement on these terms for ten to twenty years and send its troops to protect Christendom from the Muslims. The titles of both Stefan and Ivan IV were to include 'Livonian'. Moscow was ready to recognise its loss of Polotsk and its environs (Kopye, Ula, Krasny, Turovlya, Sokol, Kozyan, Sitna, Ozerishche and Usvyat) as well as Velizh, Luki the Great, Nevel, Zavolochye and Holm. For his part, Stefan was to give up the lands with settlements near Pskov ('the environs of Pskov').

The second option covered the situation in which Stefan would insist on taking the whole of Livonia, and Possevino would not be able to convince him to compromise. This option comprised a truce for seven to twelve years, ceding the whole of Livonia to Rzeczpospolita, evacuation of the property of the Russian church from Livonia and withdrawal of garrisons with their artillery. In exchange, Russia demanded the return of all Stefan had conquered in the border region (except Polotsk and its environs), and the retention of Sebezh by Russia. The possibility of Russia taking part in a campaign against Turkey was ruled out.

The third option outlined in Yeletsky's instructions envisaged the worst-case scenario: Stefan would refuse to give up Luki the Great and the environs of Pskov and would demand the whole of Livonia. In this case the ambassadors were to turn to Possevino, to underline the willingness of Russia to fight with the Muslims and insist on the retention of a portion of Livonia almost identical to the one described in the first option. However, Ivan was ready to give up towns but not the land around them. The lands of Luki the Great and the environs of Pskov would be ceded to Stefan.

The papal legate took up the challenge of reconciling the two warring states with great zeal. In his letter of 22 October, Possevino alleged that he had saved Pskov from bombardment by new guns that had been moved to Pskov from Riga (whereas, in fact, no guns had been moved to Pskov). In a letter to the tsar of 16 November the legate acted almost as a Russian spy. He informed the tsar about the plans of the Polish–Lithuanian commanders and about movements of troops. In his letters, Possevino always addressed Ivan IV as either 'Your Majesty' or 'Tsar and Grand Prince of the whole of Russia', which was not usual for imperial or papal diplomats.

The talks began on 13 December 1581 in the village of Kivereva Gora, not far from the small town of Yam Zapolsky. The talks were very difficult. The Lithuanian diplomats declared that Bathory was willing to give up the Pskov environs (Voronach, Velizh, Ostrov and Krasny), but Russia was to return the whole of Livonia. They also said that they were to conclude the deal within three days and if the Russian diplomats had objections the talks could be broken before they had begun. Then the ambassadors of Rzeczpospolita started asking crucial questions. Did Yeletsky have any instructions regarding the ceding of the whole of Livonia to Stefan? Did he have any instructions relating to the war of Russia against Sweden, which at that moment was an ally of the Polish–Lithuanian Commonwealth? Was Moscow willing to pay the soldiers of Rzeczpospolita for their military feats in Russia?

As Yeletsky could give only negative answers to these questions and the conditions of Rzeczpospolita were unacceptable, he countered that if Russia ceded Livonia to Rzeczpospolita, then Russia would be left without sea ports. In this case it would not be able to help the Holy Roman Empire and the

Vatican in their war against Turkey, for the land route from the Holy Roman Empire and Vatican to Russia was blocked by the hostile Rzeczpospolita. Incidentally, this is the only instance in which Russian documents mention the need to gain access to the Baltic Sea. However, this need had a peculiar explanation. Russia needed access to the Baltic Sea for regular communication with the pope.

According to Yeletsky's report, Possevino did his best to fulfil his mission, influenced the Lithuanian diplomats and made sure they did not break off the talks. The legate tried to discover chancellor Jan Zamojski's secret instructions to the ambassadors and promised to pass this confidential information to the Muscovite diplomats.

The talks went on all December and brought only modest results. The Lithuanians demanded the whole of Livonia while Russia demanded the return of the occupied territories. Then, one dark night in January 1582, the Russian ambassadors came to Possevino and 'with a great and very sore weeping' said that it was impossible for them to conclude a peace treaty without giving up Yuryev, whereas the tsar forbade them to give up that town. Yeletsky begged Possevino to intercede for them with the tsar so that they should not be punished. Possevino promised to help. The next day, the Russian diplomats said they were willing to become martyrs for the sake of peace with Rzeczpospolita; they would run counter to the will of the tsar and give up Yuryev. Yeletsky, of course, was being insincere; the tsar's instructions did allow for ceding Yuryev, so the diplomats were not disobeying his orders. Yeletsky put on this act before Possevino and the Lithuanians to show how much they risked and to make the Lithuanians more yielding. The show produced the desired effect on the Lithuanian diplomats, who knew what Ivan the Terrible could do to diplomats who did not follow his instructions. Yeletsky's ploy succeeded.

By 9 January a number of issues had already been settled. 'Tsar' was to be used as part of the title of Ivan the Terrible only in Russian versions of documents. The Lithuanians did not recognise 'of Smolensk' as part of Ivan's IV title at all, whereas the Russians did not recognise 'of Livonia' as part of Bathory's. The 'eternal peace', suggested by the Lithuanian party and Possevino, was rejected and Yeletsky succeeded in concluding a ten-year truce. Yeletsky considered it a success that the negotiating parties agreed that Stefan's ambassadors would come to Moscow first, and only then would the Russian delegation go to Vilno to ratify the agreement.

Unfortunately, a number of problems remained unresolved. The Russian delegation objected to a nominal list of all towns and to the presence of Possevino's signature on the agreement documents, as the papal legate was only a mediator. The terms and conditions of the withdrawal of the Polish–Lithuanian army from near Pskov and of the Russian army from Livonia remained unconfirmed. The issue of the exchange of prisoners was not settled. The Lithuanians demanded 300,000 golden coins and the release of prisoners in exchange for the release of all captive Russians and the return of the castles of Opochka and Sebezh.

The debates got so heated that the diplomats sometimes came to blows. On one occasion Possevino took offence and stormed out of the room because the diplomats did not listen to him and, especially, because he and the pope were not mentioned in the peace treaty. The Russian ambassadors remained calm and reminded him that he had promised to serve the tsar and that he, instead of swearing, had to convince the Lithuanian delegation to do what was good for the Russian party; for that, in the end, was what his service to the tsar implied. In a temper, the legate snatched the draft of the treaty from the hands of Roman Alferyev and hurled it through the door, then grabbed Alferyev by the lapels of his fur coat and pulled so that buttons came off, according to Alferyev's later report to the tsar. After this fight the legate, shouting all the while, kicked the Russian delegation out of his house. To this the Russian diplomats bravely responded: 'It is not proper, Antonio, to throw the tsar's document on the floor and compromise us'.[10]

Although the atmosphere was extremely heated, everybody realised that the negotiations had to be continued. The parties forced themselves to make concessions and on 15 January the peace agreement was signed. The agreement was close to the second option outlined in Ivan's instructions. Russia gave up Livonia but regained towns lost during the war with Bathory (except Polotsk with Velizh and other environs). The destiny of the territory captured by Sweden remained undecided. The order of withdrawal of Russian and Lithuanian troops was determined. Yeletsky had coped with his task. The results of the defeat were not catastrophic. Russia did not lose vital territory, but could not keep the lands captured in 1558–78.

Ambassador Yeletsky returned to Russia on 11 February and brought the the peace treaty document. Then a delegation from Rzeczpospolita was to be received which would witness the ratification of the agreement by Ivan the Terrible. Then Moscow diplomats would go to witness ratification of the agreement by Stefan Bathory.

The Rzeczpospolitan delegation of Jan Zbarazhsky, Mikolaj Talvash and Mikhail Garaburda, sent to confirm the agreement concluded at Kivereva Gora, was in Moscow from 18 June to 17 July 1582. The parties discussed the issue of the coming war against Sweden. The ambassadors decided to refrain for a while from discussing which country should possess Narva and other

Livonian towns occupied by Sweden. On 20 October Stefan confirmed the documents by oath.[11]

While the dispute between Russia and Rzeczpospolita was temporarily settled, there remained one more enemy, the one that had made the most profit from the Baltic wars of the second half of the sixteenth century: Sweden. Neither Sweden nor Russia wanted to continue the war. It was expedient to find a solution and define the spheres of influence in the Baltic region. The first talks between Swedish and Muscovite diplomats took place in May 1583. At these talks a truce for two months was concluded and both sides expressed willingness to meet for talks at a higher level, which took place in August on the Plyussa river. The Swedish delegation included Pontus Delagardi and Klaus Tott; Russia was represented by Prince Ivan Lobanov-Rostovsky, nobleman Ignaty Tatishchev and clergyman Druzhina Petelin. The solution for the issues of territory and the exchange of prisoners was postponed, though not shelved, and a three-year truce was signed. In December 1585 the truce would be extended for another three years.

HOW THE WARS OF IVAN THE TERRIBLE OPENED UP RUSSIA FOR EUROPE

The wars of Ivan the Terrible have not been treated well by history. It is the figure of Ivan, the bloody tyrant, who comes to the fore when one thinks about his military policy. This image overshadows the personal courage and high tactical skill of the sixteenth-century Russian commanders. The evil deeds of the tyrant have even diminished the Russian military victories.

More than that, the negative characterisation of Ivan the Terrible, very often deserved, has been extended to the results of his strategy. The victories were hushed up, the defeats were emphasised and often exaggerated. A parable with a deep subtext resulted, saturated with Christian ideas such as 'God's millstones are grinding slowly, but they do so to the very end' or 'The requital is inevitable'. According to this traditional history, Tsar Ivan the Terrible had been punished for his tyranny and crimes with his military defeats and his shame. All his most important wars had been lost. The subjects of the Russian tsar had been punished by the very same defeats, because they suffered from such a cruel monarch, not even trying to overthrow his tyranny. So, in general, Ivan the Terrible's wars are considered to be nothing more than a number of shameful defeats, which have illuminated the bloody and cruel image of the Russian tsar.

Such an approach, persisting to the turn of the twentieth century, has its genesis in the Polish and German propaganda of the Livonian War period. And it was the 'Propaganda War' that Russia, in the sixteenth century, had lost completely. Sixteenth-century Russia had nothing to set against the enormous stream of newspapers, pamphlets and so-called *flugschriften* (propaganda flyers or leaflets, often illustrated, for the poor) that were addressed to the common people of Europe. Lengthy printed stories were also widely distributed all over Europe in the second half of the century. But it was only in the middle of the century that book printing had first come to Russia. Russia, with its backwardness, its handwritten books, absence of printing and no knowledge of foreign languages had nothing to counter this literature. So, Russia was a very weak fighter in this propaganda war.

It was not in vain that Stefan Bathory carried a field printing press in his rear guard. After each battle with the Russians a propaganda leaflet was immediately published. It would tell how a few Polish warriors crushed several hundred or even several thousand Russians, performing a great number of feats which were to be compared only with the valiant deeds of ancient heroes. It was the Poles that zealously spread the legends of the inborn Russian hostility to the Catholics, saying that Muscovites were praised and given absolution for their sins if only they could kill a Roman Catholic. It was the Poles who wrote that the Russians were dirty, wild, uncivilised barbarians, inclined to violence and dangerous to highly developed nations. It was the Polish propaganda that revealed to the West the Tatar tradition of selling people to slavery and attributed it to the Muscovites. They propagated the idea that the Muscovites were culturally and politically more similar to the Turks and Asiatics than to the civilised Europeans.[12]

This propaganda, fuelled especially by the events of the Livonian War, was a complete success. By attacking Livonia, Lithuania and Poland, Muscovy made itself known all over Europe for the first time. Albert Schlichting, a German contemporary of Ivan the Terrible, wrote:

Nobody could have known before the character and the cleverness of the Moscow Prince Vasilievich, what power he possessed and what cruelty against his subjects he demonstrated. His deeds have come to be known only when he captured Polotsk. Since that time, with his wars never ceasing, the prince's cruelty, his tyranny overpassing those of Nero were revealed. They had been hidden before, because of human ignorance.[13]

The role of these leaflets in creating the negative attitude to 'Muscovite aggressors' in the West is hard to overestimate. The very form of them added a certain tint to the information; they were preceded by verbose headlines, where the main events were described. This description was accompanied by a moral evaluation of the event, sometimes with a suitable quotation from the Bible or some historical analogy. In these compositions Russia had been

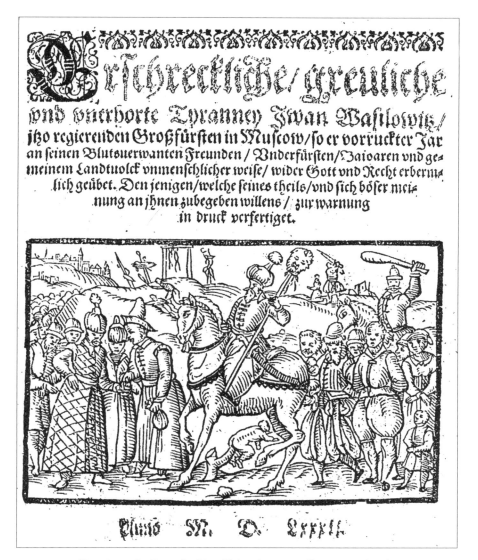

'Russia under Ivan the Terrible' – the cover illustration for the
German edition of George von Hoff's Erschreckiche, Grewliche und Nic Erhörte
Tyranney'n Johannis Basilidis *(Naumburg, 1582)*

compared with Turkey (in the engravings of that time the Russians were
very often identified with the Turks). Authors wrote that the Russians were
comparable with the Turks in their cruelty and barbarism. They were supposed
to represent a threat for the civilised European Christian world equal to that
of Muslim fanatics from the Orient. Russia was attributed that image of 'the

'Crimes of the Turks' – *an engraving by Leonhardt Fronsperger*
from The Book of War, *1596*

enemy' which had been formed during the wars of Europe and the Muslim
Orient in the age of the Crusades.

The particularly colourful figure of the tyrant 'Vasilievich' was a favourite
subject of European political writing.[14] A new genre of 'Ivaniana' took its
place in European historiography. It started with blood-curdling stories
about the *oprichniki* written by the Germans Albert Schlichting (1571–2)
and Heinrich Staden (1578), and also by Livonians Johann Taube and Helert
Krause (1572). For example, according to Taube and Krause, 'the final
destruction of the whole Christian World, the Kingdom of Poland, Lithuania
and our ill-starred land [Livonia]' was the aim of the Russian attack upon
Livonia, and 'all these actions were directed against God, against honour,
against the Christian Church'. The Danish diplomat Yakob Ulfeldt also called
Ivan IV 'the bitterest enemy of Christendom'. Only a gloomy desert was left in
Livonia as a result of the Russian tsar's attack. Ulfeldt described the dreadful
picture of the town of Oberpahlen, captured by the Russians, where dogs
were eating the corpses of those hanged and gnawed them to their bones. On

the road one could see the heads of those killed impaled on the fences and unburied bodies everywhere.

In a German leaflet of 1578 the rescue of Livonia from the Muscovites was equated with the salvation of Israel from the pharaoh in the Bible. The third part of the very first biography of Ivan the Terrible, published by a German pastor, Paul Oderborn, in 1585, described the Russian army's defeats in Livonia. It started with the motto: 'Vengeance is mine, I will repay' (Hebrews 10:30). Oderborn treated the Russian defeat in the Livonian War as God's retribution against the sinner and the tyrant, emphasising that the tsar had been defeated by the Christian king, Stefan Bathory. Heaven itself was against the tyrant. Oderborn wrote of a comet, hanging in the sky over Moscow and about the fall of a meteorite near the village of Nalivka, claiming 'a gravestone with strange letters had fallen from the heavens'. Ivan the Terrible, ordered its destruction, proving himself, to the German pastor's mind, 'the worthless man, who dared to rise against his own fate'.

Speaking about these discourses, the American historian William Urban pointed out that all European countries experienced the horrors of war at that time. Any army on the enemy's territory was equally merciless. Why was there such a reaction against the Russian invasion of Livonia? The scholar explained that it was because the reputation of the Russians as barbarians had already been formed by that time. And barbarians were expected to be crude and cruel.[15]

The German reseacher Thomas Ott wrote that the touching image of the innocent victim of the heathen barbarian attack, illustrated with parallel examples from ancient and biblical history was merely 'the performance or the object of demonstration'. That was the material which could serve as a basis for the effective moralising on European themes. These events were the subject for discussion of the German Reformation thinkers with their anxiety, which troubled them enough without even philosophising about the Livonian War. These themes were the purity of faith, humanism, eschatology, violence, sin and so on. Poor Livonia's calls for help, contained in the leaflets, were not supposed to raise any activity of those called and they didn't act. Despite the demonstration of compassion, neither the Holy Roman Empire, nor the Kingdom of Poland, nor Rzeczpospolita, nor Sweden had ever tried to save the perishing Livonian Order. On the contrary, they used the Livonian tragedy to illustrate their own intellectual and spiritual learning, or to defend their own aggression and territorial expansion.

Thomas Ott singled out three types of storytelling in the leaflets. The first was the description of the cruelties of war and the sufferings of the victims of Russian agression, accompanied by moralising with an eschatological subtext. The second contained a chronological description of the military actions along with some ethical subtext. The whole plan of the author was usually subjected to this subtext. The factual subject matter was no more than a cover (a 'foil' according to Ott) for moral maxims. The third type of storytelling was the apotheosis of both the new martyrs and the heroes who had saved the Christian world from the 'Russian barbarians'. For that they deserved eternal glory and remembrance by their descendants.[16]

The principle of European authors' reasoning on the political structure of Ivan the Terrible's Muscovy was founded on counterpoising the positive political experience in their own country and the negative one in Russia. Such is, for example, Giles Fletcher's *Of the Russian Commonwealth*, written in 1589, which was to oppose Thomas Smith's *The Commonwealth of England*, published in 1583. Smith praised English parliamentarism as an example of social partnership between the monarchy, aristocracy and democratic forces. Using Russia as an example, Fletcher tried to show a contrary political regime.[17]

The book of the Swede Erik Falk, *Panegyric* was very similar to that of Fletcher's. He juxtaposed Moscow's tyranny with the 'perfect' Swedish political organisation. The same idea, this time compared with European (mostly German) political structure, was the basis of Paul Oderborn's book about the reign of Ivan the Terrible.

In 1585 Oderborn had published the first biography of Ivan the Terrible, a certain condemnation of the Russian tsar. He characterised the tsar with a lot of cruel epithets and comparisons, the kindest of them being 'a wild, mad tyrant'. It is worth noticing that Oderborn's accusations were rather serious. He wrote that the tsar forced people to play chess with him. Those who refused were executed on the spot, while those who played and lost had their ears, noses and lips cut off. The book contained some risky allusions. The legend about the cut lips, noses and ears was closely connected with the eschatological prophecies of the prophet Ezekiel (Ezekiel 23:25), which meant that the tsar played the role of Antichrist or his closest servant. Ivan, the tsar, was described by the German clergyman as a person actively using senseless cruelty. Oderborn quoted a famous legend about the elephant he received as a gift from Tachmasp, the Persian shah. The great prince of Moscow wanted the elephant to be made to kneel before him. When various tortures failed, the tsar ordered the dumb beast cut to pieces.

The connection of the Livonian War with the merciless character of the Russian state, which attacked the Livonian Order because of its own aggressiveness was another variation on the same theme. The Livonian chronicler Balthazar Ryussov directly explained that, with the occupation of Kazan and Astrakhan, 'the Muscovites became too powerful not only for the province of Livonia, but for other neighbouring states'. The conquest of the nearest peoples by the Russians was supposed by Albert Schlichting and Alexander Gvanini to have brought tyranny upon Russia: 'In 1563 AD when the Great Prince of Muscovy Ivan Vasilievich occupied the former Lithuanian town of Polotsk, widely known at the time [sic!], he became very proud of the success of his campaign'. That is why the tsar, following his grandfather and father, 'took the fortress and the estates. Later all the males from the noble and ancient families who were supposed by him to be the enemies of his tyranny, were killed or eliminated'. This was followed by a description of the atrocities of the *oprichniki.*

The inevitable punishment followed these enormous villainies, never before seen in the history of the world. The prayers of the murdered innocents reached the Divine ears. Ivan the Terrible, as Oderborn remarked, had died in the second year of the war, taken away by a cruel disease. It happened because of his dejection after military defeat. The appeals to God by the prisoners of war, praying for Ivan's death, played their part, for while he was living and was violent, the World in its own essence could not exist. Oderborn continued that friendship, brotherhood and peace had been destroyed in Russia, the churches and altars had been trampled down and no single law was preserved. Everyone waited for the death of the tyrant in the hope that something would change for the better, but the Russian people were usually frightened upon the death of the tsar, afraid that the enemies of Muscovy 'would grow stronger, they would come and conquer us'. Oderborn let his imagination run away, claiming that on the burial day, 30 March 1584, Ivan's body had disappeared, never to be seen again.* As soon as 'the beast had died', the law, brotherhood, friendship, peace and holiness were restored.

In decribing the tyranny of Ivan the Terrible, special attention was paid to the feminine theme. Europeans saw a special example of his tyranny in his attitude to women. Schlichting even devoted a special section to Ivan's 'tyranny against women' in his revelatory book about the tsar. As was noticed by Taube and Krause: 'God must have wished to reveal his anger and tyranny through the weak feminine nature'. Oderborn related how, after the fall of Polotsk in 1579, Moscow's women revolted, demanding that they should have their husbands recalled from the war or be given other husbands. A clergyman, Schelkalov, suppressing the revolt, called for the menfolk of the town, saying, that 'these Amazons' would unite and 'throw the government over altogether'. And the townsmen dissipated the rebelling women with swords and whips.

---

* In reality, Ivan the Terrible was buried in the Archangels Cathedral in the Kremlin, Moscow.

IOANNIS
BASILIDIS MA-
GNI MOSCOVIAE
Ducis vita,

A

PAVLLO ODERBORNIO
tribus libris conscripta.

AD

HENRICVM IVLIVM EPISCO-
pum Halberstadensem, Brunonisuicanorum
& Luneburgensium Ducem magnani-
mum & illustrissimum.

ANNO M. D. LXXXV.

The cover illustration from Oderborn's book on Ivan the Terrible

European authors paid special attention to Russian excesses, their destruction of Livonia and the execution of prisoners of war. Their leaflets are full of such descriptions. The Muscovites demonstrated great inventiveness in the means of execution. They crucified their victims, burnt them alive, hanged them or shot them with arrows; they cut out the hearts and pushed them into each corpse's mouth. For Europeans this symbolism of Russian cruelty was directed first of all against the weakest (children and women), then against the courageous fighters and noblemen (the defenders of the cities), and finally against the priests. For example, English ambassador Jerome Gorsey wrote:

> O the lamentable outcries and cruel slaughters, drowning and burning, ravaging of women and maids, stripping them naked, without mercy or regard of frozen weather, tying and binding them by three and by four at their horses' tails, dragging them, some alive, some dead, all bloodying the ways and streets, lying full of carcasses of the aged men and women and infants; some goodly persons clad in velvet, damask and silks, with jewels, gold and pearls hid about them; the fairest people in the world, by reason of their generation, country and climate, cold and dry. There were infinite numbers thus sent and dragged into Russia. The riches, in money and merchandises and other treasure, that was conveyed and carried out of these cities and country and out of six hundred churches robbed and destroyed, was invaluable.[18]

Yakob Ulfeldt's book described the Livonian prisoners of war, who had been forced into the depths of Russia:

> The Tatars were taking some of them to Moscow, others were being sold in the city; they had been brought near the entrance of the church, for them to be seen properly. The purchasers and the salesmen were gathering in front of our house. The first bought the prisoners cheap, having chosen those they wished. These unfortunate people were dirty, naked or ragged, which you may believe me made us have great compassion for them.

Ulfeldt also described the hunger problems in Livonia when under occupation by the tsar's army:

> The hunger had been so hard that they were found to eat the bread made of crumbled bran, hay and straw; in many places on our way we saw people eating grass, picked up in the fields and pastures. One can only sympathise seeing the great sufferings of the Livonians and damn the cruelty of Russians, who were like roaring lions, and eat them, captured, like mad dogs or pigs.[19]

In his book published in 1615, Peter Petrey, a Swede, gave a great number of graphic descriptions of the evil deeds of the Russians in the Baltic countries. The Tatars raped and murdered 500 noble women and maidens during the seizure of the town of Ascherot, for example. In Moscow 378 prisoners from Livonia and Lithuania were executed, during which crime the brave Livonian maidens cursed the evil deeds of the Russian monarch. They blamed him for his order to torture them constantly and cruelly, to drown them, break their knees, cut pieces of flesh from their bodies, put them between boards and bars, whip them, rape them and roast them. Petrey wrote: 'But the maidens called for their God, praying with all their hearts and souls; unable to speak, they showed with their eyes that the Godless tyrant gave them pain and unjustice and will be punished for that.'

Petrey quoted some verses written in honour of women murdered by the Russians after the seizure of Weissenstein:

Two women and a maiden
Were captured by the tyrant, while being quite innocent,
The men shared their captivity.
He [Ivan the Terrible] ordered them to be tortured
And to make fire,
For them to be completely burnt.
When one of the maidens came to the fire,
She said fearlessly and courageously to the Prince:
'Oh, Cruel Ruler, you look in delight
At the tortures of the victims
Don't even try to forget my words!
When the Son of God comes to the Last Judgement
And gives his just sentence,
You'll be doomed to terrible sufferings.
But these children of God alive and me among them
Will see you in the hands of the tortures.
Glad and merry I will be to see
Your execution and your eternal suffering'.
Having finished her speech, the innocent maiden
Went to her execution with great piety
And died to lead an eternal life then
As the adherent of the holy and true faith.

Petrey's judgement on these women was that:

The punishment of Livonian women and children by Russian troops
(engraving from German leaflet)

These staunch and pious women and maidens might be truly compared with the Saint and unshakeable maiden-sufferers: Blandine, Dorothy and that woman in the Book of Maccabeus, who had been consoling and encouraging with the Divine word her seven sons, mercilessly tortured by the tyrant Antiochus, though they were quite innocent'.[20]

According to Petrey, the inhabitants of the town of Wenden preferred to be blown up in the mined cathedral rather than be tortured by the tyrant. On this occasion the Jesuits had been ashamed, because they were laughing at the Protestants for their not having any wine for their last Eucharist, but God had made a miracle and given a barrel of wine for the devotion.

Europeans were sure that such a bloody tyrant had no support in his own country.* All Russians dreamt of freedom and liberty, but dreaded their tsar. This assurance generated the myth of strong political opposition in

---

* In reality, no information existed about this opposition (only about individuals, such as Prince Andrey Kurbsky, for example). It was a paradox, but the bloody tyrant Ivan the Terrible was one of the most popular rulers in Russian history. This was strikingly illustrated in folklore: Tsar Ivan was the positive hero of folk songs and tales of the sixteenth century. See: Perrie, Maureen, *The Image of Ivan the Terrible in Russian Folklore* (Cambridge: Cambridge University Press, pb 2002), Cambridge Studies in Oral and Literate Culture vol. 16.

Russia against Ivan the Terrible. Allegedly, Muscovites dreamt of the tyrant's dethronement and would support the assistance of the West with great pleasure, to the point of welcoming foreign occupation. Europeans expected the Russian people to meet the invading forces with enthusiasm. According to the Western authors, the Muscovites were the main victims of their tsar. It was he who 'started all the evil'. The Russian people might easily come to an agreement with Europeans. For example, they could make a covenant against the tsar and hand him over to the Poles. According to Paul Oderborn, it was only necessary to wake people up, as all Russians were surprised with the apathy of the tsar and his lack of resistance to the enemy during the last years of the war. But the fear of the tyrant, the people's feeble-mindedness and their mutual suspicion didn't allow them to organise; 'the insane silence' reigned in Russian society.

For these authors the main problem was to ensure the overthrow of Ivan the Terrible himself, and the neutralisation of his supporters, since ordinary Russians didn't want to fight for their motherland. The appearance of the plans to occupy Moscow marked the high point of the development of this discourse. These plans were minutely developed by the team of Pfalzgraf Georg Hans von Pheldentz (count of Alsace). In 1578 the plan for transforming Muscovy into a province of the Holy Roman Empire was put forward by the count's adherents. Its main author was the tsar's former *oprichnik*, the fugitive Heinrich Staden. In 1578–9 this project was sent to the emperor, to the duke of Prussia and to the kings of Sweden and Poland. It was discussed in 1581 in Lübeck at the *Hanzestag*, a conference of the members of the Hanseatic League, and in 1588 at the court of Emperor Rudolf II, but in both cases it was rejected. The Empire was a politically weak state and did not dare to fight Russia.

Staden supposed just 200 ships, 200 guns and 100,000 soldiers would be enough to occupy Muscovy. They would not be necessary, he thought, to fight the enemy, but to occupy and keep the country subjugated. Staden wrote: 'These should be such warriors, who would leave the Christian World devastated, leaving no people alive, or any estates undestroyed. There are many of them in the Christian World.'* The Empire itself should provide half the vessels, the Hanseatic League, Spain or France should lend the second half. So, in Staden's opinion, the whole war would cost about 100,000 thalers.

---

* The term 'Christian World' was used here as a synonym of the term 'Europe'. Staden interpreted it as the Catholic lands of Europe, that is, the possessions of the Habsburgs, predominantly the great territory of the Holy Roman Empire as well as Spain and France.

One hundred missionaries should follow the army; they were easy to find in German universities.

Staden offered to start from Hamburg, Bremen or Emden and first of all attack the town of Kola in Laplandia. Then Solovky monastery, Cholmogory and Key Island in the mouth of the River Onega would follow; later Turchasov and Kargopol' were to be occupied. These should be followed by Vologda and St Kirill monastery on the White Lake. Then Staden grew more ambitious: 'Go farther and devastate Alexandrov!' This would be followed by the destruction of St Trinity monastery, the towns of Volock Lamsky, Zvenigorod and Kolomna, the village of Kolomensky and the outskirts of Moscow. Finally, Moscow itself could then be occupied without firing a shot.

Staden was sure that it would only be necessary to explain to the Russians everything about the great tyranny of their grand prince and to promise that they could retain their estates in order for the Russian nobles to stop fighting for Ivan the Terrible. The tsar should be arrested and sent to the Holy Roman Empire. One of the brothers of the German emperor should become the ruler of the new Russia. Local authorities should be the imperial commissars. It would be necessary to forbid the building of stone Orthodox churches, allowing only wooden ones, while Catholic churches should be built solely of stone. After several years all Orthodox churches would decay and the Muscovites would have to change their religion, converting smoothly to Catholicism.

If this plan had been activated, the world map would be transformed. Staden wrote: 'When the Russian lands would be captured, the borders of Holy Roman Empire should be coincided with the Persian frontier'. Staden was sure that it was easy to reach America through Persia. In alliance with Persia, the Holy Roman Empire would win an easy victory over Turkey. The conquest of Russia should be the first step to world supremacy of the Holy Roman Empire.

Of course, Staden's plan was adventurist, imaginary and fantastical. But it was very indicative of his understanding of the discourses and political mythology that were in use during the propaganda war against Russia in the second half of the sixteenth century.

This brief review allows us to reach some conclusions. During the Livonian War a massive explosion in the publication of anti-Muscovite works took place in the Western intellectual world. They blackened the Russians and their country, their rulers and their aggression against small, defenceless Livonia, and so on. It was not until the Livonian War that the idea of the imminent threat of 'Asiatic Russia' to civilised Europe became one of the main principles of European policy.

The extension of the European Union on 1 May 2004 was accompanied by a number of declarations by high-ranking politicians. Some of them openly, some secretly, expressed one and the same thought: Russia will never become an EU member, as its difference from the European world is too great. The characteristics of this difference had changed but little as to their meaning (only in the specific details of each age). The sources of the stereotypical attitude to Russia are to be found in Ivan the Terrible's wars and in the way they were reflected in sixteenth-century European thought.

This reflection possessed such a strong initial impulse that it predetermined the Europeans' attitude to Russia from the sixteenth century to the present day; and Russia has constantly reinforced this opinion through its policy, which has been far from humble since that time. European intellectuals have used the example of Russian history to demonstrate what the Europeans should not do, what behaviour was incompatible with being European. Russia was held up as the 'antiEurope'. European authors revealed the essence of their own Christian world through the descriptions of non-European negative qualities of their neighbours and antagonists, mostly the Muslims, the Turks and, since the second half of the sixteenth century, the Russians. This cultural mechanism turned out to be so effective and demanded by Europe that American historian Larry Wolff's statement that 'if Russia had not existed, it should have been invented by the West', which he applied to European attitudes to Russia in the Enlightenment of the eighteenth century, ought to be repeated while thinking about those of the sixteenth century.[21]

Finally, one last point should be emphasised. Most European comments about the Russia of Ivan the Terrible contain negative characterisations of Muscovy and the Muscovites. But it is impossible to answer the following question: what is exaggerated in European studies of Russia and where is the sixteenth-century reality reflected truly? Regarding these issues, the greatest difficulty in the study of this epoch was very accurately characterised by the Russian historian Alexey Miller:

> We know that they [the foreigners' stories] are tendentious, we know that the observers' eyes are directed by the prevailing discourses. But the degree and the character of the tendentiousness as a rule remain unclear . . . The overall assertion, that Russia was backward and uncivilised, is not wrong . . . But in every concrete case – how much sincere delusion is there, how much conscious inventiveness, how much suppression? Up to now we don't have any papers attempting to answer these questions.[22]

We might add that in many cases there is no possibility of checking this information objectively. It is quite clear that Ivan the Terrible was a tyrant and his military policy was aggressive. At the same time, it's quite clear that its negative evaluation in European thinking has a highly ideological and discursive character. It is not objective; both the level of the Russian tsar's cruelty, and very often the cruel episodes themselves, are full of myth and fantasy. The history of Ivan the Terrible's military policy was much more complicated. It is impossible to describe it in black and white only. But leaving aside emotions, however important they might be, we will see in the epilogue how Ivan the Terrible's wars really ended.

Epilogue

Ivan the Terrible's military policy can be evaluated under three categories:

- results of his Eastern policy;
- results of his Western policy;
- results of his military policy for his own country.

In terms of his Eastern policy, Ivan the Terrible achieved at least three results which may be considered as true victories and successes. The capture of Kazan (1552) and Astrakhan (1556), along with the beginning of the occupation of Siberia (1582), paved the way for the transformation of Russia into an empire. Moreover, it became a Eurasian empire, composed of the peoples of both Europe and Asia. Russia finally became a true empire in the seventeenth century, after the completion of the conquest of Siberia and the Far East and the annexing of Ukraine after the defeat of Rzeczpospolita in 1654–67. But the first step towards empire was taken by the strategy of Ivan the Terrible.

The Eastern policy of Ivan IV had been a complete success because it strengthened Russian statemanship, extended Russian territory, glorified Russian arms and helped to achieve great political results. The victories over the Tatar states, the heirs of the Golden Horde, allowed the Russians to overcome the enduring inferiority complex instilled in them by the Tatar yoke of the thirteenth and fourteenth centuries. The Kazan, Astrakhan and Siberian Tatars might have deserved better than the cruel and aggressive policy of Ivan the Terrible, but these people proved to have been ground by the millstones of history. The Russians believed it to be a historical revenge; once the Russians had been the Tatar slaves, now history turned and the Tatars became subject to the Russians. In the sixteenth century they were not the same Tatars, they were innocent of the Tatar yoke of the Middle Ages, but historical revenge is rarely accurately aimed or completely just, and very often turns against innocent parties.

The military policy of Russia in the Crimea had also been a success. Russia did not manage to conquer and enslave the Crimea, but this had only been a hypothetical objective during Ivan the Terrible's reign. Russia had no practical means of conquering the Crimea, which would have entailed involvement in a very dangerous military confrontation with Turkey. With the exception of this ambitious aim, Russia had been successful everywhere. It could not overcome the Crimea, but it successfully repelled all its attacks, defending itself capably. In 1571 the Crimean Tatars had burnt Moscow down, but in 1572 their army was completely destroyed halfway to the city.

The first Russian–Turkish war in 1569 was also victorious for Muscovy. Last but not least, in 1571 Russian troops entered the steppe and formed the future border of Russia by cutting crosses on very old oaks. Thus was initiated the programme of invading the *Pole*, which, after Ivan the Terrible's death, would force the Crimean Tatars out, as began to be evident as early as the end of the sixteenth century.

As for his Western policy, the Livonian War was one of Russia's minor wars. One can easily characterise it with the words 'a failure, a defeat, a loss'. In the long run it has been overshadowed by more momentous events, such as the *Oprichnina* of Ivan the Terrible (1565–72), the Time of Troubles (1604–18) and the introduction of serfdom (at the end of the sixteenth century). The Livonian War only gets a mention in three regards. Firstly, it is considered to be an unfortunate attempt to reach the Baltic Sea, which anticipated the feat of Peter the Great by about 150 years; secondly, for historians of a certain political view the Livonian War is a good example of a stupid, irresponsible, crazy enterprise, which was the result of Ivan the Terrible's tyrannical regime and which brought Russia to military and political collapse; thirdly, the Livonian War serves as an example of an aggressive war waged by Russia against peaceful neighbouring states.

All these conclusions look biased. Their supporters adjust the facts to their own point of view and organise the events to support their favourite idea. All the ideological labels may be torn off if one remembers that the Livonian War is an artificial construct by which a series of Baltic wars appear unified into a single war that lasted for twenty-five years. This was done by the Russian imperial historians of the eighteenth and nineteenth centuries, Mikhael Scherbatov and Nicholas Karamzin. In reality it consisted of the Russian–Swedish War (1555–7); the Livonian War proper (1556–61, involving the Livonian Order, Poland, Grand Duchy of Lithuania (GDL), Russia, Sweden and Denmark, and ending with the destruction of the Livonian Order); the Russian–Lithuanian War (1561–70); the Swedish–Danish War (1563–70); the 'Moscow War' between Russia and Rzeczpospolita (1578–82); and two

Russian–Swedish wars (1579–83 and 1589–95). Only after the last of these were the Baltic wars of the sixteenth century completed.

Let us try to test the three formulae mentioned above:

'Russia lost the Livonian War'

The war of Russia against Sweden in 1555–7 was won by Russia. The war of 1556–61 for the division of Livonia ended with the collapse of the Livonian Order; its lands were divided among neighbouring states, the greatest part of them passing to Russia. So Russia could not possibly have been among those countries that had lost the war. Moscow also won its war with the Grand Duchy of Lithuania in 1561–70, obtaining Polotsk and its surroundings. Russia lost the 'Moscow War' of 1578–82 with Rzeczpospolita and the war with Sweden of 1579–83. However, Muscovy practically returned to the positions on which it had stood before the disastrous year of 1578. Russia had occupied part of Livonia and Polotsk and lost them by 1582–3. Some of the Russian Baltic fortresses that were lost in 1578–83 were gained back during the Russian–Swedish war of 1589–95. So, strictly speaking, the overall territorial result of the Baltic wars of the second half of the sixteenth century was not a failure for Russia. It had neither gained nor lost anything important.

'The Livonian War is a good example of a stupid, irresponsible, crazy enterprise'

The actions of the Muscovite government, diplomatic service and military command were not always effective and successful, but it is hardly possible to represent the events of the war only as a series of shameful mistakes and failures.

The measures of mobilisation taken by the central govenment may be evaluated in differing ways, but it is clear that, somehow or other, sufficient human and material resources were collected to allow the country to wage a whole series of hard wars without subjecting Russia to a military catastrophe and complete foreign occupation. The Russian government proved equal to this task.

The really negative aspect of Ivan the Terrible's reign was the *Oprichnina*. It was a real terror against Ivan's own subjects, spying mania and the struggle with imaginary traitors and so on. As a result, a traditional Russian question arises when evaluating the Baltic wars. It is the eternal question of the high and bloody price paid by the Russian people for the mistakes of those in power. Alas! Such a question may be asked about many events in Russian history, not only about the epoch of Ivan the Terrible.

Russian diplomacy had both some successes and some great mistakes and failures. The breaking of the anti-Russian alliance of Lithuania and Crimea is among the former. The alliance with Denmark in 1562, which greatly facilitated Russian actions on the Baltic, also belongs among the successes, as does the involvement of the Vatican and the Holy Roman Empire in a manner favourable to Russia's political interests in the 1580s. Russia managed to persuade the pope and the emperor not with certain promises but also with some shadowy hints of promises.

As a result the Christian world helped Moscow to sign a treaty with Rzeczpospolita on quite acceptable terms. But Ivan the Terrible didn't repay his debts. Russia withheld both from the Catholic Union and from its role in the anti-Muslim league. In his talks with Antonio Possevino, the papal legate who anticipated the glory of the Catholic faith and the conversion of the tsar, Ivan called the pope a wolf. Being at quite a loss, the dismayed legate could only murmur: 'Well, if the pope is a wolf, there is nothing to talk about.'

Among the diplomatic failures were the unfortunate attempt to create an anti-Lithuanian league of Russia and the Crimea; the wrong policy towards the 'Livonian king', Magnus, which contributed to his turning traitor; and the failure of the election campaigns during the Polish interregnum. There were many more small defeats, and they were the results of the ineffectual style of the Muscovite diplomatic service. Their adherence to the old customs and rituals, their self-importance and the dogmatism of thought overpowered their common sense and the art of diplomacy. It was easier for a Russian envoy to suffer heroically 'for the sake of his tsar', than to conjure some clever diplomatic combination.

The military results of the Baltic wars of the second half of the sixteenth century were not so distressing. The commanders were at their best and often won the battles. The wars were lost by the politicians, but that was a characteristic feature of many more periods of human history. One of the greatest victories was won by the Russian army at Ermes (1560). It was the Russian army that put the final full stop to the history of the Northern Crusaders. The march to Polotsk in 1563 and the invasion of Livonia in 1577 were absolutely victorious. The defence of Pskov in 1581 brought its protectors eternal glory.

Among the serious military defeats were the battle of the Ula (1564) and the losses of Polotsk (1579), Luki the Great (1580) and Narva (1581). It is worth mentioning, however, that this list itself shows that Russia had hardly lost any major field battle (we leave open the question whether the Ula battle could be considered to be major). The fighting was waged around towns and the territories attached to them.

'The Livonian War serves as an example of an aggressive war waged by Russia against peaceful neighbouring states'

Was it Russia alone that was annexing Livonian lands? The country was invaded simultaneously by Poland, Lithuania, Sweden and Denmark, each of which created their own zones of occupation. The German Hanseatic League also had some aggressive intentions towards the Baltic lands. As for the wars between Russia and Lithuania or Russia and Sweden, all the countries involved were equally guilty of militarism. For example, in 1561, the military operations were started by Lithuania against Russia; in 1579, 1580 and 1581 it was the troops of Rzeczpospolita that began the invasion of Russia and occupied its lands for three years. All participants in the Baltic wars divided the spheres of influence, established the borders of possible expansion and defined the zones of occupation. The search for guilty parties is not the job of a historian, but of a lawyer. A historian should not judge, but comprehend. Yet it should be emphasised that to blame Russia for its aggressive policy and to consider it to be the only cause of the wars of the sixteenth century would be ahistorical and would contradict well-proven facts. Not only Russia but also several European countries at the same time claimed the Baltic lands and wished to occupy them.

What, then, was the result of the Livonian War and the other Baltic wars of the second half of the sixteenth century? Let us consider the gains and losses of each of the countries involved.

The Livonian Order

The Order collapsed and lost its official meaning. Its lands were divided among the neighbouring countries. Part of the population was exterminated, part of it emigrated and some of it was assimilated socially and culturally by the invading countries (principally Sweden and Poland). This marks the end of the epoch of the Northern Crusaders.

Rzeczpospolita (the kingdom of Poland and Grand Duchy of Lithuania)

It turned out that Poland gained much from the Baltic wars. It was this country that dominated in the Polish–Lithuanian union founded in Lublin in 1569 as a result of the incapacity of the GDL to stand up to the Russian enemy alone. Although it would be incorrect to speak of the annexation of Lithuania, the prevailing role of the Polish component in Rzeczpospolita, that unique cultural and historical formation, is indisputable.

As for territorial acquisitions, Rzeczpospolita gained more lands than any of the other combatants. The rulers of Courland and Semigalia became vassals of the kings of Poland. Letlandia and most of Estlandia (with the exception of its eastern part), Riga included, were subjected to Poland. So, one can speak about the incorporation of the Baltic lands into the Polish–Lithuanian state as a result of the Baltic wars. The English historian Robert Frost was quite correct in calling the sixteenth century the time of Polish domination of the Baltic.

But the fact is that the memory of Polish rule disappeared because it lasted for only a short time. As early as the first quarter of the seventeenth century, Poland was practically ousted from the region by Sweden. To continue Robert Frost's thought, one hundred years of Swedish rule came to the Baltic, to be substituted later in the eighteenth century by the 'Russian epoch'. But this seems to be the subject of a different book.

Sweden

This country profited immensely from the Baltic wars, but, unlike those of Rzeczpospolita, these gains were not momentary, but long-lasting. Having obtained independence in 1523, Sweden swiftly passed on its way from a peripheral state to the mighty sovereign of the Baltic. In fact, the construction of the famous Swedish Empire, dominating the region throughout the whole seventeenth century and then destroyed by Peter the Great in 1700–21, began in the second half of the sixteenth century with the occupation of Northern Estlandia by the Swedes.

Denmark

Judging by the result of the Baltic wars, Denmark looks more like a loser, though its losses weren't symbolised by its great military failures or territorial losses. Denmark had failed to stay in the Baltic and make a bridgehead against Sweden there. The kingdom of Prince Magnus in Estlandia was destroyed. It is worth noting, however, that this result corresponds with the minor effort invested; the Livonian theatre was not a priority for Danish policy in the sixteenth century.

The Holy Roman Empire

The Empire lost its easternmost colony, which showed once again its political weakness, though in the sixteenth and seventeenth centuries territorial losses on an even greater scale became traditonal for the Habsburg family. Indeed, other factors than the loss of territory deserve special attention. The Baltic wars revealed that the authority of the emperor in the Christian world was still great, in spite of military impotence. It was constant awareness of the opinion of the imperial court at Vienna that prevented Denmark from making its policy more active. The role of the Empire, the Vatican and legate

Antonio Possevino's mission in the background of the Moscow war are hard to underestimate. It was Germany that became a battlefield in the propaganda war against Russia in the second half of the sixteenth century (most of the leaflets were written in German or Latin). The Empire, therefore, rose from the Baltic wars reclaiming its reputation as a player; militarily weak, but still preserving its art in the field of diplomatic struggle and intrigues, and preserving its authority in the spiritual and ideological spheres.

Russia

What had really Russia gained and lost during the wars of Ivan the Terrible? The first gain was some political experience, which was quite new. These were the first Russian wars against Europe. They demonstrated the technical and tactical deficiency of the Russian army in comparison with the Western mercenaries. They revealed the lack of an actual propaganda mechanism and the old-fashioned principles of the army's formation. However, the solutions materialised very slowly, over a century later, the immense resolve and ruthlessness of Peter the Great being necessary to begin the reconstruction of the Russian military machine.

For the first time the Russian army was fighting in Europe as part of a military coalition (albeit a pitiful one, with Prince Magnus of Denmark their only ally) and against other coalitions. Muscovite envoys mastered high diplomatic arts, taking part in the competition for the Polish crown (during the interregnum) and discussing the project of the division of western Europe between Germany and Russia, the first in its history, with the lords of the Holy Roman Empire.

Ivan the Terrible determined the direction of Russia's geopolitical ambitions for centuries: towards the Baltic and eastern Europe. His actions also predestined for ages the historical fate of this region as a border, an unstable zone between the European and Russian civilisations. Scholars used to call this zone the 'Limitrophe' (from the Latin word *limes* – the name of the borders of the ancient Roman Empire). From the seventeenth to the twentieth centuries, the main opposition was between western Europe and Russia. The nations and states within the Limitrophe zone (the Baltic peoples, Poles, Lithuanians, Ukrainians, Byelorussians and so on) proved to be the cards to change hands in big political games. They were 'thrown' from one side to the other, being attached sometimes to Russia, sometimes to the West. That was the source of tragedy for many peoples and many nations which disappeared, victims to the ambitions and desires of the big players: for example, the Prussian Order disappeared in 1525 annexed by Poland; the Livonian Order in 1561, annexed by Poland, Sweden, Denmark and Russia; and Rzeczpospolita in 1795, annexed by Austria, Prussia and Russia.

The wars of Ivan the Terrible gave Russia some negative experiences as well. Alas, they quite clearly demonstrated that the Russians' greatest enemies were themselves. It's not quite certain who damaged the Russian army more, the soldiers of King Stefan Bathory or the terror of the *Oprichnina* of Ivan the Terrible. Intellectual inefficiency, ignorance, the lack of professionalism, technical and cultural backwardness were far worse enemies of Russia than the Poles, the Tatars and the Swedes.

How far did Russian armies develop under Ivan the Terrible? The Russian army had reached the state in which it functioned until the 1630s more than a half a century before. During the wars of Ivan the Terrible the role of fire-arms increased. If there were only specialised detachments possessing guns at the beginning of Ivan's reign, by the 1580s firearms were the basic equip-ment of infantry and increasingly in use among the cavalry. In these wars the control of military administration was refined and models developed for military organisation in different situations: campaigns, small raids, sieges, offensive defence, defence-in-depth and so on. The foundation of special for-tified defensive zones — the abatis lines at the southern borders — brought great advantages. Owing to these zones, Russia was able to pass over to the offensive in the south in the 1580s, after the death of Ivan the Terrible.

In conclusion, let us remark that Ivan the Terrible's military policy did not bring about the large-scale reconstruction of the European world. However, his wars pointed the way for the future conflicts and wars of the seventeenth and eighteenth centuries: the Turkish, Baltic, Ukrainian, Polish and Swedish ones. It was not in vain that the allegorical figures of Ivan the Terrible and Peter the Great were carved on the Triumphal Arch erected in honour of the Niestadt peace treaty, signed after the Northern War between Russia and Sweden (1700–21), which ended with a complete victory for Emperor Peter the Great. The figures of Ivan the Terrible and Peter I were accompanied, respectively, by the inscriptions '*Incipit*' ('He began') and '*Perficit*' ('He perfected').

Notes

Introduction

1. Karl Marx, *Secret Diplomatic History of the 18th Century* at: http://www.marxists.org/archive/marx/works/1857/russia/ch04.htm (last visited 14 August 2007).
2. Vadim Tsymburski, 'Zemlja za Velikim Limitrofom', in *Bizness i Politika*, 9 (1995), p 56.
3. John Fennell (ed., trans), *The Correspondence between Prince A.M. Kurbsky and Tsar Ivan IV of Russia, 1564–1579* (Cambridge, 1963), pp 6 and 8.
4. The papers of negotiations with the Lithuanian embassy of Stanislav Kryski, *1578* (unpublished), Russian State Archive of Ancient Acts, fond 79, inventory no. 1, document no. 10, pp 381 and 384.
5. David Miller, 'The Coronation of Ivan IV of Moscow', in *Jahrbücher für Geschichte Osteuropas*, 16 (1968), pp 562–3.
6. 'The Report of Russian Ambassador in England Fyodor Pisemski, 1582', in *Sbornik Russkogo istoricheskogo obschestva*, vol. 38 (St Petersburg, 1883), p 46.
7. The speech of Russian boyar Vasiliy Yuriev at the negotiations with the Crimean envoy Akinchey, June 1565 (unpublished), Russian State Archive of Ancient Acts, fond 123, inventory no. 1, document no. 11, p 352.
8. Sergey Bogatyrev, 'Battle for Divine Wisdom: The Rhetoric of Ivan IV's Campaign against Polotsk', in Erik Lohr and Marshall Poe (eds), *The Military and Society in Russia, 1450–1917* (Leiden, Boston and Köln, 2002), p 341.
9. For more details, see Alexander Filjushkin, 'Problema genezisa Rossijskoj imperii', in Iliya Gerasimov, Sergey Glebov, Alexander Kaplunovskiy, Marina Mogilner and Alexander Semenov (eds), *Novaya Imperskaya istoriya post-sovetskogo prostranstva* (Kazan, 2004), pp 375–408.

Chapter 1

1. Michael Roberts, 'The Military Revolution 1560–1660', in Michael Roberts, *Essays in Swedish History* (Minneapolis, 1967), pp 195–225; John Lynn (ed.), *Tools of War: Instruments, Ideals and Institutions of Warfare, 1445–1871* (Urbana, 1990); Clifford Rogers (ed.), *The Military Revolution Debate: Readings on the Military Transformation of Early Modern Europe* (Boulder, 1995); Geoffrey Parker, *The Military Revolution: Military Innovation and the Rise of the West 1500–1800* (Cambridge, 1996).
2. Richard Hellie, *Enserfment and Military Change in Muscovy* (Chicago and London, 1971), pp 164 and 267; Sergey Kaštanov, 'Zu einen Besonderheiten der Bevölkerungssituation Russlands im 16. Jahrhundert', in *Jahrbücher für Geschichte Osteuropas*, 43 (1995) pp 338–9; Michael Krom, 'O chislennosti russkogo vojska v pervoj polovine XVI v', in *Rossijskoe gosudarstvo v XIV-XVII vv.: Sbornik statej, posvjaschennyj 75-letiu so dnja*

rozhdenija U.G. Alexeeva (St Petersburg, 2002), pp 67–82.

3. Richard Hellie, 'Why did the Muscovite Elite Not Rebel?', in *Russe History*, 25 (1998), no. 1–2, pp 155–62; Marshall Poe, 'What did Russians Mean, When They Called Themselves "Slaves of the Tsar"?', in *Slavic Review*,57 (1998), no. 3, pp 585–608.

4. Arkadiy Mankov, *Ceny i ich dvizhenie v Russkom gosudarstve 16-go veka* (Moscow and Leningrad, 1951), pp 37, 45, 50, 53, 91, 121, 126 and 140.

5. For more details, see Anatoliy Chernov, *Vooruzhennye sily Russkogo gosudarstva v XVI-XVII vekach* (Moscow, 1954); Maria Denisova, 'Pomestnaya konnitsa i ee vooruzhenie v XVI-XVII vekach', in Trudy Gosudarstvennogo, *Istoricheskogo Muzeya*, vol. 20: *Voenno-istoricheskiy sbornik* (Moscow, 1948).

6. *Razryadnaya kniga 1475–1605*, vol. 2, no. 1 (Moscow, 1981) pp 91–2; 'Dopolneniya k Nikonovskoy letopisi', in *Polnoe sobranie Russikich letopisej*, vol. 13 (Moscow, 1965), p 339.

7. Giles Fletcher, 'Of the Russian Commonwealth', in Lloyd Berry and Robert Crummey (eds), *Rude and Barbarous Kingdom: Russia in the Accounts of Sixteenth Century English Voyagers* (Madison, Milwaukee and London, 1968), p 180.

8. Jerome Gorsey, 'Travels', in Berry and Crumney (eds), *Rude and Barbarous Kingdom*, p 289.

9. This is the author's translation from Sergey Shokarev (ed), *Genry Shtaden: Zapiski nemtsa-oprichnika* (Moscow, 2002), p 84.

Chapter 2

1. Fletcher, op. cit., p 195.

2. Evliya Cheleby, *Kniga Puteshestviy (The Book of Travels)*, at http://www.vostlit.info/Texts/rus8/Celebi2/frametext1.htm (last visited 14 August 2007).

3. Ghulnara Aminova, 'K methodike sostavleniya administrativnoy karty Kazanskogo Khanstva', in Sergey Alishev and Ilidus Zaghidullin (eds), *Kazanskoe Khanstvo: Aktualnye problemy issledovaniya* (Kazan, 2002), pp 117–34.

4. Damir Islhakov, 'Demographicheskaya situatsiya v tatarskikh khanstvakh Povolzhiya', in Alishev and Zaghidullin (eds), *Kazanskoe Khanstvo*, p 143.

5. Iliya Zaytsev, *Astrakhanskoe Khanstvo* (Moscow, 2004), pp 30–62.

6. Anna Khoroshkevich, *Rus' i Krym: ot souza k protivostoyaniju. Konec XV – nachalo XVI veka* (Moscow, 2001), p 103.

7. Georgy Gontsa, 'K istorii moldavsko-turetskich otnoshenij nachala XVI veka', in Boris Rybakov (ed), *Rossia, Polsha i Prichernomorie v XV – XVIII vekach* (Moscow, 1979), pp 40–7.

8. Robert Frost, *The Northern Wars: War, State and Society in Northeastern Europe, 1558–1721* (Harlow, 2000), pp 8–9.

9. Andrzej Walicki, 'The Political Heritage of the Sixteenth Century and its Influence on the Nation Building Ideologies of the Polish Enlightenment and Romantism', in Samuel Fiszman (ed), *The Polish Renaissance in its European Context* (Bloomington, 1988), pp 35–6.

10. *Relacje nuncjuszów apostolskich i innych osób o Polsce od r. 1548 do 1690*, vol. 1, (Berlin-Poznań, 1864), p 199.

11. Stanisław Bodniak, *Polska a Bałtyk za ostatniego Jagiellona* (Kórnik, 1947), pp 57 and 59–60; Kazimierz Lepszy, *Dzieje Floty Polskiej* (Gdańsk, Bydgoszcz and Szczecin, 1947), p 84–6.

12. Frost, op. cit., p 7.

13. Walther Kirchner, *The Rise of the Baltic Question* (Westport, 1970), pp 4–11; William Urban, *The Livonian Crusade* (Washington, 1981), pp 430 and 432.

14. Arvo Viljanti, *Gustav Vasas ryska krig 1554–1557* (Abo, 1955), pp 42 and 776.

Chapter 3

1. Yuri Seleznev, 'Otvetnyj udar: Russkie napadeniya na Zolotuu Hordu', in *Rodina. Russky istorichesky journal*, 11 (2003), pp 95–7 and 102–4.
2. See the following articles in *Slavic Review*, 26 (1967), no. 4: Edward Keenan, 'Muscovy and Kazan: Some Introductory Remarks on the Patterns of Steppe Diplomacy', pp 548–58; Jaroslav Pelensky, 'Muscovite Imperial Claims to the Kazan Khanate', pp 559–76; Omeljan Pritsak, 'Moscow, the Golden Horde and the Kazan Khanate From a Polycultural Point of View', pp 577–83; Ihor Shevchenko, 'Moscow's Conquest of Kazan: Two Views Reconciled', pp 541–7. See also: Jaroslav Pelensky, *Russia and Kazan. Conquest and Imperial Ideology (1438–1560s)* (Mouton, 1974), pp 65–138; Frank Kampfer, 'Die Eroberung von Kazan 1552 als Gegenstand der zeitgenossischen rusischen historiographie', in *Forschungen zur osteuropaischen Geschichte*, 14 (1969), pp 7–161.
3. John Fennell (ed., trans), *Prince A.M. Kurbsky's History of Ivan IV* (Cambridge, 1965), p 31.
4. Anon., 'Nikonovskya Letopis', in *Polnoe sobranie Russikich letopisej*, vol. 13 (Moscow, 1965), p 206.
5. Fennell (ed., trans.), *Prince A.M. Kurbsky's History of Ivan IV*, p 41.
6. Ibid., p 49.
7. Ibid., p 53.
8. Ibid., p 57.
9. Ibid., p 61.
10. Ibid., p 63.
11. Ibid., p 51.
12. Zaytsev, op. cit., pp 142–5.
13. Vasiliy Smirnov, *Krymskoe Khanstvo pod verkhovenstvom Ottomanskoj Porty do nachala XVIII veka* (St Peterburg, 1887), pp 425–6.
14. Anon., 'Nikonovskya Letopis', p 271.

Chapter 4

1. Boris Florya, 'Proekt antituretskoj koalicii serediny XVI veka', in Boris Rybakov (ed.), *Rossia, Polsha i Prichernomorie v XV – XVIII vekach* (Moscow, 1979), pp 74–9.
2. For the history of Pselsky Town, see Vladimir Zagorovskiy, *Istoriya vkhozhdeniya Centralnogo Chernozemiya v sostav Rossijskogo gosudarstva v XVI veke* (Voronezh, 1991), pp 138–43.
3. The report of Russian ambassador Athanasius Nagoy, September 1563 (unpublished), Russian State Archive of Ancient Acts, fond 123, inventory no. 1, document no. 10, p 161, inner face.
4. The message of Devlet-Girei to Ivan the Terrible, August 1563 (unpublished), Russian State Archive of Ancient Acts, fond 123, inventory no. 1, document no. 10, pp 173–5, inner face.
5. The report of Russian ambassadors Athanasius Nagoy and Fyodor Pisemsky, October 1564 (unpublished), Russian State Archive of Ancient Acts, fond 123, inventory no. 1, document no. 11, pp 138–40.
6. The report about negotiations with Crimean envoy Yelyushka, January–February 1567 (unpublished), Russian State Archive of Ancient Acts, fond 123, inventory no. 1, document no. 12, pp 344–59.
7. The message of Devlet-Girei to Ivan the Terrible, 3 October 1570 (unpublished), Russian State Archive of Ancient Acts, fond 123, inventory no. 1, document no. 13, pp 309–12.
8. Zagorovskiy, op. cit., pp 165–8.
9. Smirnov, op. cit., pp 426–8.
10. The report about negotiations with Crimean ambassador Devlet-Kildei, June 1571 (unpublished), Russian State Archive of Ancient Acts, fond 123, inventory no. 1, document

no. 13, pp 401–5.

11. Alexander Filjushkin, 'Kholop tvoj vinovatyj: Prestuplenie i raskayanie Kudeyara Tishenkova', in *Rodina. Russky istorichesky journal*, 12 (2004), pp 68–70.

12. Ruslan Skrynnikov, *Tsarstvo terrora* (St Petersburg, 1992), pp 453–66.

Chapter 5

1. Kirchner, op. cit., pp 3 and 105; Urban, op. cit., p 465; Frost, op. cit., pp 11–12.

2. Vigantas Stancelis, 'The Annexation of Livonia to the Grand Duchy of Lithuania: Historiographical Controversies', in *Lithuanian Historical Studies*, 5 (2000), p 21; Erich Donnert, *Der Livändische Ordenstritterstaat und Russland. Der Livändische Krieg und die baltische Frage in der europäischen Politik 1558–1583* (Berlin, 1963), pp 37–8.

3. Alexander Filjushkin, 'Diskourses Livonskoj vojny', in *Ab Imperio. Studies of New Imperial History and Nationalism in the Post-Soviet Space*, 4 (2001), pp 43–80.

4. Anon., 'Nikonovskya Letopis', p 260.

5. Viljanti, op. cit., pp 371–700.

6. Knud Rasmussen, *Die Livländische Krise 1554–1561* (Copenhagen, 1973), pp 28–9; Erik Tiberg, *Zur Vorgeschichte des Livländischen Krieges: Die Beziehungen zwischen Moskau und Litauen 1549–1562* (Uppsala, 1984), pp 63 and 85–87; Jan Olewnik, 'Polsko-Pruski plan inkorporacji Inflant do Monarchii Jagiellohskiej z lat 1552–1555 i jego pierwsze stadium realizacji', in *Komunikaty mazursko-warmihskie*, 4 (146) (1979), pp 396–8.

7. Norbert Angermann, *Studien zur Livländpolitik Ivan Groznyj's* (Marburg, 1972), pp 15–16; Kirchner, *The Rise of the Baltic Question*,pp 96–98; Erich Tiberg, *Om Villkoren för Moskoviens Baltiska handle 1487–1547 jch handelns roll I utrikespolitiken*,book I, (Stochkholm, 1975), pp 2 and 9–228; Urban, 'The Origin of the Livonian War, 1558', in *Lituanus, the Lithuanian Quarterly Journal of Arts and Sciences*, 29 (1983), no. 3; Urban, *The Livonian Crusade*, pp 474–6.

8. Stanislav Karwowski, *Wcielenie Inflant do Liwy i Polski 1558–1561 roku* (Poznah, 1873); Rasmussen, op. cit., pp 21–33; Urban, *The Livonian Crusade*, pp 482–4.

9. Rasmussen, op. cit., pp 83–5; Tiberg, *Zur Vorgenschichte des Livländischen Krieges*, pp 90–4

10. Anon., 'Nikonovskya Letopis', p 295.

11. Balthasar Ryussov, 'Livonskaya khonika', in *Sbornik materialov i statej po istorii Pribaltijskogo Kraya*, 2, (1879), pp 387–8.

12. Tiberg, *Zur Vorgenschichte des Livländischen Krieges*, pp 168–73.

Chapter 6

1. Bogatyrev, op. cit., pp 341–5.

2. Konstantin Petrov (ed.), *Kniga Polotskogo pokhoda 1563 goda (Issledovanie i text)*, (St Peterburg, 2004), pp 31–86.

3. The speech of Vasilij Yuryev at the Russian–Lithuanian negotiations, 11 December 1563, in *Sbornik Russkogo istoricheskogo obschestva*, vol. 71 (St Petersburg, 1892), p 270.

4. Andrey Yanushkevich, 'Vulskaya bitva 1564', in *Polatskiya gistarychnyja zapiski. Navukovy Chasopis*, 1 (2004), pp 32–42.

5. The speeches of Russian and Danish diplomats at the negotiations, July 1562 (unpublished), Russian State Archive of Ancient Acts, fond 53, inventory no. 1, document no. 1, pp 190–204.

6. Ibid., pp 234–41.

7. Anna Khoroshkevich (ed), 'Statejnyj spisok Rossijskogo posolstva v Daniu v 1562–1563 godach', in Jakob Ulfeld, *Puteshestvie v Rossiju* (Moscow, 2002), pp 520–46.

8. Sture Arnell, *Bidrag till belysning av den baltiska fronten under det nordiska sjuårskriget*

1563–1570 (Stockholm, 1977); Knud Jespersen, 'Rivalry without Victory: Denmark, Sweden and the Struggle for the Baltic 1500–1720', in Göran Rystad et al (eds), *In Quest of Trade and Security. The Baltic Power Politics 1500–1900*, book 1 (Lund, 1994), pp 137–76; Frede Jensen, *Danmarks konflikt med Sverige 1563–1570* (Copenhagen, 1982).

9. 'Odprava Cesarza Maximiliana II do Cara Ivana IV, 1576' (unpublished), Archiwum Główne Akt Dawnych w Warszawie (Central Archives of Historical Records in Warsaw), Archive of Dukes Radzivill, Dz II, no. 89a, p 10.

10. Alexander Zimin, *V kanun groznykh potryasenij. Predposylki pervoj krestianskoj vojny v Rossii* (Moscow, 1986), pp 47–51; Boris Florya, *Ivan Grozny* (Moscow, 1999), pp 344–7.

11. Rheinhold Heidenstein, *Zapiski o Moskovskoj vojne (1578–1582)*, at http://www.vostlit. info/Texts/rus9/Geidenstein/text1 (last visited 14 August 2007).

12. Ibid.

13. The papers of Russian–Lithuanian negotiations in 1578 (unpublished), Russian State Archive of Ancient Acts, fond 79, inventory no. 1, document no. 10, pp 315–84.

14. The papers of the embassy of Mikhail Karpov and Peter Golovin, 1578–79 (unpublished), Russian State Archive of Ancient Acts, fond 79, inventory no. 1, document no. 10, pp 1–118 and 415–56.

Chapter 7

1. Heidenstein, op. cit.
2. Ibid.
3. Ibid.
4. The papers of the embassy of Ivan Sitsky, 1580 (unpublished), Russian State Archive of Ancient Acts, fond 79, inventory no. 1, document no. 12, pp 21–77.
5. The instructions to the delegation of Eustaphy Pushkin and Fyodor Pisemsky, April 1581 (unpublished), Russian State Archive of Ancient Acts, fond 79, inventory no. 1, document no. 12, pp 252–62.
6. The message of Ivan IV to Stefan Bathory, 29 June 1581, in Dmitry Likhachev and Yakov Lurie, *Poslaniya Ivana Groznogo* (Moscow and Leningrad, 1951), pp 213–238.
7. The message of Stefan Bathory to Ivan IV, 2 August 1581, in Michael Pogodin and Dmitry Dubensky (eds), *Kniga posolskaya Metriki Velikogo knyazhestva Litovskogo, soderzhaschaya v sebe diplomaticheskie snosheniya Litvy v gosudarstvovanie korolya Stefana Bathoria (s 1573 po 1580 god)* (Moscow, 1845), pp 177–206.
8. Heidenstein, op. cit.
9. Ibid.
10. The message of Prince Dmitry Eletsky to Tsar Ivan IV, 12 January 1582, in Fyodor Uspensky (ed.), *Peregovory o mire mezhdu Moskvoj i Polshej v 1581 – 1582 godach* (Odessa, 1885), pp 63–74.
11. Izabel de Madariaga, *Ivan the Terrible* (New Haven and London, 2006), pp 334–40.
12. Ekkehard Klug, 'Das "asiatische" Russland Ueber die Entstehung eines europaischen Vorurteils', in *Historische Zeitschrift*, 245 (1987), pp 265–89.
13. The author's translation from Albert Schlichting, 'Kratkoe skazanie o charactere i zhestokom pravlenii Vasilievicha, Tyranta Moscovii', at http://www.vostlit.info/Texts/rus10/ Schlichting/frametext.htm (last visited 14 August 2007).
14. Andreas Kappeler, *Ivan Grozny im Spiegel der ausländischen Druckschriften seiner Zeit. Ein Beitrag zur Geschichte des westlichen Russlandbildes* (Frankfurt/Mein, 1972), pp 9, 237 and 239; Stefan Mund, *Orbis russiarum: Genèse et development de la representation du monde 'russe' en Occident à la Renaissance* (Geneva, 2003), pp 270–4; Thomas Ott, 'Livonia est propugnaculum Imperii': *Eine Studie zur Schilderung und Wahrnehmung des Livländischen Krieges (1558–1582/83) nach den deutschen und lateinischen Flugschriften der Zeit* (Munich, 1996), pp 7–8 and 63–5.

15. Urban, *The Livonian Crusade*, pp 489.
16. Ott, op. cit., pp 53–4.
17. Richard Pipes, in his introduction to Giles Fletcher (ed. Richard Pipes), *Of the Russian Commonwealth* (Harvard, 1966), pp 26–8.
18. Gorsey, op. cit., p 267.
19. Anna Khoroshkevich and John Lind (eds), *Jakob Ulfeld: Puteshestvie v Rossiju*,(Moscow, 2002), pp 290 and 339–40.
20. Peter Petrey, 'Istoriya o velikom knyazhestve Moskovskom', in Sergey Dubov, *O nachale vojn i Smut v Moscovii* (Moscow, 1997), pp 242–5.
21. Larry Wollf, *Izobretaya Vostochnuu Europu: Karta civilizacii v soznanii epochi Prosvescheniya* (Moscow, 2003), Introduction to the Russian edition, p 14.
22. Ibid., Alexey Miller's introduction, pp 7–8.

Appendix I
Chronology

1530, 25 August – birth of Grand Prince Ivan IV.

1533, 4 December – Ivan IV becomes official ruler of Russian state. He was three years old. All power was in the hands of the regency council.

1538, 3 April – death of Ivan's mother, Grand Princess Elena Glinskaja. She was poisoned.

1543, 29 December – Ivan IV orders the execution of Prince Andrey Shuysky, his first order of punishment. Ivan was thirteen years old.

1545, 2 April – beginning of the Russian–Kazan War (ends in 1552). First Russian raid on Kazan.

1547, 16 January – Coronation of Ivan the Terrible in the Cathedral of the Mother's Assumption in Moscow.

1547, February – second Russian raid on Kazan.

1547, November–March 1548 – third Russian raid on Kazan.

1548 – Russian Orthodox church of St Nicholas, in the Livonian town Dorpat, forcibly closed by Livonians.

1549 – beginning of military cooperation between Moscow government and Don Cossacks. Ivan the Terrible commands Cossacks to ravage the territories of the Crimean khanate.

1549, November–February 1550 – fourth Russian raid on Kazan.

1549–50 – Cossacks capture Astrakhan for a short time.

1550 – founding of *streltsy* forces.

1551 – foundation of the fortress of Michailov in southern Russia. The Russian border advanced southward into the wilderness area of the so-called *Pole*.

1551, 24 May–2 October 1552 – the great campaign to conquer Kazan (from the foundation of the siege fortress of Sviyazhsk to the capitulation of Kazan).

1552 – King Sigismund II Augustus of Poland, and Duke Albert of Prussia plan the annexation of the Livonian Order during secret meetings in

Krupishki and Breitenstein.

1554, 28 April–1 June – negotiations between Russia and the Livonian Order in Moscow. Livonia undertook to pay tribute for three years, until 1557.

1554, 29 July – Russian troops capture Astrakhan for the first time.

1554, August – secret Polish–Prussian memorandum prepared, outlining a plan for the subjugation of Livonia.

1554 – first negotiations between Russia and the Grand Duchy of Lithuania about alliance against Muslim countries.

1555, July – Battle of Sudbishchi between Russian and Crimean troops, the first success of Muscovite army in a field battle.

1555, September – Swedish force led by Jakob Bagge attacks Russian fortress of Oresheck. Beginning of the Russian–Swedish War.

1555, November – some tribes of the Nogays pledge loyalty to Ivan the Terrible.

1556, January – siege of Swedish fortress of Vyborg by Russian troops.

1556, May–June – so-called War of Coadjutors in Livonia: rebellion of supporters of Wilhelm, archbishop of Riga. Rebels ask Polish king to intervene in Livonia.

1556, June – assault of Don Cossacks and Cossack *atamans* from Cherkassy, Mlyn and Kanev upon the Crimean *ulusy* and Turkish fortresses on Black Sea coast.

1556, June – beginning of peace negotiations between Russia and Sweden.

1556, July – Russian troops capture Astrakhan for the second time. Astrakhan khanate destroyed.

1556 – issue of law on military service – *Ulozhenie o Sluzhbe*.

1557, February – Russia and Sweden make peace. End of Russian–Swedish War.

1557, May, October – Battle of Khortitsa Island between Crimean Tatars and troops of Prince Dmitry Vishnevetsky.

1557, 5 September – Pozvol peace treaty between Livonia and Poland. Livonia becomes subject to the Polish crown.

1557, December – negotiations in Moscow between Russian and Livonia regarding Livonian non-payment of *Yuryevskaya* tribute.

1558, January – Russian invasion of Livonia. Beginning of Livonian War and Russian occupation of its share of Livonia.

1558, January–April – 'siege' of Crimea by the detachment of Prince Dmitry Vishnevetsky, Cossacks and Muscovite troops.

1558, 11 May – Russian troops capture important Livonian fortress of Narva.

1558, 18 July – Russian troops capture Dorpat and rename it Yuryev. It becomes capital of Russian possessions in Livonia.

1558 – second attempt by Russia to enter into an anti-Muslim alliance with the Grand Duchy of Lithuania.

1559, January – German Reichstag in Augsburg decides to help Livonia by urging Ivan the Terrible to stop military operations in Livonia and asking German towns for a loan of 100,000 *guldens* for the hiring of troops. These measures were not realised.

1559, January–February – second great Muscovite invasion of Livonia. 50,000 Russian troops cross the Livonian border in seven different places.

1559, February–June – Muscovite troops and Don Cossacks attack the Crimea. High point of Russian success in their campaign against the Crimean khanate.

1559, 10 March – Lithuanian delegation officially accuses Ivan the Terrible of violating the peace between Christian states and assaulting Wilhelm, archbishop of Riga, King Sigismund's relative.

1559, 31 August – the First Vilna Pact between Livonia, Poland and the Grand Duchy of Lithuania. King of Poland takes the lands of Livonia under his protection.

1559, September – the Treaty of Neubourg. Danish King Frederick II buys the Livonian island of Ösel, and decides to send his younger brother Duke Magnus there with the title of bishop of Ösel and Courland.

1559, November – counterattack by the Livonian Order. Siege of Yuryev.

1560, February – third major Russian invasion drives deep into Livonia.

1560, April – Danish Duke Magnus landed at Arensburg to start implementation of Treaty of Neubourg. Denmark begins the occupation of its share of Livonia.

1560, July – Polish and Lithuanian troops start implementing the First Vilna Pact and invade Livonia.

1560, 2 August – Battle of Ermes, the last great fight of the Northern Crusaders. The military forces of the Livonian Order are totally destroyed.

1560, September – Revel's citizens and nobility of Harrien ask for Swedish aid.

1560, September – Reichstag of Speyer decides to ask for support of Livonia from England, Poland, Denmark, Sweden and cities of the Hanseatic League. None materialises.

1561, 30 May – King Sigismund declares the Polish sovereign should be high commander of all troops fighting the Russians in Livonia, regardless of who hired the soldiers. Beginning of the Russian–Polish–Lithuanian War.

1561, June – knights and citizens of Revel and northern Estonia sign an agreement making themselves subjects of the Swedish crown. Beginning of Swedish occupation of its part of Livonia.

1561, 28 November – Second Vilna Pact officially recognises partition of the Livonian Order's territory; all its possessions formally pass under jurisdiction of Lithuania and Poland.

1562, March–August – Russian–Danish negotiations. Ivan IV confirms treaty on **7 August**; King Frederick ratifies it on **3 December**. It was the first international document declaring Livonia to be the legitimate possession of the Russian tsar.

1562, 30 November–15 February 1563 – raid and siege of Polotsk by Russian troops. Capitulation of Polotsk.

1563–64 – Russian diplomatic attempts to enter alliance with Crimean khanate, directed against the Grand Duchy of Lithuania.

1563–70 – war between Sweden and Denmark.

1564, 26 January – battle of the Ula in which the Grand Duchy of Lithuania was victorious over the Muscovites.

1564, 30 April – flight of Prince Andrey Kurbsky from Russia to the Grand Duchy of Lithuania.

1565 – establishment of the *Oprichnina* of Ivan the Terrible.

1566 – completion of the *zasechnaja cherta*, the fortified line in southern Russia consisting of barricades of felled trees.

1566–67 – Crimean attempts to enter alliance with Russia, directed against the Grand Duchy of Lithuania.

1569 – first Russian–Turkish War over Astrakhan; glorious victory for Russia.

1569, 28 June – Union of Lublin. Foundation of the Polish–Lithuanian Commonwealth (Rzeczpospolita).

1570, 24 June – Russia and the Grand Duchy of Lithuania conclude a three-year truce, ending the Russian–Polish–Lithuanian War.

1570, August–March 1571 – siege of Revel by Russian and Danish troops.

1571 – institution of Russian frontier military service in southern Russia. Russia actually marks its southern boundaries officially on the upper Mius and Orel rivers.

1571, 24 May – Moscow set on fire by Tatars and burnt to the ground.

1572, 7 July–14 May 1573 – first Polish interregnum. First attempt by Ivan the Terrible to ascend the Polish throne.

1572, 23 July–2 August – Battle of Molodi, a glorious Russian victory against the Tatars.

1574, 29 June–4 March 1576 – second Polish interregnum. Second attempt by Ivan and his son Fyodor Ivanovich to ascend the Polish throne.

1576 – division of eastern Europe between Russia and Germany (Holy Roman Empire) discussed.

1577, 13 June–August – victorious raid by Russian troops into Livonia. The last Muscovite victory in Livonia.

1577, November – counterattack by Lithuanian troops in Livonia captures Dinaburg and Wenden.

1578, 30 January – truce between Russia and the Grand Duchy of Lithuania signed in Moscow, later annulled by Stefan Bathory.

1578, January–March – the Warsaw *sejm* decides to start war against Russia and recapture Polotsk and Livonia; beginning of the 'Moscow War' between Russia and Rzeczpospolita.

1578, February, June and October – three sieges of Wenden, Muscovites defeated.

1579, 26 June – Stefan Bathory sends Ivan an official declaration of war.

1579, 30 June–October – Stefan Bathory's first invasion of Russia.

1579, July – Swedish invasion of northern Estonia. Siege of Narva.

1579, 1 September – Bathory captures Russian fortress of Polotsk.

1580, August–October – Bathory's second invasion of Russia.

1580, November – Swedish invasion of Russian region of Karelia.

1581, August–February 1582 – Stefan Bathory's third invasion of Russia. The raid of Krzysztof Radzivill's unit on inner Russia reaches the tsar's residence, Staritsa. Famous unsuccessful siege of the Russian stronghold of Pskov.

1581, 5 September – Bathory captures Russian fortress of Luki the Great.

1581 – Sweden conducts active military operations in Livonia, capturing Narva, the main Russian fortress on **6 September**.

1581, 13 December–15 January 1582 – negotiations between Russia and Rzeczpospolita in Yam Zapolsky. Stefan Bathory and Ivan the Terrible conclude a ten-year truce, ending the 'Moscow War'.

1583, May–August – Russian–Swedish negotiations take place on the Plyussa river, resulting in a three-year truce.

1584, 18 March – death of Ivan the Terrible.

1585 – publication of first European biography of Ivan the Terrible, written by German pastor Paul Oderborn.

Appendix II
Rulers

Grand princes, sovereigns of all Russia and tsars of all Russia

1462–1505 Ivan III Vasilievich, Grand Prince, Sovereign of all Russia

1505–1533 Vasiliy III Ivanovich, Grand Prince, Sovereign of all Russia

1533–1584 Ivan IV Vasilievich, Grand Prince, Sovereign and Tsar of all Russia

1584–1598 Fyodor Ivanovich, Grand Prince, Sovereign, Tsar and Autocrat (*samoderzhec*) of all Russia

Masters of the Livonian Order

1494–1535 Walter von Plettenberg

1535–1549 Hermann Hasenkamp von Brüggeneye

1549–1551 Johann von der Recke

1551–1557 Heinrich von Galen

1557–1559 Johann Wilhelm von Fürstenberg

1559–1561 Gotthard (Godert) Kettler

Grand princes of Lithuania

1492–1506 Alexander Kazimirovich, simultaneously the king of Poland from 1501

1506–1548 Sigismund I the Old, simultaneously the king of Poland

1548–1572 Sigismund II Augustus, simultaneously the king of Poland; from 1569, king of Rzeczpospolita

Kings of Poland

1492–1501 Jan Olbracht

1501–1506 Alexander Kazimirovich, simultaneously grand prince of Lithuania

1506–1548 Sigismund I the Old, simultaneously grand prince of Lithuania

1548–1572 Sigismund II Augustus, simultaneously grand prince of
           Lithuania; from 1569, king of Rzeczpospolita

Kings of Rzeczpospolita

1569–1572 Sigismund II Augustus
1573–1574 Henry Valois
1576–1586 Stefan Bathory
1587–1632 Sigismund III Vasa; from 1592, simultaneously king of Sweden

Emperors of the Holy Roman Empire

1493–1519 Maximilian I Habsburg
1519–1556 Charles V Habsburg, (1519–30 formally 'King of the Romans')
1556–1564 Ferdinand I Habsburg
1564–1576 Maximilian II Habsburg
1576–1612 Rudolf II Habsburg

Rulers of Prussia

1498–1510 Frederick of Saxony, grandmaster of the Teutonic Order
1511–1568 Albert of Brandenburg-Ansbach, grandmaster of the Teutonic
           Order; from 1525, simultaneously first duke of Prussia
1568–1618 Albert Frederick, Duke of Prussia

Kings of Sweden

1523–1560 Gustav I Vasa (Gustav Eriksson)
1560–1568 Erik XIV
1568–1592 Johan III
1592–1599 Sigismund III Vasa, simultaneously king of Rzeczpospolita

Kings of Denmark

1481–1513 Hans Oldenburg
1513–1523 Christian II
1523–1533 Frederick I
1534–5159 Christian III
1559–1588 Frederick II
1588–1644 Christian IV

Kings of England

1509–1547 Henry VIII
1547–1553 Edward VI

1553–1558 Mary I
1558–1603 Elizabeth I

Popes
1492–1503 Alexander VI
1503 Pius III
1503–1513 Julius II
1513–1521 Leo X
1522–1523 Adrian VI
1523–1534 Clement VII
1534–1549 Paul III
1550–1555 Julius III
1555 Marcellus II
1555–1559 Paul IV
1559–1565 Pius IV
1566–1572 Pius V
1572–1585 Gregory XIII
1585–1590 Sixtus V
1590 Urban VII
1590–1591 Gregory XIV
1591 Innocent IX
1592–1605 Clement VIII

Sultans of Turkey
1481–1512 Bayezid II
1512–1520 Selim I
1520–1566 Suleyman I 'the Magnificent'
1566–1574 Selim II
1574–1595 Murad III
1595–1603 Mehmed III

Khans of the Crimean khanate
1466–1513 Mengli-Girei
1513–1523 Mohammed-Girei I
1523–1532 Saadat-Girei I
1532–1551 Sagib-Girei I
1551–1577 Devlet-Girei I
1577–1584 Mohammed-Girei II
1584–1588 Islam-Girei
1588–1608 Kazy-Girei

Khans of the Kazan khanate

1495–1502 Abdull-Latiph
1502–1518 Mohammed-Emin
1519–1521 Shahghali
1521–1524 Sagib-Girei
1524–1531 Safa-Girei
1531–1536 Dzhan-Aly
1536–1546 Safa-Girei
1546   Shahghali
1546–1549 Safa-Girei
1549–1551 Utamesh
1551–1552 Shahghali
1552   Yadegar

Khans of the Astrakhan khanate

1502–1514 Abd al-Kerim
1514–1521 Janibek
1521-?   Khuseyn
? – 1528 Sheykh-Akhmet
? – 1531 Kasim
1531–1532 Islam-Girei
1532   Kasim
1532–1533 Akkubeck
1533–1537 Abd ahr-Rakhman
1537–1539 Derbish-Ghali
1539–1543 Abd ahr-Rakhman
1545–1546 Akkubeck
1546–1554 Yamghurchi
1554–1556 Derbish-Ghali

Appendix III

State of Troop Alertness and the Mobilisation Potential of the Armies of Countries Participating in the Wars of Ivan the Terrible

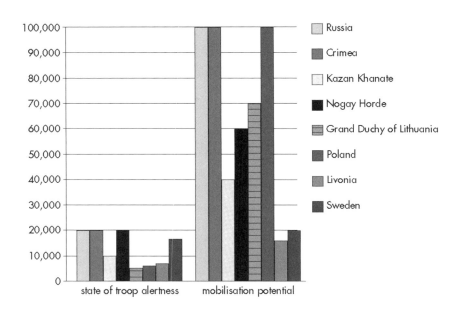

Appendix IV

Comparison of Eastern European Armies
of the Sixteenth Century

Country	The basic force of the army	Characteristics of cavalry	Characteristics of infantry
Russia	Cavalry. Recruitment: noble militia; military service is obligatory for every nobleman	Heavy and light cavalry; Basic armament: cold steel and bows; firearms rare	Auxiliary role. *Streltsy* – equipped with matchlock firearms; *Posokha* – irregulars armed with various light armament. No pikemen
The Crimean khanate	Cavalry. Recruitment: militia	Light cavalry; Cold steel and bows; No firearms	Only in garrisons in the Crimea itself; No firearms
The Kazan khanate	Cavalry. Recruitment: from specialised military class (*oglans*) or from irregulars	Light cavalry; Cold steel, bows; Firearms rare	Ceremonial and court troops, militia; Scarce in peacetime
The Astrakhan khanate	Cavalry. Recruitment: militia	Light cavalry; Cold steel and bows; No firearms	Scarce; Only in garrisons; Limited use of firearms
The Nogay Horde (Great and Small ones)	Cavalry. Recruitment: militia.	Light cavalry; Cold steel and bows; No firearms	No infantry
Turkey (only the troops stationed in the Crimea and the northern Black Sea region)	Infantry	For the most part light cavalry; Small in number cavalry was rarely engaged in special operations; Armed both with cold steel and firearms	Janissaries and irregulars; Armed with cold steel and firearms; Light armour; The most part of infantry detachments are attached to garrisons
The Grand Duchy of Lithuania	Cavalry. Recruitment: noble militia	Heavy and light cavalry; Cold steel and firearms; Light and heavy armour	Auxiliary role; Used mainly in the defence of fortresses and performing technical tasks; Cold steel and firearms
The Polish Kingdom	Cavalry	Heavily armed hussars' cavalry; Lancers armed with cold steel and firearms as well; Light cavalry is less common	Lancers and arquebusiers; Importance of infantry increased since the last third of sixteenth century after introduction of *haiduks* by Stefan Bathory
Livonia	Knights' cavalry	Heavily armed cavalry, very rare use of light cavalry; Armament: mostly cold steel; firearms were known but archaic, medieval tactics of battling did not allow frequent use	*Knechts*; Cold steel and firearms
Sweden	Infantry; Irregulars were gradually replaced by mercenaries during the century	Auxiliary role; Cold steel and firearms	Lancers and arquebusiers; Cold steel

Characteristics of artillery	The system of defence	Navy	Use of mercenaries
Siege, field and fortress artillery highly developed; Extensive use of foreign specialists to teach Russians until they reached European standards in the use of artillery	Well thoughtout; border defence duties; early warning of incursions; On state level: elaborate defensive system using large forces on south and east border; Special system of border fortifications – abatis barriers	None	Military personnel from Europe; Use of Tatar units from subjugated Kazan and Astrakhan khanates, the Nogay Horde and peoples of northern Caucasus in westward operations
Not used in field battles; Most of the artillerymen in the Crimean fortresses are Turks	Perekop (the Crimean Isthmus) is blocked; The rest of the territories are not being defended systematically (not counting the Ottoman fortresses)	None	The Nogays are invited for joint campaigns; Turkey's aid is used especially in technical sphere (artillery, navy, art of fortification)
Some evidence of fortress artillery, but not widely used	No system of frontier defence	None	The Nogays are invited from time to time
Possibly some fortress artillery, but not widely used	No system of frontier defence	No navy, excluding minor piracy on Caspian Sea	The Nogays are invited from time to time
No artillery	No system of frontier defence	None	Did not bring in foreigners; Sometimes participated in joint campaigns with other Tatar states and more often hired themselves out
Field and fortress artillery is highly developed	A system of fortresses, most of which are stone	The Black Sea navy consisting mainly of galleys with sails	Foreigners were not employed in the Black Sea region (if not to regard local militiamen as mercenaries)
Siege, field and fortress artillery is highly developed	A system of small permanent garrisons in boundary fortresses that did not provide safety, however	No navy	Mercenaries from European countries were invited; Hiring for remuneration
Siege, field and fortress artillery highly developed	A system of small permanent garrisons in boundary fortresses that did not provide safety, however	Small navy; Use of privateers	The number of mercenaries in the army had been increasing throughout sixteenth century till it reached its highest number in the last third of the century under Stefan Bathory
Fortress artillery mainly, though familiar with the other types of artillery	Garrisons in castles. The system of the castles was oriented towards keeping control over the territory and suppression of the local tribes and not towards repulse of the outer aggression	No navy excluding military ships aimed for trade fleet guarding large trade cities (Riga, Revel etc.)	Mostly mercenaries from Germany though the practice of hiring was not widespread due to scarcity of means allotted by the grandmaster, bishops and cities
Siege, field and fortress artillery highly developed	A system of small permanent garrisons in boundary fortresses that did not provide safety, however	The second mightiest navy in the Baltic region after Denmark's	Recruiting of mercenaries was a widespread practice

Bibliography

Aksan, Virginia, 'Ottoman Wars and Warfare, 1450–1812', in Jeremy Black (ed), *War in the Early Modern World* (London: University College London Press, 1999).

Angermann, Norbert, *Studien zur Livländpolitik Ivan Groznyj's* (Marburg and Lahn: J G Herder-Institut, 1972).

Arbusow, Leonid, *Grundriss der Geschichte Liv-, Est- und Kurlands* (Riga: Jonck u. Poliewsky, 1908).

Attman, Artur, *The Russian and Polish Markets in International Trade: 1500–1650* (Gothenburg: Institute of Economic History of Gothenburg University, 1973).

——, 'The Struggle for Baltic Markets: Powers in Conflict 1558–1618', in *Acta Regiae Societatis Scientiarum et Litterarum Gothoburgensis. Humaniora, 14* (Gothenburg: Kungl, Vetenskapsoch vitterhets-samhället, 1979).

Baron, Samuel, *Explorations in Muscovite History* (Norfolk: Brookfield, 1991).

Biskup, Marian (ed.), *Inflanty w średniowieczu: Władstwa zakonu krzyżackiego I biskupów /Pod redahcią Mariana Biskupa* (Toruh, Towarzystwo Naukowe: Uniwersytet Mikołaja Kopernika, 2002).

Bobrick, Benson, *Fearful Majesty: The Life and Reign of Ivan the Terrible* (New York: Putnam, 1987).

Bodniak, Stanisław, *Polska a Bałtyk za ostatniego Jagiellona* (Kórnik: 1947).

Bogatyrev, Sergei, 'Battle for Divine Wisdom: The Rhetoric of Ivan IV's Campaign against Polotsk', in Eric Lohr and Marshall Poe (eds), *The Military and Society in Russia, 1450–1917* (Leiden and Boston, Mass: Brill, 2002).

——, 'The Sovereign and His Counsellors: Ritualised Consultations in Muscovite Political Culture, 1350s–1570s', in *Suomalaisen Tiedekatemian Toimituksia. Annales Academiæ Scientiarum Fennicæ.*

Sarja-ser. Humaniora nide-tom 307 (Helsinki: Academia Scientiarum Fennica, 2000).

Butterwick, Richard (ed.), *The Polish–Lithuanian Monarchy in European Context, c.1500–1795* (Basingstoke: Palgrave, 2001).

Chirot, Daniel (ed.), *The Origins of Backwardness in Eastern Europe. Economics and Politics from the Middle Ages until the Twentieth Century* (Berkeley: University of California Press, 1989).

Christiansen, Eric, *The Northern Crusades* (London: Penguin, 1997).

Collins, L.J.D., 'The Military Organisation and Tactics of the Crimean Tatars, 16th–17th Centuries', in Vernon Perry and Malcolm Yapp (eds), *War, Technology and Society in the Middle East* (London: Oxford University Press, 1975).

Crummey, Robert, *The Formation of Muscovy: 1304–1613* (London: Longman, 1987).

Davies, Brian, *Warfare, State and Society on the Black Sea Steppe, 1500–1700* (London and New York: Routledge, 2007).

Delius, Walter, *Antonio Possevino SJ und Ivan Groznyj: Ein Beitrag zur Geschichte der kirchlichen Union und der gegenreformation des 16. Jahrhunderts* (Stuttgart: Evang. Verl. Werk, 1962).

Derbov, Leonard, 'K istorii padeniya Livonskogo Ordena', in *Uchenye zapiski Saratovskogo gosudarstvennopgo universiteta*, vol. 17 (Saratov: izdatelstvo Saratovskogo universiteta, 1947).

Donnert, Erich, *Der Livändische Ordenstritterstaat und Russland: Der Livändische Krieg und die baltische Frage in der europäischen Politik 1558–1583* (Berlin: Rütten and Loening, 1963).

Duffy, Christopher, *Siege Warfare: The Fortress in the Early Modern World* (New York: Barnes and Noble, 1979).

Dvorkin, Alexander, *Ivan the Terrible as a Religious Type: a Study of the Background, Genesis and Development of the Theocratic Idea of the First Russian Tsar and His Attempts To Establish 'Free Autocracy' in Russia* (Erlangen: Lehrstuhl für Geschichte und Theologie des christlichen Ostens, 1992).

Dzyarnovich, Aleg, ' . . .in nostra Livonia'. *Dakumentalnye krynitsy pa gistoryi palitychnykh adnosinav pamizh Vyalikim Knyastvam Litovskim i Livoniyaj v kantsy 15 – pershej palove 16 stoletij: Sistemetizaciya i aktavy analyz* (Minsk, 2003).

Eckardt, Hans von (trans. Catherine Phillips et al.), *Ivan the Terrible* (New York: Alfred A Knopf, 1949).

Esper, Thomas, 'Military Self-Sufficiency and Weapons Technology in Moscovite Russia', in *Slavic Review*, 28 (1969), no. 2.

Filjushkin, Alexander, 'Diskursy Livonskoj vojny', in *Ab Imperio: Studies of New Imperial History and Nationalism in the Post-Soviet Space*, 4 (2001).

——, 'Der Diskurs von der Notwendigkeit des Durchbruchs zur Ostsee in der russischen Geschichte und Historiographie', in Karsten Brüggemann (ed), *Narva und die Ostseeregion: Beiträge der II. Internationalen Konferenz über die politischen und kulturellen Beziehungen zwischen Russland und der Ostseeregion (Narva, 1.-3. Mai 2003)* (Narva: Narva College, 2004).

——, 'Vglyadyvayas' v oskolki razbitogo zerkala: Rissijskij diskurs velikogo knyazhestva Litovskogo', in *Ab Imperio: Studies of New Imperial History and Nationalism in the Post-Soviet Space*, 4 (2004).

——, *Tituly russkikh gosudarej* (Moscow and St Petersburg: Al'yans-Arkheo, 2006).

Fisher, Alan. *The Crimean Tatars* (Stanford: Hoover Institution Press, 1978).

Florya, Boris, *Ivan Grozny* (Moscow: Molodaya Gvardiya, 1999).

Forsten, Georgy, 'Bor'ba iz-za gospodstva na Baltijskom more v 15 i 16 stoletiyakh', in *Zapiski istoriko-filologicheskogo fakulteta imperatorskogo Sankt Petersburg universiteta*, vol. 14 (St Petersburg, 1893).

——, 'Baltijskij vopros v 16 i 17 stoletiyakh (1544–1648). T. I: Bor'ba iz-za Livonii', in *Zapiski istoriko-filologicheskogo fakulteta imperatorskogo Sankt-Peterburgskogo universiteta*, vol. 33 (St Petersburg, 1893).

Frost, Robert, *The Northern Wars: War, State and Society in Northeastern Europe: 1558–1721* (Edinburgh and Harlow: Longman, 2000).

Graham, Hugh, 'How Do We Know What We Know About Ivan the Terrible? (A Paradigm)', in *Russe History*, vol. 14 (1987), no. 4.

Grant, Jonathan, 'Rethinking the Ottoman "Decline": Military Technology Diffusion in the Ottoman Empire, Fifteenth to Eighteenth Centuries', in *Journal of World History*, vol. 10 (1999), no. 1.

Grzybowski, Stanisław, *Henryk Walezy* (Wrocław: Zakład Narodowy im. Ossolińskich-Wydawnictwo, 1980).

Król i kanclerz (Krakow: Krajowa Agencja Wydawnicza, 1988).

Hall, Bert, *Weapons and Warfare in Renaissance Europe: Gunpowder, Technology and Tactics* (Baltimore: Johns Hopkins University Press, 1997).

Hellie, Richard, 'What Happened? How Did He Get Away With It?: Ivan Groznyi's Paranoia And the Problem of Institutional Restraints', in *Russe History*, vol. 14 (1987), no. 4.

Hellie, Richard, 'The Costs of Muscovite Military Defence and Expansion' in Lohr et al (eds), *The Military and Society in Russia, 1450–1917* (Leiden: Brill, 2002).

Hrala, Ieronim, *Ivan Mikhajlov Viskovaty* (Moscow: Radiks, 1994).

Huttenbach, Henry, *Muscovy's Conquest of Muslim Kazan and Astrakhan, 1552–1556*, in Michael Rywkin (ed.), *Russian Colonial Expansion to 1917* (London: Mansell, 1988).

Inalcik, Halil, 'The Origin of the Ottoman–Russian Rivalry and the Don–Volga Canal (1569)', in *Annals of the University of Ankara, 1946–47*, vol. 1.

Kappeler, Andreas, *Ivan Grozny im Spiegel der ausländischen Druckschriften seiner Zeit. Ein Beitrag zur Geschichte des westlichen Russlandbildes* (Frankfurt: Peter Lang, 1972).

——, 'Die Deutschen Flugschriften über die Moskowiter und Iwan den Schrecklichen im Rohmen der Russlandliteratur des 16 Jahrhunderts', in Mechthild Keller (ed.), *Russen und Russland aus deutscher Sicht: 9–17 Jahrhundert* (Munich: Fink, 1988).

Karttunen, Kaarlo, 'Jean III et Stefan Batory: Études sur les relations politiques entre la suede et la Pologne de 1576 a 1583', in *Annales Academiae Scientiarum Fennicae*, series B. vol. V.1 (Genève: Imprimerie Chaulmontet, 1911).

Karwowski, Stanisław, *Wcielenie Inflant do Liwy i Polski: 1558–1561 roku* (Poznań: 1873).

Keep, John, *Soldiers of the Tsar: Army and Society in Russia, 1462–1874* (Oxford: Clarendon Press, 1985).

Khodarkovsky, Michael, *Russia's Steppe Frontier: The Making of a Colonial Empire, 1500–1800* (Bloomington: Indiana University Press, 2002).

Khoroshkevich, Anna, *Rossija v systeme mezhdunarodnykh otnoshenij serediny 16 veka* (Moscow: Nauka, 2003).

Kiaupa, Zigmantas, Jūratė Kiaupienė and Albinas Kuncevičius, *The History of Lithuania Before 1795* (Vilnius: ARLILA Press, 2000).

Kirby, David, *Northern Europe in the Early Modern Period: The Baltic World. 1492–1772* (London: Longman, 1990).

Kirchner, Walther, *The Rise of the Baltic Question* (Westport, Conn.: Greenwood Press, 1970).

Klug, Erik, 'Das "asiatische" Russland. Ueber die Entstehung eines europaischen Vorurteils', in *Historische Zeitschrift*, 245 (1987).

Koc, Leon, *Szlakiem Batorego: Wojna Moskiewska 1577–1582* (Wilno: 1926).

Koroljuk, Vladimir, *Livonskaya vojna: Iz istorii vneshnej politiki Russkogo centralizovannogo gosudarstva vo vtoroj polovine 16 veka* (Moscow:

izdatelstvo Akademii nauk SSSR, 1954).

Kotarski, Henryk, 'Wojskowość Polsko-Litewska doby Batorianskiej (1576–1586)', in Witold Bieganski (ed.), *Historia wojskovości Polskiej* (Warszaw: Ministerstwa Obrony Narodowej, 1972).

Kurukin, Igor, 'K izucheniu istochnikov o nachale Livonskoj vojny i deyatelnosti pravitelstva Adasheva i Silvestra', in *Istochnikovedcheskie issledovaniya po istorii feodalnoj Rossii* (Moscow: Institut istorii SSSR Akademii nauk, 1981).

Lamb, Harold, *The March of Muscovy: Ivan the Terrible and the Growth of the Russian Empire, 1400–1648* (New York: Doubleday, 1948).

Lepszy, Kazimierz, *Dzieje Floty Polskiej* (Gdansk; Bydgoszcz; Stettin: 1947).

Lepyavko, Sergey, *Ukrainskoe kozatstvo v mizhdunarodnikh vidosinakh (1561–1591)* (Chernigiv: Siveryanska dumka, 1999).

Lloyd, Berry and Robert Crummey (eds), *Rude and Barbarous Kingdom: Russia in the Accounts of Sixteenth-Century English Voyagers* (Madison: University of Wisconsin Press, 1968).

Loit, Alexander, 'Die Baltischen Länder im Schwedischen Ostseereich', in Alexander Loit and Helmut Pirimäe (eds), *Die schwedischen Ostseeprovinzen Estland und Livland im 16–18 Jahundert* (Stockholm: Almquist och Wiksell Internat, 1993).

McNeill, William, *Europe's Steppe Frontier, 1500–1800* (Chicago: University of Chicago Press, 1964).

Madariaga, Isabel de, *Ivan the Terrible: First Tsar of Russia* (New Haven and London: Yale University Press, 2005).

Majewski, Wieslav, 'The Polish Art of War in the Sixteenth and Seventeenth Centuries', in Jan Fedorowicz (ed.), *A Republic of Nobles. Studies in Polish History to 1864* (Cambridge: Cambridge University Press, 1982).

Mund, Stéfane, *Orbis Russiarum: Genèse et development de la representation du monde 'russe' en Occident à la Renaissance* (Geneva: Lirairie Droz S.A., 2003).

Murphey, Rhoads, *Ottoman Warfare, 1500–1700* (London: University College London Press, 1999).

Natanson-Leski, Józef, *Epoka Stephana Batoriego w dzieach granicy wschodniej Rzeczypospolitej* (Warsaw: 1930).

Niedzielski, Kazimierz, *Batory i car Iwan w zapasach o Inflanty: (1579–1581)* (Warszawa: 1916).

Novoselsky, Alexey, *Bor'ba Moskowskogo gosudarstwa s tatarami v pervoj polovine 17 veka* (Moscow and Leningrad: izdatelstvo Akademii Nauk SSSR, 1948).

Ott, Thomas, *'Livonia est propugnaculum Imperii': Eine Studie zur*

Schilderung und Wahrnehmung des Livländischen Krieges (1558–1582/83) nach den deutschen und lateinischen Flugschriften der Zeit (Osteuropa-Institut München: Mitteilungen 16/1996) (Munich: Osteuropa-Inst, 1996).

Paul, Michael, 'The Military Revolution in Russia, 1550–1682', in *Journal of Military History*, vol. 68 (2004), no. 1.

Pavlov, Andrei and Maureen Perrie, *Ivan the Terrible* (London: Pearson/ Longman, 2003).

Perrie, Maureen, *The Image of Ivan the Terrible in Russian Folklore* (Cambridge: Cambridge University Press, 1987; pb 2002).

—, *The Cult of Ivan the Terrible in Stalin's Russia* (Basingstoke and New York: Palgrave, 2001).

Rasmussen, Knud, *Die livländische Krise 1554–1561* (Copenhagen: Universitetsforlaget, 1973).

Roberts, Michael, *The Early Vasas: A History of Sweden, 1523–1611* (Cambridge: Cambridge University Press, 1968).

Roggers, Clifford (ed.), *The Military Revolution Debate. Readings on the Military Transformation of Early Modern Europe* (Boulder: Westview Press, 1995).

Sikorski, Janusz, *Polskie tradycje wojskowe. T. I: Tradycje walk obronnych z najazdami niemców, krzyżaków, szwedów, turków i tatarów* (Warsaw: Wyd. Ministerstwa Obrony Narodowej, 1990).

Skrynnikov, Ruslan (ed. and trans. Hugh Graham), *Ivan the Terrible* (Gulf Breeze, Florida: Academic International Press, 1981).
Tsarstvo terrora (St Petersburg: Nauka, 1992).

Śliwiński, Artur, *Jan Zamoyski: Ranclerz i Hetman Wielki Koronny* (Warsaw, 1947).

Smith, Dianne, 'Muscovite Logistics, 1462–1598', in *Slavonic and East European Review*, vol. 71 (1993) no. 1.

Staemmler, Klaus-Dietrich, *Preussen und Livland in ihrem Verhältnis zur Krone Polen. 1561 bis 1586* (Marburg: Lahn, 1953) *Wissenschaftliche Beiträge zur Geschichte und Landeskunde Ost-Mitteleuropas*, no. 8.

Stancelis, Vigantas, 'The Annexation of Livonia to the Grand Duchy of Lithuania: Historiographical controversies', in *Lithuanian Historical Studies*, 5 (2000).

Stone, David, *A Military History of Russia: From Ivan the Terrible to the War in Chechnya* (Westport, CT: Praeger, 2006).

Sucheni-Grabowska, Anna, 'Starania Iwana Grożnego o rękę Katarzyny Jagiellonki a konflikt z Rosią o Inflanty (1560–1561)', in *Homines et Societas: Czasy Piastów i Jagiellonów* (Poznan, 1997).

Sunderland, Willard, *Taming the Wild Field: Colonization and Empire on the Russian Steppe* (Ithaca, NY: Cornell University Press, 2004).

Szelągowski, Adam, *Walka o Bałtyk* (Lvov and Poznan: 1921).

Thaden, Edward, 'Ivan IV in Baltic German Historiography', in *Russe History*, vol. 14 (1987), no. 4.

Tiberg, Erik, 'Die politik Moskaus gegenüber Alt-Livland: 1550–1558', in *Zeitschrift für Ostforschung*, 25 (1976).

——, *Zur Vorgeschichte des Livländischen Krieges: Die Beziehungen zwischen Moskau und Litauen 1549–1562* (Stockholm: Almqvist och Wiksell, 1984) Acta Universitatis Upsaleinsis. Studia Historica Upsaliensia, vol. 134.

——, *Moscow, Livonia and the Hanseatic League: 1487–1550* (Stockholm, 1995) Akta Universitatis Stockholminesis. Stidia Baltica Stockholmiensia, vol. 15.

Troyat, Henri (trans. Joan Pinkham), *Ivan the Terrible* (London: New English Library, 1985).

Urban, William, *The Livonian Crusade* (Washington, DC: University Press of America, 1981).

Viljanti, Arvo, *Gustav Vasas Ryska Krig 1554–1557*, vols 1 and 2 (Stockholm, 1957).

Vinogradov, Alexander, 'Vneshnyaya politika Ivana IV Groznogo', in Gennadiy Sanin (ed.), *Istoriya vneshnej politiki Rossii, Konets 15–17 vek* (Moscow: Mezhdunarodnye otnosheniya, 1999)

Wijaczka, Jacek, *Prusy książęce a Polska, Litwa i Inflanty w połowie XVI w. Działalnosč dyplomatyczna Arsenusa von Brandta w 1544–1558* (Kielce: Wyższa Szkoła Pedagogiczna im. Jana Kochanowskiego, 1992).

Wimmer, Jan, 'Piechota w wojsku polskim XV-XVIII w', in Witold Bieganski (ed), *Historia wojskowości polskiej* (Warszaw: Ministerstwo Obrony Narodowej, 1972).

Yanov, Alexander (trans. Stephen Dunn), *The Origins of Autocracy: Ivan the Terrible in Russian History* (Berkeley and London: University of California Press, 1981).

Yanushkevich, Andrey, *Vyalikae Knyastva Litovskae i Inflyantskaya vajna 1558–1570* (Minsk: Medisont, 2007).

Zagorovsky, Vladimir, *Istoriya vkhozhdeniya Tsentralnogo Chernozemiya v sostav Rossijskogo gosudarstva v 16 veke* (Voronezh: izdatelstvo Voronezhskogo universiteta, 1991).

Zawadski, Konrad, *Początki Prasy Polskiej: Gazety ulotne i seryjne XVI-XVIII wieku* (Warsaw: Biblioteka Narodowa, 2002).

Zernack, Klaus, *Polen und Russland: Zwei Wege in der Europaischen*

Geschichte (Berlin: Propylaen Verlag, 1994).

Zimin, Alexander, *V kanun groznykh potryasenij: Predposylki pervoj krestianskoj vojny v Rossii* (Moscow, 1986).

Index

Aa (river) 198
Abd ahr-Rakhman (khan of
    Astrakhan) 281
Abd al-Kerim (khan of
    Astrakhan) 281
Abdull-Latiph (khan of Kazan)
    281
Abo (Swedish town) 147, 190
Ack-Mechet' (Crimean town)
    60
Adashev, Alexey (Russian
    nobleman) 98, 99, 103, 120,
    147, 165–6, 168
Adashev, Danila (Russian
    nobleman) 115, 116, 159
Adezh see Etz
Adrian VI (pope) 280
Adyghes 133
Adzel (Livonian town) 224
Aidar (Tatar town) 116
Akhmat (khan of the Great
    Horde) 32
Akinchey (Crimean envoy) 267
Akkerman (Belgorod, Turkish
    fortress) 36, 58, 72, 116,
    119, 180
Akkubeck (khan of Astrakhan)
    281
Aksan, Virginia (historian) 287
Albert Frederick (duke of
    Prussia) 279
Albert Hohenzollern
    (grandmaster of Teutonic
    Order and duke of Prussia)
    143, 147, 150, 155, 156,
    273, 279
Aleksin (Russian town) 128
Alexander I (Russian emperor)
    35
Alexander the Great
    (Macedonian tsar) 214
Alexander Kazimirovich (grand
    prince of Lithuania) 278
Alexander VI (pope) 280

Alexandrov (Russian town)
    205, 255
Alexeev Yuri (Russian
    historian) 268
Alferyev, Roman (Russian
    ambassador) 119, 228, 242
Alishev, Sergey (Tatar historian)
    268
Allentaken (Livonian district)
    160, 161
Altyul'sky Horde 65
Alyst see Marienburg
America 255
Aminova, Ghulnara (Tatar
    historian) 268
Angermann, Norbert (German
    historian) 270, 287
Ankara (Turkish city) 2
Anna Jagiellonka (Polish
    princess) 172
Anykščiai (Onikszty)
    (Lithuanian town) 155
Apennines 52
Arabath (Crimean town) 72
Arak-bahadir (Tatar
    commander) 96
Arbusow, Leonid (Baltic
    historian) 287
Arctic Ocean 236
Arensburg (Livonian town)
    168, 193, 275
Arginy (Tatar clan) 59
Armenians 58, 72
Arnell, Sture (Swedish
    historian) 270
Arseny (bishop of Polotsk) 177
Arsk (the field) 96, 97, 102
Ascheraden (Livonian castle)
    163, 200, 232
Ascherot (Livonian town) 252
Ashibash Faruh (Tatar
    ambassador) 122
Asia 92, 258
Asiatics 244

Astel, Franz von Segenhagen
    Genant (commander of Revel)
    161
Astrakhan (capital of the
    Astrakhan khanate) 14, 36,
    38, 65, 66, 69–71, 74, 108–
    11, 114, 125–7, 131, 133,
    137, 139, 225, 273, 274, 276
Astrakhan khanate xi, 12, 14,
    15, 19, 68, 70, 71, 93, 94,
    107, 109, 111, 112, 115, 118,
    122, 124, 125, 140, 249, 258,
    274, 281, 282, 284
Atachik (commander of the
    Cheremises) 95
Attman, Artur (Swedish
    historian) 287
Augsburg (German town) 164,
    275
Augustus (Roman emperor) 197
Austria 265
Avraamov, Sevastyan (Russian
    ambassador) 108, 109
Azov (Turkish fortress) 36, 72,
    109, 116, 126, 127
Azov, Sea (the Sea of Azov) 13,
    58, 65, 72, 109, 112, 114–16,
    126

Bagge, Jakob (Swedish
    commander) 146, 192, 274
Bakhchisarai (capital of the
    Crimea) 60, 119, 123, 125,
    128
Balaklava (Crimean town) 72
Baltic region 13, 142, 144, 156,
    175, 197, 202, 214, 223, 243,
    252, 262
Baltic Sea 13, 145, 175, 192,
    241, 259
Barbely, Georgy (Hungarian
    commander) 220
Baron, Samuel (historian) 287

Baryatinsky, Peter (Russian
  nobleman) 233
Baryny (Tatar clan) 59
Barysh (river) 99
Bashkirs 68
Basmanov-Pleshcheev, Alexey
  (Russian nobleman) 96, 113,
  123, 159, 190
Bathory, Stefan see Stefan
  Bathory
Batu (Mongol khan) 93, 181
Bauske (Livonian castle) 166
Bayezid (Bajazet) (sultan of
  Turkey) 1
Bayezid (Bajazet) II (sultan of
  Turkey) 280
Belev (Russian town) 115
Belgorod see Akkerman
Beloozero (White Lake) (lake)
  255
Belsky, Bogdan (Russian
  nobleman) 200
Belsky, Dmitry (Russian prince)
  96
Belsky, Ivan (Russian prince)
  129–31
Bendery (Turkish fortress) 72
Beran (Livonian castle) 199
Berezina (river) 181
Berlin (German city) xiv
Beznin, Mikhail (Russian
  commander) 208, 214
Bichura (Nogay envoy) 111
Bieganski, Witold 293
Bill, Peter (Danish ambassador)
  161
Birzhi (Lithuanian town) 155
Biskup, Marian (Polish
  historian) 287
Black Island 109
Black, Jeremy (historian) 287
Black Sea 13, 58, 60, 72, 114,
  116, 274
Bobrick, Benson (historian) 287
Bodniak, Stanislaw (Polish
  historian) 268, 287
Bogatyrev, Sergey (English
  historian) xiii, 13, 267, 270,
  287
Bogdan (artillery master) 43
Bolhov (Russian town) 129,
  130
Böll, Werner (Livonian
  commander) 172
Bong, Jonson (Swedish
  commander) 192
Borholm (island) 89
Borisenok, Yury (editor) xiii
Bornemissza, Johann
  (Hungarian commander) 216,
  219, 220, 234

Borovsk (Russian town) 138
Bosnia 2
Boye, Georg (Swedish
  commander) 204
Bratoshino (village) 132
Breitenstein (Prussian town)
  150, 274
Bremen (German town) 255
Brest (town of the Grand Duchy
  of Lithuania) 181, 188
Brüggeneye von, Hermann
  Hasenkamp (Livonian master)
  278
Bryansk (Russian town) 165
Bryullov, Karl (Russian painter)
  238
Bulgaria 1
Bundov, Yakov (Russian
  nobleman) 33
Butterwick, Richard (historian)
  288
Buttler, Bartholomäus (Prussian
  commander) 228
Buturlin, Ivan (Russian
  nobleman) 159
Buturlini (Russian nobles) 29,
  30
Byelorussians 197, 264
Bykovsky, Yury (Lithuanian
  ambassador) 119, 122
Byzantium 2, 10, 11, 119

Caesar, Gaius Julius (dictator of
  the Roman Republic) 214
Canol, Geronimo (Italian
  commander) 232
Casimir IV Jagiellon (Polish
  king) 148
Caspian Sea 65, 72, 107, 109,
  110, 126
Catherine II (Russian empress)
  25, 58
Cedzhety (Tatar clan) 59
Charlemagne (king of Franks)
  214
Charles V Habsburg (German
  emperor) 279
Charles IX (king of France) 194
Chebukov, Ivan (Russian
  nobleman) 125
Chegilek (Tatar prince) 110
Cheleby, Evliya (Turkish
  traveller) 65, 268
Chelibay, Halil (Crimean
  ambassador) 138
Cherckess-Kermen (Turkish
  fortress) 72
Cheremises (nation of the Volga
  region) 14, 68, 95, 97
Cheremisin, Dementy (Russian
  commander) 219

Cheremisinov, Ivan (Russian
  nobleman) 33, 116
Cheremisov, Ivan (Russian
  commander) 111
Cherkashenin, Bor (Tatar
  ambassador) 128
Cherkashenin, Mikhail
  (Cossack ataman) 114, 116
Cherkasskaya, Maria (Russian
  tsarina) 129
Cherkassky, Mikhail (Russian
  nobleman) 129, 130
Cherkassky, Temryuk
  (Caucasian nobleman) 129
Cherkassy (town of the Grand
  Duchy of Lithuania) 114,
  115, 274
Chernigov (Ukrainian town) 84,
  165, 175, 180, 213
Chernov, Anatoliy (Russian
  historian) 268
Chigirin (Ukrainian town) 127
Chingiz Khan (Mongol khan)
  91, 94
Chirot, Daniel (historian) 288
Chohov, Andrey (artillery
  master) 43
Cholmogory (Russian town)
  255
Christian II (king of Denmark)
  279
Christian III (king of Denmark)
  161, 165, 279
Christian IV (king of Denmark)
  279
Christiansen, Eric (historian)
  288
Christopher (prince of
  Transylvania) 207, 228
Christopher of Mecklenburg
  (coadjutor of bishop of Riga)
  154, 155
Chulkov, Danila (Russian
  commander) 115
Chuphut-Kale see Kyrk-Er
Chuvashes 68, 97
Circassians (inhabitants of
  eastern Ukraine) 52, 180
Circassians (inhabitants of
  northern Caucasia) 114, 116,
  133
Clement VII (pope) 280
Clement VIII (pope) 280
Collins, L. (historian) 288
Constantinople (capital of
  Byzantium) 11, 15
Copenhagen (capital of
  Denmark) 191, 200
Courland (Kurlandia) 87, 161,
  166, 174, 193, 199, 203, 208,
  214, 218, 262, 275

Crimea (peninsula) 58, 72, 112, 274, 275
Crimean khanate xi, 12, 13, 37, 38, 47, 57–60, 62, 65, 66, 70, 71, 74, 93, 94, 108, 111–20, 122–5, 127, 129, 131–3, 138–40, 165, 259, 261, 268, 273–6, 280, 282, 284
Crummey, Robert (historian) 268, 288
Cyprian (bishop of Polotsk) 212

Daghestan 72
Danes 52, 168, 170, 188, 190, 193, 199, 200
Dankov (Russian fortress) 129, 133
David (biblical king of Ancient Israel) 12
Davies, Brian (American historian) 288
Dedilov (Russian fortress) 40, 129
Delagardi, Pontus (Swedish commander) 223, 224, 232, 243
Delius, Walter (historian) 288
Dembinski, Matthias (Polish commander) 202, 204, 232
Denisova, Maria (Russian historian) 268
Denmark xii, 15, 88, 89, 139, 142, 143, 145, 161, 164–6, 168–70, 173, 175, 188–93, 198–200, 259, 261–5, 271, 275, 276, 279
Derbish-Ghali (khan of Astrakhan) 14, 108–12, 281
Derbov, Leonard (Russian historian) 288
Derzhek, Krzysztof (Lithuanian ambassador) 225–7
Desht-y-Kypchack 72
Devlet-Girei I (khan of Crimea) 113, 114, 117–23, 125, 127–33, 135, 137, 138, 225, 269, 280
Devlet-Kildei (Tatar ambassador) 125, 131, 269
Dinaburg (Livonian castle) 166, 198, 201, 203, 204, 277
Divei-murza (Tatar nobleman) 135, 136
Dnieper (river) 35, 37, 58, 72, 114–16, 123, 138, 181, 188, 213, 225
Dnieper Cossacks 35, 58, 74, 115, 118
Dniester (river) 72, 180
Don (river) 35–8, 109, 114, 116, 126

Don Cossacks 36, 58, 74, 114, 115, 273–5
Donnert, Erich (German historian) 270, 288
Dorogobuzh (Russian town) 206
Dorogostajski-Monivid, Mikolaj (Lithuanian nobleman) 213, 220
Dorpat (Livonian city, in Russian period – Yuryev) 87, 150, 152, 153, 156, 158, 160, 163, 167, 171, 224, 241, 273, 275
Dovojna, Stanislav (voevode of Polotsk) 177
Drissa (Lithuanian fortress) 185, 225, 239
Drutsk (town of the Grand Duchy of Lithuania) 182
Dubensky, Dmitry (Russian historian) 271
Dubna (Russian fortress) 233
Dubov, Sergey (publisher) 272
Dubrovna (town of the Grand Duchy of Lithuania) 224
Duffy, Christopher (historian) 288
Dunn, Stephen (translator) 293
Durasov, Fyodor (Russian nobleman) 33
Dutch 52
Dvorkin, Alexander (historian) 288
Dzhan-Aly (khan of Kazan) 281
Dzyarnovich, Aleg (Belarusan historian) 288

Eastern Europe 36, 57, 72–4, 81, 93, 121, 264, 272
Eckardt, Hans von (historian) 288
Edward VI (king of England) 279
Egypt 93
Eletsky, Dmitry (Russian ambassador) 228, 271
Elizabeth I (queen of England) 13, 280
Emden, Thomas von (Polish commander) 232
Emden (German town) 255
England 13, 131, 170, 192, 248, 275, 279
English 52
Enikale (Crimean town) 72
Erik XIV (Swedish king) 192, 279
Erlaa (Livonian castle) 163
Ermes (Livonian castle) 171, 172, 261, 275

Ernest (German prince) 197
Esper, Thomas (historian) 289
Estlandia (Estonia) 86, 169, 170, 190, 201, 223, 262, 263, 276, 277
Ests 87, 88
Etz (Livonian town) 160, 224
Eurasia 2
Europe xi, 1, 16, 17, 19, 20, 22, 23, 36, 40, 56, 74, 80, 89, 112, 131, 140, 143, 150, 195, 218, 220, 228, 238, 244, 246, 254–6, 258, 264, 272, 277
Europeans 24, 51, 159, 230, 236, 237, 244, 249, 251, 254, 256
Evsta (river) 163
Ezel (episcopacy) 87
Ezel (island) 87

Fahrensbach, Jürgen (commander of mercenaries) 215, 220, 228, 234
Falk, Erik (Swedish writer) 248
Fedorowicz, Jan (Polish historian) 291
Fellin (Livonian castle) 168, 171, 172, 225
Fennell, John (English historian) 267, 269
Ferdinand I Habsburg (emperor of the Holy Roman Empire) 171, 279
Fessalia 2
Filimonov, Lyapun (Cossack ataman) 111
Finland 89
Finns 89, 145
Fiorovanti, Aristotle (Italian architect) 52
Fisher, Alan (historian) 289
Fiszman, Samuel (historian) 268
Fleming, Gerhard (Livonian ambassador) 156
Fletcher, Giles (English ambassador) 52, 64, 248, 268, 272
Florya, Boris (Russian historian) 269, 271, 289
Forsten, Georgy (Russian historian) 289
France 15, 68, 74, 194, 197, 254
Frederick I (king of Denmark) 279
Frederick II (king of Denmark) 165, 166, 170, 188, 191, 192, 275, 276, 279
French 52, 236
Fridrich Saxon (grandmaster of Teutonic Order) 279

Fronsperger, Leonhardt (German writer) 246
Frost, Robert (English historian) 89, 263, 268, 270, 289
Funikov-Pronchischev, Vasily (Russian nobleman) 33
Fürstenberg, Gotthard (Livonian ambassador) 158
Fürstenberg, Johann Wilhelm von (Livonian master) 153, 155, 160, 171, 193, 278
Fustov, Ivan (Russian commander) 214
Fyodor Ivanovich (Russian tsar) 3, 39, 194, 277, 278

Galen, Heinrich von (Livonian master) 153, 155, 156, 172, 278
Galich (Russian town) 69, 96
Garaburda, Mikhail (Lithuanian clergyman) 180, 181, 242
Garaburda, Peter (Lithuanian ambassador) 203, 205, 233
Gayka, Jan (Lithuanian ambassador) 172
Gazi (Nogay prince) 65
Gdansk (Polish city) 74, 190, 198
Gdov (Russian fortress) 231, 235
Genoa (Italian city) 72
Gerasimov, Iliya (Russian historian) 267
Germans 15, 52, 211, 220, 223, 228, 234, 236, 246
Germany see Holy Roman Empire
Ghezlyov (Crimean town) 60, 72
Glebov, Sergey (Russian historian) 267
Glinskaja, Elena (grand princess) 48, 273
Glinsky, Vasiliy (Russian prince) 175
Golden Horde 2, 36, 57, 58, 65, 69, 91–4, 112, 132, 133, 140, 256, 269
Golitsin, Yury (Russian prince) 98
Golokhvastov, Ivan (Russian commander) 177
Golovin, Mikhail (Russian nobleman) 109
Golovin, Peter (Russian ambassador) 203–6, 271
Golubok, Gabriel (Polish commander) 223

Gontsa, Georgy (Moldavian historian) 268
Gorbaty, Alexander (Russian prince) 95, 102, 103
Gornaya Storona ('High Side') 97, 98
Gorodets (Russian town) 36
Gorsey, Jerome (English ambassador) 52, 53, 251, 268, 272
Gotland (island) 89
Great Horde 32, 57, 68–70, 109, 121
Great Nogay Horde 65, 66, 129, 133
Great Poland 74
Great Tataria see Golden Horde
Greeks 52, 58
Gregory XIII (pope) 280
Gregory XIV (pope) 280
Gregory Korinfsky (medieval writer) 11
Graham, Hugh (historian) 289, 292
Grant, Jonathan (historian) 289
Grzybowski, Stanisław (historian) 289
Gulf of Finland 89, 143, 144, 146
Gusevskoye Field 96
Gustav I Vasa (king of Sweden) 145, 147, 268, 279
Gvanini, Alexander (Polish historian) 249

Habsburgs (dynasty) 2, 74, 263
Hadji-Girei (khan of Crimea) 57
Hadzi-Tarhan see Astrakhan
Hall, Bert (historian) 289
Hamburg (German city) 255
Hans Oldenburg (Danish king) 279
Hapsal (Livonian castle) 225
Harrien (Livonian district) 169, 170, 171, 275
Heidenstein, Rheinhold (German historian) 200, 201, 210, 216, 219, 232, 234, 236, 237, 271
Hellie, Richard (historian) 267, 268, 289, 290
Helmet (Livonian castle) 171
Henning, Solomon (Livonian ambassador) 164
Henry Valois (king of Rzeczpospolita) viii, 194, 195, 279
Henry VIII (king of England) 279

Herberstein, Sigismund von (ambassador of the Holy Roman Empire) 56
High Side see Gornaya Storona
Hildesheim, Rombert (Livonian ambassador) 164
Hlebowicz, Jan (Lithuanian nobleman) 208
Hoff von, George (German writer) 245
Holland 192, 228
Holm (Russian town) 223, 224, 239
Holstein (region in Denmark) 166
Holy Roman Empire 52, 54, 74, 131, 150, 156, 158, 163, 164, 166, 170, 176, 194, 195, 228, 238, 241, 247, 254, 255, 261, 263, 264, 277, 279
Holzschuher, Jurgen (Livonian chancellor) 156
Horn, Heinrich (Swedish commander) 214
Hrala, Ieronim (Polish historian) 290
Hrodno (city of the Grand Duchy of Lithuania) 185
Hungarians 208, 211, 212, 216, 219, 220, 223, 230–4, 236
Hungary 2, 15, 80, 197, 228
Huttenbach, Henry (historian) 290
Hwoynitsa (Polish town) 190

Ilmen (lake) 229
Inalcik, Halil (historian) 290
Innocent IX (pope) 280
Innsbruck (German town) 56
Islam-Girei (khan of Astrakhan) 281
Islam-Girei (khan of Crimea) 280
Islam-Kermen (Turkish fortress) 114
Islhakov, Damir (Tatar historian) 268
Ismail (Nogay prince) 65, 108–11, 116
Israel (biblical) 247
Istanbul (capital of Turkey) 72
Italians 39, 52, 233, 236
Italy 15, 52
Ivan III Vasilievich (grand prince of all Russia) vii, 1–3, 12, 14, 31, 37, 66, 93, 121, 239, 278
Ivan IV Vasilievich (Ivan the Terrible) (tsar of all Russia) v, vii–ix, xii, 3–5, 9–17, 20, 22, 26, 30, 32, 37–40, 43, 48,

49, 52, 53, 67, 68, 71, 72, 74,
78, 82, 84, 89, 91–5, 97–100,
102–8, 110–33, 137–42, 146,
152, 156, 159–61, 163–6,
168–72, 175, 177, 180, 181,
185, 186, 188, 190, 191,
193, 194, 197–207, 214, 216,
225–229, 231–233,
238–50, 253–60, 264, 265,
267, 269–71, 273, 275–8
Ivangorod (Russian fortress) 40,
49, 89, 159, 214
Izmail (Turkish fortress) 72
Izoras 89

Jagiellons (Polish dynasty) 176,
186
Jan, Olbracht (king of Poland)
278
Janibek (khan of Astrakhan)
281
Jashlavy (Tatar clan) 59
Jenkinson, Antonio (English
ambassador) vii, 18
Jensen, Frede (Danish historian)
271
Jerwen (Livonian district) 168
Jespersen, Knud (Swedish
historian) 271
Jesus Navin (Joshua) (biblical
king of Israel) 12
Jews 58, 72, 93, 98, 180
Johan III (Swedish king) 279
Julius II (pope) 280
Julius III (pope) 280

Kaban (lake) 100
Kabarda 129
Kabardins 114, 116
Kadysh (Tatar nobleman) 95
Kaftyrev, Gregory (Russian
nobleman) 110
Kaluga (Russian town) 128,
130, 133
Kama (river) 68, 95, 97
Kampfer, Frank (German
historian) 269
Kanev (town of the Grand
Duchy of Lithuania) 114,
115, 180, 274
Kanukov, Kanklych (Russian
commander) 115
Kapha (Crimean town) 72,
125, 126
Kaplunovskiy, Alexander
(Russian historian) 267
Kappeler, Andreas (German
historian) 271, 290
Karaims 58
Karamzin, Nicholas (Russian
historian) 259

Karasabazar (Crimean town) 60
Karela (Russian fortress) 89,
223
Karelia 89, 145, 147, 223, 277
Karelian Isthmus 147
Karelians 89
Kargopol' (Russian town) 255
Karkus (Livonian castle) 171
Karpov, Mikhail (Russian
ambassador) 203, 204, 205,
271
Karttunen, Kaarlo (historian)
290
Karwowski, Stanislav (Polish
historian) 270, 290
Kashin, Mikhail (Russian
nobleman) 219
Kashira (Russian town) 113,
128, 131, 135
Kasim (khan of Astrakhan) 281
Kasimov (Tatar town) 94
Kaštanov, Sergey (Russian
historian) 267
Katarzyna Jagiellonka (Polish
princess) 172
Kazan (capital of Kazan
khanate) xi, 14, 52, 66–9,
95–104, 106, 107, 111, 114,
126, 131, 133, 137, 139, 273
Kazan khanate xi, 12, 15, 19,
32, 36, 47, 66–9, 93–5, 99,
107, 108, 112, 115, 116, 124,
125, 140, 249, 258, 268, 269,
281, 282, 284
Kazanka (river) 95, 102
Kazy-Girei (khan of Crimea)
280
Keenan, Edward (American
historian) 269
Keep, John (historians) 290
Kerch (Crimean town) 72,
114–16
Kerch Straits 114
Kettler, Gotthard (Livonian
master) 160, 161, 163, 164,
166, 168, 171, 172, 183, 193,
199, 278
Key (island) 255
Khabarov, Ivan (Russian
nobleman) 98
Khilkov, Dmitry (Russian
prince) 208, 214, 219, 220
Khilkov, Vasiliy (Russian
prince) 214
Khodarkovsky, Michael
(historian) 290
Khodkevich, Yuri (Lithuanian
nobleman) 180
Khodkevich, Grzegorz
(Lithuanian nobleman) 182,
198

Khoroshkevich, Anna (Russian
historian) 268, 270, 272, 290
Khortitsa (island) 114, 115, 274
Khoruzhy, Andrey (Lithuanian
ambassador) 168
Khrushchev, Alexander
(Russian nobleman) 237
Khuseyn (khan of Astrakhan)
281
Khvorostinin, Andrey (Russian
nobleman) 230, 237
Khvorostinin, Dmitry (Russian
prince) 135, 137, 178
Kiaupa, Zigmantas (Lithuanian
historian) 290
Kiaupienė, Jūratė (Lithuanian
historian) 290
Kiev (Ukrainian city) 84, 124,
176, 181, 186, 188
Kiliri (river) 102
Kiliya (Turkish fortress) 72
Kinevel (Livonian castle) 163
Kirby, David (historian) 290
Kirchner, Walther (historian)
268, 270, 290
Kirrumpäh (Livonian town)
160, 224, 225, 232
Kivereva Gora (Russian village)
240, 242
Klug, Ekkehard (German
historian) 271, 290
Kmita, Filon (Lithuanian
nobleman) 206, 212, 213,
220, 233
Knut of Abo (Swedish
ambassador) 147
Kobelev, Sergey (Russian envoy)
138
Kobets (Lithuanian fortress)
185
Kobyakov, Shyryay (Russian
commander) 115
Koc, Leon (Polish historian)
290
Kochanowski, Jan (Polish poet)
233
Koiva (river) 163
Kokenhusen (Livonian castle)
viii, 153, 154, 163, 200, 203,
208, 232
Kola (Russian town) 255
Kolki (estate in Livonia) 190,
192
Kolomensky (village) 130, 255
Kolomna (Russian town) 47,
128, 133, 134, 255
Kolupayev, Mikhail (Cossack
ataman) 111
Konskiye Vodi (river) 58
Koporje (Russian fortress) 47,
89, 232

Kopye (Russian fortress) 239
Korff, Nikolay (Livonian commander) 204
Koroljuk, Vladimir (Russian historian) 291
Kostroma (Russian town) 25, 69
Kotarski, Henryk (Polish historian) 291
Kotoshikhin, Gregory (clerk) 24
Kozelsk (Russian town) 129, 130
Kozyan (Russian fortress) 49, 208, 239
Krakow (capital of Poland) viii, xiv, 60, 74, 76, 147, 153, 205
Krasnaya (Russian fortress) viii, 49
Krasny (Russian town) 163, 167, 208, 239, 240
Krause, Helert (Livonian nobleman) 246, 249
Kremon (Livonian castle) 153
Kreutzburg (Livonian castle) 199
Krivoborsky, Vasily (Russian commander) 212
Krom, Michael (Russian historian) 267
Kromer, Martin (Polish historian) viii, 74
Kruglaya, Mount 96
Krumhausen, Joachim (burgomaster of Narva) 159
Krupishki (Polish town) 150, 274
Kryski, Stanislaw (Lithuanian ambassador) 202, 205, 267
Kulikovo (field in Russia) 93
Kuncevičius, Albinas (Lithuanian historian) 290
Kuns, Kaspar (artillery master) 43
Kurbsky, Andrey (Russian prince) 5, 24, 99, 100, 102–5, 107, 160, 171, 253, 267, 269, 276
Kuremsha (Crimean ambassador) 139
Kurshes 87
Kurukin, Igor (Russian historian) 291
Kurz, Martin (Polish commander) 223
Kvashnin, Zhdan (Russian ambassador) 238
Kyrk-Er (Crimean town) 60

Ladoga (lake) 144, 145
Ladoga (Russian fortress) viii, 47,

Lais (Livonian town) 224
Lamb, Harold (historian) 291
Laplandia 255
Latvia 197
Latvians 202
Laudohn (Livonian castle) 199
Lennewarden (Livonian castle) 232
Leo X (pope) 280
Lepszy, Kazimierz (Polish historian) 268, 291
Lepyavko, Sergey (Ukrainian historian) 291
Lesser Poland 74
Letlandia (Letland, Livonian district) 86, 161, 166, 168, 262
Letts 87
Leventhal, Michael (publisher) xiii
Likhachev, Dmitry (Russian philologist) 271
Lind, John (historian) 272
Lingett, Jamie (Scottish officer) 53
Lithuania (Grand Duchy of Lithuania) v, viii, xi, xii, 1, 10, 12, 13, 17, 37, 38, 59, 60, 74, 77–80, 83, 84, 88, 91, 115, 118–25, 128, 131, 138, 140, 143, 150, 155, 158, 165, 167, 168, 170, 171, 173–7, 180–2, 185–8, 190, 192, 194, 195, 198, 199, 203–5, 207, 214, 216, 234, 239, 244, 252, 259–62, 270, 271, 274–9, 282, 284
Lithuanians 1, 15, 30, 52, 78, 114, 121, 163, 165, 171, 181, 182, 185, 187, 201–4, 218, 223–5, 233, 236, 241, 242, 264
Livni (Russian fortress) 140
Livonia viii, xi, xii, 14, 17, 85–8, 124, 129, 137, 139, 143, 144, 148, 150, 152, 153, 155–8, 160–71, 174, 175, 181, 186, 188, 190, 192, 193, 197–201, 203, 204, 207, 208, 214, 216, 218, 224–7, 232, 238–42, 244, 246, 247, 249, 251, 252, 255, 260, 261, 270, 271, 274–7, 282, 284
Livonian Order 3, 15, 84, 87, 88, 119, 142–4, 148, 150, 152–6, 158, 160, 161, 163–6, 168, 170–2, 174, 175, 193, 247, 248, 259, 260, 262, 264, 273–6, 278
Livonians 15, 150, 152–4, 158–60, 164, 167, 171, 193,

194, 199, 200, 204, 246, 251, 273
Livs 87, 88
Lloyd, Berry (historian) 268
Lobanov-Rostovsky, Ivan (Russian prince) 243
Lobin, Alexey (Russian historian) xiii
Lohr, Erik (historian) 267, 287
Loit, Alexander (historian) 291
Lopasna (river) 134
Lopatinski, Wenclaw (Lithuanian ambassador) 206
Lübeck (German town) 228, 254
Lublin (Polish town) 185, 187, 204, 276
Lüdinhausen, Wolf Heinrich von (Livonian *vogt*) 168
Ludsen (Livonian castle) 166, 198, 225
Luki the Great (Russian town) ix, 176, 181, 216–18, 220, 221, 223–8, 239, 240, 261, 277
Lukoml (town of the Grand Duchy of Lithuania) 182
Lurie, Yakov (Russian historian) 271
Lviv (Polish city) 74, 188, 204
Lyko-Obolensky, Fyodor (Russian nobleman) 219
Lykov, Mikhail (Russian commander) 212
Lynn, John (historian) 267

McNeill, William (historian) 291
Macarius (Moscow metropolitan) 11, 93, 96
Macedonia, 1
Madariaga, Izabel de (English historian) 271, 291
Magnus (Danish prince) viii, 137, 166–70, 189, 193, 198, 200, 201, 224, 232, 261, 263, 264, 275
Majewski, Wieslav (Polish historian) 291
Malezky, Jan (Polish commander) 155
Mankov, Arkadiy (Russian historian) 268
Mansurov, Leonty (Russian ambassador) 110, 111
Marcellus II (pope) 280
Mari 68
Marienburg (Livonian town) 168, 224
Marienhausen (Livonian town) 198

Marx, Karl (philosopher) 1, 267
Mary I (queen of England) 280
Matejko, Jan (Polish painter) 148, 238
Maximilian I Habsburg (emperor of the Holy Roman Empire) 279
Maximilian II Habsburg (emperor of the Holy Roman Empire) ix, 194, 196, 197, 238, 271, 279
Mazovia 74
Mecca (Muslim religious centre) 111
Mediterranean Sea 146
Mehmed III (sultan of Turkey) 280
Mekhovsky, Matvey (Polish historian) 69
Melchior, Valentin (Livonian ambassador) 156
Mengly-Girei (khan of Crimea) 121, 280
Meschera (land in Russia) 36, 99, 176
Meschersky, Vasiliy (Cossack ataman) 38
Michailov (Russian town) 129, 273
Mielecki, Mikolaj (Polish commander) 207, 211, 212
Mikulinsky, Semen (Russian prince) 95, 99
Miller, Alexey (Russian historian) 256, 272
Miller, David (historian) 267
Mingrelians 72
Minsk (city of the Grand Duchy of Lithuania) 182
Mitrophanov, Alexander (translator) xiii
Mius (river) 58, 114, 129, 276
Mlyn (town of the Ukraine) 114, 274
Mogilev (town of the Grand Duchy of Lithuania) 224, 232
Mogilner, Marina (Russian historian) 267
Mohammed-Emin (khan of Kazan) 66, 281
Mohammed-Girei I (khan of Crimea) 57, 71, 280
Mohammed-Girei II (khan of Crimea) 138, 139, 280
Moldavia 72
Molochnaya (river) 58
Molodi (village) xi, 53, 133–7, 140, 276
Molotov, Vyacheslav (Russian minister) 195

Mongol–Tatars 92
Mordvinians 97, 99, 102, 103, 176
Morozov, Mikhail (Russian nobleman) 100
Morozov, Peter (Russian nobleman) 100
Mosalsky, Vladimir (Russian ambassador) 138, 139
Moscow (capital of Russia) vii, 6, 12, 14, 15, 17, 26, 29, 32, 33, 38, 39, 41, 43, 47, 48, 52, 56, 60, 65, 66, 84, 89, 95, 97, 98, 108–11, 114, 115, 118–22, 124–6, 128, 130–3, 135, 136, 138, 139, 147, 150, 152, 153, 156, 158–61, 164–7, 170, 172, 173, 176, 180–2, 186–8, 190–3, 197, 202–6, 218, 225, 227, 233, 236, 238, 239, 241, 243, 247–9, 251, 252, 254, 255, 259–61, 273, 274, 276, 277
Mozhaysk (Russian town) 176, 224, 228
Mstislavsky, Feydor (Russian prince) 208
Mstislavsky, Ivan (Russian prince) 214
Mtsensk (Russian town) 113
Münchhausen, Christopher von (vogt of the bishop of Ösel) 161
Münchhausen, Johann von (archbishop of Ösel and Courland) 161
Mund, Stefan (historian) 271, 291
Munkeben, Jan (Polish commander) 193
Münster, Kasper von (Livonian commander) 153
Murad III (sultan of Turkey) 280
Murat (Crimean envoy) 122
Muravskaya Road 113
Murom (Russian town) 69, 96
Murphey, Rhoads (historian) 291
Murtaza-murza (Tatar nobleman) 95
Muscovites see Russians
Muscovy see Russia

Nagoy, Athanasius (Russian ambassador) 120, 121, 123, 124, 127, 128, 269
Nagoy, Feydor (Russian nobleman) 96
Napoleon Bonaparte (French emperor) 35

Nara (river) 135
Narova (river) 49, 143, 159
Narva (Livonian fortress) 49, 158–60, 170, 192, 193, 214, 224, 232, 243, 261, 274, 277
Narykov, Chyura (Tatar nobleman) 95
Natanson-Leski, Józef (historian) 291
Nero (Roman Emperor) 244
Neubourg (Danish town) 166, 168, 275
Neuhausen (Livonian town) 150, 152, 160, 224
Neuschloss (Livonian town) 160, 224
Neva (river) 89, 143, 144, 146
Nevel (Lithuanian town) 40, 84, 185, 208, 220, 224, 225, 239
Nisha (Russian fortress) 212
Nizhni Novgorod (Russian city) 51, 69, 95, 96
Nogay Horde xi, 19, 38, 47, 65–7, 69–71, 98, 109–12, 116, 117, 126, 133, 135, 227, 274, 282, 284
Northern Caucasia 17, 65, 72, 114, 116, 126, 127, 129, 132, 133, 136
Norway 89
Novgorod the Great (Russian city) viii, 6, 9, 14, 16, 25, 32, 39, 44, 47, 89, 131, 132, 144, 145, 147, 150, 152, 153, 156, 158, 173, 181, 188, 198, 216, 227, 236
Novgorod-Seversky (Russian town) 84, 122, 165, 173, 175, 180, 181, 203, 216, 225
Novogrudok (town of the Grand Duchy of Lithuania) 182
Novoselsky, Alexey (Russian historian) 291
Novoseltsev, Luka (Russian ambassador) 124
Novosil (Russian fortress) 133
Nozdrovaty, Mikhail (Russian nobleman) 233
Nuraddine (Nogay prince) 65

Oberpahlen (Livonian castle) 163, 171, 247
Ochakov (Turkish fortress) 58, 72, 114, 116
Oderborn, Paul (German pastor) ix, 247–50, 254, 277
Odinpe (Livonian district) 160, 161

Odoyevsky, Nikita (Russian prince) 134, 135
Oka (river) 29, 84, 128, 129, 133, 133, 135
Olewnik, Jan (Polish historian) 270
Onega (river) 255
Opochka (Russian fortress) 233, 242
Orel (river) 129, 276
Orel (Russian fortress) 133
Oresheck (Russian fortress) viii, 47, 89, 144, 146, 274
Orishovsky, Ivan (Lithuanian commander) 220
Orsha (Lithuanian town) 176, 182, 202, 206, 212, 213, 220, 224, 227
Orthely, Abraham (Flemish cartographer) viii, 91
Orzhekhovsky, Andrey (Polish commander) 231
Ösel (island) 161, 166, 168, 200, 275
Ostrometsky, Jan (Polish nobleman) 236, 237
Ostrov (Russian fortress) 208, 228, 240
Ostrozhsky, Konstantin (prince of the Grand Duchy of Lithuania) 119, 213
Ott, Thomas (German historian) 247, 248, 271, 272, 291
Ottomans see Turks
Ovchina, Dmitry (Russian prince) 178
Ozerishche (Lithuanian fortress) 183, 188, 220, 224, 225, 239

Padis (Livonian fortress) 223
Pakhra (river) 136
Paletsky, Andrey (Russian commander) 212
Paletsky, Dmitry (Russian nobleman) 146, 153
Paris (capital of France) 35, 194, 228, 231
Parker, Geoffrey (historian) 267
Paul III (pope) 280
Paul IV (pope) 280
Paul, Michael (historian) 292
Pavlov, Andrei (Russian historian) 292
Pavlov, Fedka (Cossack ataman) 97
Pechevily (Turkish historian) 131
Peipus (lake) 158, 160
Pelensky, Jaroslav (historian) 269

Penyonzhek, Prokopy (Polish commander) 231
Perekop (Crimean town) 72, 112, 115, 116, 119
Perevoloka (confluence of Volga and Don rivers) 109, 126
Pernau (Livonian town) 158, 173, 183, 190, 232
Perrie, Maureen (English historian) 253, 292
Persia 68, 114, 255
Perry, Vernon (historian) 288
Petelin, Druzhina (Russian clergyman) 218, 243
Peter the Great (Peter I) (Russian emperor) 25, 259, 263-5
Petrey, Peter (Swedish writer) 252, 253, 272
Petrov, Konstantin (Russian historian) 270
Petrov, Peter (Russian commander) 146
Petrov, Stepan (artillery master) 43
Petrovski, Ioann (Polish royal secretary) 231
Pheldentz, Georg Hans von (German pfalzgraf) 254
Philimonov, Lyapun (Cossack ataman) 38
Philophey (Russian monk) 15
Pimen (archbishop of Novgorod the Great) 93
Pinkham, Joan (translator) 293
Pipes, Richard (American historian) 272
Pirimäe, Helmut (historian) 291
Pisemsky, Fyodor (Russian nobleman) 111, 124, 128, 224, 225, 267, 269, 271
Pius III (pope) 280
Pius IV (pope) 280
Pius V (pope) 280
Pivov, Roman (Russian nobleman) 218
Platter, Wilhelm (Polish commander) 201
Plettenberg von, Walter (Livonian Master) 278
Plyussa (river) 242, 277
Podolia 181, 207, 218
Poe, Marshall (American historian) 267, 268, 287
Pogodin, Michael (Russian historian) 271
Poland v, viii, xi, xii, xiv, 13, 68, 74, 76-80, 84, 88, 115, 120, 131, 138, 140, 142, 143, 148, 150, 153-155, 158, 165-71, 173-5, 180, 185-8,

190, 192-4, 197-9, 205, 210, 214, 244, 246, 247, 254, 259, 262-5, 268, 273-6, 278, 282, 284
Pole ('The Wild Steppe') 58, 72, 128, 129, 140, 259, 273
Poles 15, 52, 78, 193, 194, 202, 204, 211, 212, 218, 220, 224, 225, 228, 230-2, 236, 244, 254, 264, 265
Polish–Lithuanian Commonwealth (see also Rzeczpospolita) 74, 138, 139, 140, 185, 194, 197, 198, 203-5, 212, 213, 224, 233, 240, 276
Polota (river) 177
Polotsk (city of the Grand Duchy of Lithuania) viii, ix, 49, 78, 84, 122, 175-82, 185, 186, 188, 199, 202-4, 207-12, 218, 225-7, 239, 240, 242, 244, 249, 260, 261, 267, 276, 277
Polubensky, Alexander (Lithuanian commander) 198
Porkhol (Livonian town) 225
Porkhov (Russian fortress) 231, 235
Possevino, Antonio (papal legate) 239-42, 261, 264
Potemkin, Grigory (Russian prince) 58
Poznan (Polish city) 74
Pozvol (Lithuanian town) 155, 161, 164, 166, 274
Prevozsky, Matvey (Lithuanian ambassador) 227, 228
Pritsak, Omeljan (historian) 269
Pronsk (Russian fortress) 40
Pronsky, Yury (Russian nobleman) 102, 109
Prussia 143, 147, 153, 154, 176, 254, 264, 265, 273, 279
Pselsky Town (Russian fortress) 115, 120, 269
Psiyol (river) 115
Pskov (Russian city) ix, 15, 32, 47, 150, 152, 158, 167, 168, 181, 188, 198, 200, 207, 208, 214, 216, 225, 228-36, 238-40, 242, 261, 277
Pskovo-Pechersky monastery 234, 235
Pushkin, Eustaphy (Russian ambassador) 224-7, 271
Putivl (Russian town) 36, 133, 180
Putivlets, Pitchuga (Cossack ataman) 38

Pyatigorsk (highlands at the northern Caucasia) 114

Rabotka (river) 95
Radzivill, Krzysztof (Lithuanian prince) 207, 208, 212, 232, 233, 277
Radzivill, Mikolaj (prince of the Grand Duchy of Lithuania) 78, 174, 177, 182, 185, 207, 212
Ragnit (Prussian castle) 155
Randen (Livonian castle) 160
Rasmussen, Knud (Danish historian) 270, 292
Recke, Johann von der (master of Livonian Order) 278
Repnin, Andrey (Russian prince) 134
Revel (Livonian city) 87, 88, 129, 158, 161, 163, 164, 170, 171, 192, 193, 201, 275, 276
Rezanov, Afanasy (Russian ambassador) 238
Ribbentrop, Joachim von (German minister) 195
Riga (Livonian city) viii, ix, 87, 88, 148, 153, 155, 158, 161, 163–5, 171, 173, 190, 201, 203, 232, 240, 263, 275
Ringen (Livonian castle) 160, 163
Rjurikovichi (Russian dynasty) 181
Roberts, Michael (American historian) 267, 292
Rodenpois (Livonian castle) 163
Rogers, Clifford (historian) 267, 292
Roman Empire 264
Rome (Italian city) 11, 15
Romodanovsky, Anton (Russian ambassador) 192
Ronneburg (Livonian castle) 153, 225
Rositten (Livonian castle) 166, 198, 225
Rostov the Great (Russian town) 14, 93, 130
Rozhay (river) 136
Rozrazhevsky, Christopher (Polish nobleman) 207
Rujery (nuncio) 78
Rudolf II Habsburg (emperor of the Holy Roman Empire) 238, 254, 279
Rus' see Russia
Rusa the Old (Russian town) 223, 233, 235

Russia v, ix, xi, xii, 1–3, 5–19, 23, 24, 28, 31, 32, 35, 37, 39, 42, 43, 47, 49, 52–60, 65, 67, 68, 71, 74, 77, 80, 83, 84, 88, 92–4, 97, 98, 108, 109, 112–19, 121, 122, 124–9, 131–3, 137–40, 142, 144, 145, 147, 150, 153, 155, 156, 158–61, 165, 167–73, 176–8, 180–2, 185–95, 198, 201–4, 206, 208, 212–15, 218, 223, 224, 226–8, 231, 232, 238–49, 251, 254–6, 258–65, 267–70, 273–8, 282, 284
Russians vii, 2, 20, 23, 64, 68, 71, 93, 94–8, 100, 102, 104, 105, 107, 109–11, 113–16, 121, 124, 126–8, 135–7, 145, 152, 158–60, 164, 165, 168, 172, 174, 175, 181–3, 186, 188, 190, 200, 201, 204, 207, 212, 216, 218–25, 227, 230–4, 236, 237, 241, 242, 244–7, 249, 251–6, 258, 264, 265, 276, 277
Ruyen (Livonian castle) 171
Ryasan (Russian city) 36, 38, 99, 113, 123, 131, 135
Rybakov, Boris (Russian historian) 268, 269
Rystad, Göran (Swedish historian) 271
Ryussov, Balthazar (Livonian chronicler) 152, 158, 168, 249, 270
Rywkin, Michael (historian) 290
Rzeczpospolita (see also Polish–Lithuanian Commonwealth) 77, 175, 185, 187, 188, 194, 197, 202, 205, 206, 214–16, 218, 220, 223–8, 231, 233, 236–43, 247, 258–63, 265, 276–9
Rzevsky, Matvey Diyak (Russian nobleman) 33, 114, 129
Rzevsky, Yelizar (Russian envoy) 138
Rzhev (Russian town) 233

Saadat-Girei I (khan of Crimea) 280
Sabyrov, Andrey (Russian nobleman) 27
Safa-Girei (khan of Kazan) 67, 95, 281
Sagib-Girei (khan of Crimea) 71, 280
Sagib-Girei (khan of Kazan) 66, 281

Salaty (Lithuanian town) 155
Salis (Livonian castle) 232
Salman (Tatar commander) 109
Saltykov, Lev (Russian nobleman) 113
Samara (river) 68
Sapieha, Andrzey (Lithuanian commander) 204
Saray (capital of the Golden Horde) 109
Sari-Tau (Saratov, town) 68
Sass, Reinhold (Livonian commander) 172
Sava, Boris (Polish commander) 201
Saxony 279
Schelkalov, Andrey (Russian clergyman) 249
Scherbatov, Mikhael (Russian historian) 259
Schlichting, Albert (German writer) 244, 246, 249, 271
Schujen (Livonian castle) 163
Schwanenburg (Livonian castle) 161, 163, 199
Scotland 15, 192
Scots 52, 53, 236
Sebezh (Russian town) 176, 225, 239, 240, 242
Selart, Anti (Estonian historian) xiii
Selburg (Livonian castle) 166, 208
Seleznev, Yuri (Russian historian) 93, 269
Selim I (sultan of Turkey) 280
Selim II (sultan of Turkey) 125, 280
Semenov, Alexander (Russian historian) 267
Semigalia 87, 174, 193, 262
Semigals 87
Serben (Livonian castle) 163
Serbia 1
Serbians 80
Serebryany, Peter (Russian prince) 96, 102, 126, 127, 175
Serebryany, Vasily (Russian prince) 103, 182
Serpukhov (Russian town) 26, 27, 128, 130, 133, 135
Sesswegen (Livonian castle) 163, 199
Severga (Cossack ataman) 97
Seversky Donets (river) 115, 116
Seyid-Muhammed-Riza (Turkish historian) 131
Shahghali (khan of Kazan) 66, 95–9, 108, 116, 281

Shapilov, Armenin (Russian envoy) 138, 139

Shapkin, Grigory (Russian clegyman) 172

Shatsk (Russian town) 129

Shchenyatev, Peter (Russian nobleman) 102, 105, 146

Shein, Boris (Russian commander) 212

Shemyakin, Yury (Russian nobleman) 100, 109

Sheremetyev, Feydor (Russian commander) 208, 212

Sheremetyev, Ivan (Russian nobleman) 113, 114, 120

Sheremetyev, Semen (Russian commander) 146

Shevchenko, Ihor (historian) 269

Shevrigin, Istoma (Russian ambassador) 238, 239

Sheydyakov, Peter (Russian commander) 208

Sheykh-Akhmet (khan of Astrakhan) 281

Shich-Mamay (Nogay prince) 65

Shimkov, Jan (Lithuanian ambassador) 172

Shiriny (Tatar clan) 59

Shklov (town of the Grand Duchy of Lithuania) 224, 232

Shokarev, Sergey (Russian historian) 268

Shuysky, Andrey (Russian prince) 273

Shuysky, Ivan (Russian prince) 135, 230, 231, 237

Shuysky, Peter (Russian prince) 160, 182

Siberia 15, 47, 258

Siberian khanate 17, 67

Sikorski, Janusz (Polish historian) 292

Sidnell, Philip (editor) xiii

Sieberg, Christopher (Livonian commander) 172

Sigismund I the Old (king of Poland) 57, 143, 147, 278

Sigismund II Augustus (king of Poland) viii, 14, 115, 118–21, 123, 125, 149, 150, 155, 156, 161, 164–6, 170–3, 177, 180–3, 185, 193, 194, 273, 275, 278, 279

Sigismund III Vasa (king of Rzeczpospolita, king of Sweden) 279

Simeon Bekbulatovich (Tatar prince) 198

Sitna (Russian fortress) viii, 49, 50, 208, 239

Sitsky, Ivan (Russian prince) 218, 224, 271

Sixtus V (pope) 280

Skrotoshin, Jan (Lithuanian ambassador) 187

Skrynnikov, Ruslan (Russian historian) 270, 292

Słonim (Polish town) 204

Śliwiński, Artur (Polish historian) 292

Small Nogay Horde 65, 66, 129, 133

Smilten (Livonian castle) 154, 163, 224

Smirnov, Vasiliy (Russian historian) 269

Smith, Dianne (historian) 292

Smith, Thomas (English writer) 248

Smolensk (Russian city) ix, 32, 84, 122, 165, 173, 176, 181, 188, 203, 212, 213, 216, 222, 224, 225, 241

Sokol (Russian fortress) viii, 49, 50, 208, 212, 239

Sokolinsky, Yury (Lithuanian commander) 216

Solary, Antonio (Italian architect) 52

Solkhat (Crimean city) 60

Solomon (biblical king of Ancient Israel) 12

Solovjov, Sergey (historian) 60

Solovky (monastery) 255

Sophia Jagiellon (Polish princess) 148

Soyembika (Tatar tsarina) 97, 98

Spain 68, 74, 254

Speyer (German town) 170, 275

St Kirill (monastery on the White Lake/Beloozero) 255

St Petersburg (Russian city) xiii, xiv, 143

St Trinity (monastery near Moscow) 255

Staden, Heinrich (German mercenary) 54, 246, 254, 255, 268

Staemmler, Klaus-Dietrich (historian) 292

Stalin, Joseph (ruler of the USSR) 1

Stancelis, Vigantas (Lithuanian historian) 270, 292

Staritsa (Russian town) 227, 233, 277

Starodub (Russian town) 165, 220

Stefan Bathory (king of Rzeczpospolita) ix, 17, 82, 138, 139, 194, 197, 198, 201–3, 205–8, 210–12, 214–20, 224–34, 236–44, 247, 265, 271, 277, 279

Stockholm (capital of Sweden) 190, 192

Stone, David (historian) 292

Streshnev, Ivan (Russian clergyman) 206

Sucheni-Grabowska, Anna (Polish historian) 292

Sudak (Crimean town) 72

Sudbishchi (locality) 113, 114, 120, 274

Sukin, Fedor (Russian nobleman) 168, 172

Suleshevy see Jashlavy

Suleyman I Kanuny (sultan of Turkey) 280

Sunderland, Willard (historian) 292

Sunzel (Livonian castle) 163

Sunzensky town (Russian fortress) 132

Sura (river) 68, 99

Susha (Russian fortress) 49, 213

Suzdal (town) 66

Svinaya road 130

Sviyaga (river) 95, 96

Sviyazhsk (Russian fortress) 96–8, 100, 114, 273

Sweden xii, 88–90, 132, 143–5, 147, 164, 170, 173, 175, 188, 190, 192, 232, 240, 243, 247, 254, 259, 260, 262, 263, 265, 271, 274–6, 279, 282, 284

Swedes 15, 52, 53, 89, 145–7, 175, 186, 193, 204, 223, 224, 232, 263, 265

Syrensk see Neuschloss

Syvash (lake) 112

Szelągowski, Adam (Polish historian) 293

Tachmasp (Persian shah) 248

Tallinn see Revel

Talvash, Mikolaj (Lithuanian ambassador) 242

Taman (Turkish fortress) 72

Tarnovsky, Stanislaw (Polish commander) 228

Tartu see Dorpat

Tarusa (Russian town) 134

Tarvast (Livonian castle) 30, 171, 175, 225

Tatars viii, 1, 7, 17, 19, 32, 36, 38, 47, 50, 52, 53, 57–65, 68–72, 78, 80, 92, 93, 94–100, 102, 103, 105,

108–21, 123, 124, 126, 129,
130, 132, 134–7, 139, 140,
146, 164, 176, 180, 200, 204,
207, 227, 251, 252, 258, 259,
265, 276
Tatev, Peter (Russian
commander) 200
Tatishchev, Ignaty (Russian
nobleman) 243
Taube, Johann (Livonian
nobleman) 158, 246, 249
Temnikov (Tatar town) 94
Temreon (Turkish fortress) 72
Temryuk (Tatar town) 114
Tereberdey-murza (Nogay
nobleman) 135, 136
Terek (river) 125
Terpigorev (a cellarer from
Novgorod the Great) 156
Teterin, Timofey (Russian
commander) 111
Teutonic Order 84, 142, 143,
147, 185, 279
Thaden, Edward (historian) 293
Theodosius (archbishop of
Novgorod the Great) 93
Tibay-murza (Nogay prince)
116
Tiberg, Erik (Swedish historian)
270, 293
Tikhaja Sosna (river) 2
Timur-i-Lenk (Tamerlane)
(Asiatic conqueror) 2, 68
Tirsen (Livonian castle) 164
Tisenhausen, Fabian (Livonian
nobleman) 153
Tishinkov, Kudeyar (Russian
nobleman) 130, 132, 270
Tishkevich, Skumin (Polish
ambassador) 118
Tishkevich, Vasily (Lithuanian
ambassador) 165
Tishkov, Andrey (Russian
ambassador) 111
Tmutarakan (Russian town)
109
Tokhtamysh (Nogay prince)
114
Tokhtamysh (Tatar khan) 93
Tokmakov, Yury (Russian
nobleman) 137
Tolmachevo (Russian village)
xiv
Tolsburg (Livonian castle) 163
Toman (Tatar town) 114
Toropets (Russian town) 176,
181, 219, 220, 233
Torun (Polish town) 190
Tott, Klaus (Swedish
ambassador) 243
Transylvania 194, 207

Trikaten (Livonian castle) 171,
225
Troecourovi (Russian nobles)
29
Troyat, Henri (historian) 293
Troyekurov, Fyodor (Russian
nobleman) 100, 102
Trubetskoy, Fyodor (Russian
nobleman) 129
Tsimburski, Vadim
(philosopher) 2, 267
Tula (Russian town) 49, 113,
135
Turchasov (Russian town) 255
Turgenev, Peter (Russian
nobleman) 110
Turkey 1, 38, 57, 58, 60, 66,
68, 72–4, 86, 92, 108, 125,
126, 138, 139, 197, 239–41,
245, 254, 259, 280, 284
Turks ix, 11, 58, 59, 64, 72, 80,
114, 116, 125–7, 131, 133,
180, 202, 238, 239, 244–6,
256
Turovlya (Russian fortress) viii,
49, 50, 212, 239
Tver (Russian city) 14, 25, 236
Tyufyakin, Mikhail (Russian
prince) 129
Tyutev, Ivan (Russian
ambassador) 119

Udmurts 68
Uglich (town) 96
Ugra (river) 32
Ukraine 197, 258
Ukrainians 264
Ula (Russian, then Lithuanian
fortress) viii, 182, 183, 185,
204, 239
Ula (river) viii, 184, 212, 261,
276
Ulanka (Cossack commander)
111
Ulfeldt, Yakob (Danish
diplomat) 246, 251, 270, 272
Ulken, Kordt (townsman of
Narva) 159
Ulug-Mohammed (khan of
Kazan) 66
Umny-Kolychev, Fyodor
(Russian ambassador) 185
Ural (mountains) 67
Ural (river) see Yaik
Urban VII (pope) 280
Urban, William (historian) viii,
247, 268, 270, 272, 293
Urne, Klaus (Danish
ambassador) 161, 165

Urovetsky, Nikolay (Polish
commander) 216, 222, 223,
228
USA (United States of America)
xiv
Uspensky Fyodor (Russian
historian) 271
USSR 197
Ustjug (Russian town) 39, 69
Usvyat (Russian fortress) 216,
224, 225, 239
Utamesh (khan of Kazan) 97,
98, 281
Uverskaya, Olga (translator)
xiii
Uzbek (Tatar khan) 93

Vasiliy II (grand prince of
Moscow) 66
Vasiliy III Ivanovich (grand
prince of all Russia) vii, 3,
188, 239, 278
Vasilsursk (Russian town) 95
Vassian Rylo (Russian bishop)
93
Vatican 15, 72, 238, 239, 241,
261, 263
Velikaya (river) 232
Velizh (Russian fortress)
215–17, 219, 224, 225, 239,
240, 242
Veshnyakov, Ignaty (Russian
nobleman) 109
Victorin, Mefody see Mefody
Victorin
Vienna (capital of Habsburg's
state) 238, 263
Viljanti, Arvo (Swedish
historian) 89, 268, 270, 293
Vilno (capital of the Grand
Duchy of Lithuania) viii, 60,
74, 78, 118, 119, 155, 166,
174, 176, 180, 186, 188, 203,
205, 214, 225, 241, 275, 276
Vinogradov, Alexander (Russian
historian) 293
Vishnevetsky, Dmitry (prince
of the Grand Duchy of
Lithuania) 58, 114–16, 180,
274
Vishnevetsky, Mikhail (prince
of the Grand Duchy of
Lithuania) 213
Viskovaty, Ivan (Russian clerk)
120, 147, 153, 168
Vitebsk (city of the Grand
Duchy of Lithuania) 176
Vladimir (prince of Ancient
Russia) 11, 181
Vods 89

Voksherin, Fyodor (Russian envoy) 118
Volchek, Jan (Lithuanian ambassador) 119
Volga (river) 13, 14, 17, 35, 37, 38, 65, 66, 68, 69, 94, 96, 97, 99, 109–11, 126, 133, 233
Volga Bulgaria 66
Volhynia 79, 181, 188
Volkhov (river) 145
Volock Lamsky (Russian town) 255
Vologda (Russian town) 255
Volovich, Grigory (Lithuanian ambassador) 180
Volynsky, Jakov (Russian nobleman) 130
Vorobjova Sloboda 33
Voronach (Russian fortress) 185, 228, 240
Voronezh (Russian city) xiii, 140
Vorotynsky, Mikhail (Russian prince) 104, 128, 129, 132–4, 136, 137
Votjaks see Udmurts
Voyeykov, Baim (Russian nobleman)
Voyeykov, Ivan (Russian nobleman) 219
Vuoksi (river) 147
Vyatka (river) 68, 95, 97, 109, 111
Vyatka (Russian town) 95
Vyazemsky, Alexander (Russian nobleman) 109
Vyazma (Russian town) 165
Vyborg (Swedish fortress) 89, 143, 146, 147, 190, 274
Vyrodkov, Ivan (Russian clerk) 96, 98, 104
Vyshgorod (Russian town) 163

Walicki, Andrzej (Polish historian) 268
Walk (Livonian castle) 225
Warsaw (Polish city) 204, 224, 277
Weissenstein (Livonian castle) 171, 172, 225, 232, 252
Wenden (Livonian town) 161, 163, 168, 190, 198, 200–2, 204, 253, 277
Wesenberg (Livonian castle) 163, 224

Western Dvina (river) 163, 166, 171, 177, 181, 182, 185, 188, 199–202, 207, 208, 212, 216
Westphalia 87
Weyer, Ernst (Polish commander) 207
White Lake see Beloozero
Wiek (Livonian district) 168
Wijaczka, Jacek (Polish historian) 293
Wilhelm of Brandenburg (archbishop of Riga) 148, 153, 155, 165, 166, 274, 275
Wimmer, Jan (historian) 293
Winter, Heinrich (Livonian ambassador) 156
Wirland (Livonian district) 160, 169
Wolff, Larry (American historian) 256, 272
Wolmar (Livonian castle) 155, 158, 171, 198, 200, 225

Yadegar (khan of Kazan) viii, 99, 102, 105–7, 281
Yadwiga (Polish queen) xiv
Yaik (river) 38, 65
Yakovlev, Vladimir (Russian nobleman) 129
Yakovleva, Galina (translator) xiii
Yakovlya, Zakharij (Russian nobleman) 96, 103
Yam (Russian fortress) 47, 89, 232
Yam Zapolsky (settlement) 228, 237, 240, 277
Yam Zubtsovsky (Russian town) 233
Yamghurchi (khan of Astrakhan) 108, 109, 281
Yan-Bolduy (Tatar ambassador) 128
Yan-Magmet (Tatar ambassador) 121
Yanov, Alexander (historian) 293
Yanushevsky, Jan (Polish poet) 214
Yanushkevich, Andrey (Belarussian historian) xiii, 270, 293
Yapp, Malcolm (historian) 288

Yaroslav the Wise (prince of Ancient Russia) 12, 181
Yeletsky, Dmitry (Russian prince) 239–42
Yelyushka (Tatar ambassador) 123, 269
Yenbars (Tatar nobleman) 98
Yepifan (Russian town) 129
Yezevka (river) 96
Yuryev see Dorpat
Yuryev, Nikita (Russian nobleman) 163
Yuryev, Vasilij (Russian nobleman) 181, 267, 270
Yusuf (Nogay prince) 109–11

Zabolotsky, Ignatiy (Russian commander) 115
Zabolotsky, Peter (Russian commander) 163
Zaghidullin, Ilidus (Tatar historian) 268
Zagorovskiy, Vladimir (Russian historian) 269, 293
Zamojski, Jan (chancellor of Poland) ix, 211, 214–16, 219, 222, 223, 229, 231, 233–7, 241
Zaporozje (Cossack settlement) 39
Zavolochye (Russian fortress) 220, 222, 223, 225, 228, 239
Zawadski, Konrad (Polish historian) 293
Zaytsev, Iliya (Russian historian) 268, 269
Zbarazhsky, Jan (Polish commander) 220, 242
Zelobov-Pusheshnikov, Grigory (Russian nobleman) 33
Zernack, Klaus (German historian) 293
Zholkevsky, Stanislaw (Polish nobleman) 236
Zimin, Alexander (Russian historian) 271, 294
Zlobin, Grigory (Russian envoy) 122
Zlynsky Field 130
Zonenborg (Livonian castle) 168
Zuzin, Bahteyar (Russian commander) 97
Zvenigorod (Russian town) 255